on 1/94

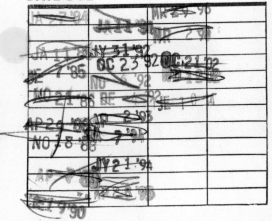

CHEKHOV
A study of the major stories and plays

Odette de Mourgues: *Racine, or The Triumph of Relevance*
Ronald Gray: *Goethe: A Critical Introduction*
C. B. Morris: *A Generation of Spanish Poets 1920–1936*
R. F. Christian: *Tolstoy: A Critical Introduction*
Richard Peace: *Dostoyevsky: An Examination of the Major Novels*
John Bayley: *Pushkin: A Comparative Commentary*
Dorothy Gabe Coleman: *Rabelais: A Critical Study in Prose Fiction*
W. E. Yates: *Grillparzer: A Critical Introduction*
Ronald Gray: *Franz Kafka*
John Northam: *Ibsen: A Critical Study*
Geoffrey Strickland: *Stendhal: The Education of a Novelist*
Ronald Gray: *Brecht the Dramatist*
Henry Gifford: *Pasternak: A Critical Study*
J. P. Stern: *A Study of Nietzsche*
Other volumes in preparation

CHEKHOV

A study of the major stories and plays

BEVERLY HAHN

CAMBRIDGE UNIVERSITY PRESS

CAMBRIDGE

LONDON · NEW YORK · MELBOURNE

Published by the Syndics of the Cambridge University Press
The Pitt Building, Trumpington Street, Cambridge CB2 1RP
Bentley House, 200 Euston Road, London NW1 2DB
32 East 57th Street, New York, NY 10022, USA
296 Beaconsfield Parade, Middle Park, Melbourne 3206, Australia

First published 1977
First paperback edition 1979

Printed in Great Britain at the
University Press, Cambridge

Library of Congress cataloguing in publication data
Hahn, Beverly, 1947–
Chekhov: a study of the major stories and plays.
(Major European authors)
Bibliography: p.
Includes index.
1. Chekhov, Anton Pavlovich, 1860–1904 – Criticism and interpretation.
PG3458.Z8H3   891.7′2′3   75–22557
ISBN 0 521 20951 X hard covers
ISBN 0 521 29670 6 paperback

CONTENTS

GENERAL PREFACE TO THE SERIES

The *Major European Authors* series, as the name implies, considers the most important writers of the European literatures, most often giving a volume to each author, but occasionally treating a group or a genre. The basic assumption is that the general reader and the student will be able to find information on biography and literary history fairly easily elsewhere: that what he will look for in this series is a single volume which gives a critical survey of the entire oeuvre or the most important works. Authors of books in the series are asked to keep this general critical objective in mind, to write critical introductions which will help the reader to order his impressions of the works of art themselves, to assume little prior knowledge, and so far as possible either to quote in English or to translate quotations.

It is hoped that the series will help to keep the classics of European literature alive and active in the minds of present-day readers: both those reading for a formal literary examination, and those who in the original languages and in translation wish to keep in touch with the culture of Europe.

ACKNOWLEDGMENTS

I would like to thank the editors of *The Critical Review*, Melbourne, for permission to reprint articles on *Three Sisters* and *The Cherry Orchard* which appeared in a preliminary form in that journal, in June 1972 and June 1973 respectively.

I would also like to thank my parents for their encouragement and for their practical generosity, which took so many different forms and made it so much easier for me to undertake this work; Mr Robin Grove of the English Department at the University of Melbourne, for the time and energy he gave in reading through the manuscript and for the extremely valuable suggestions he made; and Mr Graham Burns of the English Department at La Trobe University, for his generous help and support all during the writing of the book.

I am grateful to Miss Jean Slaifstein and Miss Sheila Casey for typing the original manuscript, and to my teachers in the Russian Department at Melbourne University.

B. H.

A NOTE ON TRANSLATIONS

Any work which attempts to deal with an author writing in a foreign language and in the context of a foreign culture will necessarily discover limitations and difficulties. These are not lessened by the critic's need – as distinct from that of the historian of ideas – to attend at all times to precise stylistic qualities of the writing (as something inseparable from its imaginative 'content') and to the subtleties of nuance which probably escape any but the natives of a culture. I am therefore aware that, in the present work, there are limitations on what I may do in the way of close textual commentary, accepting these as an inevitable disadvantage of a subject too compelling in other respects for me to discard.

However, in Chekhov's case there are some special factors to help mitigate the difficulties. In the first place, Chekhov's art is almost always highly structured, requiring, for a full understanding, a response to the way detail is organized in an overall pattern. Speeches, images and even whole scenes are carefully, and often ironically, juxtaposed against one another, so that one rarely finds any single set of values or single emotion holding sway. These formal properties naturally survive translation intact and are thus available for comment by the non-native critic. Secondly, the prevalence of simile rather than metaphor in the language of the original means that poetic effects themselves are more easily and reliably translatable, and that they too are generally accessible to a reader who is not a Russian-speaker. The 'big white birds' of *Three Sisters*, for example, ultimately take on a broadly metaphoric force, but they are first introduced through simile:

Скажите мне, отчего я сегодня так счастлива? Точно я на парусах, надо мной широкое голубое небо и носятся большие белые птицы.

Tell me, why am I so happy today? *As if* I were sailing, above me a wide blue sky and big white birds moving about.

Indeed, though they are present here only figuratively, these birds later become real creatures (invisible from the stage, but nonetheless indicated as physically flying overhead) whom Masha addresses longingly in Act IV when Vershinin's departure is imminent:

The migratory birds are already in flight. . . (*looks up*). Swans or geese . . . my beloved, happy ones.

In nearly every example I can recall, the major images in Chekhov's work are natural images which are to some extent independent of the figures of speech which embody them from point to point. Thus, if the precise effect of one simile (or the less frequent metaphor) is lost in translation, it is likely that the non-native reader can still feel the composite poetic effect of (say) the falling snow in 'Misery', the cherry orchard in *The Cherry Orchard* or, in *Three Sisters*, Moscow's blossoms, sunlight and warmth. Moreover, even less central images, like the recurrent water images in 'Easter Eve' or the surreal imagery of the moonlight shining through the window-bars in 'Ward No. 6', seem to survive translation more or less intact.

Perhaps most important of all, there exists in English a standard translation of the main body of Chekhov's stories, novellas and plays, completed by a single translator and therefore preserving a certain uniformity of sensibility: Constance Garnett's translations of prose works, published between 1916 and 1923, and of the major plays, published in the early 1920s.* (At the time of writing, Ronald Hingley's new edition of Chekhov's works, the 'Oxford Chekhov', is still incomplete. However, I have

---

* *The Tales of Tchehov*, 13 vols. (London, 1916–23): I. *The Darling and Other Stories*, 1916. II. *The Duel and Other Stories*, 1916. III. *The Lady with the Dog and Other Stories*, 1917. IV. *The Party and Other Stories*, 1917. V. *The Wife and Other Stories*, 1918. VI. *The Witch and Other Stories*, 1918. VII. *The Bishop and Other Stories*, 1919. VIII. *The Chorus Girl and Other Stories*, 1920. IX. *The Schoolmistress and Other Stories*, 1920. X. *The Horse-Stealers and Other Stories*, 1921. XI. *The Schoolmaster and Other Stories*, 1921. XII. *The Cook's Wedding and Other Stories*, 1922. XIII. *Love and Other Stories*, 1923.

    The Plays of Tchehov, 2 vols. (London, 1922–3; reprinted 1965–70): I. *The Cherry Orchard and Other Plays*, 1922. II. *Three Sisters and Other Plays*, 1923.

    In the present essay, references to the Garnett edition of Chekhov's stories are made in parentheses, by volume and page number only: thus, '(VII.28)' means '*The Bishop and Other Stories*, p. 28'. (Stories marked with an asterisk * are not included in the Garnett edition; their sources are identified in the endnotes in the usual way.)

consulted such volumes as were available and am grateful for the opportunity of comparison they provided.) The Garnett translations, and especially her translations of the plays, have hardly, of course, been immune from attack; and the most recent has come from David Magarshack in his 'Introduction' to his *The Real Chekhov* (London, 1972). But while it is true that Mrs Garnett does occasionally take liberties with Russian colloquialisms and other idioms, the question of their 'quaintness' or otherwise seems to me a matter of taste; and, allowing for the fact that there are probably better translations of the plays, still the number of Garnett's 'misconceptions' (if we consider her translations overall) seems to me to have been exaggerated. She has, at the least, a fine ear for English cadence; and since for more than fifty years after Chekhov's death hers was the only substantial selection of Chekhov's stories available in English, her *Tales* have themselves attained something of the status of an English classic. For this reason, and although I have consulted the originals at points where definite differences occur between current English translations, the following accounts of works and of the development of Chekhov's art take the Garnett version of him as their basis.

Even so, I do think that a distinctively 'Chekhovian' sensibility emerges through a whole range of English translations of Chekhov's work. In part, this has to do with the structural emphases of which I have already spoken, which I shall attend to subsequently. But as well as this there are consistencies of tone and of manner from one translator to another which emerge despite inevitable differences in the translators' sensibilities. If this is not conspicuously so with the overall narrative tone and stance of the stories, it is largely because their narrative style is a 'neutral' one, without the obvious stylistic formality of (say) Pushkin or even, to some extent, of Lermontov. The narrative does not draw attention to its own 'manner'. But, particularly with the plays, it is surely possible to feel different textures of speech associated with different characters, which a variety of English translators succeed in capturing. Even a non-native reader can feel the differences deriving from the original Russian. For example, take these two speeches from *The Cherry Orchard*, placed side by side and out of context. I quote them first in Russian, from *Вишневый сад* (Letchworth: Bradda Books, 1965):

Епиходов. Я пойду. (*Натыкается на стул, который падает.*) Вот...
(*Как бы торжествуя.*) Вот видите, извините за выражение, какое обсто-
ятельство, между прочим... Это просто даже замечательно! (*Уходит.*)
(p. 17)

Любовь Андреевна (*глядит в окно на сад*). О, мое детство, чистота
моя! В этой детской я спала, глядела отсюда на сад, счастье просыпа-
лось вместе со мною каждое утро, и тогда он был точно таким, ничто
не изменилось. (*Смеется от радости.*) Весь, весь белый! О, сад мой!
После темной ненастной осени и холодной зимы опять ты молод,
полон счастья, ангелы небесные не покинули тебя... Если бы снять с
груди и с плеч моих тяжелый камень, если бы я могла забыть мое
прошлое! (p. 28)

Both of the translations which follow (by Constance Garnett in
The Cherry Orchard and Other Plays (London, 1922) and by Elisaveta Fen in *Chehov Plays* (Harmondsworth, 1971)) capture the
staccato and comically pompous quality of Epihodov's speech on
the one hand, and the lyrical but partly sentimental and theatrical
quality of Lyubov's address to the orchard on the other:

GARNETT:

EPIHODOV. I am going (*stumbles against a chair, which falls over*). There!
(*as though triumphant*). There you see now, excuse the expression, an
accident like that among others... It's positively remarkable (*goes out*).
(p. 5)

LYUBOV (*looking out of the window into the garden*). Oh, my childhood, my
innocence! It was in this nursery I used to sleep, from here I looked
out into the orchard, happiness waked with me every morning and in
those days the orchard was just the same, nothing has changed (*laughs
with delight*). All, all white! Oh, my orchard! After the dark gloomy
autumn, and the cold winter; you are young again, and full of happiness,
the heavenly angels have never left you... If I could cast off the burden
that weighs on my heart, if I could forget the past! (p. 20)

FEN:

YEPIHODOV. I'll leave you now. (*Bumps into a chair which falls over.*) You
see! (*Triumphantly.*) You can see for yourself what it is, I mean to say
...so to speak... It's simply extraordinary! (*Goes out.*) (p. 335)

LIUBOV ANDRYEEVNA (*looks through the window at the orchard*). Oh, my
childhood, my innocent childhood! I used to sleep in this nursery; I used
to look on to the orchard from here, and I woke up happy every
morning. In those days the orchard was just as it is now, nothing has
changed. (*Laughs happily.*) All, all white! Oh, my orchard! After the dark,

stormy autumn and the cold winter, you are young and joyous again;
the angels have not forsaken you! If only this burden could be taken
from me, if only I could forget my past! (pp. 347–8)

Though in this instance the Garnett translation is generally more
accurate to the original, surer and more eloquent, both versions
manifest in each passage a common impulse derived from the
stylistic texture of the original, so that although our valuation of
Chekhov's power as a writer (in the local characteristics of the
writing) might vary slightly according to whether he were being
received through the Garnett version or the Fen, there are, I
think, sufficient grounds for confidence about what *kind* of writer
he is at any given point. It is also possible to make fairly confident
interpretative judgments about the quality of the characters'
emotions (even down to its rhythmic manifestations) conveyed
through such speech.

It is, at any rate, on such a basis that some elements of my
accounts will rest.

Part I

I am not a liberal, not a conservative, not a believer in gradual progress, not a monk, not an indifferentist...I regard trade-marks and labels as a superstition. My holy of holies is the human body, health, intelligence, talent, inspiration, love, and the most absolute freedom – freedom from violence and lying, whatever forms they may take. This is the programme I would follow if I were a great artist.

Letter to A. N. Pleshcheyev (Moscow, October 1889)

INTRODUCTION

Ever since the expatriate Prince Mirsky in 1927 placed Chekhov in the context of the 'twilight years' of Russian history and of the 1890s generally, readers in English seem to have approached Chekhov with a slight mistrust. The two major plays, *Three Sisters* and *The Cherry Orchard*, are perennially popular; but even they (not to mention the whole body of quite neglected prose behind them) have not had the critical acceptance they deserve. To Mirsky, the Chekhov 'cult' was itself a reflection of the dangerous state of post-war English psychology. It signified to him 'an unusually complete rejection of what we may call the heroic values', the literary counterpart of which was what he calls 'negative gentlemanism'.[1] And, although more recent critics from Ronald Hingley to Maurice Valency and Logan Speirs[2] have sought in part to counteract this view, it still persists in the clichés we are likely to hear about Chekhov's negativity, his proneness to indulge in unexamined mood, his anticipation of 'the absurd' and the impression of formlessness one is presumed to take from his work. The currency of these clichés is regrettable, for it not only distracts attention from the real fineness of the late plays but also discourages wide acquaintance with the varied range of Chekhov's work, on the assumption that what he has to offer is essentially repetitive and static.

The irony of the present general attitude to Chekhov is that this very assumption, which prevents readers from getting to know him, lies at the core of a misplaced popular acclaim of him. To the extent that his works seem to abstract their characters from the rhythms of purposeful action and the flow of communication between people – to that extent he is celebrated as a man of peculiarly modern perception. His people, it is said, cannot communicate with each other in a satisfactory manner, since conversations proceed to some extent by misunderstandings or half-understandings, and listeners seem not to give that attention which, in drama particularly, we expect them to give to speakers. But if there is a surface truth in this, it should also be said that these conversations and inattentive groupings are governed by a controlling irony, and in any case that they appear almost exclusively in the late plays, where Chekhov is dealing with highly individualized figures from the non-aristocratic landed gentry. Many of the stories, on the other hand, are unusually successful in revealing communities or elements of communities functioning in an animated and communicative way, even if individual figures are displaced within them. And what we have in the plays is not typically that feeling for the extreme isolation of the individual that is associated with Western European literature as it becomes self-conscious about the 'culture of cities' and urban impersonality, but something rather different. Chekhov is 'modern' in that he has assimilated, to the point of its becoming an imaginative assumption, the Romantic emphasis on the essential individuality of persons; but the egos of his characters are not customarily undernourished, and the threat they seem to feel is not that of anonymity. They are not wastelanders; nor do they seem threatened by the blankness of a metaphysically meaningless existence. In fact, their situation is rather the opposite. In the late plays they seem haunted by the memory (often a recent one, if we can tell from the quality of their nostalgia) of how a community conducive to the shape of their personalities ought to function, and they seem never to question the human value of energy, purposive activity and work. The current tendency to impute to Chekhov a 'modern' sympathy for the 'absurd' elements of life, aggravated by the isolation of consciousness in the mass agglomerations of the modern city, is doing again what the old criticism did in linking Chekhov with impressionist modes of art and Russia's 'twilight years'.[3] It involves a familiar process of transference whereby the reader, or critic, recognizes certain signals, without taking the trouble to read them properly. That process has already done Chekhov a disservice for three-quarters of a century.

Chekhov is an author who must be seen whole if he is to be properly understood at all; and seeing him whole involves not merely tracing his development through the short stories, the novellas and finally the plays, but feeling what it is that he achieves, positively, with each new turn. His is, after all, an unprecedented case (qualitatively, in his native tradition; absolutely, in ours) of an excellent prose writer who was also an excellent dramatist – an author who made important contributions first to the short story, then to the novella, and finally to the dramatic form. What is more, although a clear line of development can be discerned through these forms, no one form emerges as in any sense simply the workshop for the others. His fundamentally dramatic talent reached its definitive form in the last two plays; but few authors have managed the novella form to such purpose as he, and he did so in a peculiarly fruitful climate of ideas.

At a time when English letters were at a low ebb and American literature (with the special exception of Henry James) was temporarily exhausted after its great classical phase, Chekhov's prose work undertook a task of cultural definition and revaluation in relation to earlier images of his culture which is no less important, I think, than the one Lawrence was to undertake, in his turn, in relation to English civilization. So, if only to give a perspective to Lawrence's (or, for that matter, James's or Conrad's) short fiction, it is essential that Chekhov's novellas be read and known. The novella form is not one that the English imagination has inhabited much, perhaps because it tends so strongly towards polemics,[4] and the English have shown themselves less ready to adopt a polemical stance in literature than – for historical–cultural reasons[5] – their Russian counterparts have done. But in the climate of ideas in the latter part of the last century, with old truths being either complicated or shattered and new dogmas beginning to arise, the novella seems to have become, internationally, increasingly important and popular. For Tolstoy in Russia, as much later for Lawrence in England, it was a weapon of polemical power, wielded often with a fair degree of malice. But for Chekhov, with the scientific materialism of Spencer and Darwin pressing upon him on the one hand and Tolstoy's beliefs on the other, the novella became a means to combat the whole polemical cast of mind. In his novellas he meticulously opposes what is essentially a *novelist's* concern for psychological verisimilitude against some inflexible core of dogma derived from outside the work but re-presented within it. This is not to say that Chekhov's works are counter-polemical in any narrow sense; against polemics, they postulate a profound and lasting observation of how people think and behave and what happens to them. But I do not deny that the fictional works convey a peculiar excitement from their own sense of occasion, the sense – unusual to anyone acquainted only with Chekhov's plays – of works shaped by a fighting spirit. Part IV of this book is given over to an account of the major novellas in which this occurs: 'A Dreary Story', 'Ward No. 6', 'Peasants' and 'The Duel'. The combatants are Chekhov and Tolstoy, and behind them Spencer, Darwin and Nietzsche. Two of these works, 'A Dreary Story' and 'The Duel', deserve a place among the great works of short fiction in the world.

Chekhov, then, is not a writer who can only give dramatic and poetic representation to the predicament of one particular class – projecting a 'vague charm', as Raymond Williams calls it,[6] which he has not the resources to examine stringently. He is in no sense an aesthete of the kind generally associated, in Western Europe, with the 1890s. The achievement of the middle-period novellas is, rather, to bring a strong moral preoccupation to bear, through intense observation, on a whole range of contemporary ideas. More generally, I would claim that Chekhov's work belongs to that European tradition of humanist literature, classical in spirit and often centring in comic modes of perception, which links Pope and Swift with Jane Austen, Henry James and James Joyce. For, like those authors, Chekhov is steadfastly preoccupied with man, and the values which interest him are those inhering in the diverse possibilities of ordinary human lives. He has none of the impulse of his fellow-countrymen Dostoevsky and Tolstoy to feel human situations in the light of powerfully intuited metaphysical facts, which is possibly one of the reasons why he seems, at first glance, not so compelling or profound. His earliest stories were comic, and the comedy came from a delighted and satirical observation of pompous or otherwise absurd behaviour and gesture. And even when the ironic observation of human behaviour had grown into a compassionate insight into the essential pathos of such manners and mannerisms, Chekhov never went so far as to suggest a further religious dimension behind or above human activity itself by which life (or art) might ultimately be justified.

Much Chekhov criticism stresses his *sadness*: the vein of near-complaint in the sisters' cry 'If only we knew, if only we knew!' or the sense of solitude one feels when, after the momentous human changes in 'The Duel', the little boat disappears among the high waves and the surrounding world indifferently pursues its own laws, quietly beginning to 'spot with rain'. As I shall argue in chapter 14, *Three Sisters* is a very sad play: almost inevitably, given his humanist orientation, Chekhov is painfully aware throughout his work of human limitations and the fact of death. Such things weigh heavily with him, as do poverty and grief, because in his view there is no restitution for them. Often, too, Chekhov expresses the pain of grief or the finality of death against a background of indifference in the natural world – of softly but constantly falling snow or unwavering, eerie moonlight – which heightens our sense of life's cruelty. As his works and the details of his life both make clear, Chekhov was actually highly responsive to the varying atmospheres of landscape, both emotionally and imaginatively. There is a strong correlation in his work between particular kinds of landscape and the exploration of particular kinds of concern. In Part III of this book I shall discuss some of the stories set in the steppe country, where the varying moods of the steppe and the effects of light and darkness playing across it operate as powerful philosophical metaphors; and in Part V I shall take up the question of Chekhov's interest in feminine sexuality, which he consistently associates in its intensity with Southern summers. But as Chekhov presents it in his work, landscape never takes on the numinous potency which it can assume in Wordsworth and even sometimes in Lawrence. There is no sense of spiritual co-operation between men and the energies of nature, of nature having some interior power. On the contrary, though the sense of natural potencies varies, there are times in Chekhov's work when nature seems no more than a surface, a spectacle, which Chekhov, through his characters, watches with a sad equanimity:

MASHA. But still there is a meaning?
TUSENBACH. Meaning...Here it is snowing. What meaning is there in that? (*a pause*)[7]

Yet, if this seems a denial of life's values and energies, it should also be remembered that the same sense of human beings themselves having to determine whatever life is about is behind Chekhov's hope in human purposiveness and progress. The balances emerging from this are precarious and the emphasis shifts from work to work. In the late plays, where speeches about the necessity of toil and the progress of humanity towards 'the highest happiness on earth' are most frequent and conspicuous, such hopes are fenced in by irony. They are most often voiced by characters who don't work and never will, and they are largely subverted, in context, by an over-riding, sad sense of unfulfilled aspirations in the characters before us. 'The Duel', however, is tentatively optimistic about men's capacity to change and thus to find new and better terms for their lives; and other stories, including 'Ward No. 6' and 'Peasants', are driven by a moral passion which originates in Chekhov's strong personal conviction of the worth of social progress.

It is true, I think, that Chekhov sometimes over-emphasizes work as a way of giving meaning to life and that certain more personal and spiritual manifestations of energy seem outside the range of what he can convincingly represent. That is, partly because he is a non-religious writer, Chekhov seems to find it difficult to create characters whose own spirits are almost religiously intense, characters like Alyosha Karamazov in *The Brothers Karamazov* or, on the negative side, Dolohov in *War and Peace*. He creates good men, men with social ideals, like Misail Polozniev of 'My Life', but there are no true Chekhovian saints. Likewise, though Chekhov can conceive of people propelled by a deep-seated, anarchically destructive personal energy, like Aksinya in 'In the Ravine' or Solyony in *Three Sisters*, he finds it very hard to give them continuous and humanly credible narrative life. With the special exception of Von Koren, whose potential destructiveness never finds full expression in any case, these characters are presented in a conspicuously stylized way which acknowledges their possibility but does not make them particularly real. So Solyony in Act IV of *Three Sisters* is effectively reduced to the tokenism of his recitations and his attempts to rid his hands of the smell of a corpse. Chekhov's imagination, one might say, is profoundly democratic: he looks not to the extremities of the human personality but to ordinary people and the daily conditions of their lives. None of his figures emerges with the almost demonic vitality of a Dostoevsky character to challenge and disrupt the broader emphases of Chekhov's art. He puts so much faith in work because he believes in the human element in human progress, even if he is simultaneously aware of the limited benefits which that progress yields to any individual life. He is deeply, democratically, concerned for ordinary people's welfare. He has the strengths and the limitations of the classical humanist.

Even Chekhov's exploration of philosophical questions involves no impulse to settle a metaphysical truth. His interest, as a humanist, is in the different ways different men feel about the world. Thus his steppe stories, while they pose all sorts of questions about the purpose of life, do so through the minds of, and in relation to, particular characters, and the value of their revelations is psychological as much as anything else. But 'Lights' (which is discussed in some detail in Part III) gives a fascinating sense of the kinds of issue with which Chekhov's imagination was engaged, and of his way of feeling those issues, as he said, 'through images'. 'What is life's purpose?' 'If there is no purpose, how important is the moral life?' 'What is the relation of sexual desire to love, and of love to life's purpose?' 'What is truth and what is illusion, and how long may illusions last?' These and other questions course through the longer stories and novellas, though always embodied in particular situations and only ever answered in relation to this figure or that. Furthermore, in 'Lights' the questioning is done at its deepest level through alternate landscape images, first at night and then at dawn, which project different senses of the world to complicate the spoken sense of it by the story's speakers.

This structural counterpointing of different images of the world, which happens not only in 'Lights' but in 'Easter Eve' and (less successfully) in some other stories, highlights the need for the critic of Chekhov to pay close attention to structure. Unfortunately, the cliché which calls Chekhov the formless imitator of formless lives has inhibited this kind of Chekhov criticism in the past. It is true that the structural ironies on which the stories of 1886–90 depend are often curiously unemphatic, and that one is not alerted to them by any supportive irony in the prose itself. Yet to see that the irony is unemphatic is as important to becoming inward with Chekhov's sensibility as is initially perceiving its presence. For there is at all times something of the man of science about Chekhov, a quiet going about his business in which he is concerned more for the integrity of the facts and for their proper weighting in the narrative than for an audience who must be *made* to understand. The ironic patterns are so broad and under-dramatized, compared with those of the plays, that Chekhov could perhaps be charged with being structurally (and even morally) vague. But it is at least equally plausible that the quiet irony which completes (say) 'Vanka' or 'Enemies' derives instead from a clear sense of artistic proportion and tact. After all, when irony is not based on a sense of human folly but on an incipiently tragic sense of how the world works – by mutual frustration of people's lives – it achieves more for the human spirit by being dignified than by overt protest. It is not that the significances are blurred: the limitations met by the characters in each case are unambiguously clear. It is just that Chekhov relies on one's noticing, as derived from the structuring of the tales, ironic details that have the special force of not actually being stated. The effect is to create an air of moral reticence which, in literary terms, becomes a kind of morality itself, a way of asserting human dignity and an unsentimental intelligence against the cruelty of the facts.

Yet a different account has to be given of the plays. Their imaginative structuring is just as important, as I attempt to show in chapter 1 on *The Cherry Orchard* and in chapter 14 on *Three Sisters*. But, by comparison, the ironic patterns in the plays tend to be more immediate and obvious, and the moral emphases within the conflicts of class interest (and of cultural interest) are more clearly defined. In fact, the late plays reveal a shift in preoccupations and a re-invigoration of Chekhov's purpose. He becomes unusually identified with the interests of a single class – significantly, one not his own. He takes up much more explicitly the question of what characteristics in the people he represents are national characteristics – a question Tolstoy made virtually inevitable for any Russian writer after him, and one which drama, by its ritual and communal nature (being aware of its audience, and making its audience aware of itself), was particularly suited to explore. And in his last work, *The Cherry Orchard*, he resumed something of the distinctly comic spirit with which, in an extremely coarse form, his career had begun.

In the chapters which follow, I shall be intent on making a case for Chekhov's positive achievements at each point. While I shall mention critical defects and problems as I see them, and while I shall indicate which I consider to be lesser works in the total body, I have made it my objective to account for the best of Chekhov's achievement within the scope of this work. The reason for this will, I hope, be clear. The critic who wrote on the defects of *The Excursion* while *The Prelude* lay unknown would do service to no one. In the case of Chekhov, the stories have received scant formal attention outside Russia and the Russian departments of universities, where they are of course well known. However, I begin not at the beginning but at the end, since it is from *The Cherry Orchard*, made so fortuitously topical by the events in Russia some fourteen years later, that so many of the disabling clichés surrounding Chekhov's work have originated. Only by looking more closely at that play, associated so strongly with the sentimental conception of Chekhov as the 'poet of Russia's twilight years', can we begin to gain a more robust and challenging and, I think, more appropriate view of him.

I

'The Cherry Orchard'

The Cherry Orchard is not the easiest of Chekhov's works with which to begin a reassessment of him. Because it is his last work, composed in illness and apparently in a psychological state of unusual detachment from the particulars of the life around him, its created world does feel somewhat brittle, and it is visually and dramatically exceptionally stylized. In this sense it seems to confirm those elements of the popular conception of Chekhov which involve his being charming but lacking imaginative strength, an orchestrator of 'mood' (*nastroenie*), but mood without content. But precisely because it does conform, more than any other Chekhov piece, to this conception of him as a melancholy and merely impressionistic dramatist, it is a useful starting-point from which to begin a fresh approach to him.

In a letter to Olga Knipper on 25 November 1903, before the première of *The Cherry Orchard*, Chekhov commented prophetically: 'So Nemirovich-Danchenko did not read my play to the Society of Lovers of Russian Literature? We began with misunderstandings and we shall end with them – such, it seems, is the fate of my play.'[1] The misunderstandings in question were principally those between himself and the co-directors of the Moscow Art Theatre, Stanislavsky and Nemirovich-Danchenko, as to the prevalent spirit of this last and perhaps most intriguingly original of his plays. As early as September 1903, while he was still in the process of writing, Chekhov had said 'I shall call the play a comedy';[2] and later he added, 'It has turned out not a drama, but a comedy, in parts a farce, indeed...'[3] Never did he renounce this conviction that *The Cherry Orchard* was, above all things, a comedy. But Stanislavsky, from the moment of first reading the play, had very different ideas about it: 'This is not a comedy or a farce, as you wrote, it is a tragedy whatever the solution you may have found for the better life in the last act.'[4] During the rehearsals for the première on 17 January 1904, there was considerable antagonism between author and director,

Chekhov objecting not only to the excesses of Stanislavsky's 'naturalism'[5] but also – and primarily – to the sad and wistful mood which he felt was being falsely projected onto his play. (In some of the performances under Stanislavsky's direction, the duration of the fourth act was extended from twelve to forty minutes to make the utmost of the 'tragedy' of the final scene.)[6] Nor was Chekhov's anger quick to subside. As late as April 1904 he was still complaining to Olga:

Why is it that my play is persistently called a drama in posters and newspaper advertisements? Nemirovich-Danchenko and Stanislavsky see in my play something absolutely different from what I have written, and I'm willing to stake my word on it that neither of them has once read my play through attentively. Forgive me, but I assure you it is so.[7]

The Cherry Orchard, then, was first staged amid a controversy about its basic mood, a controversy which even today remains unresolved. But the irony of the situation is that, despite all Chekhov's protestations, the popular conception of Chekhov until very recently has been Stanislavsky's Chekhov: that wistful lyricist whom so many writers have characterized as negative, as being incapable of giving expression to human will or to purposeful human energy. It is this conception of Chekhov which David Magarshack, untypically, perpetuates in the following description:

The dying, melancholy sound of a broken string of a musical instrument. . .is all Chekhov needed to convey his own attitude to the 'dreary' lives of his characters. . .With the years this sound acquired a nostalgic ring, and it is this sad, nostalgic feeling Chekhov wanted to convey by it. It is a sort of requiem for the 'unhappy and disjointed' lives of his characters.[8]

The peculiar thing about Magarshack's account is that this paragraph comes in the midst of an argument that *The Cherry Orchard* is a farce; and this perhaps typifies the strain evident in a number of critical accounts as they attempt to accommodate Chekhov's intentions to a basic seriousness in their own response. In recent years a number of critics have reacted against the older view which took Stanislavsky's side in the debate – doing so, however, in a way which seems slightly forced. Apart from David Magarshack's account of the play as farce, Maurice Valency discovers it to be, of all things, 'cosmic *vaudeville*',[9] and Logan Speirs finds it 'astonishingly light and fresh'.[10] Only two accounts – those of J. L. Styan and Harvey Pitcher[11] – seem to come close to the true spirit of the play; but neither of them views it, as I think it should finally be viewed, as comedy in a strictly classical sense.

Traditionally, *The Cherry Orchard* has been seen as the poetic elegy which Stanislavsky claimed it was: a play of nostalgic regret for the passing of the landed gentry, cultivated but passive, from control of the Russian land. Its characters, it has often been said, are appealing but weak, unable to act or even to recognize the vulnerability of their position; and in the orchard itself Chekhov has given a somewhat uncritical image of the gracious old order, wantonly destroyed by the new. Clearly, this account has a partial truth: the play is indeed about a world in the process of change, the major characters do seem mysteriously unable to save their orchard, and the loss of the orchard at the end is felt with something like nostalgic regret. But a close look even at the major characters should reveal that their so-called weakness and lack of will is actually something much deeper and much more interesting: in Lyubov and Gaev it amounts to a complex sense of guilt and self-degradation which is both personal and yet obscurely the product of their situation of privilege. Lyubov's addiction to pills and her incessant coffee-drinking suggest, obliquely, something disturbed and guilty about her worldliness; and Gaev's incongruous references to billiards (while disconcertingly unrealistic and obtrusive in the play) represent his attempt to deflect his particular sense of self-degradation into harmless and apparently meaningless verbal gesture. Nor are these characters simply illustrative 'types' of upper-class decadence (though they are certainly closer to being that than the characters of *Three Sisters*). For although Gaev really is, in one way, the 'superfluous man of the eighties' so solemnly imputed to Chekhov as his characteristic 'type', the fact that he himself perceives his relation to that type liberates him, comically, from it:

I'm a man of the eighties. They run down that period, but still I can say I have had to suffer not a little for my convictions in my life. It's not for nothing that the peasant loves me. One must know the peasant![12]

The comedy, and the resilience in Gaev himself which will later find him returning home from the sale of the orchard drying his tears with one hand and in the other clutching anchovies and Kertch herrings, give the lie to any account that would make the characters simply stereotypes of upper-class decadence and the art correspondingly predictable or moralistic.

As has often been noticed, the cherry orchard captures, as an image, something of the past glory of the Russian estates, focusing the different feelings of the characters towards that past. It forms the centre of a carefully balanced composition which begins as soon as Lopahin suggests his plan to cut the orchard down:

LYUBOV. Cut down? My dear fellow, forgive me, but you don't know what you are talking about. If there is one thing interesting – remarkable indeed – in the whole province, it's just our cherry orchard.

LOPAHIN. The only thing remarkable about the orchard is that it's a very large one. There's a crop of cherries every alternate year, and then there's nothing to be done with them, no one buys them.

GAEV. This orchard is mentioned in the 'Encyclopaedia'.

LOPAHIN (*glancing at his watch*). If we don't decide on something and don't take some steps, on the 22nd of August the cherry orchard and the whole estate too will be sold by auction. Make up your minds! There is no other way of saving it, I'll take my oath on that. No, no!

FIRS. In [the] old days, forty or fifty years ago, they used to dry the cherries, soak them, pickle them, make jam too, and they used –

GAEV. Be quiet, Firs.

FIRS. And they used to send the preserved cherries to Moscow and to Harkov by the waggon-load. That brought the money in! And the preserved cherries in those days were soft and juicy, sweet and fragrant ...they knew the way to do them then...

LYUBOV. And where is the recipe now?

FIRS. It's forgotten. Nobody remembers it.[13]

The voices on the stage come from three directions in time. Firs's voice is from the past, when the orchard was abundant with life and work, beautiful but also productive. Lyubov and Gaev speak from the present of an orchard already more important for private reasons than for itself: it is a landmark mentioned in the 'Encyclopaedia', a spectacle that is no longer useful, but one intimately associated with their childhood. Finally, in Lopahin we have the voice of the future, which assures us of the necessity of sacrificing the orchard. The voices play effectively around one another, while each is heard separately and remains distinct. And what they give us, as they emerge relative to each other, is a significantly deepening perspective on the centrally placed image of the cherry orchard. Like the gentry themselves, the orchard is a touching relic of the past: glorious in blossom, an image of a gracious and leisurely age, but essentially of no use. Its vulnerability to the axe is sad, but its unproductiveness, compared with the juicy harvests of the past, partly qualifies the loss. Compared with it, Lopahin's projected villas will be ugly and perhaps vulgar, but they will at least have their use and take their vitality (however purely notional that vitality is in the actual world of the play) from a new and growing class.

This much is indicated very early in the first act. But it is characteristic of Chekhov criticism generally that very few accounts of *The Cherry Orchard* go much beyond this sense of things (mixed up with discussions of character) and a definition of the 'comic' or 'tragic' or 'tragi-comic' response Chekhov is supposed to have had to it. It is here that the disputes arise. For on the one hand, Chekhov creates a sense of social transition and of its cost, showing a serious interest in the nature and process of social evolution and change. The financial ruin of the old estates, the changing economics associated with the emancipation of the serfs and the growth of a new merchant class out of the ranks of the former serfs, all are mentioned in the play and are in some ways the central psychic facts under whose impetus the characters act:

FIRS. I've had a long life. They were arranging my wedding before your papa was born...(*laughs*). I was the head footman before the emancipation came. I wouldn't consent to be set free then; I stayed on with the old master...(*a pause*). I remember what rejoicings they made and didn't know themselves what they were rejoicing over.
LOPAHIN. Those were fine old times. There was flogging anyway.
FIRS (*not hearing*). To be sure! The peasants knew their place, and the masters knew theirs; but now they're all at sixes and sevens, there's no making it out.
GAEV. Hold your tongue, Firs. I must go to town tomorrow. I have been promised an introduction to a general who might let us have a loan.
LOPAHIN. You won't bring that off. And you won't pay your arrears, you may rest assured of that.[14]

But, on the other hand, Firs's subservience, Lopahin's rather aggressive autonomy, and Gaev's failure to be realistic about his debts are not the deeply (even tragically) consequential states which *Three Sisters* might have made of them. In fact, the lightness of texture in *The Cherry Orchard* is very finely achieved. Like *Three Sisters*, the play is imbued with a sense of social and cultural tension, which the breaking string and the thud of the axe express at snapping-point. But the heartfelt agreement between Firs and Lopahin which Firs's deafness makes possible gives the dialogue a comic touch; and even at the first ominous sound of that breaking string, a lighter note is not far away:

(*All sit plunged in thought. Perfect stillness. The only thing audible is the muttering of* FIRS. *Suddenly there is a sound in the distance, as it were from the sky – the sound of a breaking harp-string, mournfully dying away.*)

LYUBOV. What is that?

LOPAHIN. I don't know. Somewhere far away a bucket fallen and broken in the pits. But somewhere very far away.

GAEV. It might be a bird of some sort – such as a heron.

TROFIMOV. Or an owl.

LYUBOV (*Shudders*). I don't know why, but it's horrid (*a pause*).

FIRS. It was the same before the calamity – the owl hooted and the samovar hissed all the time.

GAEV. Before what calamity?

FIRS. Before the emancipation (*a pause*).[15]

The way the sound is placed, at an impasse in the conversation and immediately after the sun has set, gives it clear symbolic force. It is the sound of social transition, of the passing away of a particular class, as the wheels of a society begin to turn. As the string snaps in the sky over characters momentarily silent and stilled, the historical process that will absorb them is almost palpable. There is a strong premonition of the defeat of the play's major characters – of all, that is, except Lopahin. Yet the social significance of the snapping string is suggested and at the same time lightened by Firs's reference to similar omens before the emancipation. The long perspective of time returns to the immediate comedy of Firs's remark.

In view of this careful balance between comic possibilities and the seriousness of Chekhov's social and cultural preoccupation, it is hard to see how the overall structure of his art could be called loose. Furthermore, what emerges from the play is a characteristic division of Chekhov's sympathies, in this case between the claims of the old social order and those of the new. *Three Sisters* contains Chekhov's closest act of identification with people of any class, and the sisters belong to that same class of which Lyubov and Gaev are a decadent extreme. Yet Chekhov, himself the grandson of a serf, was also aware of the positive achievements of social change and of the social value of the energetic, egoistic thrust of his lower-class characters. The old order in *The Cherry Orchard* certainly had its bitterness, which Chekhov presents through Trofimov's outraged social conscience:

Think only, Anya, your grandfather, and great-grandfather, and all your ancestors were slave-owners – the owners of living souls – and from every cherry in the orchard, from every leaf, from every trunk there are human creatures looking at you. Cannot you hear their voices? Oh, it is awful.[16]

And, maintaining the balance, the new order has its positive side:

LOPAHIN. I sowed three thousand acres with poppies in the spring, and now I have cleared forty thousand profit. And when my poppies were in flower, wasn't it a picture! So here, as I say, I made forty thousand, and I'm offering you a loan because I can afford to. Why turn up your nose? I am a peasant – I speak bluntly.[17]

Though Lopahin's practicality makes him blunt in manner, and even downright destructive, he can be generous, and he is not utterly impervious to beauty. His honesty and openness in the play can be as refreshing as a cool wind; and if his poppies are more flamboyant than the stately cherry orchard and more transient in blossom, they are nevertheless what the cherry orchard no longer is. Lopahin's poppies, though they lack the historical and in a sense cultural permanence of the orchard (the fact that the orchard feels permanent and so much a part of the past is why its actual destruction at the end of the play comes as such a shock), have a more colourful vitality; and, along with their beauty, they are – importantly – profitable. Their beauty *is* their 'use', a beauty for which, unlike that of the orchard, people are prepared to pay.

The earliest plays Chekhov wrote were vaudeville and farce, and the comic sense of behaviour he exploited there was never far from his work. In the early stories his sense of humour, while often expressed as irony, also involved a keen sense of the ridiculous in human gesture. So it is interesting that, after the intense seriousness of some of the middle-period novellas and the predominant sadness of *Three Sisters*, Chekhov should revert in his last play to the comic mode. As several writers have noticed, individual effects in *The Cherry Orchard* even border on burlesque, as for example the whole conception of Epihodov, 'two and twenty misfortunes', which makes for a fairly primitive kind of comedy at points throughout the play:

EPIHODOV. I am going (*stumbles against a chair, which falls over*). There! (*as though triumphant*). There you see now, excuse the expression, an accident like that among others . . . It's positively remarkable (*goes out*).[18]

Epihodov squashes, breaks and falls over everything. Trofimov, too, falls downstairs at the point of his indignant exit in Act III; Varya wields a stick that almost hits the wrong man. While there is a more sinister significance attaching to the distasteful Pishtchik and Yasha, still the comic vein continues. Yasha, with his affectations, provides a quite robust verbal comedy:

DUNYASHA. I'm passionately in love with you, Yasha; you are a man of culture – you can give your opinion about anything (*a pause*).
YASHA (*yawns*). Yes, that's so. My opinion is this: if a girl loves anyone, that means that she has no principles (*a pause*).[19]

The characters of *The Cherry Orchard* are, as Valency remarks, more formulaic than those of Chekhov's other major plays; in fact, Lyubov Andreyevna is the only figure who is even potentially tragic. But even Lyubov, if she is not herself comic, is set in a context where comedy is always likely to arise. When she pronounces herself so glad to find old Firs alive, he responds deafly 'the day before yesterday', and her worldly, rather heavy-handed 'wit' is made humorous, if it is not already, by the solemnity with which it is received:

PISHTCHIK (*to* LYUBOV ANDREYEVNA). What's it like in Paris? Did you eat frogs there?
LYUBOV. Oh, I ate crocodiles.
PISHTCHIK. Fancy that now![20]

These examples represent Chekhovian comedy developed from its early satirical origins, where Gogol's influence is often quite heavy, to a stylized, completely distinctive humour arising from calculated pomposities of phrasing and from amusing disjunctions of logic which one almost feels crystallizing in the space of the indicated pauses.

For these reasons, Chekhov's description of the play as 'a comedy, in parts a farce indeed' has an obvious truth. Any play which has such elements cannot consistently maintain an air of wistfulness or an aura of tragedy. Yet one notices that Chekhov does distinguish the comedy from his more farcical effects; and it is possible that he actually meant something rather special by the term. Stanislavsky's sense of the comic mode may have been limited,[21] but Chekhov had a more subtle sense of humour and a more sophisticated understanding. To him, the comic convention need neither require obvious high spirits nor preclude quite serious human and/or historical implications. For, being acquainted with a wide range of literature, including French literature and Shakespeare, Chekhov was in a position to think of 'comedy' in more classical terms: not as a mode provoking actual laughter, but as defining works of art which, while being imbued with a strong sense of the destinies of their figures, refuse to see those destinies tragically. Looked at more broadly than Stanislavsky's terms would allow, then, *The Cherry Orchard* might be said to belong to the same category as *The Winter's Tale*: it contains a tragedy but does not allow it to be fulfilled. In Chekhov's case, this is not because the ending brings partial recovery: Lyubov and Gaev do finally lose their estate. But what is lost at the end of *The Cherry Orchard* has really already been lost at the beginning. Lyubov Andreyevna and her family have been away from the cherry orchard and the play records their coming home; the pattern is primarily one of attempted return – return to a way of life which is idyllic and pure, but which there is really no hope of sustaining. So, whatever Chekhov actually meant when he said 'I shall call the play a comedy', *The Cherry Orchard* is surely best regarded as such by virtue of its affinities with the comedies of the past. In fact – as I now want to argue – it is perhaps most fruitfully regarded as embodying a unique and distinctively modern version of an almost discarded mode common to a number of those early comedies: that is, the pastoral mode.

Pastoral, of course, has taken many forms over the centuries. Wordsworth's 'nature' poetry, for example, or Corot's landscapes may not seem 'pastoral' in the classical sense at all. But there is some evidence to suggest that periods of rapid social transition are often accompanied in the arts by a renewal of interest (on the part of both artists and their audiences) in images of rural contentment. At its simplest, the contrast between an ideal of rustic goodness and the sophisticated vanities of the world may be the artist's most natural moral reaction to the inevitably competing energies of a society in rapid change. But even if the art that emerges takes a more complex form than this, the popular tendency at such times to equate the loss of an old way of life with the loss of cultural innocence may well supply the artist with a stock of potent psychological imagery. In *The Cherry Orchard* that imagery involves the orchard itself, identified by both Lyubov and Gaev with the purity of their childhood, to which, in coming back to the orchard, Lyubov is trying to return. And, together with that, Chekhov quite self-consciously includes with his usual stage effects the pastoral shepherd's pipe and wayside shrine. In effect, just before the onset of one of the most momentous social transitions in modern history, Chekhov renovated stylized elements of an old pastoral mode for his own distinctly modern purposes: to define the yearning for lost innocence that is so central to Lyubov's individual psychology, and to indicate by ironic disjunctions from the pastoral ideal the state of a culture in which innocence and energy have long since been lost.

Throughout his mature work, Chekhov is strongly aware of the formative traditions in his characters' lives and the state of the civilization in which they live. But this cultural and historical interest is unusually easy to isolate in *The Cherry Orchard* since (like *The Seagull*) the play is constructed around a central image, not (as in *Uncle Vanya* and *Three Sisters*) around a person or persons. On the whole, this has the disadvantage of robbing the drama of that interest in diverse individual personalities which makes *Three Sisters* (say) so complex and variable. But it does mean both that Chekhov can produce a tighter shape to his work and that he can focus more directly and emblematically on the social and cultural implications which he wishes to convey. *The Cherry Orchard* begins and ends with a stage without people: in each case there is only the 'nursery', cold and empty, with the cherry orchard sparkling through its windows. The orchard itself is the protagonist. For, right from the beginning of Act I, it is from the static spectacle of the orchard, white with frost, that the play takes its psychological shape:

A room, which has always been called the nursery. One of the doors leads into ANYA'S *room. Dawn, sun rises during the scene. May, the cherry trees in flower, but it is cold in the garden with the frost of early morning. Windows closed. Enter* DUNYASHA *with a candle and* LOPAHIN *with a book in his hand.*[22]

The sun is just rising as the act begins, so that the light defines the cherry orchard against the more shadowy interior foreground; and the whiteness of the blossoming trees and frosted earth gives the outdoor scene a static, timeless air. As the light gradually intensifies throughout the act, the cherry orchard pales back into the distance. But no account of the play can afford to disregard this immediate visual presentation of the orchard, impersonal and almost magically suspended in the morning frost. For its strangely timeless quality and mute purity become for a while, as in pastoral, the reference-points against which the ordinary human world seems burdened and exhausted by time. The room in which Act I takes place is a former nursery, a place full of memories. Lopahin and Dunyasha enter during those odd few minutes between night and day when time is most palpable:

LOPAHIN. The train's in, thank God. What time is it?
DUNYASHA. Nearly two o'clock (*puts out the candle*). It's daylight already.[23]

And when Lopahin begins his typically Chekhovian reverie, bringing a personal and social past simultaneously forward to sustain his anticipation of seeing Lyubov again, the complexity of human time is felt against the unvarying cycle of the cherry-blossoming, momentarily spellbound in three degrees of frost:

Lyubov Andreyevna has been abroad five years; I don't know what she is like now...She's a splendid woman. A good-natured, kind-hearted woman. I remember when I was a lad of fifteen, my poor father – he used to keep a little shop here in the village in those days – gave me a punch in the face with his fist and made my nose bleed. We were in the yard here, I forget what we'd come about – he had had a drop. Lyubov Andreyevna – I can see her now – she was a slim young girl then – took me to wash my face, and then brought me into this very room, into the nursery. 'Don't cry, little peasant,' says she, 'it will be well in time for your wedding day' (*a pause*).[24]

This kind of interest in time, in the fluidity of memory in bringing old situations forward into the present, is distinctive of Chekhov's last plays. In this instance, human time is both complicated by nostalgia and fraught with irony. This 'little peasant' will later own Lyubov's estate, and her troubles will be increased by his failure to have that 'wedding day'. But it is the *irrevocability* of time that occupies our attention in Act I, as Lyubov and her entourage arrive back from the worldliness of Paris in the hope of a new life. When, towards the end of the act, the windows are flung open to the orchard twittering with birds, the innocence of which it reminds Lyubov has an almost tragic past tense:

VARYA (*softly*). Anya's asleep. (*Softly opens the window*). Now the sun's risen, it's not a bit cold. Look, mamma, what exquisite trees! My goodness! And the air! The starlings are singing!
GAEV (*opens another window*). The orchard is all white. You've not forgotten it, Lyuba? That long avenue that runs straight, straight as an arrow, how it shines on a moonlight night. You remember? You've not forgotten?

LYUBOV (*looking out of the window into the garden*). Oh, my childhood, my innocence! It was in this nursery I used to sleep, from here I looked out into the orchard, happiness waked with me every morning and in those days the orchard was just the same, nothing has changed (*laughs with delight*). All, all white! Oh, my orchard! After the dark gloomy autumn, and the cold winter, you are young again, and full of happiness, the heavenly angels have never left you...If I could cast off the burden that weighs on my heart, if I could forget the past![25]

It is characteristic of Chekhov to avoid a surface nostalgia here (that emotion which is so attractive yet so dangerous in unskilled hands), and instead to make Lyubov's longing for childhood – albeit somewhat theatrical – a longing for innocence and escape from time. The whiteness she prizes as purity in the orchard touches her because of the loss of that quality in her own life (just as Gaev, too, values the brilliance and symmetry that are missing from his). For although Lyubov Andreyevna is an attractive character, a woman of energy of whom Chekhov said 'nothing but death could subdue a woman like that', there is a worldliness and incipient vulgarity about her that reveal how far away she is, psychologically, from the cherry-orchard world of her youth. She feels the passing of time, not in terms of age, but in terms of guilt – guilt about her lover, about the death of her son, about all that Paris has meant to her. And if, as the play goes on, she seems singularly inactive about any attempt to save the orchard that means so much to her, it is first because she feels that she does not morally deserve the orchard, and second because that is not really where she belongs. In her deepest self she regards the experience of losing the orchard, of letting it slip through her hands, as a form of penance – the loss of the emblem of that innocence whose reality has long since gone. In any case, the call of her life – and love – is to Paris. The telegrams that arrive at her estate, even before she arrives herself, are a persistent cause of tension, of a self-division which under the trying circumstances of Act III suddenly explodes into a defiant recognition of where her allegiances lie:

LYUBOV. That's a telegram from Paris. I get one every day. One yesterday and one today. That savage creature is ill again, he's in trouble again. He begs forgiveness, beseeches me to go, and really I ought to go to Paris to see him. You look shocked, Petya. What am I to do, my dear boy, what am I to do? He is ill, he is alone and unhappy, and who'll look after him, who'll keep him from doing the wrong thing, who'll give him his medicine at the right time? And why hide it or be silent? I love him, that's clear. I love him! I love him! He's a millstone about my neck, I'm going to the bottom with him, but I love that stone and can't live without it (*presses* TROFIMOV'S *hand*). Don't think ill of me, Petya, don't tell me anything, don't tell me...[26]

Harvey Pitcher has given a convincing account of what he calls the 'emotional network' of this scene,[27] where Lyubov Andreyevna first makes an appeal to Trofimov because he seems to have a stronger sense of right than she has and then, when he fails her, abandons herself to that other side of her nature which is impelling her towards Paris. In this episode (and elsewhere, through his association with Grisha, whose death Lyubov sees as her 'punishment'), Trofimov functions as an externalized figure of Lyubov's own conscience. Recognizing her love for the man who has robbed and abandoned her, she instinctively fears what Trofimov will say; and in defiantly proclaiming her love to him, she is proclaiming it to her own conscience as well. She is no longer torn between shame and desire in deciding what to do; and after this, the lines recited in the background from A. K. Tolstoy's 'The Magdalene' simply reinforce our impression that – paradoxical as it may seem – the cherry orchard, with all its metaphoric connotations of innocence for Lyubov, simply must be lost if she is to have peace of mind.

I have explored this whole area of suggestion in some detail because it highlights several features of Chekhov's dramatic art: the forceful visual suggestion of his stage images, the way that suggestion is complicated by the dialogue which takes place across and around it, and the simultaneous dramatization of social fact and the very personal psychological situations of individual characters. It is the work of a consummate artist whose control is everywhere evident in the work at large. For Lyubov's lost innocence is, in a sense, embodied before both her and us in Anya, the daughter who bears so much likeness to Lyubov's younger self. In Act I all hope seems centred on her. Significantly, the shepherd's pipe plays as she retires to bed, and the last words of the act are a spoken tribute to her (ordinary metaphors, perhaps, but meaningfully suggestive of natural radiance in this carefully established context):

TROFIMOV (*tenderly*). My sunshine! My spring.

When, therefore, Anya subordinates her natural goodness to a shaky ideal in welcoming the 'new dawn' with Trofimov, the sense of defeat is both personal (in what it implies for Lyubov, whom Anya comforts at the end of Act III with promises that are plainly empty) and in a broad sense cultural. Anya succumbs to the new ideology; the pastoral shepherd's piping is not heard again after the end of Act I.

Chekhov, as I have said, is renovating certain elements of pastoral to define a process of cultural transition. The whole opening scene of Act II, as a pictorial composition, is pastoral in character – the initial illusion of purity about the pastoral setting becoming only gradually and subtly ironic as we discern the presence of the 'great town' in the background. Then, more particularly, the ironic intention manifests itself through the disintegration of the pure and exact visual impression into an incongruous awkwardness of movement and modernity of dialogue when the action actually begins. The entire opening scene, beginning with the visual contrivance in the stage directions, demands the most absolute precision for its effect:

The open country. An old shrine, long abandoned and fallen out of the perpendicular; near it a well, large stones that have apparently once been tombstones, and an old garden seat. The road to GAEV's house is seen. On one side rise dark poplars; and there the cherry orchard begins. In the distance a row of telegraph poles and far, far away on the horizon there is faintly outlined a great town, only visible in very fine clear weather. It is near sunset. CHAR-LOTTA, YASHA and DUNYASHA are sitting on the seat. EPIHODOV is standing near, playing something mournful on a guitar. All sit plunged in thought. CHARLOTTA wears an old forage cap; she has taken a gun from her shoulder and is tightening the buckle on the strap.[28]

These stage directions are, clearly, much more elaborate than is usual and more precise in their disposition of the figures and properties. Chekhov mentions them specifically in a letter to Nemirovich-Danchenko: 'In the second act I substituted for the river an old chapel and a well. This is better. But in the second act you will make provision for a real green field, and a path, and an horizon wider than is usual on the stage.'[29] This 'wider horizon' provides an urban perspective to the pastoral image, foreshadowing the end of a country idyll. Even more importantly, the human groupings in the foreground (framed, in this case, by the wayside shrine and the well, so clearly reminiscent of pastoral) recall Watteau's famous painting, *Les Charmes de la vie*, bringing to mind also the subtle melancholy of that picture. Like Watteau's figure with the lute, Epihodov is set apart with his guitar, while the others are clustered on the garden seat. The setting seems initially to invite delight and the pleasures of courtly love. But while there is a love-triangle of a kind between Yasha, Dunyasha and Epihodov, it is not one that radiates innocence and joy. The divisions of attention and intention among this peculiar assortment of characters have the same effect as the preoccupied bodily attitudes of Watteau's figures. Just as Watteau's figures are subtly turned away from one another, Chekhov's characters are absorbed in their separate thoughts; and both scenes make us feel the absence of any truly functioning community between individual persons. The painting and the stage setting have in common an air of mournful distraction and even lassitude in the characters, which suggests their oppression by something both inside and outside themselves. Like Yasha's and Epihodov's singing, something in the stage setting is vaguely off-key: there is a sense of disquiet, and each figure, 'plunged in thought', seems oddly absorbed in himself.

Like Watteau's *Gilles*, Chekhov's composition shows his feeling for the fate of those secondary characters, like the artificer and the clown, who have been genially parasitic on a high culture which is now entering a phase of decline. For before the lifelessness of a culture is generally recognized, these people instinctively reflect the fact by a certain stiffness of posture and (in some cases) artlessness of gesture. Their demeanour reveals the emptiness of their art, which, in no longer serving something vital, no longer serves them. Thus, it is no small calculation on Chekhov's part that Act II should begin with Charlotta – governess, conjurer and ventriloquist – captured at an artlessly confessional moment, speaking (unheard) to other subordinate and dependent people, all of whom seem, despite their stylized postures, lonely and bereft of resource:

CHARLOTTA (*musingly*). I haven't a real passport of my own, and I don't know how old I am, and I always feel that I'm a young thing. When I was a little girl, my father and mother used to travel about to fairs and give performances – very good ones. And I used to dance *salto-mortale* and all sorts of things. And when papa and mamma died, a German lady took me and had me educated. And so I grew up and became a governess. But where I came from, and who I am, I don't know... Who my parents were, very likely they weren't married... I don't know (*takes a cucumber out of her pocket and eats*). I know nothing at all (*a pause*). One wants to talk and has no one to talk to . . . I have nobody.

EPIHODOV (*plays on the guitar and sings*). 'What care I for the noisy world! What care I for friends or foes!' How agreeable it is to play on the mandoline!

DUNYASHA. That's a guitar, not a mandoline (*looks in a hand-mirror and powders herself*).[30]

It is part of the comic convention that the sorrows of which Charlotta speaks are itemized rather than felt, partly balanced by, and partly deflected into, her cucumber-eating. The expressions of melancholy are stylized. But the fact that feelings are formalized in this arrangement does nothing to discount the fact that they are there. Though lacking the emphasis on personality and the sense of life's active cruelty which we associate with tragedy, the scene gives classical expression to a state of cultural decay by which the characters are tangibly but unconsciously oppressed. With the setting sun, in deliberate contrast to the sunrise of Act I, Chekhov prepares imaginatively for the demise of the landed class in this play and for the loss of everything which that class has contributed, positively, to the culture.

Act II as a whole assumes a processional character which is consistent with this stylized beginning: three groups of figures in turn arrive to converse by the abandoned shrine, before the sun finally sets and the string is heard snapping in the sky. The last of these groups includes Trofimov, the 'perpetual student' whose opinions (were it not for their often ironic context in the play) are fairly close to what Chekhov's letters suggest were his own.[31] Trofimov's speeches widen the specific social reference of the play:

The vast majority of the intellectual people I know, seek nothing, do nothing, are not fit as yet for work of any kind. They call themselves intellectual, but they treat their servants as inferiors, behave to the peasants as though they were animals, learn little, read nothing seriously, do practically nothing, only talk about science and know very little about art.[32]

But it is characteristic of Chekhov's irony – here and throughout his work – that this character, who so often accords with his own attitudes, is a conspicuously inadequate person, embodying more than anyone the inactivity of which he speaks. What Trofimov advocates in his most rhetorical speeches is embodied before him in Lopahin; and though he himself cannot recognize it, Chekhov clearly does so in creating that symbolic stalemate between Lopahin and Lyubov on the subject of Russia's 'giants':

LOPAHIN. You know, I get up at five o'clock in the morning, and I work from morning to night; and I've money, my own and other people's, always passing through my hands, and I see what people are made of all round me. One has only to begin to do anything to see how few honest, decent people there are. Sometimes when I lie awake at night I think: 'Oh! Lord, thou hast given us immense forests, boundless plains, the widest horizons, and living here we ourselves ought really to be giants.'
LYUBOV. You ask for giants! They are no good except in story-books; in real life they frighten us.
(EPIHODOV *advances in the background, playing on the guitar*)
LYUBOV (*dreamily*). There goes Epihodov.
ANYA (*dreamily*). There goes Epihodov.
GAEV. The sun has set, my friends.[33]

Epihodov steps forth as if in answer to Lyubov's call: the most absurd representative of the old order, passing across the stage in the last rays of light. The sounds of his guitar give way to silence, which, in turn, is broken by the sound of the snapping string. David Magarshack has pointed out how much the force of this moment depends on Chekhov's stilling his characters into a state of 'suspended animation',[34] a trance-like frame of mind which is somehow induced by the spectacle of Epihodov silhouetted against the setting sun and signalled first by Lyubov's and Anya's dreamily repeating 'There goes Epihodov' and then by Gaev's softly chanted apostrophe to Nature. As the sun sets over Epihodov the characters again sit 'plunged in thought'. But this time it is with an unspoken community of feeling, at least for the duration of the string snapping in the sky. Here, especially, one is aware of Chekhov's special instinct for dramatic timing. The subtly ritual casting of the act has prepared for some such moment, and it comes immediately after a discussion of the 'giants' which Lopahin, at least, thinks Russians ought to be, which heightens our awareness of what these people actually are. The sound of the snapping string feels like the triumph of some impersonal process over these characters' lives. It is like a forewarning of the judgment of history on their lifelessness and decadence. And as soon as that sound is heard in the play, a whole series of changes occurs. A wayfarer enters, begging and then ridiculing Varya's money; Lopahin taunts her openly about the general presumption that they will marry, which he has never quite done before; and Trofimov decisively wins Anya's loyalty. Although Lopahin's 'giants' would at least be decent and incorruptible men, and although Trofimov the idealist prophesies happiness, there is nothing in the play's structure to endorse either hope. In fact, the rising moon, the poplars, Epihodov's melancholy tune, and the echo of Varya's voice at the end of the act – 'Anya! Anya!' – say otherwise.

At this point, from the beginning of Act III, Chekhov has effectively moved the drama beyond the situation in which the pastoral suggestions had their meaning. With the fate of the old class all but sealed, he turns more directly to give an image of shifting power and social disintegration. From a beginning in which what is essentially a family is re-united in a setting of shared memories, the play accumulates people – only to loosen the bonds between them; and, as part of that process, the emphasis shifts from Lyubov's personal longing for lost innocence to the power-dynamics of social change. In Acts I and II Yasha and Dunyasha, coming only gradually into their own right as characters, are disruptive presences among the cherry-orchard people, breaking up any sense of those people as forming a stable, self-contained community. Though officially subordinate in station, they dress and act like the class they serve; and often Yasha's service to that class is performed insolently and ironically. In Act III, however, with the introduction of the post-office clerk and station-master as reluctant guests at Lyubov's party, Chekhov brings directly into focus the stages of Lyubov's and Gaev's loss of power and the greater importance of a new factor in the determination of status – money. In no other of Chekhov's plays is money so important, so insidiously dominating the characters' lives. Pishtchik can think of nothing else, as he himself says. And the unusually nervous balance of relationships in Act III derives from the fact that, although the scales of power are presumed to have tipped with the sale of the orchard, no one knows exactly which way.

Like its counterparts in Chekhov's other major plays, Act III brings the drama to a climax by collecting its characters together in strained and untypical circumstances. Almost always, these occasions have the inbuilt irony of being gatherings that should not have taken place. Like Serebryakov's meeting to propose the sale of the estate in *Uncle Vanya*, or the accidental fire in *Three Sisters* (so wholly inappropriate to the sisters' state of feeling at

that moment that it seems as if it has been lit 'on purpose' to
spite them), the party in Act III of *The Cherry Orchard* takes place
at 'the wrong time to have the orchestra, and the wrong time to
give a dance'.[35] In every detail the occasion is an affront to all
that Lyubov and Gaev have represented in the past:

> *A drawing-room divided by an arch from a larger drawing-room. A chandelier*
> *burning. The Jewish orchestra, the same that was mentioned in Act II, is heard*
> *playing in the ante-room. It is evening. In the larger drawing-room they are*
> *dancing the grand chain. The voice of* SEMYONOV-PISHTCHIK: 'Promenade*
> à une paire!' *Then enter the drawing-room in couples, first* PISHTCHIK *and*
> CHARLOTTA IVANOVNA, *then* TROFIMOV *and* LYUBOV ANDREYEVNA,
> *thirdly* ANYA *with the Post-Office Clerk, fourthly* VARYA *with the Station-*
> *Master, and other guests.* VARYA *is quietly weeping and wiping away her tears*
> *as she dances. In the last couple is* DUNYASHA. *They move across the drawing-*
> *room.* PISHTCHIK *shouts:* 'Grand rond, balancez!' *and* 'Les Cavaliers
> à genou et remerciez vos dames.' FIRS *in a swallow-tail coat brings in*
> *seltzer water on a tray.* PISHTCHIK *and* TROFIMOV *enter the drawing-*
> *room.*[36]

The very presence of the post-office clerk and the station-master
is a sign of change, a disappointment in terms of what has been
prepared for by the double drawing-room, the arch and the
burning chandelier. After the outdoor setting of Act II, this
indoor scene is burdened with the accessories of a past age,
oppressing the non-aristocratic present with their disproportionate formality and weight. The dance, designed to promote
high spirits, can only manage a forced gaiety, beneath which lie
frustration and a flickering aggression. No one in the room
(except perhaps the silly Dunyasha) is really happy, and only a
convention of mock abuse, freely indulged in, covers – or partly
covers – the personal aggressions that are going on:

TROFIMOV (*teasing*). Madame Lopahin! Madame Lopahin!
VARYA (*angrily*). Mangy-looking gentleman![37]

This propensity for aggression infects nearly all the characters,
but it is most obvious in Charlotta – that curiously displaced
and autonomous person, obscure as to class, mannish, and yet
not without a feminine quota of loneliness. Charlotta works with
artifice, she is skilled in illusion; and it is by illusion that she
distracts attention from the painful fate hanging over the cherry
orchard. In her check trousers and grey top hat, and springing
into the air to shouts of 'Bravo!', she is an unrealistic figure,

belonging, one comes to see, to the stylized tradition of mime. Yet the significance of her tricks is important and intriguing:

CHARLOTTA (*holding pack of cards in her hands, to* TROFIMOV). Tell me quickly which is the top card.
TROFIMOV. Well, the queen of spades.
CHARLOTTA. It is! (*To* PISHTCHIK) Well, which card is uppermost?
PISHTCHIK. The ace of hearts.
CHARLOTTA. It is! (*claps her hands, pack of cards disappears*). Ah! what lovely weather it is to-day!
(*A mysterious feminine voice which seems coming out of the floor answers her.* 'Oh, yes, it's magnificent weather, madam.')
CHARLOTTA. You are my perfect ideal.
VOICE. And I greatly admire you too, madam.
STATION MASTER (*applauding*). The lady ventriloquist – bravo![38]

The rapid succession of one trick after another and Charlotta's triumph in her power of command make this a *tour de force* of personal assertion which has also an edge of aggression about it. In the circumstances, with Lyubov helplessly awaiting news of what has happened to the estate, Charlotta's demonstration of her power to will the world as she wants it, and her willing a kind of anarchy, feels to the audience like an act of psychic violence. The violence is cleanly achieved: it is probably not even conscious. But Chekhov makes it impossible for us not to feel that Charlotta in some sense *wills* her employers' loss of power. It is, after all, just such a cruel, almost predestined operation of 'chance' and sudden overthrow of the old order which gives Lyubov's estate to Lopahin.

Chekhov is unusually alert to this kind of latent aggression in subordinate people; and the first definite news that the orchard has been sold provokes laughter from Yasha and, most surprising of all, irony from Firs. From then on the cherry-orchard people can do nothing but lose. And this process of loss culminates in the burlesque of Varya's taking a stick to Epihodov: her last frustrated gesture of authority, as Lopahin – the new owner of the cherry orchard – enters and is almost struck by the stick. I mentioned earlier Chekhov's sure sense of timing. Here, as Lopahin announces that he has bought the orchard, Chekhov depends for an effect on bringing the whole on-going momentum of the drama itself to a halt: there is neither action nor dialogue as the shock reverberates across the stage. Only after Varya has thrown down her keys does the action resume its progress, but

now with Lopahin in command and not Lyubov. The final shift
of power takes place, definitively, in that one moment, after which
Lyubov is left with nothing but her private hope of going to Paris
and Anya's well-intentioned but empty promises.

As far as the characters are concerned, the drama at this point
is effectively finished; and the last act is in many ways thinner
than the other three. What it does, however, is to shift the
emphasis away from people and towards social fact. The very
setting of the scene is more impersonal, with the cold, hard
reality of Lyubov's loss embodied in the new starkness of the
former 'nursery':

*Same as in First Act. There are neither curtains on the windows nor pictures
on the walls: only a little furniture remains piled up in a corner as if for sale.
There is a sense of desolation; near the outer door and in the background of
the scene are packed trunks, travelling bags, etc.*[39]

The sense of space on the stage is a sense of emptiness, an
emptiness in which Lopahin and Yasha with their glasses of
champagne are somewhat at a loss. The house already has an
abandoned and hollow air. As in Act I, the weather is sunny and
still, with three degrees of frost; but the significance of such
weather now is simply that it is 'just right for building'. A
pervasive shift has taken place in the culture represented in
the play, from originally aristocratic to bourgeois values. Yet
Chekhov's response remains ambivalent. He is too much of a
realist not to place some value simply on the continuity of life,
even as the play clearly expresses his regret at the cultural
implications of the change:

TROFIMOV. Your father was a peasant, mine was a chemist – and that
proves absolutely nothing whatever. (LOPAHIN *takes out his pocket-book*).
Stop that – stop that. If you were to offer me two hundred thousand
I wouldn't take it. I am an independent man, and everything that all
of you, rich and poor alike, prize so highly and hold so dear, hasn't the
slightest power over me – it's like so much fluff fluttering in the air. I
can get on without you. I can pass by you. I am strong and proud.
Humanity is advancing towards the highest truth, the highest happiness,
which is possible on earth, and I am in the front ranks.
LOPAHIN. Will you get there?
TROFIMOV. I shall get there (*a pause*). I shall get there, or I shall show
others the way to get there.
(*In the distance is heard the stroke of an axe on a tree*)
LOPAHIN. Good-bye, my dear fellow; it's time to be off. We turn up our

noses at one another, but life is passing all the while. When I am working hard without resting, then my mind is more at ease, and it seems to me as though I too know what I exist for; but how many people there are in Russia, my dear boy, who exist, one doesn't know what for. Well, it doesn't matter. That's not what keeps things spinning.[40]

In this exchange between Lopahin and Trofimov, two aims or styles of life are brought into confrontation, but it is a confrontation without malice. It is the last salutation between men bent on opposite ways, and it rises to the occasion with an uneasy but touching reconciliation: 'We turn up our noses at one another, but life is passing all the while.' Trofimov has the vague idealism of the old class, Lopahin the quiet, instinctive pragmatism of the new. Lopahin has money and a certain confidence in the utility of work; but his is also the axe that fells the cherry trees. Trofimov has only a great dream; and, while it is in one way a democratic dream, it is in its self-aggrandizing pride and self-assurance unmistakably aristocratic in origin. Each man is presented to us as to some extent self-deceived. Lopahin is unable to see the destructive side of his 'work', and when he says 'When I am working hard...it *seems* to me as though I too know what I exist for' (my italics), he half-recognizes that the real purpose of life eludes him. Trofimov naively trusts in his dream; but it seems, to say the least, a highly precarious dream when set against the down-to-earth question 'Will you get there?' and the distant sound of the axe.

Yet it is significant that this note of impartiality is struck in a scene involving these particular characters, Trofimov and Lopahin. Chekhov's ethical sense demands that he recognize Lopahin's basic decency and that he admire Lopahin's ability to get things done. To do so, he sets him beside Trofimov – a character who is emotionally cold and therefore not one to whom we give warm sympathy, but an idealist in his own terms and an associate of the old class. In this way a certain balance is achieved between the claims of the old order and the new, and Chekhov's presentation of the situation is demonstrably fair. For some time, in fact, the play carefully elicits responses and counter-responses so as to prevent the feelings of any one character or group of characters from holding complete sway. Lyubov and Gaev are seen to be saddened by the loss of the orchard, but they are also relieved, and not just because the tension is over but because their personal lives are somehow freed. They are freed too late perhaps, and certainly in an ambiguous way, but freed nonetheless. Lopahin, on the other hand, having triumphed in the purchase of the orchard, seems to have no private energy left. The scene where he cannot bring himself to propose to Varya, tactfully constructed as it is, makes us feel more than ever that there is something unfree about Lopahin's emotional life. It is never made clear whether that lack of freedom derives from a sense of personal insecurity which makes him afraid of marriage, or from a sentimental attachment to Lyubov which makes Varya seem inferior, or simply from his being too occupied with other things. But Chekhov makes us feel all along that Lopahin will not propose to Varya, and he confirms that feeling immediately before the 'proposal' scene when the champagne glasses are prematurely emptied by a thirsty Yasha. And in the course of the scene itself, Lopahin's inability to propose is suggestively associated with an unconscious reluctance to be controlled by those who controlled his forefathers, when he hears whisperings of connivance behind the closed door.

It is characteristic of Chekhov to keep up this dialogue of opposing values and claims for as long as his dramatic situations will allow. The emptiness of the house, left to stand during the winter to be knocked down in the spring, when 'new life' theoretically begins, makes us feel the departure from the cherry orchard to be the sad finale to a whole era of Russian life. Yet still the voices are set in dialogue:

ANYA. Good-bye, home! Good-bye to the old life!
TROFIMOV. Welcome to the new life!

There is not one response but many, deftly intertwined:

LOPAHIN. Till the spring, then! Come, friends, till we meet! (*goes out*).
(LYUBOV ANDREYEVNA and GAEV *remain alone. As though they had been waiting for this, they throw themselves on each other's necks, and break into subdued smothered sobbing, afraid of being overheard.*)
GAEV (*in despair*). Sister, my sister!
LYUBOV. Oh, my orchard! – my sweet, beautiful orchard!
Voice of ANYA (*calling gaily*). Mamma!
Voice of TROFIMOV (*gaily, excitedly*). Aa-oo![41]

This counterpointing of youth and age, hope and elegy, perfectly balances two alternative social possibilities. It is a tribute to Chekhov's intelligence that that balance should persist to the very end. But as all the voices dissolve into silence and the dull thud of the axe, the moment has come for him to abandon the previous restraints on his own sympathies:

The stage is empty. There is the sound of the doors being locked up, then of the carriages driving away. There is silence. In the stillness there is the dull stroke of an axe in a tree, clanging with a mournful lonely sound. Footsteps are heard. FIRS *appears in the doorway on the right. He is dressed as always – in a pea-jacket and white waistcoat, with slippers on his feet. He is ill.*)[42]

The sounds retreating, then silence, and finally the axe and the solitary footsteps, all echo life deserting the cherry orchard and the destruction of the orchard itself. And with the appearance of Firs, old, sick and lying motionless on the stage as the curtain drops, a chapter of history does seem to be coming to a close.

It is true, I think, that this image of Firs at the very end of the play softens and distorts our sense of the Russian past, evoking too simple a pathos. Since the cherry orchard itself is, from one point of view, a somewhat biased emblem of the past (its value, though ultimately ambiguous, is intrinsically established in its beauty, its glistening whiteness), the play's ending, which has historical, as well as cultural, implication, needs to be firmer. Firs, also, is a risky figure for Chekhov to give much importance to because he is so much a stock creation, producing only a limited comedy and always tempting Chekhov to indulge over-simple effects. We might compare the sense of the past as embodied in Firs with the sense of even the very recent past in *Three Sisters*, where it takes such a complex form in Olga's, Masha's and Irina's personalities, or with the late story 'A Woman's Kingdom', where a past style of life is seen incongruously penetrating the one that has replaced it. Fortunately, Firs lying on the stage is not the only impression with which *The Cherry Orchard* leaves us. Above him is the sound of the string snapping in the sky, and behind him the resounding strokes of the axe.

Given the usually robust conventions of the stage, the drama of *The Cherry Orchard* is unusually subtle, unusually formalized. Even the sequence of sounds with which it ends, which J. L. Styan calls 'the most daring...the naturalistic theatre has known',[43] has a curiously ambivalent effect which is difficult to define. The sound of the snapping string, with its mournful and yet impersonal quality, was an artistic possibility already present in Chekhov's mind as early as 1887, where it appears in the story

'Happiness'. But it finds its fullest realization here in the stylized world of *The Cherry Orchard*. For, although the sound was one Chekhov actually heard as a boy, its significance to his imagination was obviously both semi-mysterious and profound. It seems to have made him feel, or perhaps simply expressed for him as nothing else could have done, some harsh and sad intuition about the world and about people's lives within it which would otherwise have remained inexpressibly abstract. In *The Cherry Orchard* it combines a number of meanings. In the simplest terms, and together with the sounds of the axe on the tree, it expresses symbolically the end of a particular era: it makes us seem actually to *hear* social changes taking place, making them unusually palpable. At the same time, it also impersonalizes our responses, taking them away from the characters as individual people, and concentrating our attention more abstractly on their predicament and on the process by which they have been displaced. After the simplification of feeling introduced by the final scene with Firs, that is in part what the play needs. But the ambivalence of the sound, coming inexplicably 'out of the sky' and yet 'mournfully dying away', captures something deeper in the whole spirit of the play which relates to Chekhov's wider interest in cultural decay. Nothing could be further from the truth than the suggestion that *The Cherry Orchard* is simply a social drama weighing up the advantages and disadvantages of social change in late nineteenth-century Russia and accordingly alternating poetic elegy with sequences of farce. Nor, as I hope I have shown, is the play an evocative piece of 'mood' with little intellectual substance. Its triumph is to express, as Watteau's paintings so often express, both the social and psychological manifestations of a situation in which a sustaining and ordering culture has become defunct. And, to express this, it brilliantly assimilates comic and tragic possibilities to one another until practically every scene is both light in texture and pervaded by a subtle melancholy – a true merging of tragic and comic possibilities. *The Cherry Orchard*, then, may be unusually stylized. But the vitality it brings to elements of a neglected mode of pastoral, the rightness of what happens to its created people in terms of their individual psychology and their cultural predicament, and the cultural assessment which Chekhov undertakes in the play, give us some measure of what an instinctive and alive artist he was.

Part II

But in short stories it is better to say not enough than to say too much, because, – because – I don't know why!

Letter to I. L. Shcheglov (Moscow, 22 January 1888)

2

Beginnings

The mature Chekhov who wrote *The Cherry Orchard* and displayed there such sympathy for the estate culture[1] is a decidedly serious artist, composed and accomplished, with a range of sympathies to rival that of any of his respected compatriots. He belongs firmly in the main tradition of Russian literature as Wordsworth or George Eliot belong in the English tradition. Like theirs, his art extends the expressive possibilities of his chosen forms to the point where they seem innovatory, while at the same time drawing deeply on the resources of a civilization and its language and finally of a national history itself, embodied in character and idiom. Yet unlike most serious writers – but, surprisingly, like Dickens – Chekhov began as a popular artist. Writing for the Moscow humorous magazines of the early 1880s – *Dragonfly, Alarm Clock, Onlooker* and later *Fragments* – Chekhov had a most unorthodox beginning for a classic writer in Russia, a beginning quite opposite from that of Pushkin or Gogol and their successors of the next generation, Goncharov, Turgenev and Tolstoy. Russia's foremost writers traditionally came from the landowning class (Dostoevsky described Russian literature as 'a literature of landowners'). And although, as Irving Howe says,[2] Gogol, Leskov and Dostoevsky himself represent a decisive break from the 'literature of landowners' with their new interest in the cities and the urban poor, Gogol and Dostoevsky at least began their literary careers seriously, contributing to the 'intellectual' journals. In 1880, three years before Turgenev's death and at the precise end of the great middle period of Tolstoy's work (*War and Peace* had been published in 1869, *Anna Karenina* in 1878), the aristocratic age of Russian literature was to suffer a further challenge. The child of a merchant family and the grandson of an ex-serf, Chekhov began to make his way through the lowbrow humorous magazines that were springing up to satisfy the needs of a new class. Ernest Simmons, in his biography of Chekhov, gives an effective summary of the historical and cultural changes that were taking place:

'The reign of mediocrity has started,' Turgenev wrote in a letter in 1874; and by the beginning of the Eighties a period of extreme social and political stagnation had set in which became deeply reactionary after the assassination of Alexander II. Under the blighting influence of Konstantin Pobedonostsev, Procurator of the Holy Synod and principal adviser of Alexander III – a man who could 'stop further decay like frost but could never help a living thing to grow' – all the vital intellectual and artistic forces of the country were plunged into apathetic gloom. At his urging progressive public opinion was either severely limited or brutally suppressed. Under these conditions the growing urban middle class, divorced from the leadership of the intellectuals, developed readers for whom the literature of the landed gentry, with its concern for the great questions of the day, had become irrelevant. A new kind of reading matter which would reflect the values, interests, and way of life of the 'little people' was needed, and the humorous magazines sprang up in abundance as one of the responses to this demand.[3]

Chekhov's spirit in writing for these magazines, and indeed the spirit of the magazines themselves, is perhaps best indicated by the pseudonyms he adopted for the purpose – 'Antosha Chekhonte', 'My Brother's Brother', 'The Man Without a Spleen', 'Screw No. 6' and so on.[4] What he wrote for them was largely in line with their demands. They were stories written quickly, dashed off without much care or revision, produced to limits of a thousand words and often less, light and topical, and always in danger from the censor's pencil. Prolific as Chekhov was in these early years of writing for the humorous magazines (he produced 120 stories in the first year alone), his overall achievement in this vein is thus strictly limited. Only a year or two after his own liberation from the restrictions of the humorous magazines,[5] he said of a contributor to *Fragments*: 'Write him that to describe drunkenness for the sake of using drunkards' words is a kind of cynicism. There is nothing easier than to exploit drunkards.'[6] Yet more than once the Chekhov of *Fragments* had himself been guilty of such cynicism, sometimes in exactly the same form. In fact, the taste in humour of the Moscow magazines and their general standard probably made that cynicism unavoidable. Many of Chekhov's early contributions are simply extended jokes, hardly stories at all; and even as jokes they are banal. Hingley cites the following 'advertisement' among such instances:

IN LEUKHIN'S BOOK-SHOP there are on sale the following frightful books: *Passionate Love, Self-Taught*, or *Oh, you beast!* by Idiotov. Price 1 rouble 80 copecks... *The Memoirs of a Woman's Stocking*, or *So much for Innocence!* Price 1 rouble 50 copecks.[7]

It was from such tasteless beginnings that Chekhov's art began to develop. For even while he was still contributing to the Moscow magazines, especially during the years 1880 to 1885, there was a gradual development in Chekhov's work, changing him from a compliant contributor with the state of his family's finances most at heart to a young artist labouring under painful creative conditions. Some of the early signs of that change – to contrast with the example I have just quoted – are found in miniatures like 'The Death of a Government Clerk', 'The Chameleon' and 'Fat and Thin': miniatures which, though nowhere approaching the fullness of even the stories of 1885 ('A Malefactor', 'An Upheaval' or 'Sergeant Prishibeyev'*),[8] nevertheless have within their comic framework some of the bitterness and consequence of serious farce.

In view of Chekhov's family background, his predilection for farce is not surprising:

What writers belonging to the upper class have received from nature for nothing, plebeians acquire at the cost of their youth. Write a story of how a young man, the son of a serf who has served in a shop, sung in a choir, been at a high school and a university, who has been brought up to respect everyone of higher rank and position, to kiss priests' hands, to reverence other people's ideas, to be thankful for every morsel of bread, who has been many times whipped, who has trudged from one pupil to another without goloshes, who has been used to fighting and to tormenting animals, who has liked dining with his rich relatives, and been hypocritical before God and men from the mere consciousness of his own insignificance – write how this young man squeezes the slave out of himself, drop by drop, and how waking one beautiful morning he feels that he has no longer a slave's blood in his veins but a real man's.[9]

These remarks have a clear and acknowledged reference to Chekhov's own life, and the pain of this early degradation gives much of his youthful writing its impulse to ridicule those incorrigibly subservient people, victims of a rule of authority, who do more than anyone else to perpetuate it. Furthermore, the unpopularity of the Czarist bureaucracy among the class of likely readers of the humorous magazines probably guaranteed such broadly satirical stories an automatic welcome. Thus 'The Death

of a Government Clerk' seems to take a vengeful delight in the
swelling grotesquerie of the clerk's attempts to apologize to the
offended general, inviting the reader to mock at the clerk's
absurdity and even, finally, at his self-induced death. Similarly,
'Fat and Thin' and 'The Chameleon' make a comedy of ridicule
out of the various reversals of behaviour attendant upon unexpected changes in their characters' relative status. The thin man
of 'Fat and Thin' is 'agreeably astonished' to meet an old friend;
on learning that he is a privy councillor, he is 'agreeably overwhelmed'. The change of reaction is caught in images of spineless
malleability and in the suddenly elongated postures of the thin
man's wife and son, so that the details, while comic, ultimately
have a farcical point in capturing so extreme a contortion:

The thin man turned pale and rigid all at once, but soon his face twisted
in all directions in the broadest smile; it seemed as though sparks were
flashing from his face and eyes. He squirmed, he doubled together,
crumpled up...His portmanteaus, bundles and cardboard boxes
seemed to shrink and crumple up too... His wife's long chin grew longer
still; Nafanail drew himself up to attention and fastened all the buttons
of his uniform. (XIII.285)

Even the direct comedy of the situation does not cover the
satirical flavour of Chekhov's bitterness against this obsequiousness encouraged by the hierarchy of Czarist officialdom.

   In general, though, these early stories are quite predictable in
outcome, being structured more or less according to the principles of the popular joke – thus ending by twisting back upon
their own apparent assumptions. The figures Chekhov lampoons
are popular stereotypes, nothing more; and 'The Death of a
Government Clerk' and 'The Chameleon' (even though notable
in their way) depend almost wholly upon a comic escalation of
one plausible, but basically improbable, circumstance. The secret
of the 'art' is given away in the opening of 'Fat and Thin':

Two friends – one a fat man and the other a thin man – met at the
Nikolaevsky station. (XIII.283)

It is a simple joke form, more than usually amplified. As is
common in such jokes, the figures begin by conforming to 'fat'
and 'thin' stereotypes, diverge from this pattern for a time as
the thin man assumes some of the fat man's air of self-satisfied
affluence, and then return to their original mould in the final
comic *coup*. Apart from its farcical import, noted above, what

distinguishes the story is little more than its unwaning confidence in its capacity to juggle with stereotypes.

Yet for so young an artist working in so banal a medium, Chekhov does seem to have had a peculiar faith in his command of popular Russian stereotypes and of supposedly national 'types' in general; and on occasions that very faith gave him daring comic successes where a more practised writer would be unlikely to take the risks. I am thinking in particular of 'A Daughter of Albion'. In that story the 'typically English' appearance of the governess, who is solemnly and even disdainfully engrossed in the business of fishing, is caricatured to the point where it is hard to distinguish her Englishness from her pagan archetypal qualities as the primal fisherwoman: she has 'prominent eyes like a crab's, and a big bird-like nose more like a hook than a nose', and so on. The images are memorably comic. And, as the English governess and Russian landowner fish side by side in silence, each despising the other's parochialism and nationalistic intolerance, we see the first sign of Chekhov's celebrated ability to organize failures of communication into comic tableaux. Yet the insults to which the Englishwoman is subjected by her Russian employer quickly become offensive, and the sexual undertones in the story are objectionable. So although the English governess is allowed a triumph of indifference at the end, the weight of the story remains, in spite of Chekhov's apparent intentions, somewhat irrationally against her. As we see not only here but also in 'A Nincompoop' and in 'Ninotchka', vulnerability in certain kinds of characters sometimes impelled Chekhov, at this early stage in his career, into a kind of impatient ridicule.

By 1885, however, Chekhov was writing a quite different kind of story, aided by the new freedoms allowed him in the humorous press as a consequence of his growing reputation and by his developing association with the more respectable *St Petersburg Gazette*. Even the more comic works like 'A Malefactor' or 'Sergeant Prishibeyev', while they still have their basis in farce, have a comic buoyancy which seems to indicate a new tolerance expanding Chekhov's sympathies. Sergeant Prishibeyev's sense of the law as pronouncing things illegal unless they are positively permitted, for example, although it is the perfect sort of material for farce, transcends that to give a delighted appreciation of life's comic possibilities. The effect comes both from the natural humour of the phrasing – 'Is there a law that says people should go about in droves?' – and from the unmistakably peasant flavour of Prishibeyev's authoritarianism. And I find the moment when Prishibeyev submits to the court his daunting list of 'peasants what burn lights' one of the most truly comic highlights in Chekhov's early work. The stories may still be said to run to a formula, one epitomized by the court situations of mutual misunderstanding between people of opposite mentalities that we find in both 'Sergeant Prishibeyev' and 'A Malefactor'. Also, Gogol's influence is obviously there in the kind of humour, the comic clumsiness of the characters' inadvertent self-confessions. But now the stories are beginning to be cast as dramas in miniature. Their situations are simultaneously appalling and funny, and they would require almost no adaptation for the stage.

'He keeps pretending to be a fool! as though he'd been born yesterday or dropped from heaven! Don't you understand, you blockhead, what unscrewing these nuts leads to? If the watchman had not noticed it the train might have run off the rails, people would have been killed – you would have killed people.'

'God forbid, your honour! What should I kill them for! Are we heathens or wicked people? Thank God, good gentleman, we have lived all our lives without ever dreaming of such a thing...Save, and have mercy on us, Queen of Heaven!...What are you saying?' (VI.273)

In this sequence from 'A Malefactor', Chekhov captures both the peasant's ignorant self-righteousness and the judge's mounting annoyance, without giving all his sympathy to one or the other. His judgment at the end of the story is left open, since he recognizes the quite different human aspects of the case when viewed from the different sides. He also shows his developing psychological realism in the way he represents the peasant's slowness and genuine incredulity as sometimes verging, from his inner sense of the licence afforded by his position, on deliberate though always cautious insolence.

This change in the 1885 stories is brought about, then, by Chekhov's more sympathetic approach to people and situations, even to his by then habitual stereotypes. The sympathy which goes out to the unlikable press-secretary in 'The Milksop'*[10] makes an instructive comparison with the hard-edged treatment of the lackey in 'The Death of a Government Clerk'. But better than either is 'An Upheaval', which contains one of the first really distinctive Chekhovian male figures – in the sense that that phrase might apply to (say) the speaker in the dramatic monologue 'On the Harmfulness of Tobacco' or Kuligin in *Three Sisters*. That is, there is a type of person who seems to me to enter literature uniquely through Chekhov's art – a person whose weak or even contemptible exterior masks an unarticulated depth of inner frustration and yet who seems self-revealing enough at a superficial level because he is somewhat pompous and generally talkative. Being talkative, this sort of person gives no signal that he is holding things back, so that only an art which works with real subtlety, through structural revelation and unspoken irony, as Chekhov's does, can make us feel that there is nevertheless something more to him and thus bring him into his own. One such figure, in any case, is Nikolay Sergeitch, the crushed and brow-beaten husband in 'An Upheaval'. But, before I proceed to that particular story, a sketch for a story in Chekhov's note-books 1892–1904 may help to illustrate the kind of structural irony I have in mind:

A scholar, without talent, a blockhead, worked for twenty-four years and produced nothing good, gave to the world only scholars as untalented and as narrow-minded as himself. At night he secretly bound books – that was his true vocation: in that he was an artist and felt the joy of it. There came to him a bookbinder, who loved learning and studied secretly at night.[11]

There is a danger, of course, that this sort of broad but simple ironic construction could be applied in too many situations and thus become a sterile formula. But, in simple form, this example does illustrate one of the central habits of Chekhov's mind and art – a habit which took more and more complex forms as his career went on.

In 'An Upheaval', then, we are surely not intended (as some accounts have suggested)[12] to side wholly and moralistically with Mashenka, the young governess, as she departs in indignation from her employer's house. For although the obvious outrage in the story is the accusation of theft against Mashenka, there is, as it turns out, a much longer-standing outrage that has been committed against Nikolay Sergeitch, in the face of which Mashenka herself is unfeelingly high-handed:

'I took my wife's brooch,' Nikolay Sergeitch said quickly...
Now, after this candid avowal on the part of Nikolay Sergeitch, she could not remain another minute, and could not understand how she could have gone on living in the house before.

'And it's nothing to wonder at,' Nikolay Sergeitch went on after a pause. 'It's an every-day story! I need money, and she...won't give it to me. It was my father's money that bought this house and everything, you know! It's all mine, and the brooch belonged to my mother, and ...it's all mine! And she took it, took possession of everything...I can't go to law with her, you'll admit...I beg you most earnestly, overlook it...stay on. *Tout comprendre, tout pardonner.* Will you stay?'

'No!' said Mashenka resolutely, beginning to tremble. 'Let me alone, I entreat you!'

'Well, God bless you!' sighed Nikolay Sergeitch, sitting down on the stool near the box. 'I must own I like people who still can feel resentment, contempt, and so on. I could sit here for ever and look at your indignant face...So you won't stay, then? I understand...It's bound to be so...Yes, of course...

'Nikolay Sergeitch!' his wife's voice called from the drawing-room. 'Agnia, call your master!'

'Then you won't stay?' asked Nikolay Sergeitch, getting up quickly and going towards the door. 'You might as well stay, really. In the evenings I could come and have a talk with you. Eh? Stay! If you go, there won't be a human face left in the house. It's awful!'

Nikolay Sergeitch's pale, exhausted face besought her, but Mashenka shook her head, and with a wave of his hand he went out.

Half an hour later she was on her way. (III.60–1)

Nikolay Sergeitch's action is contemptible, he is self-pitying in speech; and one part of Chekhov reacts as Mashenka reacts. But at the same time we cannot fail to respond to that combination of resigned helplessness and hard experience which makes Nikolay Sergeitch quietly sit down on the stool in pleased contemplation of Mashenka's indignant face. The pauses in his speech convey the difficulty he feels as his frustrated being and thwarted individuality reach out to Mashenka's innocence; so it is a sad irony that Mashenka's very innocence inevitably stands in the way of her making an appropriate response. Nikolay Sergeitch's admiration for Mashenka's spirit is admiration for something he himself has lost, something 'human' which her departure will remove entirely from the house. He therefore pleads with her to stay. But in asking her to stay he is asking her to tolerate an injustice and to compromise with life as he has done. It is a paradoxical situation. Since Nikolay Sergeitch despises himself, he is both glad not to have to despise Mashenka and sorry that he must therefore lose her. Yet his ability to entertain these mixed feelings, where Mashenka reacts so purely and heartlessly, makes him a more appealing figure than she is, however superior her native spirit is to his. Compared with Nikolay Sergeitch, whom she holds in such contempt, Mashenka hardly knows what an outrage is. The supposed victim of the story's circumstances ends up the slightly callous victor: that is the irony. But in any case the sudden gesture of self-revelation, as in 'On the Harmfulness of Tobacco', where a lifetime of frustration releases itself semi-articulately and without premeditation, is a major development of lasting importance for Chekhov's art, and a distinct and dramatic departure from the manipulation of simple stereotypes in the earlier works.

Yet possibly the two best stories of the period 1880–5, both of them published in the more serious *St Petersburg Gazette*, display a poetic rather than strictly dramatic talent, conceiving the short story as a kind of poem in prose form. These two stories are 'The Huntsman' and 'Sorrow'. For, from the very beginning, 'The Huntsman' opens up for the reader a new Chekhovian landscape:

A sultry, stifling midday. Not a cloudlet in the sky...The sun-baked grass had a disconsolate, hopeless look: even if there were rain it could never be green again...The forest stood silent, motionless, as though it were looking at something with its tree-tops or expecting something.

At the edge of the clearing a tall, narrow-shouldered man of forty in a red shirt, in patched trousers that had been a gentleman's, and in high boots, was slouching along with a lazy, shambling step. He was sauntering along the road. On the right was the green of the clearing, on the left a golden sea of ripe rye stretched to the very horizon. He was red and perspiring, a white cap with a straight jockey peak, evidently a gift from some open-handed young gentleman, perched jauntily on his handsome flaxen head. (VI.243)

The sensuousness of this scene is subdued by a sultry expectancy; the carefree figure of the huntsman contends with a sense we have, conveyed through the landscape, of life being somehow unfree. The setting as a whole is much more evocative than in the stories prior to this date, and the placing of the huntsman in so noticeably wide a horizon gives a kind of pathos to his evident satisfaction with himself. For the details immediately suggest a resistant world unadapted, and even possibly hostile, to human needs, provoking for us an implied question about the terms on which people might choose to exist in such a world. And as the story goes on, Chekhov sets the contagion of the huntsman's freedom, which makes even Pelagea hide her smiling mouth, and yet the morally firmer quality of the woman's immobility, in a dialogue of claims which begins to give the narrative a quasi-parable shape:

A silence followed. Three wild ducks flew over the clearing. Yegor followed them with his eyes till, transformed into three scarcely visible dots, they sank down far beyond the forest.

'How do you live?' he asked, moving his eyes from the ducks to Pelagea.

'Now I am going out to work, and in the winter I take a child from the Foundling Hospital and bring it up on the bottle. They give me a rouble and a half a month.'

'Oh...'

Again a silence. From the strip that had been reaped floated a soft song which broke off at the very beginning. It was too hot to sing. (VI.248)

The woman equates reality with domesticity and work. For the huntsman the only reality is freedom. Their brief meeting after twelve years' nominal marriage is poetically saturated with omens of impending separation: the wild ducks trace a flight in the direction Yegor will take, the mention of the Foundling Hospital directs Pelagea in another. Like the bird-song, their conversation is only just begun when it is broken off, and the tenuousness of their contact is expressed through the awkward but touching exchange of the rouble note. The story expresses both the irreconcilable differences between Yegor's and Pelagea's senses of the world and something of the impersonality and vastness of the world itself. There is, therefore, no judgment to be made: simply a sense of the pathos of Pelagea's predicament, and the poetic logic of an ending which reflects and reverses the images with which the scene began:

He walked by a long road, straight as a taut strap. She, pale and motionless as a statue, stood, her eyes seizing every step he took. But the red of his shirt melted into the dark colour of his trousers, his steps could not be seen, and the dog could not be distinguished from the boots. Nothing could be seen but the cap, and...suddenly Yegor turned off sharply into the clearing and the cap vanished in the greenness.

'Good-bye, Yegor Vlassitch,' whispered Pelagea, and she stood on tiptoe to see the white cap once more. (VI.249)

As we see, the story form itself, its very shape, is being made to insist upon the brevity and tenuousness of this encounter as the huntsman disappears back into the silent expanse of forest from which he came. The carefully worked perspectives and the sultry ripeness of the atmosphere give an unusual potency to the sense of time and space stretching beyond the immediate scene. And the pathos of that, and of the acknowledged impossibility of the marriage ever being a real marriage, is captured movingly in the widening space between Pelagea and the man she loves.

'Sorrow', on the other hand, is less even in quality, less consistently poetic. The turner Grigory Petrov, an habitual drunkard, is taking his sick wife to hospital over roads obscured by snow. Having seen in his wife's eyes, not her usual cowed look, but the stern gaze of one who is dying, he has been suddenly awakened after forty years of neglect to the knowledge that he does indeed care for her; and now, as he drives, he masks his fear that she may 'go and...[die on him]' at just such a time with a robust, incipiently comic monologue on how he, a 'mere peasant', will deal with the doctor. But in the midst of this comic monologue his wife Matryona does die, and in his grief Grigory loses his way. Chekhov gives a powerful account of Grigory's drive through the snowstorm in the rapidly falling darkness of evening and his gradual numbness as he is overtaken by grief and the cold. But there seems to be a sudden withdrawal of sympathy from Grigory Petrov at the end, when he wakes up in hospital to find his legs paralysed with frostbite and the same doctor whom he has planned to outwit tells him that he has nothing to complain of, that he has lived long enough anyway. Even the story's own last words – 'Good-bye to the turner!' – have a sort of callousness about them. It is hard to think of another instance among Chekhov's stories of such an uncontrolled or uncontrollable combination of narrative ingredients – the various elements in the narrative so tending to confront, rather than complement, each other. In the name of ordinary realism, Chekhov has portrayed Grigory as a coarse-mannered man, but he is then faced with the difficulty of having to define externally, through imagery, the resurgence of Grigory's dormant humanity. Certainly, Grigory himself has no vocabulary in which to express it. And the result is that the rough peasant idiom and low comedy of Grigory's imagined interview with the doctor actually pull in the opposite direction from the poetic force Chekhov gives to the landscape of whirling snow around the silent sick woman. Nor does one know quite what to make of the seemingly gratuitous cruelty of the ending and the callousness of the doctor. Yet there is in 'Sorrow' a remarkable handling of the landscape images, which come to act as a composite metaphor for human states and feelings, in something like the manner of the later 'Misery' and 'Easter Eve'. Sorrow, Chekhov tells us, 'had come upon the turner unawares, unlooked-for and unexpected'; he was 'quite suddenly in the position of a busy man, weighed down by anxieties and haste, and even struggling with nature' (IX.148). The 'nature' against which he struggles is both his wife's sickness and the snowstorm which delays his progress to the much-needed hospital. So, as the story proceeds, there is a gradual identification of Matryona's suffering with the storm, and of the storm with the turmoil in Grigory's thoughts – an identification that reaches its first, strangely stilled, climax at the moment when Matryona is seen to have died:

It struck him as strange that the snow on his old woman's face was not melting; it was queer that the face itself looked somehow drawn, and had turned a pale grey, dingy waxen hue and had grown grave and solemn.

'You are a fool!' muttered the turner...'I tell you on my conscience, before God...and you go and...Well, you are a fool! I have a good mind not to take you to Pavel Ivanitch!'

The turner let the reins go and began thinking. (IX.149)

In this magnificently constructed moment, the woman's features assume the anonymity of the snow-swept landscape, while the landscape itself (or at least the snow-storm) takes on something of the peculiar coldness and vastness of death. Grigory Petrov, too, intuitively senses the moment of relaxed tension in which the suffering is over, although it is for him a moment of fear. Chekhov makes his gesture in letting the reins fall deeply expressive: in it we feel the lack of direction which Matryona's death produces in a man who has just begun to feel some sympathy for his ill-treated wife. Then, as he picks up the reins again, Chekhov has him begin a journey that quickly becomes a metaphoric one. Back and forth he drives, lost, through a snow-obliterated world that is now an inner reality as much as any external phenomenon of nature:

Grigory turned back and lashed the horse with all his might. The road grew worse and worse every hour. Now he could not see the yoke at all. Now and then the sledge ran into a young fir-tree, a dark object scratched the turner's hands and flashed before his eyes, and the field of vision was white and whirling again.

'To live over again,' thought the turner...

The white clouds of snow were beginning little by little to turn grey. It was getting dusk.

'Where am I going?' the turner suddenly bethought him with a start...

And the snow kept turning darker and darker, the wind grew colder and more cutting...

'To live over again!' thought the turner. 'I should get a new lathe, take orders...give the money to my old woman...' (IX.150–1)

Moments such as this in the early Chekhov reveal an intuitive questing after the representatively poetic occasion, one in which the contours of landscape may be called upon to produce a form of metaphoric epiphany. Here in 'Sorrow' the effect is spoilt by the puzzling harshness of the ending (which in its callousness exceeds anything the turner might conceivably have deserved) and by the vindictive application of the turner's own blunt idioms to himself. But as an early instance of Chekhov's ability to define dramatic events in terms of poetic effect, this story is clearly quite important.

It is perhaps not surprising that for some years after his discovery of this newly poetic, metaphoric art, Chekhov was inclined to give it predominance over the more purely dramatic basis of his creative temperament. In his later years, as he turned to the poetic drama of *The Seagull*, *Uncle Vanya*, *Three Sisters* and *The Cherry Orchard*, it found its most subtle form in a poetic amplification of the dramatic action, enriching and complicating its deeper implications. But before arriving at that point, Chekhov had to develop the subtlety of his images and learn to relate them more flexibly to other elements in his meaning. In the early stories poetic qualities are often too heavily interpretative: they enforce an overriding mood that is evocative and/or powerful but also somewhat limited. For all the development that occurs between 'Fat and Thin' and 'The Huntsman' or 'Sorrow', it is the development between 'Sorrow' and 'A Dreary Story' that marks Chekhov's true maturity as an artist. The years 1880 to 1885 were the years of Chekhov's artistic apprenticeship. He had yet to make his career.

3

The short story – I

The year 1886 was one of the turning-points in Chekhov's life and work. As 'The Huntsman' and 'Sorrow' show, his development from his often coarse and banal beginnings in such things as the *Dragonfly* 'advertisements' was quite rapid. But in March 1886 that development was given a sudden new impetus by the arrival of a letter from the noted older author Grigorovich.[1] The importance of this letter and of Chekhov's reply to it warrants my quoting both in full:

DEAR SIR, ANTON PAVLOVICH:

About a year ago I read by chance a story of yours in *Petersburg Gazette*; I do not recall its title. I remember only that I was struck by its qualities of outstanding originality and chiefly its remarkable accuracy and truthfulness in its descriptions of people and nature.

Since then I have read everything that bore the signature of Chekhonte, although I was inwardly vexed at a man who held so poor an opinion of himself as to consider the use of a pseudonym necessary. While reading you, I continually advised Suvorin and Burenin to follow my example. They listened to me and now, like me, they do not doubt that you have *real* talent – a talent which places you in the front rank among writers in the new generation.

I am not a journalist nor a publisher. I can be useful to you only as one of your readers. If I speak of your talent, I speak out of conviction. I am almost sixty-five, but I still feel so much love for literature and follow its success with so much ardour and rejoice when I find in it something living and gifted, that I cannot refrain – as you see – from holding out both hands to you.

But this is by no means all. Here is what I wish to add. By virtue of the varied attributes of your undoubted talent – the precise truth of your internal analysis, your mastery of description (the snowstorm, the night, the background in *Agafya* etc.), the plasticity of your feelings which in a few lines projects a complete picture (the clouds above the setting sun 'like ashes over dying coals', etc.) – I am convinced that you are destined to create some admirable and truly artistic works. And you will be guilty of a great moral sin if you do not live up to these hopes. All that is needed is esteem for the talent which so rarely falls to one's lot. Cease to write hurriedly. I do not know what your financial situation is. If it is poor, it would be better for you to go hungry, as we did in our day, and save your impressions for a mature, finished work, written not in one sitting, but during the happy hours of inspiration. One such work will be valued a hundred times higher than a hundred fine stories scattered among the newspapers at various times. In one leap you will reach the goal and will gain the notice of cultivated people and then all the reading public.

Why is it that you often have motifs with pornographical nuances at the basis of your tales? Truthfulness and realism not only do not exclude refinement but even gain from it. You have such a powerful sense of form and a feeling for the plastic, that you have no special need, for example, to speak about dirty feet with turned-in toenails or a clerk's navel. These details add exactly nothing to the artistic beauty of a description and only spoil the impression among readers of taste. Have the generosity to forgive such observations, for I resolved to make them only because I sincerely believe in your talent and with all my soul desire its fullest development.

Several days ago I was told that you are publishing a book of tales. If it is to appear under the pseudonym of CHE-KHON-TE, I beg you earnestly to telegraph the publishers to print it under your real name. After your recent stories in *New Times* and the success of *The Hunter*, the book will also have great success. It would be agreeable to have some assurance that you are not angry over my remarks, but that you accept them in the spirit that I write – not as an authority but out of the simplicity of an old heart.

Three days later, Chekhov replied:

Your letter, my kind, warmly beloved herald of glad tidings, struck me like a thunderbolt. I nearly wept, I was profoundly moved, and even now I feel that it has left a deep imprint on my soul. As you have smiled on my youth, so may God give you peace in your old age. I, indeed, can find neither words nor actions to show my gratitude. You know with what eyes ordinary people look upon such outstanding people like yourself, hence you may realize what your letter means for my self-esteem. It is worth more than any diploma, and for a beginning author it is an honorarium now and for the future. I am as in a daze. I lack the ability to judge whether or not I merit this great reward. I only repeat that it has overwhelmed me.

If I have a gift which must be respected, then before the purity of your heart I confess that I have not respected it up to now. I felt that I had such a gift, but I had grown accustomed to regarding it as insignificant. Reasons of a purely external nature suffice to render one excessively mistrustful and suspicious toward oneself. Such reasons, as I now recall, I had in abundance. My whole family have always referred condescendingly to my work as a writer and have never ceased offering me friendly advice not to give up a real profession for scribbling. I have hundreds of friends in Moscow and among them a score of writers, yet I cannot recall a single one who would read me or recognize me as an artist. In Moscow there is a so-called 'Literary Circle'. Talented and mediocre people of all kinds and ages meet there once a week to gossip in the private room of a restaurant. If I were to go there and read even a bit of your letter, they would laugh in my face. During the five years of my roaming from newspaper to newspaper, I became infected with their own common views on the triviality of literature and soon grew accustomed to regarding my own work slightingly – so I simply sat down and wrote! That is the first reason. The second is that I am a physician and up to my neck in medicine. No one has lost more sleep than I have over the fable of hunting two hares at one time.

I write all this to justify to you, in some small degree, my grievous sin. Hitherto I have treated my own literary work frivolously, carelessly, without thinking. I do not recall a *single* tale of mine over which I have worked more than a day, and *The Hunter*, which pleased you, I wrote in the bathhouse! I have written my stories the way reporters write up their notes about fires – mechanically, half-consciously, caring nothing about either the reader or myself. I wrote and tried in every way not to waste on my tales images and pictures which were clear to me and which, God knows why, I kept to myself and carefully concealed.

What first drove me to take a critical view of my writing was a very charming and, as far as I can judge, a sincere letter from Suvorin. I began to think of writing some purposeful piece, but nevertheless I did not have faith in my own literary direction.

And now, all of a sudden, your letter arrived. You must forgive the comparison, but it had the same effect on me as a government order 'to get out of the city in twenty-four hours'! That is, I suddenly felt the absolute necessity for haste, to get out of this rut, where I am stuck, as quickly as possible.

I agree with you in everything. The cynical effects which you attribute to me I myself felt when I saw *The Witch* in print. They would not have been there if this tale had been written in three or four days instead of one.

I will free myself from hurried work, but not just yet. It is not possible to get out of the rut into which I have fallen. I do not refuse to suffer hunger, for I have already gone hungry, but it is not a question of myself alone. I devote my leisure to writing, two to three hours a day and a little at night – that is, only time enough for small undertakings. In the summer, when I shall have more leisure and fewer expenses, I'll settle to work in earnest.

I cannot place my own name on my book because it is too late; the cover design is ready and the book is printed. Many Petersburgers apart from yourself advised me not to spoil the volume by using a pseudonym, but I did not listen to them, probably out of vanity. I do not like the book at all. It is a hotch-potch, an untidy accumulation of student pieces marred by the censorship and the editors of humorous magazines. I believe that many, in reading it, will be disappointed. If I had known that I was being read and that you were watching me, I would not have let the book be published.

All my hopes lie entirely in the future. I am only twenty-six. Perhaps I shall manage to do something, although time passes quickly.

Please excuse this long letter and do not blame a man who, for the first time in his life, has dared to pamper himself with the great pleasure of a letter to Grigorovich.

Send me, if possible, your photograph. I have been so encouraged and stirred up by you that I ought to write you not a mere sixteen pages but a whole ream. May God give you happiness and health, and please believe in the sincerity of a profoundly respectful and grateful A. CHEKHOV.[2]

Though Chekhov's letter itself betrays signs of immaturity in its extravagant analogies and its exaggeration of Grigorovich's authority, his artistic career did take a more serious direction from this point on. Of course, his family's financial situation prevented him from changing his working habits all at once and for years to come small stories (the well-known 'Sleepy' was one) would be dashed off for a few roubles while some larger work was in hand. But, on the whole, there is a discernible change in the stories of 1886, which are both more serious and better finished than those which preceded them.

As a serious writer of short stories Chekhov was in a slightly difficult position. Before him in the Russian tradition were Pushkin, Gogol, Lermontov, Leskov and Turgenev – a formidable line of authors, all of whom had achieved very real triumphs in the short-story form. Chekhov's 'The Huntsman' was inspired by Turgenev's 'The Tryst', from *The Hunting Sketches*. His early farcical works continue the Gogol influence; and his sometimes mythically intense environments, particularly at the climaxes of the later novellas, probably originate from his admiration of Lermontov's 'Taman' from *A Hero of Our Time*. But Chekhov was really a different kind of writer from his predecessors, and if they were influences upon him, they nevertheless never became models. Like them, he is not a metaphysical writer in any real sense: his basic interest is in the terms on which ordinary people live out their finite and often frustrated lives. But he differs from his predecessors in that the scope of his vision nevertheless takes in more than the purely social or psychological. This extra dimension in Chekhov's work, which is extremely subtle and therefore difficult to define, has, perhaps, something to do with the kinds of interest natural to him as a dramatist: interest, for example, in the way figures are disposed within a larger scene and thus in the imaginative and psychological effects of different spatial perspectives, or his sense of the dramatic potency that pauses or extended silences may assume at particular intervals in an action or speech. Whatever its origins, its presence in the early stories is as a wider ambience surrounding the human action, an ambience which seems to be expressing the impersonality of time and space. A brief comparison of a passage from 'The Tryst' (1852) with the one discussed in the last chapter from 'The Huntsman' (1885) may help to illustrate what I mean. Here, first, is Turgenev:

Victor languidly put out his hand, accepted the offering, sniffed negligently at the flowers, and fell to twiddling them in his fingers, now and then turning his eyes upward in thoughtful dignity. Akulina was contemplating him...There was in her melancholy gaze so much of tender devotion, of adoring submission and love. She loved him, and she dared not weep, and was saying farewell to him and admiring him for the last time; but he lay there, lolling like a sultan, and with magnanimous patience and condescension was tolerating her adoration. It was with indignation, I confess, that I studied his red face, through the affectedly disdainful indifference of which a satisfied, sated self-conceit was peering. Akulina was so splendid at that instant: all her soul was trustingly, passionately unfolding before him, was drawn to him, was yearning to caress and be caressed, but he...he let the cornflowers drop on the grass, pulled out of a side pocket of his overcoat a round bit of glass rimmed with bronze, and began trying to squeeze it in over his eye; however, no matter how he strove to retain it with the help of a frowning eyebrow, a pursed-up cheek, and even his nose, the monocle kept right on popping out and falling back into his hand.[3]

And now Chekhov:

A silence followed. Three wild ducks flew over the clearing. Yegor followed them with his eyes till, transformed into three scarcely visible dots, they sank down far beyond the forest.

'How do you live?' he asked, moving his eyes from the ducks to Pelagea.

'Now I am going out to work, and in the winter I take a child from the Foundling Hospital and bring it up on the bottle. They give me a rouble and a half a month.'

'Oh...'

Again a silence. From the strip that had been reaped floated a soft song which broke off at the very beginning. It was too hot to sing. (VI.248)

Though the Turgenev is obviously good, the Chekhov has a much more dramatic basis and is more deft, managing without the rather clumsily dramatized author-presence that obtrudes through *The Hunting Sketches*. Furthermore, Chekhov conveys a strange silence around and through the scene, so that we feel the difficulty with which the characters reach out to one another and the tenuous conditions on which their lives meet. There is nothing to match this in Turgenev's more conventionally social and psychological narrative. All of Turgenev's attention is occupied by the social and sexual demeanour of a particular man to the peasant girl who loves him. The narrative voice in 'The Tryst' conveys a continuous moral reaction to what it records: '...through the affectedly disdainful indifference of which a satisfied, sated self-conceit was peering.' Chekhov, on the other hand, though interested in the relationship between the man and woman and sympathizing with the woman's plight, makes his reader so conscious of the contingency of their meeting that one is disinclined to judge either of them. The poignancy of the encounter comes not from the woman's violated trust but from the fact that these people inhabit a world in which it is the natural fate of things to be dispersed, like the bird-song, and lost, like the ducks, in time and space. The very expanse of that world, which should open into freedom, seems to disperse the elements of a possible and more positive human intimacy. So that if Chekhov is not a metaphysical writer in Tolstoy's or Dostoevsky's sense, neither is he, like Gogol or Turgenev, basically confined in range to social and psychological insight. His interest in setting his characters in a poetically created context of time and space, with the landscapes projecting a sense of the world as unyielding to human pressures and needs, infuses his early stories with a spirit which is not simply 'neutral' in some indefinable sense but consciously and perceptibly agnostic.

Being a more serious artist therefore meant for Chekhov, after Grigorovich's letter of 1886, registering more fully in his work his intense consciousness, as an agnostic and developing humanist, of suffering, grief and death. It was not open to him – nor, I should think, to any Russian author – to write stories of manners in the English sense. Russian society was, of course, divided into recognizable classes which could be identified by differences of manners and dress, but it appears to have lacked a broad middle class, and this presumably had important consequences both for literary subjects and for literature's expectations of its audience. The 'literature of landowners' was preoccupied with the great social, moral and theological issues of the day. Its upper-class audience was apparently assured enough of its own polite codes simply to take them for granted and to look beyond them to more important concerns. Upper classes in general probably have less cause for self-scrutiny about manners than the more mobile middle and upper-middle classes, precisely because upper classes are less constantly invaded by 'newcomers'. These 'newcomers' are the people whom, by their inferior manners, the more established members of a middle class will usually be jealously on the alert to detect. Perhaps more importantly, it is the middle class, as the most energetic class in society and the one most challenging to old class dominances, which provides the most sustained context for observing the interaction between different classes and hence for clarifying differences of manners. In classic Russian literature, social classes are represented as being unusually discrete. There are the peasants (rural and urban), the non-aristocratic landed gentry and the aristocrats: between them, a middle ground of students, clerks, merchants and officials who do not cohere as a definite class at all. The social energy seems to come from the merchant group, but that group, on the whole, seems fairly small and much more limited in its mobility than the equivalent class in England. So it is probably significant that Russian literature generally is more preoccupied with its *national* codes and 'types' than with those of a class or classes, even allowing that an interest in 'class', as it is defined in the English tradition, is never merely that. The fact that Chekhov himself attempted so early to portray facets of the Russian national character (as he did seriously in 'The Steppe', 1888) and only belatedly – at the height of his career – engaged with the subtleties of class situations and conflicts, also suggests that the Russian literary environment was, in this respect, virtually the antithesis of the English.

With that sense of literary integrity and of literature's seriousness which Chekhov came to share with other great Russians, he saw it as literature's task to depict 'truth, unconditional and honest'[4] – the truth of life itself; but as he conceived that truth, there were no literary models for him to follow. He most admired Maupassant, but unlike Maupassant he had no particular, prejudicial view of the human personality to put forward. Among Russia's own writers there were none who shared quite his sense of the world. Pushkin in 'The Station-Master' and Gogol in 'The Overcoat' had conveyed suffering as it arises in particular social contexts; and, of course, stoicism in the face of the harshest circumstances is one of the hallmarks of Russian literature's images of its own national types. But there seems to have been no precedent in Russian literature for Chekhov's compassionate presentation of human suffering which recognizes and captures also the surrounding impersonality of time and space. This is particularly so when one thinks of the way Chekhov's compassion is combined with a highly developed sense of irony: for irony, in Chekhov, is not simply a 'method' but is intrinsic to his vision. It is something he perceives in life itself, in the way lives are turned and twisted from their hoped-for direction – as, for example, when a long-standing wish is fulfilled at the very moment when it is no longer wished for. This kind of perception gives his art both its distinctive ironic shape and its compassionate tone. So it is perhaps no wonder that, even after Chekhov began to be more serious about his work, it took some time and further practice for his vision to find its most appropriate forms. He had to learn to by-pass the obvious opportunities for capturing the reader's sympathy, to get away from that sort of conventionality, and to convey instead, through the peculiar directions taken by his tales, a more complex understanding of the precise conditions and restrictions of his characters' lives. Many of the early stories, at their more serious moments, tend to offer simple, affecting images of suffering through strongly realized (but incipiently sentimental and inherently limited) visual scenes. Only very gradually, as we shall see, was Chekhov able to realize the seriousness of his vision actually through his distinctive sense of irony.

We have already seen the beginning of this serious and sad sense of the world, and a non-ironic, imagistic definition of it, in 'Sorrow'. In 1886 a number of the same elements were reproduced in another story, 'Misery'. From the comparison one can see an initially instinctive image – that of falling snow – taking on a steady, conscious metaphoric force; and in the later story the character's grief, rather than being gradually unfolded, is made immediately apparent in a suggestive visual scene:

The twilight of evening. Big flakes of wet snow are whirling lazily about the street-lamps, which have just been lighted, and lying in a thin soft layer on roofs, horses' backs, shoulders, caps. Iona Potapov, the sledge-driver, is all white like a ghost. He sits on the box without stirring, bent as double as the living body can be bent. If a regular snow-drift fell on him it seems as though even then he would not think it necessary to shake it off...His little mare is white and motionless too. Her stillness, the angularity of her lines, and the stick-like straightness of her legs, make her look like a halfpenny gingerbread horse. She is probably lost in thought. Anyone who has been torn away from the plough, from the familiar grey landscapes, and cast into this slough, full of monstrous lights, of unceasing uproar and hurrying people, is bound to think.

It is a long time since Iona and his nag have budged. (IX.57)

Though there is a touch of sentimentality about the nag 'lost in thought', the total effect is quite powerful. The feeling of the passage comes from the suggestiveness of the immobilized postures – the sledge-driver 'bent as double as the living body can be bent', and the angular outline of the little mare – as these are progressively defined at the centre of a whitening world of steadily falling snow. For, given the lightness of texture associated with the lazy whirling of the snow around the street-lamps, the still, hunched figure of the sledge-driver covered with fallen snow becomes the centre of gravity, its weight and immobility seeming to abstract it from the snow-measured passing of time. The quietude suggested by the snowflakes and the newly lit lamps deepens into a burdened intuition of the muteness of suffering (gently connecting the man with the horse), which the bustle of the city noise further defines by contrast. As the story proceeds, Iona is roused three times from his desolation to take a fare, and each time he begins to tell of the death of his son. But no one wants the discomfort of another man's personal tragedy; and after each fare Chekhov returns Iona, with a sense of its ever deepening poignancy, to the same hunched immobility as at the opening:

Putting his fare down at Vyborgskaya, Iona stops by a restaurant, and again sits huddled up on the box...Again the wet snow paints him and his horse white. One hour passes, and then another...(IX.59)

Iona on the box epitomizes the loneliness of sorrow implied in the epigraph – 'To whom shall I tell my grief?' The snow falling around him intensifies that sense of Iona's aloneness by giving a constant visual sense of the world apart from Iona going on as before. This composite image is the one to which the story constantly returns. For it is in the nature of things that no one can really share Iona's sense of what has happened to him; and the recurrence of that one image is Chekhov's way of making us feel the pathos of such a fact. As we come to realize, even when Iona is finding a kind of relief in the companionship of the officer or the 'merry gentlemen', he is, in his deepest self, still huddled up on his box.

Unfortunately, there is a damaging weakness in the way the story presents Iona's second fare. The vulgarity and violence of the young men and the pathos of Iona's trying to laugh at their aggression against him are both too extreme to be properly convincing. There is, I think, some power in the way Iona and the hunchback are brought into a desperate accord by the threat which his own isolation presents to each:

Iona feels behind his back the jolting person and quivering voice of the hunchback. He hears abuse addressed to him, he sees people, and the feeling of loneliness begins little by little to be less heavy on his heart. The hunchback swears at him, till he chokes over some elaborately whimsical string of epithets and is overpowered by his cough. (IX.61)

The hunchback's abuse is virtually impersonal: in a strange way it satisfies a deep need in Iona as well as in himself. But Iona's repeated laugh, even after he has been struck, is overdone:

And Iona hears rather than feels a slap on the back of his neck.
   'He-he!...' he laughs. 'Merry gentlemen...God give you health!' (IX.61)

In one of his letters Chekhov says about writing stories: 'One must not humiliate people – that is the chief thing.'[5] In this part of 'Misery' he unconsciously falls into that trap. Iona is the most vulnerable kind of character, a victim, inarticulate about his actual suffering though desperate to talk. In trying to enter into his feelings, Chekhov is undertaking, more successfully, something like what Dickens tried to do with Jo in *Bleak House*. Whole paragraphs, though bordering on sentimentality in some of the phrasing, are intensely moving:

Again he is alone and again there is silence for him...The misery which has been for a brief space eased comes back again and tears his heart more cruelly than ever. With a look of anxiety and suffering Iona's eyes stray restlessly among the crowds moving to and fro on both sides of the street; can he not find among those thousands someone who will listen to him? But the crowds flit by heedless of him and his misery... His misery is immense, beyond all bounds. If Iona's heart were to burst and his misery to flow out, it would flood the whole world, it seems, but yet it is not seen. It has found a hiding-place in such an insignificant shell that one would not have found it with a candle by daylight...(IX.62)

But, elsewhere in the story, in the process of evoking the pathos of this 'insignificant shell', Chekhov robs Iona of some of his early dignity. And the 'solution' the story finds to Iona's loneliness is perhaps a rather obvious one, which partly lets down the powerful beginning. In order to carry the effect through at all, Chekhov has to rely on small emotive details, like the mare's 'shining eyes' and her munching and listening, to suggest more sympathetic attention from the animal than can realistically be there:

He puts on his coat and goes into the stables where his mare is standing. He thinks about oats, about hay, about the weather...He cannot think about his son when he is alone...To talk about him with someone is possible, but to think of him and picture him is insufferable anguish...

'Are you munching?' Iona asks his mare, seeing her shining eyes. 'There, munch away, munch away...Since we have not earned enough for oats, we will eat hay...Yes...I have grown too old to drive...My son ought to be driving, not I...He was a real cabman...He ought to have lived...

Iona is silent for a while, and then he goes on:

'That's how it is, old girl...Kuzma Ionitch is gone...He said good-bye to me...He went and died for no reason...Now, suppose you had a little colt, and you were own mother to that little colt...And all at once that same little colt went and died...You'd be sorry, wouldn't you?...'

The little mare munches, listens, and breathes on her master's hands. Iona is carried away and tells her all about it. (IX.64–5)

An essentially sentimental writer would probably have gone on; but after that suggestive silence in which Iona seems to wonder whether he will continue and then abandons himself to the emotional situation, Chekhov quickly closes off the narrative. Having indicated what is to be the general quality of Iona's speech and taking warning from what might happen if he were to over-elaborate that touching but incipiently sentimental analogy of the boy and the 'little colt', he ends the story deftly and tactfully in a summarizing statement: 'Iona is carried away and tells her all about it.'

'Misery', then, is a quite important early story. It reveals already a strong human and moral concern in Chekhov's work, and it projects a quite forceful sense of his basic view of the world through its imagery. The falling snow around Iona seems neither a response to his misery nor something that can change it. It is just part of an unconscious process which would be the same if men did not exist. And as it slowly obliterates colours and shapes, falling evenly across the sky, it feels imaginatively analogous to the passing of time. Significantly, one of the best short stories of our own century by an agnostic writer – Joyce's 'The Dead', from *Dubliners* – depends upon a very similar effect: there too the falling snow, all over Ireland, at Gabriel Conroy's window and over the churchyard where Michael Furey is buried, is made to convey a similar sense of time passing and of a universe indifferent to men.

Yet, as I have suggested, the extent of Chekhov's reliance on suggestive imagery in these early stories can be a limitation. In the late plays there is a great range of pictorial effects, enriching and ramifying action which is dramatically alive with emotional currents and cross-currents as complex as any the theatre has seen. But in some of this earlier work the imagery over-dominates the whole, and by doing so it seems to deny the reader the intellectual participation he expects and requires of such an art. I think we miss the sense of challenge: the challenge to see the ramifying implications of the way situations are dramatized and the way they are structured to interact. The imagery is over-insistent, over-obvious; and it insists on just one thing. What is more, this static, pictorial definition of human predicaments involuntarily gives the impression of unusual human passivity – whence, no doubt, derives the criticism that Chekhov's characters are somehow will-less and negative. Both charges would undoubtedly be difficult to deny in the case of 'Dreams' (1886). The situation there (of two peasant constables escorting a prison escapee through a landscape of sticky mud and ragged autumn trees) is much too obviously contrived, designed deliberately to crush all hopes of a better life, while simultaneously investing those hopes with pathos. The immediate landscape is, in fact, heavy-handedly symbolic:

The travellers had been a long while on their way, but they seemed to be always on the same small patch of ground. In front of them there stretched thirty feet of muddy black-brown mud, behind them the same, and wherever one looked further, an impenetrable wall of white fog. They went on and on, but the ground remained the same, the wall was no nearer, and the patch on which they walked seemed still the same patch. (vi.88)

It is not difficult to see that this potentially imprisoning landscape, in which progress feels illusory and in which the clinging mud makes every step an effort, is being offered as a composite metaphor of the restrictive reality within which dreams are both powerful and completely unreal. The recaptured escapee-tramp has a dream, predictable in the circumstances, of escaping from custody to the tall forests and plentiful life of Siberia; but no sooner is the dream conveyed than the barriers to its realization are erected with even greater vividness:

All three were pondering. The peasants were racking their brains in the effort to grasp in their imagination what can be grasped by none but God – that is, the vast expanse dividing them from the land of freedom. Into the tramp's mind thronged clear and distinct pictures more terrible than that expanse. Before him rose vividly the picture of the long legal delays and procrastinations, the temporary and permanent prisons, the convict boats, the wearisome stoppages on the way, the frozen winters, illnesses, deaths of companions...(vi.98)

This catalogue of obstacles in the tramp's mind has immediate power, touching deftly as it does on the known brutalities of the Russian penal system. But to use those physical obstacles indirectly to reinforce a more abstract and basic sense of men's lack of freedom seems rather wilfully pessimistic. Chekhov's supposed interest in the wider nature of the conditions inhibiting all men's lives is narrowed and prejudiced by the extreme physical adversity in this one case. Pondering the vast distance separating them from freedom, all three men are robbed of any air of effective initiative, while the deliberately archetypal ingredients of the scene (the clinging mud, the primitive mound on which the three men sit) attempt, spuriously, to enlarge one extreme of physical bondage into a pessimistic general image of human fate.

Apart from the problem of the over-pictorial nature of the art, there is, then, the further problem of what is generally referred to as Chekhov's 'negativity' in the defeat he constructs for the tramp's dreams. But one such case, or even more, is hardly sufficient foundation for a whole characterization of Chekhov, such as Lev Shestov's in an almost wholly impressionistic essay (favourably reviewed some years ago, on the occasion of its republication, in the *New York Review of Books*), 'Anton Tchekhov (Creation from the Void)'. Since Shestov's views seem to have gained some general currency, it is worth quoting him at this point:

To define his tendency in a word, I would say that Tchekhov was the poet of hopelessness. Stubbornly, sadly, monotonously, during all the years of his literary activity, nearly a quarter of a century long, Tchekhov was doing one thing alone: by one means or another he was killing human hopes.[6]

If this were true, Chekhov could never have written 'The Duel'; and 'The Party', 'The Lady with the Dog' and *The Cherry Orchard* (to mention just a few) would have to be much simpler than they in fact are. Certainly, he could not be the humanist my account makes him out to be. But since this view may superficially seem appropriate to some of the early work, I want to take issue with it in relation to 'Vanka', one of the most perfect little stories of 1886. Apart from its intrinsic interest and its suitability for raising this issue of Chekhov's supposed 'negativity', 'Vanka' is also one of the few works of this period which rely more for their meaning on capturing a voice and on the irony inherent in their organization than on the visual suggestion of the imagery.

'Vanka' is a simple tale, relaxed and emotionally straight-forward. Yet the kind of reverberation set up by the simple situation of a child writing a letter of love to his grandfather far away is one of those small accidents of genius. Vanka's plea, written amid the shelves of lasts in the shoemaker's shop on Christmas Eve, is a desperate plea to be allowed to return to his child's life; and the letter he writes, with its intense child-like conviction that he simply cannot survive the Moscow life, captures a note that is unbearably genuine:

'Dear grandfather, show the divine mercy, take me away from here, home to the village. It's more than I can bear. I bow down to your feet, and will pray to God for you for ever, take me away from here or I shall die.' (xii.91)

His whole letter movingly combines his childishly respectful mode of address to someone much older with his intense love of and respect for his grandfather, and associates his feeling for his grandfather with a whole former sense of the world to which Moscow just does not measure up. Chekhov captures superbly the emphatic emotional imperatives of the child's voice, and in Vanka's testing of Moscow against the village life we find a touching echo of a child's habits of thought:

'And in the butcher's shops there are grouse and woodcocks and fish and hares, but the shopmen don't say where they shoot them.' (xii.92)

But most impressive, given the obvious dangers of the story's situation, is the complete absence of sentimentality in the images given of Vanka's past. Vanka's memory is vivid: his longing is a quite different thing from adult nostalgia. He is close enough to the reality of his past for it to remain in his mind vibrantly crisp and impregnated with primitive vigour:

He remembered how his grandfather always went into the forest to get the Christmas tree for his master's family, and took his grandson with him. It was a merry time! Grandfather made a noise in his throat, the forest crackled with the frost, and looking at them Vanka chortled too. Before chopping down the Christmas tree, grandfather would smoke a pipe, slowly take a pinch of snuff, and laugh at frozen Vanka...The young fir trees, covered with hoar frost, stood motionless, waiting to see which of them was to die. Wherever one looked, a hare flew like an arrow over the snowdrifts...Grandfather could not refrain from shouting: 'Hold him, hold him...hold him! Ah, the bob-tailed devil!' (xii.93)

Vanka 'chortling' epitomizes the unself-conscious vitality of the whole scene. Similarly, the images of grandfather in the imagined present, joking with the servants and pinching the maids, wearing felt boots and carrying his little mallet, are extremely vivid and yet in no way sentimental. In fact, grandfather himself – as distinct from Vanka's feeling for him – emerges through the story as somewhat banal, so that a part of the effect Chekhov eventually achieves here comes from the poignant disproportion which we are made progressively to sense between Vanka's love and the merits of the person to whom it is given.

Vanka's love gets its special intensity from its being strongly associated with a sense of belonging. It is typical of Chekhov's instinctive psychological understanding that he brings in as he does, through the child's touching egoistic trust in the power of his own name, the way that loving is bound up with self-identity:

'Dear grandfather, when they have the Christmas tree at the big house, get me a gilt walnut, and put it away in the green trunk. Ask the young lady Olga Ignatyevna, say it's for Vanka.' (XII.92)

Later in the story, too, Vanka's desperate insecurity is conveyed as he tries to reassert his connection with grandfather's world by citing his association with its people and objects:

'I send greeting to Alyona, one-eyed Yegorka, and the coachman, and don't give my concertina to anyone. I remain, your grandson Ivan Zhukov. Dear grandfather, do come.' (XII.94)

Yet it is the painful fate of childhood to end, at one point or another, when that loving protection which has given power and a sense of 'specialness' to one's name recedes into the background, when the world becomes a place of many names and of men all fending for themselves. So the sad, ironic twist of events at the end, by which the same childish vulnerability underlies Vanka's not knowing how to address the letter, is – though cruel – consistent with the psychological facts of growing up. The deft downward turn in the story's direction is what Shestov would no doubt point to as the moment when Chekhov 'kills' Vanka's hope:

After thinking a little, he dipped the pen and wrote the address:
   To grandfather in the village.
  Then he scratched his head, thought a little, and added: *Konstantin Makaritch.* Glad that he had not been prevented from writing, he put on his cap and, without putting on his little great-coat, ran out into the street as he was in his shirt...(XII.94)

But the emphasis here is light; and, rather than being a gratuitously imposed 'Chekhovian cruelty', it is a way of realizing, through a turn of events rather than by overt statement, the irrecoverability of that special sense of childhood belonging in any life to which it has been lost. Vanka's childhood is as irrecoverable as Lyubov Andreyevna's innocence in *The Cherry Orchard.* Moreover, in 'Vanka' as in *The Cherry Orchard* there is, behind the psychological insight, an implied recognition (in the details about grandfather and the background of Vanka's life) of economic realities determining people's fates. Chekhov does not wilfully deny Vanka his hope, but his intensely sympathetic portrayal of the child's loneliness and insecurity is combined with a realistic sense both of the inevitability of painful psychological changes in life and of the web of social restriction in which Vanka is caught.

That this realism is not, ultimately, a denial of the value of life, but simply the context for a poignant appreciation of what positive qualities remain in it, is evident from the stress Chekhov places on the intensity of Vanka's feeling. While he reveals the frustration of Vanka's hope of release, he never underplays or undervalues the intensity (and the partial mystery) of his generous love. Rather, it is Chekhov's sense of the worth of that love which lies at the source of his compassion, and indeed at the source of his animated portrayal of the child, who is one of the most 'living' characters in minor fiction. Chekhov does not 'kill' human hopes; but he knows that, all too often, life itself thwarts them; and whether or not it is of practical value to alert the reader to such frustrations of people's hopes and the situations that are decisive for them, Chekhov ensures, at the very least, that we will view such frustrations with compassion. Time and time again in his works he returns to situations in which a love might be seized and confirmed but is not; and he depicts such missed opportunities not in order to win a victory over his characters' happiness, but to show the pathos of such a moment's being allowed to slip by – whether because the people involved are not quite sure of what they feel, or because they cannot express it at the right time, or simply because they are by nature inhibited.

To the humanist writer, for whom the most immediate personal value in life will probably be love and fulfilled relationships generally, there is a special pathos about lives which lack love or in which love is frustrated, and even about simple misunderstandings between people. Each instance of these is a lost opportunity for understanding or fulfilment which can never be regained. In some cases, as in 'The Kiss' and 'Verotchka', it is virtually a lost life. If, then, Chekhov's art is unusually preoccupied with the frustrations of loving purpose at the points where human lives intersect, it is because of the value that such relationships must bear in his view of things, and the waste of love that he must quietly deplore. The capacity for love in people who lack the opportunity for it, and the deprivation of love in those who have known it, are things of which he is unusually and painfully aware. It is in this context, and not one of morbid negativity, that Chekhov's presentation of 'frustrated lives' should be viewed.

4

The short story – II

Among the very finest stories of 1886 and 1887 are 'Easter Eve' and the better-known 'Enemies'. In their different ways they show Chekhov to be already a master of the short-story form. The limitations to which I have been pointing in the minor but serious stories up to this period – chiefly the over-dependence on a single landscape metaphor – are overcome here, and both stories make a positive value out of a creative tension now evident in Chekhov's artistic temperament. In 'Misery', the falling snow and the lights of the impersonal city, unheedful of Iona, insist imaginatively upon the transience of life and the loneliness of sorrow. That sense of things, and the images through which it is felt, are persistent elements throughout Chekhov's work. But in his longer and more significant stories he remains open also to other senses of life coming out of particular scenes and occasions, so that his works begin progressively to take shape as dialogues, behind which duelling elements of Chekhov's own temperament play themselves out.

Chekhov's demeanour in his life seems to have been that classically associated with the medical profession, which he entered from Moscow University in 1884. It embodied, on the one hand, a belief in the aspirations of science and, on the other, a resigned sense of the points beyond which nothing could be done. So that there is in Chekhov's whole intellectual temperament a basic tension between the man committed to a form of ideal and the realist painfully aware of its limitations. However conscious he was of this tension, it is one which he often reproduces in his doctor characters (and sometimes in his clerics). It is also, more importantly, the tension that dictates the very shape of his art in 'Easter Eve' and, in a different way, in 'Enemies'. 'Easter Eve' captures the special atmosphere of the eve of Easter. In its evocation of the religious celebrations and in its obvious appreciation of the lines from Nikolay's canticles, the story reveals Chekhov's attraction to the aesthetic aspects of the ceremony and to the hope of human perfectibility embodied in Nikolay's images. But equally important to the whole sense of life in 'Easter Eve' is Chekhov's sympathetic portrayal of Ieronim's pain and suffering and his lonely plying of the river-ferry – all of which seem to exist outside the terms of the religious ceremony; and the scenes outside the church, where the celebrations are viewed across the water and through the darkness of night, are pervaded by a strong sense of transience. Furthermore, the story ends, after the religious exultations of the night, with a scene rendered (in a spirit much closer to that of ordinary realism) as exhausted and bleak. The story's meaning comes from this major tension between the night-sense of human states, which gives them a religious intensity and potency, and the dawn-sense of them, in which they are numbed and mute, and bearing them is simply a necessity. 'Enemies', on the other hand, is structurally more akin to 'Vanka', with a deft, ironic twist in the course of events in mid-story. The admirable selflessness of the doctor Kirilov, in tearing himself away from the scene of his son's death to attend to Abogin's dying wife, becomes a censurable arrogance when he finds out that the 'tragedy' in Abogin's house is different from the one he expected and decides that it is an outrage on his dignity. What looks like a study of ethical idealism in the intensified atmosphere of tragedy becomes a realistic scrutiny of men's motives and of their missed opportunities for helping one another. And with the twist in outcome begins a slow but deliberate redistribution of the story's sympathies. Though the procedures in the two stories are very different, each involves a genuine division and tension in Chekhov's sympathies; and the fact that his own commitments are so deeply involved, that resolutions are not easy, ensures a depth and fairness in the represented situations – what Chekhov called '*stating a problem correctly*'.[1]

It was the impartial scientist in Chekhov who felt the need to entertain the possibility that the world might be other than as he generally perceived it; and 'Easter Eve', as I have suggested, gives quite sustained credence – in tension with other possibilities – to a basically Christian, religious view of the world. But it would be wrong to think of this tension between a Christian acceptance of the world and a more agnostic – hence ultimately more tragic – sense of it as being the basic tension in Chekhov's work. That is the form which the tension takes in 'Easter Eve'; but even there Chekhov is not so much interested in the actual content of such differing beliefs as in the puzzling variety and contradictoriness of the evidence which life presents. His response to the heightened atmosphere of the Easter ceremony and to the poetic language of the canticles indicates, not an attraction specifically towards the Christian religion, but the value he places on any kind of higher aspiration or idealism. Equally, he is not setting out to demonstrate the superiority of an agnostic perception of the world by juxtaposing the celebrated triumph of the Resurrection and Ieronim's unmitigated grief: those facts are simply recognized and recorded by the uncompromising realist in him. So the basic tension is temperamental rather than ideological – a tension (which the plays – particularly *Uncle Vanya* and *Three Sisters* – embody in a rather different form) between Chekhov's idealism and optimism about human capabilities and his resigned realism about the conditions and restrictions on life as things are. Needless to say, in this form it is a tension belonging classically to the humanist. In both 'Easter Eve' and 'Enemies' Chekhov is holding in a complex balance competing facts and intuitions about the kind of place the world is and what the people are like who inhabit it. He is attempting to '*stat[e] a problem correctly*', reflecting the full variety of the evidence (the very phrasing '*stating a problem correctly*' suggests scientific inquiry and reminds us that, as a nineteenth-century humanist, Chekhov saw the whole scientific enlightenment as central to human progress). In these two stories, therefore, he creates a complex arrangement of scenes and perspectives designed to reflect on both the kinds of people perceiving the world in certain ways and the different kinds of reality that world assumes at different times. In the shape of such art, Chekhov contributed to Russian literature a distinct – and distinctly valuable – new kind of literary humanism and realism.

Rarely in the stories is the emotional pitch so high, or the imagery so poetically intense, as in 'Easter Eve'. The Russian Easter gives the story a very special atmosphere of festive excitement, of ceremony and of religious emotions being dissipated but strangely infused through the crowd. Even the opening scene, before the Easter ceremony has begun, anticipates the later heightened atmospheres through the stark contrast between the darkness and the brightness of the stars and the sense of a brimming to overflowing abundance in all nature:

The weather seemed to me magnificent. It was dark, yet I could see the
trees, the water and the people...The world was lighted by the stars,
which were scattered thickly all over the sky. I don't remember ever
seeing so many stars. Literally one could not have put a finger in
between them. There were some as big as a goose's egg, others tiny as
hempseed...They had come out for the festival procession, every one
of them, little and big, washed, renewed and joyful, and every one of
them was softly twinkling its beams. The sky was reflected in the water;
the stars were bathing in its dark depths and trembling with the quivering eddies. The air was warm and still...Here and there, far away on
the further bank in the impenetrable darkness, several bright red lights
were gleaming...(VII.51–2)

The image is not cloying, as it might easily have been; it strangely
combines the sense of intimacy created by the warm air and
crowded stars with the remoteness and impenetrable darkness
of the opposite flood-bank where bright but distant lights gleam.
In fact, as we will see, this effect of peculiar intensity and yet of
sombre space is integral to the story. The stars are 'washed,
renewed and joyful' – an image which, though it is perhaps
slightly affected, clearly suggests an analogy with the human
crowd celebrating Easter – its aspiration for spiritual renewal
from the ceremony. There is also a sense of unusual elation in
the passage, as if the speaker himself is caught up in the general
Easter mood. But some intimation is simultaneously given, in the
image of the 'impenetrable darkness' on the other bank and the
dark distance between the church and the story's speaker, of a
different set of facts about the world from those about to be
celebrated in the church; and this is the source of the story's
tension.

Throughout most of its length, 'Easter Eve' presents two
simultaneous, but essentially opposite, realities of this special
night. It unfolds both the strange exuberance of the religious
occasion and the unmitigated suffering of the monk who, working the ferry back and forth across the dark water, seems to be
enacting his own private ritual of grief. But, rather than allow
these conflicting senses of the night simply to discount one
another, Chekhov gives each a vivid purchase on our imagina-
tions and actually constructs his scenes in such a way that each
is intensified by the other's presence. For example, the religious
ceremony, as Chekhov presents it, has a celebratory richness of
colour and sound, particularly at the moment when the Resur-

rection is announced. Seen and heard from across the water, though, it is filtered through a more sombrely suggestive atmosphere of darkness and of human voices calling for the lost monk:

The peasant went up to the water's edge, took the rope in his hands, and shouted: 'Ieronim! Ieron—im!'

As though in answer to his shout, the slow peal of a great bell floated across from the further bank. The note was deep and low, as from the thickest string of a double bass; it seemed as though the darkness itself had hoarsely uttered it. At once there was the sound of a cannon shot. It rolled away in the darkness and ended somewhere in the far distance behind me. The peasant took off his hat and crossed himself.

'Christ is risen,' he said.

Before the vibrations of the first peal of the bell had time to die away in the air a second sounded, after it at once a third, and the darkness was filled with an unbroken quivering clamour. Near the red lights fresh lights flashed, and all began moving together and twinkling restlessly.

'Ieron—im!' we heard a hollow prolonged shout. (VII.52–3)

The sense of distance here comes from a sensitively created illusion of different auditory spans and then, of course, from the visual image of the twinkling lights. The Easter significances are maintained by the ceremony and the peasant in the foreground uttering the response 'Christ is risen'. But the imaginative direction of the passage, with its suggestive distances and hollow sounds, is away from the Christian symbolism to a more sombre but still peculiarly 'heightened' symbolism of its own.

These opening scenes are clearly most important in establishing the strange ambiguity of the story's created world. In them the world is transfigured with sometimes a religious, and sometimes a tragic, intensity – and sometimes, curiously, with both. The result is that, even as they record the Easter ceremony, a number of these scenes emerge as oddly and paradoxically pagan in feeling. The religious jubilations in the outdoor atmosphere, observed from a distance and surrounded by the darkness of night, seem curiously relaxed and formless; and the fact that the ceremony is being seen from such a distance, where the figures are engulfed by the darkness, surrounds it with a strong irrational reminder of death and of life's transience:

At the water's edge barrels of tar were flaring like huge camp fires. Their reflections, crimson as the rising moon, crept to meet us in long broad streaks. The burning barrels lighted up their own smoke and the long shadows of men flitting about the fire; but further to one side and behind them from where the velvety chime floated there was still the same unbroken black gloom. All at once, cleaving the darkness, a rocket zigzagged in a golden ribbon up the sky; it described an arc and, as though broken to pieces against the sky, was scattered crackling into sparks. There was a roar from the bank like a far-away hurrah.

'How beautiful!' I said. (VII.54)

The positive assertion is there in the golden rocket zigzagging up the sky. The atmosphere is festive, full of colour and surprise, with a quality of joyous superfluity in its expenditure of energy. Yet its context is a deep solidity of darkness against which the rocket breaks and other energies are partly dispelled. It is, then, against such an emotionally ambiguous background that Chekhov sets the contending images of Ieronim grieving on the ferry and the peculiar hubbub in the church.

Since the story has to be mobile between very different settings – the river and the church – the narrator here is a dramatized character who boards the ferry to take him to the Easter ceremony. This is important because the ferry itself, despite its superficial connotations, does not actually connect one 'world' with the other: rather, it is strictly and poignantly confined to a ritual of its own. Moreover, the dramatized narrator ensures that we are only gradually eased into sympathy with Ieronim by meeting him through someone who is himself on guard:

'All the creatures are keeping holiday. Only tell me, kind sir, why, even in the time of great rejoicing, a man cannot forget his sorrows?'
I fancied that this unexpected question was to draw me into one of those endless religious conversations which bored and idle monks are so fond of. I was not disposed to talk much, and so I only asked:
'What sorrows have you, father?'
'As a rule only the same as all men, kind sir, but to-day a special sorrow has happened in the monastery: at mass, during the reading of the Bible, the monk and deacon Nikolay died.'
'Well, it's God's will!' I said, falling into the monastic tone. 'We must all die. To my mind, you ought to rejoice indeed...They say if anyone dies at Easter he goes straight to the kingdom of heaven.'
'That's true'.
We sank into silence. (VII.55)

Ieronim is specifically acknowledged to have a somewhat feminine sensibility and to have been fascinated by Nikolay's eloquence, and we require some dramatic reassurance that we are not being asked to acquiesce wholly and immediately in his particular sense of things. It is not, in fact, until the scene in the church, when the Easter hymn is being sung, that we come to sympathize with him entirely. But within the distance preserved from him by the story's speaker, he does emerge as movingly responsive to the poetry of Nikolay's canticles, in which the conventional imagery of the Eastern church is infused with a touching freshness and innocence:

'In the canticle to the Holy Mother are the words: "Rejoice, O Thou too high for human thought to reach! Rejoice, O Thou too deep for angels' eyes to fathom!" In another place in the same canticle: "Rejoice, O tree that bearest the fair fruit of light that is the food of the faithful! Rejoice, O tree of gracious spreading shade, under which there is shelter for multitudes!"'

Ieronim hid his face in his hands, as though frightened at something or overcome with shame, and shook his head.

'Tree that bearest the fair fruit of light...tree of gracious spreading shade...' he muttered. 'To think that a man should find words like those! Such a power is a gift from God! For brevity he packs many thoughts into one phrase, and how smooth and complete it all is! "Light-radiating torch to all that be..." comes in the canticle to Jesus the Most Sweet. "Light-radiating!" There is no such word in conversation or in books, but you see he invented it, he found it in his mind! Apart from the smoothness and grandeur of the language, sir, every line must be beautified in every way; there must be flowers and lightning and wind and sun and all the objects of the visible world. And every exclamation ought to be put so as to be smooth and easy for the ear. "Rejoice, thou flower of heavenly growth!" comes in the hymn to Nikolay the Wonder-worker. It's not simply "heavenly flower", but "flower of heavenly growth". It's smoother so and sweet to the ear. That was just as Nikolay wrote it! exactly like that! I can't tell you how he used to write!'

'Well, in that case it is a pity he is dead,' I said; 'but let us get on, father, or we shall be late.' (VII.58–9)

This poetically infused language of worship and the intensity of Ieronim's response to it are intrinsic to the story's power. But it is the aesthetics of his religion that Ieronim finds compelling, not its faith. Ieronim's speeches take up broadly Christian imagery with an eloquence generally absent from the Easter ceremony itself (apart from one important moment) as recorded in the story. Yet Ieronim plying the ferry, gibbet-like in shape, back and forth across the flood-waters and mourning the death of his friend, is in the story a potent figure of loneliness and suffering. And, though the Easter ceremony does not, of course, exclude recognition of such facts, the contrast between the jubilations on shore and Ieronim's private mourning makes that loneliness and suffering seem outside the normal framework of Christian reconciliation. As he starts the ferry back to the far side, Ieronim's bending to the rope becomes a heart-breaking gesture of resignation, an act of mute endurance:

The ferry ran into the bank and stopped. I thrust a five-kopeck piece into Ieronim's hand for taking me across, and jumped on land. Immediately a cart with a boy and a sleeping woman in it drove creaking onto the ferry. Ieronim, with a faint glow from the lights on his figure, pressed on the rope, bent down to it, and started the ferry back... (VII.61)

The immediate repetition of the ferry-run, the primitive manual nature of the work, and the reinforcement (by the details of the sleeping woman and the creaking cart) of an incipient sense of exhaustion all do much to make this a counter-image of life to the one being celebrated inside the church.

In the scene within the church, the strange intensity of this warm ceremonial night expresses itself as a restless, anarchic energy. It is not necessarily a more trivial scene than the one by the river, but it does have a quite different quality of chaotic and jostling joyousness:

This path led to the dark monastery gates, that looked like a cavern through a cloud of smoke, through a disorderly crowd of people, unharnessed horses, carts and chaises. All this crowd was rattling, snorting, laughing, and the crimson light and wavering shadows from the smoke flickered over it all... A perfect chaos!... But nowhere was the excitement and restlessness so marked as in the church. An unceasing struggle was going on in the entrance between the inflowing stream and the outflowing stream. Some were going in, others going out and soon coming back again to stand still for a little and begin moving again. People were scurrying from place to place, lounging about as though they were looking for something. The stream flowed from the entrance all round the church, disturbing even the front rows, where persons of weight and dignity were standing. There could be no thought of concentrated prayer. There were no prayers at all, but a sort of continuous, childishly irresponsible joy, seeking a pretext to break out and vent itself in some movement, even in senseless jostling and shoving. (VII.61–3)

The stress of the writing is not evaluative in any obvious sense: Chekhov is clearly just interested and excited by the startling human incongruity of the scene. The preternatural air that surrounds the river scene has given way to hubbub and disorder, but in a peculiar way the exaltation of ordinary feelings is still there. In fact, the streams of people flowing in and out of the church are given a strange continuity with the river experience by being imaged in terms of moving currents of water. Theirs is a primitive energy of a completely instinctive kind: a ubiquitous, de-personalized and restless vitality, which thus seems to our imaginations like the diverse, surface eddying of a stream whose powerful undercurrent we have felt to be embodied in Ieronim's isolated sensibility. And the two – the fast-moving currents and the swollen flood-waters – are brought together at one of the high points of the Easter ceremony to give a particularly intense and complex sense of the world on this special Easter night:

As I mingled with the crowd and caught the infection of the universal joyful excitement, I felt unbearably sore on Ieronim's account. Why did they not send someone to relieve him? Why could not someone of less feeling and less susceptibility go on the ferry? 'Lift up thine eyes, O Sion, and look around,' they sang in the choir, 'for thy children have come to thee as to a beacon of divine light from north and south, and from east and from the sea...'

I looked at the faces; they all had a lively expression of triumph, but not one was listening to what was being sung and taking it in, and not one was 'holding his breath'. Why was not Ieronim released? I could fancy Ieronim standing meekly somewhere by the wall, bending forward and hungrily drinking in the beauty of the holy phrase. All this that glided by the ears of people standing by me he would have eagerly drunk in with his delicately sensitive soul, and would have been spell-bound to ecstasy, to holding his breath, and there would not have been a man happier than he in all the church. Now he was plying to and fro over the dark river and grieving for his dead friend and brother.

The wave surged back. A stout smiling monk, playing with his rosary and looking round behind him, squeezed sideways by me, making way for a lady in a hat and velvet cloak. A monastery servant hurried after the lady, holding a chair over our heads. (vii.63–4)

The song of praise in the church, which goes unnoticed, calls to mind Ieronim, who is sadly deprived of this joy. The rhythms are those of the canticles he loves, and the image of the beacon calling the faithful from across the sea cannot help recalling the flood-waters and distant lights of the opening scene. Of all people, Ieronim feels the attraction of the 'divine light' – in aesthetic terms – most strongly; but it is Ieronim who is left to travel the river alone in the story's most poignant image of inconsolable suffering and loss: 'Now he was plying to and fro over the dark river and grieving for his dead friend and brother.' Thus, when the next paragraph begins 'The wave surged back', the emotional reference is, for a moment, curiously double. It seems to refer most immediately to Ieronim and his grief; but it does, in fact, open syntactically onto the most incongruously *merry* image of the entire church scene – the monk playing with his rosary, the lady in velvet, and the monastery servant carrying a chair above the worshippers' heads.

The achievement so far would be enough to mark Chekhov as one of the true masters of the short-story form; but 'Easter Eve' has not two highly metaphorical scenes but three. The third is a scene on the river in the grey light of dawn: and what that scene does is to recognize that both scenes of the night have been unusually intense – impregnated with either religious or tragic intensities – and so to replace them (without entirely subverting them) by a more ordinary image whose details are suddenly more sparse and realistic. This new image is not necessarily offered as conveying *the* truth about the world; but the morning-after feeling of unspecified disappointment is the appropriate resolution of the unstable intensities of the night, and so this landscape feels in one way more 'real':

When we came out of church after mass it was no longer night. The morning was beginning. The stars had gone out and the sky was a morose greyish blue. The iron slabs, the tombstones and the buds on the trees were covered with dew. There was a sharp freshness in the air. Outside the precincts I did not find the same animated scene as I had beheld in the night. Horses and men looked exhausted, drowsy, scarcely moved, while nothing was left of the tar barrels but heaps of black ash...

Now I could see both banks of the river; a faint mist hovered over it in shifting masses. There was a harsh cold breath from the water. When I jumped on to the ferry, a chaise and some two dozen men and women were standing on it already. The rope, wet and as I fancied drowsy, stretched far away across the broad river and in places disappeared in the white mist.

'Christ is risen! Is there no one else?' asked a soft voice.

I recognized the voice of Ieronim. There was no darkness now to hinder me from seeing the monk. He was a tall narrow-shouldered man of five-and-thirty, with large rounded features, with half-closed, list-less-looking eyes and an unkempt wedge-shaped beard. He had an extraordinarily sad and exhausted look. (VII.65–6)

The note of exaltation has gone entirely. The imagery is not concentrated into a core of intensity but is dispersed, detail after detail being recorded almost listlessly in the movement of the prose. The river scenery now feels quite different – not warm, dark and romantically intense, but bleak, cold and grey. There is still a strange beauty about it, now felt in the dewy buds and the mists over the waters, a hint of renewal that pulls against the suggestion of weary repetition in the ferry metaphor. But the overall feeling is one of exhaustion and resignation. Of the three 'landscapes' in 'Easter Eve', this is the one on which the story comes to rest. Unfortunately, it is softened by a note of senti-mentality at the end, as Ieronim is seen searching intently for his friend's features in a woman's face. But the damage done by that effect is small. For the final sense of things in the dawn scene is not offered as the one sense of things held by the story as a whole. It is, perhaps, of the three, the atmosphere most likely to express the usual reality of life. But it is the purpose and value of 'Easter Eve' to enter imaginatively into the spirit of each piece of evidence provided by these different scenes – to recognize the existence of contrary sets of evidence about the world, and to convey each as having its own kind of power. If, because of the time-sequence involved in the story, the dawn landscape literally replaces the others, it still does not replace them in our imagina-tions. The order of the scenes is not designed to allow one landscape image – and by implication one particular sense of life – to replace or discount another. Instead, the story holds its three quite distinctive atmospheres in tension against one another to give an appropriately complex statement to the mystery of the kind of place the world is, or may be.

This is not the art of a sceptic, since the questions it implicitly raises about the nature of life are not raised in a spirit of scepticism. It is the art of an extremely sensitive empiricist, whose interest in the way life *feels* at different times, and in the relation-ship between men's aspirations and the limitations life imposes on them, has no doctrinaire limitations one way or the other. Chekhov's medical training taught him to weigh the facts care-fully and dispassionately, and not to diagnose prematurely. His art can be intensely poetic and emotionally very warm; but something of the scientific spirit finds its way into his wariness about just how much truth is or can be expressed by single intuitions and/or images. Here and in the later 'Lights', he gives us a number of images projecting quite different senses of the world, holding these in balance by means of a highly complex narrative structure. The effect of the sequence in both these works is gently to endorse the sadness and sense of exhaustion of the dawn scenes. But Chekhov would never make those scenes a simple 'answer' to those of the night. His own temperamental attraction to both kinds of night-evidence as presented in 'Easter Eve' – his love of the Easter ceremony and of its power to make human beings what ordinarily they are not, and his tragic sense of the loneliness and cruelty of life – gives those images a potency that survives the morning in memory, even if there is a more familiar, and therefore more realistic, quality about the world revealed at dawn.

To discuss 'Enemies' at all requires a shift in terms. The cast of this story is directly moral, and its appeal is to more abstract sympathies than those elicited by 'Easter Eve'. In some ways it seems more thought-out, more cerebral and planned. But its very difference from 'Easter Eve' makes its own point: that Chekhov was by this time (1886–7) versatile enough to make real successes out of markedly different conceptions and forms. For, surprising as it may at first seem, especially after 'Easter Eve', 'Enemies' has something in common with the work of George Eliot. That is, it is primarily concerned with the intersecting needs of different lives and consequently with the relativity of moral claims; and there are even reminders of George Eliot in the way the recounting voice is prone at points to adopt a moralizing tone:

Abogin and the doctor stood face to face, and in their wrath continued flinging undeserved insults at each other. I believe that never in their lives, even in delirium, had they uttered so much that was unjust, cruel, and absurd. The egoism of the unhappy was conspicuous in both. The unhappy are egoistic, spiteful, unjust, cruel, and less capable of understanding each other than fools. Unhappiness does not bring people together but draws them apart, and even where one would fancy people should be united by the similarity of their sorrow, far more injustice and cruelty is generated than in comparatively placid surroundings. (XI.35)

I don't think one would be quite in danger of mistaking this for George Eliot. Nevertheless, the rounding-out of the particular situation in the passage into general truths whose cadences seem to carry such authority, and the pondered and weighty syntax, do remind one of her. And with both writers the psychological behaviour which is being generalized about is felt to be inevitable, the prose-voice having a fatalistic tone ('Unhappiness does not bring people together but draws them apart...'), at the same time as the very existence of the art – exhorting its readers to do better – seems to contradict that fatalism. Neither writer is religious in the sense of looking beyond human lives themselves for meaning or for salvation: in each, the impulse seems to be to promote an awareness in the reader of what the possibilities and conse-quences of action are within a small, flexible space of human self-determination which has fixed limits at both ends. Moreover, those limits are defined by both writers, not as conditions meta-physically ordained by God or by an impersonal fate, but at one end as the psychological propensities of particular sorts of indi-viduals, and at the other other as the way life is constituted, socially, so that no man's life is wholly his own.

We see the latter clearly in the very opening of 'Enemies'. No sooner has the doctor's son died than Abogin rings at the door:

Between nine and ten on a dark September evening the only son of the district doctor, Kirilov, a child of six, called Andrey, died of diphtheria. Just as the doctor's wife sank on her knees by the dead child's bedside and was overwhelmed by the first rush of despair there came a sharp ring at the bell in the entry. (XI.17)

The timing of this new demand on Kirilov's attention just when he needs time to react to his son's death is cruelly precise. The grief-stricken parents have hardly begun to realize what has happened before Abogin is there, pleading for the doctor to attend to his sick wife. It is the kind of moral construct one associates with the novel: a situation in which equally compelling human needs are found to be diametrically at odds, with no possible resolution that will not involve denying one person or the other. The novel is the favoured milieu for such a situation, because it is the novelist's special task to observe cross-sections of humanity with a view to their cross-purposes. But 'Enemies' is unusual in compressing this novelistic vision into the short-story form (gaining in immediacy what it loses in scope). And the story gives this dilemma of human needs crossing one another a special intensity because of the life-and-death nature of Kirilov's occupation as a doctor. One feels this immediately, as each character begins to invoke the term 'humanity':

Abogin followed him and caught hold of his sleeve.

'You are in sorrow, I understand. But I'm not asking you to a case of toothache, or to a consultation, but to save a human life!' he went on entreating, like a beggar. 'Life comes before any personal sorrow! Come, I ask for courage, for heroism! For the love of humanity!'

'Humanity – that cuts both ways,' Kirilov said irritably. 'In the name of humanity I beg you not to take me. And how queer it is, really! I can hardly stand and you talk to me about humanity! I am fit for nothing just now...Nothing will induce me to go, and I can't leave my wife alone. No, no...'

Kirilov waved his hands and staggered back.

'And...and don't ask me,' he went on in a tone of alarm. 'Excuse me. By No. XIII of the regulations I am obliged to go and you have the right to drag me by my collar...drag me if you like, but...I am not fit...I can't even speak...excuse me.'

'There is no need to take that tone to me doctor!' said Abogin, again taking the doctor by his sleeve. 'What do I care about No. XIII! To force you against your will I have no right whatever. If you will, come; if you will not – God forgive you; but I am not appealing to your will, but to your feelings. A young woman is dying. You were just speaking of the death of your son. Who should understand my horror if not you?' (XI.23)

Not only is there no course of action that will avoid doing one man a wrong: there is also none that will not violate some basic respect due to human life. To have to decide whether to let Abogin's wife die or abruptly and immediately to leave the scene of his son's death and his grieving wife is a terrible decision for Kirilov to have to make. Indeed, so cruel is the coincidence of circumstances that it is another of those Chekhovian occasions when things seem to have happened 'on purpose' to make life less bearable. George Eliot's sense of the web-like pressures exerting their influence over a person's life does not extend to this: in her work the lines of mutual frustration are less direct, and the influence of one life on another is more gradually cumulative. But it is, I think, not simply the dramatist in Chekhov showing himself in this cruelly exact timing of the two crises, but also the doctor in him who knows all too well the possibility of such simultaneous, contradictory and equally imperative demands. Since one of the story's characters is a doctor, the presented coincidence of circumstances is neither gratuitous nor implausible; and, in any case, it is a part of Chekhov's tact that although Abogin intrudes immediately upon the scene with his demand, there is actually a significant interval of time before he and Kirilov set off to attend Abogin's wife. Between Abogin's intrusion and Kirilov's agreement to go with him there is a strange sense almost of time-suspension as Kirilov is possessed by his grief, wandering in an abstracted and will-less way through the house, leaving Abogin forgotten in the hall. While Abogin's waiting figure expresses the concentration of *his* purpose, Kirilov is memorably represented as unable even to manage his usual bodily co-ordination:

Judging from his unsteady, mechanical step, from the attention with which he set straight the fluffy shade on the unlighted lamp in the drawing-room and glanced into a thick book lying on the table, at that instant he had no intention, no desire, was thinking of nothing and most likely did not remember that there was a stranger in the entry. The twilight and stillness of the drawing-room seemed to increase his numbness. Going out of the drawing-room into his study he raised his right foot higher than was necessary, and felt for the doorposts with his hands, and as he did so there was an air of perplexity about his whole figure as though he were in somebody else's house, or were drunk for the first time in his life and were now abandoning himself with surprise to the new sensation. (XI.19–20)

Abogin and Kirilov have opposite senses of urgency and hence opposite senses of time; and the understandable absorption of each by his own needs is captured here and given some weight before Kirilov reluctantly agrees to Abogin's demand.

In view of Chekhov's own occupation as a doctor, one would expect his basic sympathies in such circumstances to go to Kirilov. The incidental details of the doctor's study, his books, the mute way in which he and his wife suffer, all establish Kirilov as educated and austere, a proud man conscious of his own dignity. His initial reticence and his strong ethical sense of the code by which he is bound are known aspects of Chekhov's own demeanour. Furthermore, Chekhov's personal experience as a doctor is clearly behind the exhaustively particular details of the disarray of the room around the dead boy and the left-over medicaments, which is the background to the numbed exhaustion of Kirilov's grief. Abogin, on the other hand, is an opposite kind of character from Chekhov himself. He lives in a world of agreeable candlelight and striped linen curtains, and he is somehow childish, bourgeois, pampered. Even in appearance Kirilov and Abogin are opposites, and Kirilov bears the marks of a deeper and more suffering consciousness of himself and the world around him:

The doctor was tall and stooped, was untidily dressed and not good-looking. There was an unpleasantly harsh, morose, and unfriendly look about his lips, thick as a negro's, his aquiline nose, and listless, apathetic eyes. His unkempt head and sunken temples, the premature greyness of his long, narrow beard through which his chin was visible, the pale grey hue of his skin and his careless, uncouth manners – the harshness of all this was suggestive of years of poverty, of ill-fortune, of weariness with life and with men... Abogin presented a very different appearance. He was a thickset, sturdy-looking, fair man with a big head and large, soft features: he was elegantly dressed in the very latest fashion. In his carriage, his closely buttoned coat, his long hair, and his face there was a suggestion of something generous, leonine; he walked with his head erect and his chest squared, he spoke in an agreeable baritone, and there was a shade of refined almost feminine elegance in the manner in which he took off his scarf and smoothed his hair. (XI.27–8)

But it is obvious from this description that Chekhov is deliberately creating opposites (as he does with Ananyev and Von Schtenberg in 'Lights', and with Laevsky and Von Koren in 'The Duel'), and that he is – perhaps unexpectedly – actually dividing his sympathies more or less evenly between the two. Though Kirilov the doctor shares much in common with Chekhov, he shares less with him as a man. Kirilov is unkempt, his expression is 'unpleasantly harsh', and he is limited by his own proud arrogance. Abogin is the kind of man one might easily dismiss as superficial, a person whose manners and values seem to be very far from those of Chekhov himself. Yet there is obvious approval in Chekhov's description of him as 'generous, leonine', and he is created as having (again, despite our expectations) a genuine inner life:

Abogin was sincere, but it was remarkable that whatever he said his words sounded stilted, soulless, and inappropriately flowery, and even seemed an outrage on the atmosphere of the doctor's home and on the woman who was somewhere dying. He felt this himself. (XI.24)

To see through such mannerisms to the character's inner sincerity involves a humane extension of the range of Chekhov's natural sympathies. It involves recognizing that one sort of temperament is not inherently superior to another: thus the relative virtues of the two men remain to be tested. But more important is the situation Chekhov develops for testing Kirilov and Abogin, and the reversal that takes place in our sense even of the kind of story this is. 'Enemies' begins with a situation of tragedy in which life itself seems terribly cruel and people its victims. In the context of his own son's death, Kirilov's decision finally to go to Abogin's wife's aid is a triumph of compassion and idealism. But, while Chekhov responds to that idealism and gives it its full weight, he is interested here in just how far – from a realist's viewpoint – this sort of compassion and idealism will extend. As the story goes on, then, and even as it partially confirms shallowness and moral squalor as characteristic of Abogin's way of life (his flighty wife, whose infidelity he has been prepared to tolerate, has sent him on a hoax-call to the doctor in order to gain time to elope with her lover), it questions more and more the true nature of Kirilov's apparent selflessness at the beginning. Its purpose in doing so is not, of course, to deny the value of Kirilov's action: rather, by scrutinizing the situation in this way, it offers a more discerning sense of the real occasions and conditions of moral heroism, outside the heightened atmospheres of situations that are overtly, and therefore immediately, recognizable as tragic. That the call which interrupts the privacy of Kirilov's grief should be a bogus one, with all the sordid facts behind it, is a cruel irony and shows Chekhov's drily pessimistic view of what life is sometimes capable of. But the irony of the story is that Kirilov's reaction to that terrible cruelty of life, his repudiation of the other man's occasion for sadness as simply a 'vulgar farce', is more damaging than what has initially happened to either of them. Initially Kirilov commands most of our sympathy, and Abogin takes the little that is left; but although events show that Kirilov has cause for great sorrow, while Abogin is simply the victim of domestic trickery, it is Abogin who progressively gains the story's sympathy and Kirilov, in his arrogant rejection of Abogin's suffering, who loses some of it.

The point of equilibrium, where Kirilov and Abogin seem to share a common kind of sorrow and hence seem to command the same sympathy, is the episode of the carriage-ride to Abogin's house. At least at some moments during that carriage-ride the predicaments of the two men seem to merge as Chekhov amplifies a general sense of sorrow and pain through the surrounding landscape. It is the one place in the story when there is any approach to the poetic procedures of 'Easter Eve', although here

4-2

there is a too-contrived 'atmosphere' and some of the detail is clichéd and self-indulgent:

On the right lay a plain as uniform and as boundless as the sky; here and there in the distance, probably on the peat marshes, dim lights were glimmering. On the left, parallel with the road, ran a hill tufted with small bushes, and above the hill stood motionless a big, red half-moon, slightly veiled with mist and encircled by tiny clouds, which seemed to be looking round at it from all sides and watching that it did not go away.

In all nature there seemed to be a feeling of hopelessness and pain. The earth, like a ruined woman sitting alone in a dark room and trying not to think of the past, was brooding over memories of spring and summer and apathetically waiting for the inevitable winter. Wherever one looked, on all sides, nature seemed like a dark, infinitely deep, cold pit from which neither Kirilov nor Abogin nor the red half-moon could escape . . . (XI.26–7)

The sense of the imprisonment of the men and of the red half-moon in the dark 'pit' of nature, the cawing crows in the previous paragraphs, and the dim lights measuring the space across the peat-marshes, all make this an ominous landscape – though ominous in a damagingly unspecific way. For all the detail of the little clouds around the moon it is hard to know what to make of them; and it is hard not to be aware of a forcing of response through the image of the earth as a fallen woman and through the interpretative 'seemed' – 'in all nature there seemed to be a feeling of hopelessness and pain', and so on. States are being projected onto the landscape rather than elicited from it, and at the same time the details seem to introduce inconsistencies. But what does emerge through the landscape of the journey is a strong sense of the actual process of travelling from one house to another, from Kirilov's house to Abogin's. From the lighted window near Kirilov's garden fence and the pale upper windows of the hospital, the carriage disappears into dense shadow and darkness to re-emerge at the lighted windows of Abogin's house. In the course of its progress through the darkness it crosses smooth sand, crunches through the pebbles of the river, and proceeds again through the smooth sand on the other side. It is this sense of transition so strongly conveyed by the crossing of the river, the sense that he is being compelled to enter another man's province when he desperately wants the privacy of his own, which presumably causes Kirilov to start and to begin to struggle once more against Abogin:

And when the carriage slowly drove over the river, Kirilov started all at once as though the splash of the water had frightened him, and made a movement.

'Listen – let me go,' he said miserably. 'I'll come to you later. I must just send my assistant to my wife. She is alone, you know!'

Abogin did not speak. The carriage swaying from side to side and crunching over the stones drove up the sandy bank and rolled on its way. Kirilov moved restlessly and looked about him in misery. (xi.26)

The reader, too, feels that the river-crossing is transitional, although he is not sure into what. In this subtle way we are prepared for something exceptional to happen at Abogin's house – though we are still surprised when the incipiently tragic intensities of the story seem to have been side-tracked into domestic melodrama. As the story subsequently makes us feel, what happens to Abogin – his discovery that his wife has left him – is *his* personal tragedy; and it is Kirilov's failure to recognize this which loses for him much of the story's sympathy. But for this to become clear, and for Kirilov's arrogance to be exposed, requires first a daring shift, and even a quite risky one, from the tragedy of the situation at Kirilov's house to the sordid deceptions at Abogin's. The landscape images partly accomplish this by making us feel the likelihood of something unexpected – but that semi-paradox is as far as the preparation goes.

Abogin's way of life is such that for sorrow to take this relatively sordid form is completely plausible – even likely, given the background of his marriage. With all its vulgar pretence, it is a form one cannot imagine sorrow taking in Kirilov's life. Likewise, Abogin's reaction to it is the very opposite of the doctor's stoically silent suffering:

'The patient! The patient!' cried Abogin, laughing, crying, and still brandishing his fists. 'She is not ill, but accursed! The baseness! The vileness! The devil himself could not have imagined anything more loathsome! She sent me off that she might run away with a buffoon, a dull-witted clown, an Alphonse! Oh God, better she had died! I cannot bear it! I cannot bear it!' (xi.30)

The offence Kirilov takes at this is completely understandable, and his incredulity may even increase our sympathy:

The doctor drew himself up. His eyes blinked and filled with tears, his narrow beard began moving to right and to left together with his jaw.

'Allow me to ask what's the meaning of this?' he asked, looking round him with curiosity. 'My child is dead, my wife is in grief alone in the whole house...I myself can scarcely stand up, I have not slept for three nights...And here I am forced to play a part in some vulgar farce, to play the part of a stage property! I don't...don't understand it!' (xi.31)

There is a terrible pathos about Kirilov's inability to grasp that life could be so cruel. But the language he is beginning to use – as when he speaks of 'some vulgar farce' – also gives offence in its arrogant indifference to another man's misery. As Chekhov presents him, Abogin is a genuinely suffering man, with a real need to talk his suffering out: Kirilov has a chance to help him which his self-absorption in his own grief and angry pride will not let him take. In fact, Chekhov is unusually explicit about this moment of missed opportunity, so that although we feel Kirilov to be in the grip of a powerful psychological mechanism which he cannot resist, the moral inference to be drawn from it is still absolutely plain:

With tears in his eyes, trembling all over, Abogin opened his heart to the doctor with perfect sincerity. He spoke warmly, pressing both hands on his heart, exposing the secrets of his private life without the faintest hesitation, and even seemed to be glad that at last these secrets were no longer pent up in his breast. If he had talked in this way for an hour or two, and opened his heart, he would undoubtedly have felt better. Who knows, if the doctor had listened to him and had sympathized with him like a friend, he might perhaps, as often happens, have reconciled himself to his trouble without protest, without doing anything needless and absurd...But what happened was quite different. (xi.32–3)

The writer of this story is Chekhov the humanist, who has nothing to do with Chekhov the 'dispassionate observer' referred to so frequently by critics. Indeed, so intense is the moral preoccupation that at points, as in the passage just quoted, the writing implicitly recommends particular selfless and considerate forms of action. But if the power of 'Enemies' is a power of moral exposition, its complete credibility nevertheless derives from the convincing psychological portrayal of the reactions of the two men. At the height of their confrontation, Chekhov seems to have an almost Tolstoyan infallibility about the precise cadences, the precise weighting of the sentences, the admixture of general with particular grievances, of an ugly anger which the reader will probably recognize. It is the irrationally intense attack of a proud and articulate man, who has known hardship and suffering, on everything and everyone associated with a bourgeois life, which he easily and automatically equates with complete superficiality:

'Why did you bring me here?' the doctor went on, his beard quivering. 'If you are so puffed up with good living that you go and get married and then act a farce like this, how do I come in? What have I to do with your love affairs? Leave me in peace! Go on squeezing money out of the poor in your gentlemanly way. Make a display of humane ideas, play' (the doctor looked sideways at the violoncello case) 'play the bassoon and the trombone, grow as fat as capons, but don't dare to insult personal dignity! If you cannot respect it, you might at least spare it your attention!'...

'You have taken leave of your senses,' shouted Abogin. 'It is ungenerous. I am intensely unhappy myself and...and...'

'Unhappy!' said the doctor, with a smile of contempt. 'Don't utter that word, it does not concern you. The spendthrift who cannot raise a loan calls himself unhappy, too. The capon, sluggish from over-feeding, is unhappy, too. Worthless people!' (xi.33–4)

Kirilov's intense disgust, coming out of a peculiarly proud self-pity and catching up all kinds of social aggression, is not in the least flattering to him. Chekhov is a long way from the terms in which he thought of grief in 'Misery'. It is with a realism obviously born of intense observation that he manages such details as Kirilov's instinctive transformation of the sight of Abogin's violoncello case into the metaphor of his 'playing the bassoon and the trombone', with its derogatory suggestion of slightly vulgar self-display. And later there is that masterly capturing of the curtailed, almost sarcastic, intonation of the voice at such times of anger, as in the sentence 'Don't utter that word, it does not concern you.' The result is that, although Kirilov retains some of our sympathy (and we cannot forget the magnitude of the provocation), his harshness and injustice forfeit him our respect. He is still presented as the deeper man, and it is in the extremity of his grief that he blindly hits out; but the very fact that he has greater personal resources to draw upon makes his attack on Abogin appear as a violation of someone defenceless.

It is, then, Chekhov's triumph in this story to have made us feel the origin and in part the justice of Kirilov's reaction, and yet to have moved beyond his instinctive sympathies and antipathies to defend the rights and dignity of a comparatively shallow man. He takes nothing for granted in the situations he develops: recognizing the sorts of assumptions we are likely to make about such different men as Kirilov and Abogin, he continuously challenges those assumptions, while slowly but deliberately challenging our initial perspectives on their situation. Chekhov is not content simply to portray Kirilov's heroism and the cruelty of the fate which has his tragedy coincide with Abogin's. Though that is a moving situation, it is too simply dialectical; and, as the rest of the story makes clear, it involves a subtle romanticizing of Kirilov's real nature and motives. Moreover, there is something gratuitous about a story insisting on the cruelty and tragedy of a conflict which human beings have no power whatever to avert. So, at the cost of dissipating the initially tragic atmosphere and of seeming to mistrust such heroism as Kirilov initially displays, Chekhov in 'Enemies' is committed to getting beyond the obvious aspects of Kirilov's tragedy to a more realistic (but also more directly humanistic) understanding. By having Abogin's plea for help for his sick wife turn into so humiliating a deception for both men, Chekhov is acknowledging, as always, that element of the unexpected in the way things turn out which is part of his realistic sense of life. But, more importantly, through it he is pointing regretfully to the deeper tragedy and irony of how much further suffering Abogin and Kirilov inflict on one another. There are more critical situations in the moral life, Chekhov seems to say, than the ones which look most obvious. Responding to other people's needs, when people themselves seem so absurd and undignified, may be more crucial and more difficult than performing acts of heroism that are obvious as such. In the interests of '*stating [the] problem correctly*' Chekhov judges neither man for having the kind of temperament he has. He sets no standards of how or to what depth men should feel. But he does ultimately insist, as a humanist and saddened moralist, on the narrowness of egoism and the tragedy of misunderstanding. Not Andrey's death nor Abogin's wife's betrayal is accorded that pressure of regret which emerges so clearly in the voice of the final paragraph:

When a little later the doctor got into the victoria and drove off there was still a look of contempt in his eyes. It was dark, much darker than it had been an hour before. The red half-moon had sunk behind the hill and the clouds that had been guarding it lay in dark patches near the stars. The carriage with red lamps rattled along the road and soon overtook the doctor. It was Abogin driving off to protest, to do absurd things...

All the way home the doctor thought not of his wife, nor of his Andrey, but of Abogin and the people in the house he had just left. His thoughts were unjust and inhumanly cruel. He condemned Abogin and his wife and Paptchinsky and all who lived in a rosy, subdued light among sweet perfumes, and all the way home he hated and despised them till his head ached. And a firm conviction concerning those people took shape in his mind.

Time will pass and Kirilov's sorrow will pass, but that conviction, unjust and unworthy of the human heart, will not pass, but will remain in the doctor's mind to the grave. (xi.36–7)

Even in the later stories, after 1890, where the moral emphasis is generally stronger than it was in Chekhov's early works, it is rare for him so to dramatize his own voice. It has the effect of making 'Enemies' feel like a plea – a plea for understanding, against prejudice, in a world over which there can only be human control if there is to be control at all. It does not deliver a judgment, exactly: there is a naturalness about each man's reaction in his particular circumstances which inclines us to a fatalistic acceptance of such an outcome. But the story certainly presents a diagnosis, and a diagnosis which gets its force from an almost relentless realism about human psychology. And no one could doubt, after reading it, that Chekhov was now taking his task as a writer seriously.

Part III

That in his sphere there are no questions, but only
answers, can be maintained only by those who have never
written and have had no experience of thinking in
images.

Letter to A. S. Souvorin (Moscow, 27 October 1888)

5

The steppe stories

It was not really until 1888 that Chekhov embarked on a full-scale work of the kind recommended in Grigorovich's letter. For a time the recognition following from that letter actually intensified the pressures preventing him from undertaking a long piece, one which would also have to be very carefully worked out. The humorous magazines were more clamorous for new stories, there were numerous social invitations for Chekhov to attend to, and the number of younger Moscow writers wanting him to comment on their work increased. But it may be that his delay in attempting something for the serious monthly journals was, after all, quite fortunate. For in 1887, on an advance of three hundred roubles from Souvorin, the editor of *New Times*, he went on a journey to the Don steppe, with apparently only half an intuition that that particular region of Russia had immense psychological importance for him: 'So that I won't dry up, at the end of March I'm going to travel South, to the Don region, in Voronezh Province, and so forth, where I'll greet the spring and refresh my memory on things that have already begun to grow dim. It seems to me that by doing this my work will get along in a more lively manner.'[1]

The visit to the steppe was perhaps more important than he anticipated. It re-opened for his imagination a potently suggestive environment, one that became a deep psychological reference-point in the whole sense of life he held. He had now a new milieu in which to work: a world of vast, unvarying expanse, monolithic and yet violently changeable with the elements, and peopled by nomadic figures (not unlike some of those in the Old Testament) who are virtual archetypes of Russian stoicism. So in 1888 we find a spate of stories set in the steppe country – 'The Steppe', 'The Beauties', 'Happiness' and 'Lights' – which as a group explore basic senses of existence and basic facets of the Russian character in landscapes that vary in nature from the nihilistically uniform and de-energized to the

picturesque and mythically intense. To anyone accustomed to
thinking of Chekhov as a writer with predominantly social concerns, essentially an urban writer, this will come as a surprise.
Nothing could be further from the steppe stories than the sense
of winter bustle in Moscow in 'The Lady with the Dog' or the
whole interest in class and cultural crisis in the late plays. But
this middle-period work is, in fact, deeply responsive to landscape, in terms both of its physical contours and its power to
suggest to the imagination different philosophical images of life.
The steppe life as represented is hard, requiring fortitude and
endurance. It is also prone to accident in the way it brings people
up against one another and against sudden squalls in nature. Its
moods, its rapid changeability, make it a powerful setting for –
even a metaphor of – human violence and endurance; and its
virgin susceptibility to changing light and seasonal variations
makes it a valuable landscape for a writer interested (as 'Easter
Eve' shows Chekhov was) in the way environment acts upon
men's basic senses of the world.

I pointed out in the last chapter that Chekhov never works
toward a final 'answer'. His concern, as a humanist, is with how
the world feels at different times, in different places, to different
men. But in the context of his national literature, with its tradition
of direct utterance and often passionate conviction about general
truths, such a concern was – and still is – frequently misunder-
stood. Hence Chekhov's need to reply to Souvorin:

What you say about 'Lights' is quite just. You write that neither the
conversation on pessimism, nor the story of Kisochka helps in the least
to solve the problem of pessimism. It seems to me that the writer of fiction
should not try to solve such questions as those of God, pessimism, etc.
His business is but to describe those who have been speaking or thinking
about God and pessimism, how, and under what circumstances.[2]

The major steppe stories enquire into the nature of life from the
point of view of various specific characters: the shepherds and
the overseer in 'Happiness', the more educated men of 'Lights',
and the child Yegorushka, travelling to an unknown future, in
'The Steppe'. Chekhov is interested in what these people think,
how they think it, and (as he says) 'under what circumstances'.
Where he himself stands in relation to what they say and think
is indicated only cautiously and tentatively (and even less confi-
dently than in 'Easter Eve') by the structure of the stories, which

inevitably gives a special significance to the images with which each story ends. But even these structures become more complex as Chekhov takes new human and moral complications into account, to the point where no certain resolution attaches to their endings. It is this especially which makes 'Lights' a challenging and difficult experience to come to terms with but also one of Chekhov's finest and most original stories, and an important one in the European tradition.

In Grigorovich's letter of 1886 he speaks of the exceptional 'plasticity' of Chekhov's feelings, his ability to evoke a whole landscape in a few lines. In a letter of his own to his brother Alexander, Chekhov stresses the need for economy and for originality of detail in natural description:

In my opinion a true description of Nature should be very brief and have a character of relevance. Commonplaces such as, 'the setting sun bathing in the waves of the darkening sea, poured its purple gold, etc.,' – 'the swallows flying over the surface of the water twittered merrily,' – such commonplaces one ought to abandon. In descriptions of Nature one ought to seize upon the little particulars, grouping them in such a way that, in reading, when you shut your eyes, you get a picture.

For instance, you will get the full effect of a moonlight night if you write that on the mill-dam a little glowing star-point flashed from the neck of a broken bottle, and the round, black shadow of a dog, or a wolf, emerged and ran, etc.[3]

In his first long story for the serious journals, 'The Steppe', there are many such individual effects (like the enchanted windmill that stays so long on the horizon, or the thunder 'as though someone very far away were walking over an iron roof' – (VII.283)) which convey the contours, distances and moods of the landscape in a lively and economical way. But, given his commitment to brevity in natural descriptions, it is surprising that Chekhov should have chosen to make his '*chef d'oeuvre*' (as he called it at the time) an extended set-piece of landscape description with so little in the way of a narrative scheme. Perhaps, indirectly, he felt the pressure of a sense, apparently quite prevalent in Russia, that the mark of a good writer was his strong communicative feeling for his native land and, secondarily, for its national types. Chekhov had spent his childhood not far from the steppe, and apart from Moscow itself it was the region he knew best. There were also classic works centred on that region – Gogol's *Taras Bulba* and

Turgenev's *A Lear of the Steppes* – which he could aim to equal and also to challenge. For Chekhov must have known intuitively that what he would portray of the steppe would reveal a way of feeling about it quite different from theirs. In Gogol's historical romance it is a place of great colour and epic action, an almost sacred place peopled with Cossack defenders. Martin Petrovich, Turgenev's 'Lear of the steppes', is a figure of rough-hewn, rather grotesque Slavic grandeur. Neither Gogol nor Turgenev finds anything perturbing in the steppe's sheer expanse, which to Chekhov's imagination is accentuated by its monotonous flatness of contour. Compare, for example, the two following passages, which are virtual set-pieces of landscape description. The first is from Gogol:

The farther they went the more beautiful grew the steppe. In those years, the entire southern part of Russia, all the way to the Black Sea, was a green, virgin wilderness. Never had a plow driven through the long waves of wild growth and only the horses, hidden in it as if among the trees of the forest, trampled the tall grass. There could be nothing more beautiful in the world: the visible surface of the earth looked like a golden green ocean, its waves topped by multicolored spume. Through the tall, slender stems of the grass showed sky-blue, marine, and purple star thistles; yellow broom thrust up its pyramidal head; the white parasols of Queen Anne's lace gleamed near an ear of wheat that had appeared there God knows how and was now growing heavy. Partridges scurried among the thin stalks of the steppe plants, their necks outstretched, and in the sky hawks hung immobile on their outspread wings, eyes glued on the ground; and from the grass rose a steppe gull and bathed herself luxuriously in the blue waves of the air. Now she dissolved in the soaring heights; now she reappeared like a little comma; now, as she turned, her wings reflected a ray of sunlight.[4]

By contrast, here is Chekhov:

The cut rye, the coarse steppe grass, the milkwort, the wild hemp, all withered from the sultry heat, turned brown and half dead, now washed by the dew and caressed by the sun, revived, to fade again. Arctic petrels flew across the road with joyful cries; marmots called to one another in the grass. Somewhere, far away to the left, lapwings uttered their plaintive notes. A covey of partridges, scared by the chaise, fluttered up and with their soft 'trrr!' flew off to the hills. In the grass crickets, locusts and grasshoppers kept up their churring, monotonous music.

But a little time passed, the dew evaporated, the air grew stagnant, and the disillusioned steppe began to wear its jaded July aspect. The grass drooped, everything living was hushed. The sun-baked hills, brownish-

green and lilac in the distance, with their quiet shadowy tones, the plain
with the misty distance and, arched above them, the sky, which seems
terribly deep and transparent in the steppes, where there are no
woods or high hills, seemed now endless, petrified with dreariness.
(VII.172–3)

The difference of response in the two passages should be clear.
The spaciousness of the steppe in Gogol is caught up with a whole
sense of liberation, of natural abundance, un-fixity and fluidity.
The sustained analogy of the grass with the ocean, of the 'waves'
of wild growth, which is continued in the image of the bird
'bath[ing] herself luxuriously in the blue waves of the air', relieves any monotony in the horizontal perspectives by giving the
landscape a continuous suggestion of vertical depth. The variety
of textures and the vivid colours project a sense of vibrancy
in the landscape, even perhaps a primordial luxuriance. The
Chekhov passage, on the other hand, enacts a cycle of energies
revived in and then drained from the landscape, with the textures
of the landscape emerging as harsh and the colours faded. The
horizontal expanse of the steppe is, if anything, accentuated by
the sky being 'arched above' the plain without any real sense of
vertical continuity. The living creatures mostly hug the earth; and
Chekhov makes of their sounds (the 'trrr!' of the partridges and
the monotonous music of the insects), followed by the hush of
midday, something not quite eerie but certainly disconcerting to
ordinary human senses. Chekhov's reluctance to transmute the
landscape into metaphor as Gogol does – and thus to make his
excursion into it a 'literary' exercise, in a somewhat pejorative
sense – comes from his strong sense of the intractability of the
steppe to his imagination. There is a sense of Chekhov's separateness from the landscape, a tact in relation to it which is finally
missing in the Gogol, which suggests Chekhov's respect for – and
partial fear of – its power. Simply to feel the steppe through this
imagination, so much more perturbed about the world than
Gogol's, is a valuable thing. But, more than that, the impersonal
environment in 'The Steppe' is populated with figures who are
quite opposite in kind from Gogol's colourful Cossacks. With the
exception of Dymov, each of Chekhov's characters embodies in
his way those well-recognized conditions of Russian life and the
Russian spirit: poverty, orthodoxy and stoicism. There are, for
example, the movingly realized representative figures of Father
Christopher and old Panteley (which in themselves declare

Chekhov to be a major artist in the making). Nor can Chekhov resist the opportunity for some comment on the Russian character in general:

From this conversation Yegorushka gathered that all his new acquaintances, in spite of the differences of their ages and their characters, had one point in common which made them all alike: they were all people with a splendid past and a very poor present. Of their past they all – every one of them – spoke with enthusiasm; their attitude to the present was almost one of contempt. The Russian loves recalling life, but he does not love living. Yegorushka did not yet know that, and before the stew had been all eaten he firmly believed that the men sitting round the cauldron were the injured victims of fate. (VII.248–9)

This is predictable generalization, and hardly represents Chekhov at his best. It is noticeably less subtle than his later interest in essentially Russian character traits in the last plays. But the fact that the passage is there at all is evidence of his response to the pressures of a new audience, one which would judge him partly in terms of his portrayal of the Russian countryside and of national types, thus stimulating him with a new sense of challenge.

But despite these clear achievements and some very fine set-piece writing, the basically non-narrative character of 'The Steppe' feels unnatural for Chekhov, and the story exhibits signs of strain. His letters of this period comment on his inexperience of the mode and the fatigue of writing 'long things': 'I enjoy writing it, but I fear that, as I have little experience with these ambitious undertakings, I lose the consistent thread of the narrative, grow weary, do not speak out, and am not serious enough in manner.'[5] As is usual with Chekhov's letters, there is a certain truth and self-knowledge in this. The whole of 'The Steppe' is held together only very loosely by Yegorushka's long journey to the school that will make an educated man of him. There is, as one principle of coherence, the overall irony that the journey itself 'educates' Yegorushka probably more than any school awaiting him, by teaching him of the existence of violence and of the reality of sickness and death. The purely aesthetic response Yegorushka has to the 'gay' churchyard in his village, where the white tombstones peep from behind the fruit-laden cherry trees and where Granny lies 'sleeping', is convulsively changed by the experience of the journey to a horrified imagining of his grandmother's predicament:

Yegorushka thought of his grandmother, who was sleeping now under the cherry trees in the cemetery. He remembered how she lay in her coffin with pennies on her eyes, how afterwards she was shut in and let down into the grave; he even recalled the hollow sound of the clods of earth on the coffin lid . . . He pictured his granny in the dark and narrow coffin, helpless and deserted by everyone. His imagination pictured his granny suddenly awakening, not understanding where she was, knocking upon the lid and calling for help, and in the end swooning with horror and dying again. (VII.251–2)[6]

Though at this point his apprehension of what death means is not quite complete, there are no longer the same childish cadences captured in the earlier passage ('When Granny had died she had been put in a long narrow coffin and two pennies had been put upon her eyes, which would not keep shut' (VII.170)). Yegorushka now knows what is entailed by independent selfhood: the self being at the mercy of situations which other people haven't always the will, or the power, to help. The tales of violence told by the men around the camp-fire tell Yegorushka of factors in life which he has not yet had personally to encounter. But even they have only a remote influence on Yegorushka's development compared with his experience of being left alone in the storm and his being sick as a consequence. His steppe education is education by experience; and when he says good-bye a second time to Father Christopher it has reached a definite point:

Yegorushka kissed his hand, and shed tears; something whispered in his heart that he would never see the old man again. (VII.313)

Described like this, 'The Steppe' might seem to have the usual firm shape of Chekhov's art. But this concern with Yegorushka's growth has virtually to be pieced together from a chaotically wide range of created fact. The story is highly episodic and needlessly digressive at points (as in the whole highly detailed scene of Dymov's and Kiruha's fishing); and insufficient real development comes out of the first half. In fact, overall there is too much essentially repetitive writing, creating the steppe atmosphere in an impressionistic and highly adjectival way. The self-consciousness that came from having to write a long, serious 'literary' piece apparently deprived Chekhov of his instinctive economy and tight construction. There were also inherent difficulties in the attempt to convey the particular mood of this landscape by day: how to convey monotony and repetition as features of an atmosphere without writing monotonously and repetitiously and thus losing the interest of the reader. In 'The Steppe' Chekhov has not altogether overcome those difficulties.

The two shorter steppe stories, 'Happiness' (1887) and 'The Beauties' (1888), are more incidental by-products of Chekhov's steppe journey and as such are less beset by this self-consciousness. Both are tight in organization, and the writing in them is more relaxed than almost anything in 'The Steppe'. Even so, neither achieves a very full statement of the kind of significance Chekhov seems intuitively to have felt the steppe to have: for that, one has to wait until 'Lights'. But they do embody imaginative intuitions of an undeveloped kind which are important in the development towards 'Lights', especially those in 'Happiness'. Since it is 'Happiness' that most directly anticipates 'Lights', I shall discuss 'The Beauties' first, to make possible a greater continuity in the discussion of the two more closely related works.

Like many of Chekhov's stories at this stage, 'The Beauties' juxtaposes quite different central images, in this case different images of beauty. The image of classical beauty in the Armenian, Masha, is set against that of an irregular, distinctively Russian beauty in the girl on the station platform. However, in this particular story less is actually made of the contrast of the beauties than of the way each appears suddenly and unexpectedly out of a barren – or at best indeterminate – landscape. The steppe background gives a poignancy to the existence of these individual beauties by its harshness and desert-like expanse, having some of the connotations of Marvell's 'deserts of vast Eternity'. The narrator of the story meets Masha in the course of a carriage journey through the steppe: she comes to make tea for the travellers during their brief stay at a hot and dusty Armenian settlement whose atmosphere is no less stifling than that of the steppe itself. The Russian beauty of the second part is standing on a railway platform, admired by the passengers (including the narrator) who are continuing their train journey to the South. The journeys are therefore broadly metaphorical in that they suggest something of the way beauty appears to most people, fleetingly and accidentally, saddening them by making them aware of unpossessed possibilities which they may not even see again. These overtones are particularly clear at the end of the second episode, as the train pulls out of the station into the darkening plain and the candles begin to be lit in the carriage. The travellers' own lives, faring forward, seem sadly imperfect and time-laden, as the scene anticipates the melancholy and limitation of a joyless old age:

Putting my head out and looking back, I saw how, looking after the train, she walked along the platform by the window where the telegraph clerk was sitting, smoothed her hair, and ran into the garden. The station no longer screened off the sunset, the plain lay open before us, but the sun had already set and the smoke lay in black clouds over the green, velvety young corn. It was melancholy in the spring air, and in the darkening sky, and in the railway carriage.

The familiar figure of the guard came into the carriage, and he began lighting the candles. (ix.295)

The train leaving the beauty behind, the open plain and the guard beginning to light the candles gently suggest the span of time ahead in which things will be merely ordinary and imperfect. It is impossible not to feel the poignancy of these brief moments of delight in the presence of beauty, compared with the long hours of travelling through the night for which the train is destined.

The beauties, too, have a special poignancy in being unusually liable to waste. They are not just in unexpected places, in places without romantic opportunities; they are also captured in matured landscapes – Masha amid the mellow dryness of the steppe grasses and the Russian girl in the dying, 'rosy' light of late afternoon – where their youth and beauty seem cruelly out of place. Masha darts gracefully through a golden rain of flying chaff in the courtyard; and Chekhov makes that scene integral to the way in which we respond to Masha by having the engulfing chaff seem to etherealize her movements while also momentarily reducing her to dust. The Russian girl laughs and talks, with a coquettish self-confidence, in the late afternoon light as it mingles with the smoke of the train. Each scene is designed to give a quite strong sense of transience and of puzzling arbitrariness and waste.

But the suggestiveness of the images in 'The Beauties' seems to have lured Chekhov into trying to take up, fairly explicitly, a range of questions about beauty, its place in the world and men's reactions to it, which so short a story cannot effectively manage. It can indeed raise such questions, but it does not really clarify them in the reader's mind. We could hardly, of course, expect a resolution of them; but here Chekhov does not even correctly state the problem. When, for example, the story's narrator tries to explain his reactions to Masha's beauty and those which he observes in the Little Russian working nearby, the inconclusiveness and sheer confusion in the explanation are damaging:

And the oftener she fluttered by me with her beauty, the more acute became my sadness. I felt sorry both for her and for myself and for the Little Russian, who mournfully watched her every time she ran through the cloud of chaff to the carts. Whether it was envy of her beauty, or that I was regretting that the girl was not mine, and never would be, or that I was a stranger to her; or whether I vaguely felt that her rare beauty was accidental, unnecessary, and, like everything on earth, of short duration; or whether, perhaps, my sadness was that peculiar feeling which is excited in man by the contemplation of real beauty, God only knows. (ix.290)

Until the last clause, Chekhov seems to be examining why beauty might provoke sadness where it ought to excite delight. But when it emerges, through the elaborate syntax of the final sentence, that envy, regret and so on are being seen not as components of the 'sadness excited by real beauty' but as alternatives to it, the reader becomes confused. The question of *why* such beauty should excite sadness remains unclarified: the 'thinking in images' (as Chekhov called it) which produced the superb imagery of 'The Beauties' has allowed the intellectual concerns of the story to remain unthought-out. Even with the second beauty, the Russian girl, Chekhov seems uncertain whether to emphasize the pathos of her particular kind of beauty, a butterfly-beauty which (as so often in literature) is associated with a heightened sense of transience, or whether to locate the pathos – in social and sexual terms – in the reactions of the unkempt telegraphist and the guard, for both of whom such beauty seems 'as far away as heaven'. Having begun by invoking the fragility of the girl's delicate beauty, its apparent vulnerability even to a gust of wind from across the station platform, his introduction of these two figures – both of them ordinary, battered by life and slightly uncouth – and his pity for them shift and complicate the terms of the story in ways over which Chekhov seems to have no control. Although those final images – of the telegraphist and the guard looking wistfully after a beauty they can never hope to possess – are in themselves touching, they represent a movement right away from the kind of interest raised by the first beauty, so arbitrarily and poignantly beautiful in the midst of a wasteland of steppe.

It is probably significant that this weakness in 'The Beauties' is associated with the raising of questions for their own sake, outside the viewpoint of a strongly dramatized character. The story does have a narrator, but he is not forcefully enough distinguished from Chekhov himself. In the best of the steppe stories, on the other hand, the speakers are strongly individualized; and the questions raised are subordinated to an interest in just how these questions are raised by these particular men, how they perceive the answers, and under what pressures their perception occurs. It is in this way that 'Happiness' anticipates 'Lights'. 'Happiness' brings the shepherds and the overseer together on the steppe during the sinister and lonely time just before dawn, when each instinctively needs the company of the others; and it shows the peculiar effect of that pre-dawn light over the landscape in actively eliciting fears from the men and thus challenging them to meet and come to terms with their condition. In 'Lights' the men involved are more educated and more articulate about their impulses; in 'Happiness' the characters are primitive and superstitious. But both stories envisage the sinister austerity of the steppe, with a shadowy dusk or darkness cast over it, as provoking some primal instinct of fear or panic in human beings about the actual constitution of the world and its possible hostility to men.

'Happiness' seems, in the past, to have been generally regarded as an allegory. Ernest Simmons, for example, speaks of it as 'a sad allegory of man's eternal search for meaning, for happiness, in a world of frustrating shadows'.[7] According to this view, the treasure of which the old shepherd speaks stands for the tangible purpose and the happiness he desires from life, both of which have so far eluded him, and the shepherd himself becomes a representative figure, a kind of everyman. In one form or another we are all in quest of assurances about life's purpose: thus the shepherd speaks for us all. But it seems to me that this approach to 'Happiness' as an allegory fails to account for several of the most important things about it. In the first place, it raises the question of why Chekhov should choose so uncharacteristic a mode, especially when what he has to convey is so apparently simple and straightforward. It also makes one wonder why he should choose such primitive people to represent men

in general. And if Chekhov intends us actually to interpret each
of the story's effects – to align each one with some overall meaning which is much more abstract – then what sense are we to
make of such immediate and compelling details as the overseer's
obvious reluctance to move away from the other men, the
comfort the overseer plainly gets from the small circle of light
around his pipe, or the strange uneasiness of the dogs? I want,
therefore, to propose a quite different view of 'Happiness' – one
which recognizes these primarily sensuous effects and sees that
they only lose by being converted into the abstract. Accordingly,
I want to suggest that, in this story, Chekhov is interested in the
way the characters themselves allegorize their notion of happiness (rather than seeing Chekhov as allegorizing it for literary
purposes of his own). In other words, Chekhov, as he said, was
concerned with how particular kinds of men think. The men in
'Happiness' are uneducated and poor. The treasure is their way
of objectifying for themselves what a significant life might have
which their own lives lack. But it is not the sense that they lack
something which predominantly interests us, but the way they
represent their condition to themselves and the pressures under
which they do so.

At either end of 'Happiness' there are landscapes which are
interpretatively overloaded, artistically even a bit cynical. Take
the following, for example, from near the opening:

The sheep were asleep. Against the grey background of the dawn,
already beginning to cover the eastern part of the sky, the silhouettes
of sheep that were not asleep could be seen here and there; they stood
with drooping heads, thinking. Their thoughts, tedious and oppressive,
called forth by images of nothing but the broad steppe and the sky, the
days and the nights, probably weighed upon them themselves, crushing
them into apathy; and, standing there as though rooted to the earth,
they noticed neither the presence of a stranger nor the uneasiness of
the dogs. (VI.254)

The suggestion that the sheep have actual thoughts and are
sufficiently aware of the monotonous landscape around them for
it to 'crush them into apathy' is obviously weak – a facile and
unexpected amateurism. But the 'uneasiness' of the dogs is a
much more realistic effect and has a real imaginative impact. It
begins to give the scene an air of strange volatility, of aroused
instincts and of a quick communication of panic:

A big shaggy old sheep-dog of a dirty white colour with woolly tufts about its nose and eyes walked three times quietly round the horse, trying to seem unconcerned in the presence of strangers, then all at once dashed suddenly from behind at the overseer with an angry aged growl; the other dogs could not refrain from leaping up too.

'Lie down, you damned brute,' cried the old man, raising himself on his elbow; 'blast you, you devil's creature.' (VI.255)

The grey light before dawn has none of the intimacy or cosiness that can be associated with absolute dark. The steppe appears bleak and vast, so that in unconscious response to the double threat of the wide expanse and of the partial dark (the whole setting feeling impersonal and alien), animals and people are vaguely troubled, easily disturbed. In the men, this disturbance takes the form of a developing fear that life may have neither reward nor purpose but may be as indifferent to them as the shadowy steppe. They suddenly (and, for us, poignantly) feel the need for some tangible reassurance that life does have some value; and the whole direction of the talk between the old shepherd and the overseer is towards gaining some mutual control over these perturbing feelings.

As I have said, these are primitive people who can think only by reference to concrete things. Thus, as the darkness stimulates the old shepherd, largely through fear, into raising the question of what kind of place the world is and what kinds of potencies it contains, he does so in the only way he knows: through an abrupt, particular reference to the figure of Yefim:

'It was at Kovyli on Ascension Day that Yefim Zhmenya died. Don't speak of it in the dark, it is a sin to mention such people. He was a wicked old man. I dare say you have heard.' (VI.255)

Chekhov makes this raising of the subject of wickedness, of the demonic powers and knowledge of treasure some men seem to have, feel almost compulsive on the old shepherd's part. He is afraid to speak of Yefim in the dark, and yet he must; indeed, it is his unconscious disturbance by the night landscape that turns his thoughts that way. His whole way of thinking is superstitious rather than analytical, mythic instead of intellectual. It gives the narrative a mediaeval flavour, such is the evoked underworld of lurid supernatural sights and sounds:

'...the Evil One will begin whistling in a stone if he wants to. Before the Day of Freedom a rock was humming for three days and three nights in our parts. I heard it myself. The pike laughed because Yefim caught a devil instead of a pike.' (VI.256)

Or later:

'The treasures about here are charmed so that you may find them and not see them, but he did see them. At times he would walk along the river bank or in the forest, and under the bushes and under the rocks there would be little flames, little flames...little flames as though from brimstone. I have seen them myself.' (VI.258)

The revelation of this habit of thought, a man's convinced expression of a sense of things through mythic imagery in which literal truth is of no account, is, I think, intrinsically interesting. It is a primitive, peasant way of thinking, in this case conditioned by Russian Orthodoxy, and it does not feel implausible. Indeed, many of the images (like that of the 'little flames', where the repetition gives a gently hypnotic quality) exert a particular fascination in their colourful blending of Christian legend, folklore and demonology, which is the stuff of the old shepherd's consciousness. But even more importantly, 'Happiness' reveals something of the instinctual basis of the human psyche in general. The overseer is conscious from the beginning of his superiority to the shepherds and he is not beyond a kind of posturing and polite condescension in conversation with them. His advantage over them lies in a small resource of irony, a habit of verbal evasion by which he gives non-committal assent to everything he hears: 'It does happen...', he says. But his actual wisdom is not much greater than that of the shepherds. He too is compelled by the idea of hidden treasure, wanting tangible reassurance with which to combat his fears. Most tellingly, his lingering close to the shepherds at this stage of the night, obviously reluctant to go, reveals him to be as vulnerable to irrational fears (fears that the reader, too, surely recognizes) as are the humbler men.

During the telling of the treasure tales, whose very telling involves a mutual attempt to gain some reasurrance, the little circles of light from the overseer's pipe create a reassuring visual and human centre to the otherwise dreary and indeterminate scene. The importance of that effect to the psychological concern of the story can hardly be missed and should be further evidence against thinking of 'Happiness' as an allegory. But, in the midst of the treasure tales, when the old shepherd tells of his brother's finding a soldier standing on the very spot where there was said to be gold, there is a smoothly accomplished but imaginatively highly disruptive transition:

'A monk revealed to my brother Ilya – the Kingdom of Heaven be his – that in one place in the fortress of Taganrog there was a treasure under three stones, and that that treasure was under a charm, and in those days – it was, I remember, in the year '38 – an Armenian used to live at Matvyeev Barrow who sold talismans. Ilya bought a talisman, took two other fellows with him, and went to Taganrog. Only when he got to the place in the fortress, brother, there was a soldier with a gun, standing at the very spot...'

A sound suddenly broke on the still air, and floated in all directions over the steppe. Something in the distance gave a menacing bang, crashed against stone, and raced over the steppe, uttering, 'Tah! tah! tah! tah!' When the sound had died away the old man looked inquiringly at Panteley, who stood motionless and unconcerned.

'It's a bucket broken away at the pits,' said the young shepherd after a moment's thought.

It was by now getting light. (VI.261–2)

This mournful echo of a bucket falling in the pits, which Chekhov had heard as a child, is obviously the basis of the snapping-string sound in *The Cherry Orchard*. Here, it seems almost to mock Ilya's vain expedition with its ironically cruel end, except that the noise itself, far from having any intonation of triumph, is sad and menacing. In any case, it breaks the hold of the night and of the treasure tales both literally and symbolically. The overseer now prepares to go: there is no more comfort to be had from the shepherds' company. It is as if things have come to the worst. The tone of his comments changes to an unstable combination of regret and bitter irony:

'Yes,' he said, 'your elbow is near, but you can't bite it. There is fortune, but there is not the wit to find it.'

And he turned facing the shepherds. His stern face looked sad and mocking, as though he were a disappointed man.

'Yes, so one dies without knowing what happiness is like...' he said emphatically, lifting his leg into the stirrup. (VI.262–3)

That is not all: the imaginative perspective we have had on the steppe expanse shifts and loses its comforting human centre. Now the landscape is intriguing, yet it is pervaded by a sinister sense of complete futility:

In the bluish distance where the furthest visible hillock melted into the mist nothing was stirring; the ancient barrows, once watch-mounds and

tombs, which rose here and there above the horizon and the boundless
steppe had a sullen and death-like look; there was a feeling of endless
time and utter indifference to man in their immobility and silence;
another thousand years would pass, myriads of men would die, while
they would still stand as they had stood, with no regret for the dead nor
interest in the living, and no soul would ever know why they stood there,
and what secret of the steppes was hidden under them.

The rooks awakening, flew one after another in silence over the earth.
No meaning was to be seen in the languid flight of those long-lived birds,
nor in the morning which is repeated punctually every twenty-four
hours, nor in the boundless expanse of the steppe. (VI.263)

This dwelling on the barrows brings a kind of historical imagination into play, extending the mystery of human purpose backwards through time. The watch-mounds and tombs of an
ancient, undiscovered people excite that imagination less with a
promise of treasure than with their disconcerting testimony of
a life that has been, whose secrets have been entirely engulfed
by time. Hence the potency and poignancy of the remnants: they
have power to enforce a recognition of a whole prehistory which
it is more comfortable to forget, and they taunt those who see
them with their own terrible and unbreakable silence and with
the poverty of what is left. So it is not just the meaning of the
shepherds' lives that is in question at this point, but the meaning
of a whole span of human and natural history whose secrets are
locked tight in those unyielding mounds of earth. From a human
point of view, the landscape is heartbreaking. It has archetypal
and even nightmare properties as a composite image of human
insignificance. And it extends that sense out into the natural
world itself, where the silent flight of the rooks, the cycle of
day and night, and the steppe itself all have an automatic, unconscious quality which feels frighteningly purposeless.

The first and second landscape perspectives of 'Happiness'
thus involve a shift, from the old shepherd's and the overseer's
intuitive sense that the world is a place of strange supernatural
potencies to an author-created nihilistic image. It is the latter
that tends to excite the reader's actual sympathies where the
characters' sense of things excites his interest. But, as in 'Easter
Eve', there is no attempt to have one interpretative image of
the world cancel the other out; and Chekhov's experimentation
with the different philosophical images being projected by
the landscape as the light dawns across it is secondary to his

psychological interest in the way the night elicits fears from the men. In any case, even the image of the barrows is not actually the last, since the sun has yet to rise and reveal the steppe in a further light. Towards the end of 'Happiness', as the sun rises, there are, in fact, two separate sources of visual and psychological comfort after the bleak pre-dawn atmospheres. One is the geographically extended view from Saur's Grave, where the panoramic effect makes the landscape seem more humanly patterned and purposive:

If one clambered up on that tomb one could see the plain from it, level and boundless as the sky, one could see villages, manor-houses, the settlements of the Germans and of the Molokani, and a long-sighted Kalmuck could even see the town and the railway-station. Only from there could one see that there was something else in the world besides the silent steppe and the ancient barrows, that there was another life that had nothing to do with buried treasure and the thoughts of sheep. (VI.265)

The other is the steppe itself as the dawn light bursts across it:

An immense crimson sun came into view surrounded by a faint haze. Broad streaks of light, still cold, bathing in the dewy grass, lengthening out with a joyous air as though to prove they were not weary of their task, began spreading over the earth. The silvery wormwood, the blue flowers of the pig's onion, the yellow mustard, the corn-flowers – all burst into gay colours, taking the sunlight for their own smile. (VI.266–7)

The homely and attractive dawn scene contains hardly a trace of the sense of disturbance that has been associated with the night. The classic omens of death, the mounds and the solitary birds, have given way to the gay, ephemeral freshness of the flowers. Which is telling the truth about the world? Perhaps none of the story's landscapes, or perhaps all.

Chekhov is not really interested in settling such questions as these – in propounding 'truths'. What he has done is to dramatize how such figures as the old shepherd and Panteley confront their condition, with a special view to the way each is acted upon by the night. In doing that, he has cast 'lights' across the surrounding landscape, by which it seems to substantiate first one way of feeling about life, then another, and then a third. The effect is to disrupt the reader's sense that there is, or can be, an objective 'reality'; to open his mind to the contrary kinds of evidence that exist; and to give him sympathy for these primitive men as they have to contend with it. It is not, however, until the story actually entitled 'Lights' that these concerns with the way men think, and the conditions around them bearing on them as they think, finally take on a real ethical and moral force. Only in that story, the subject of my next chapter, are the human consequences of men's holding particular world-views thoroughly explored.

6

'*Lights*'

From the very beginnings of Western literature, there has been a tendency to associate different orders of experience with day and night, to feel that the archetype of all conflict is the conflict between darkness and light. In the Book of Genesis the light is set by God to rule over the dark, the light being the agency of order and the manifestation of God's benevolence in his satisfaction that the light is 'good':

And the earth was without form, and void; and darkness was upon the face of the deep. And the Spirit of God moved upon the face of the waters.
    And God said, Let there be light: and there was light.
    And God saw the light, that it was good: and God divided the light from the darkness...
    And God made two great lights; the greater light to rule the day, and the lesser light to rule the night: he made the stars also.
    And God set them in the firmament of the heaven to give light upon the earth,
    And to rule over the day and over the night, and to divide the light from the darkness: and God saw that it was good. (Gen. i.2–4, 16–18)

Many early myths and plays, following on from this, have expressed a sense of basic contention between darkness and light. The early English epic *Beowulf*, for example, develops a strong metaphoric opposition between the joy of the men in the lighted hall where the bard sings the song of creation, and the savagery of Grendel – fen-wanderer, creature of darkness, descendant of Cain. In the course of time, the night seems to have become more and more explicitly associated with evil forces, with the coming into operation of supernatural agencies which do harm. So that, by Shakespeare's time, night can be a metaphor for evil itself; and the power of the night is conveyed magnificently through the rhythmic rise (and hence suggestion of sinister energy) in the lines evoking it, as in the great lines from *Macbeth*:

Light thickens, and the crow
Makes wing to th' rooky wood.
Good things of day begin to droop and drowse,
Whiles night's black agents to their preys do rouse.

(III.ii.50–3)

As *Macbeth* shows, these 'black agents' include men, in whom the
night seems to release and sanction something anarchic, making
possible a bloody violence. By comparison, the modern novel
clearly has moved away from depicting evil in the metaphysical
sense and has taken up psychological and moral preoccupations
of its own; yet it still retains a sense of the night as a special time
during which particular kinds of emotions can be felt with special
intensity. Thus Lawrence's night scenes – especially the more
successful ones, like Mrs Morel's night experience in the moonlit
garden in *Sons and Lovers* and Will's and Anna's sheaf-gathering
in *The Rainbow* – involve a transfiguration of daylight reality and
a strange, almost hypnotic intensity associated with the moonlight. More relevantly, Chekhov's immediate predecessor, Tolstoy, provides in *War and Peace* what is almost a paradigm – and
surely the great model – of this kind of night-intensity as it is
found in modern literature. It is the scene where Prince Andrei
hears Natasha at the upper window:

He got up and went to the window to open it. As soon as he drew the
shutters the moonlight flooded the room as though it had long been
waiting at the window. He unfastened the casement. The still night was
cool and beautiful. Just outside the window was a row of pollard-trees,
looking black on one side and silvery bright on the other. Under the
trees grew some sort of lush, wet, bushy vegetation with leaves and stems
touched here and there with silver. Farther away, beyond the dark trees,
a roof glittered with dew; to the right was a great, leafy tree with satiny
white trunk and branches, and above it shone the moon, almost full,
in a pale, practically starless, spring sky. Prince Andrei leaned his elbows
on the window-ledge, and his eyes gazed at the heavens.

His room was on the first floor. Those above were also occupied, and
by people who were not asleep either. He heard feminine voices overhead.

'Just once more,' said a girlish voice above him which Prince Andrei
recognized at once.

'But when are you coming to bed?' replied a second voice.

'I shan't sleep – I can't, what's the use? Come, this will be the last
time...'

Two girlish voices broke into a snatch of song, forming the final phrase
of a duet.

'Oh, it's exquisite! Well, now let's say good-night and go to sleep.'

'You go to sleep, but I can't,' said the first voice, coming nearer to the window. She evidently thrust her head right out, for he could hear the rustle of her dress and even her breathing. Everything was hushed and turned to stone – the moon and her light, and the shadows. Prince Andrei, too, dared not stir, for fear of betraying his unintentional presence.

'Sonya! Sonya!' said the first voice again. 'Oh, how can you sleep? Just look how lovely it is! Oh, how glorious! Do wake up, Sonya!' and there were almost tears in the voice. 'There never, never was such an exquisite night.'

Sonya made some reluctant reply.

'No, but do look what a moon!...Oh, how lovely! Do come here. Darling, precious, come here! There, you see? I feel like squatting down on my heels, putting my arms round my knees like this, tight – as tight can be – and flying away! Like this...'[1]

I have quoted the scene in full because I believe that it had a direct and important influence on both Chekhov and Lawrence. The way the dialogue develops as the strange beauty of the night seems to stir a new potentiality in Natasha's soul is inimitably Tolstoyan in its power to suggest innocence as integral to Natasha's vitality. Chekhov's and Lawrence's characters tend to be either innocent *or* vital. The sleeplessness and the suggestive proximity of one person to another are also created with a particular Tolstoyan emphasis – more openly than would be characteristic of Chekhov, and less insistently than in Lawrence. But there can be little doubt that in the special intensity Tolstoy imparts to the scene by that curiously bright moonlight combined with extreme stillness and silence, he created not only the epitome of this night-intensity in modern literature but its influential source. The influence on Lawrence is very strongly felt in the scene already mentioned from *Sons and Lovers*, even though Mrs Morel's reaction there to the moonlight is to find it sinister and strange, a 'shock' to her soul rather than a subtle and stimulating force upon it:

The moon was high and magnificent in the August night. Mrs Morel, seared with passion, shivered to find herself out there in a great white light, that fell cold on her, and gave a shock to her inflamed soul. She stood for a few moments helplessly staring at the glistening great rhubarb leaves near the door...She became aware of something about her. With an effort she roused herself to see what it was that penetrated her consciousness. The tall white lilies were reeling in the moonlight and the air was charged with their perfume, as with a presence. Mrs Morel gasped slightly in fear. She touched the big, pallid flowers on their petals, then shivered. They seemed to be stretching in the moonlight. She put her hand into one white bin: the gold scarcely showed on her fingers by moonlight. She bent down to look at the binful of yellow pollen; but it only appeared dusky. Then she drank a deep draught of the scent. It made her almost dizzy.[2]

I think Lawrence inferior to Tolstoy here, Lawrence's details having a more strained, consciously symbolic property; but the construction of the scene, including the slow, fascinated movement from one image to another of the moonlight on the leaves and flowers, fairly obviously derives from the original imagery in *War and Peace*. In Chekhov's case, the influence is felt most strongly in his middle-period novellas, which include a great many such scenes – involving intense moonlight, where the eerie stillness seems to concentrate and yet to tease people's emotions. The following is just one example, from 'A Dreary Story':

There was a deathlike stillness, such a stillness, as some author has expressed it, 'it rang in one's ears'. Time passed slowly; the streaks of moonlight on the window-sill did not shift their position, but seemed as though frozen...It was still some time before dawn. (v.208)

What all these examples show, then, is a new psychological interest, in modern literature, in the potency of night against the 'reality' of day. Night and day are seen as giving pre-eminence to quite different sets of psychological impulses. But where, commonly, it is the night that is felt as provoking insecurity and the day that gives reassurance, Chekhov at least once – in 'Lights' – envisaged that pattern the other way around. And where Tolstoy and Lawrence made their night scenes important occasions for psychological definition – of Natasha's state of mind or of Mrs Morel's – Chekhov creates an intricate structure by which day-reality and night-reality are set against one another, and a philosophical question is implicitly posed about the substance of each.

It may help my discussion if I first outline the broad structure of 'Lights', since it contains a story within the larger story, and there is a separate narrator for each. In the main story the narrator is a doctor who, having lost his way while returning to the home of a friend, has grown fearful of what might befall him in the dark and has sought refuge in a railway workmen's hut.

There he has been welcomed by the engineer Ananyev and the student Von Schtenberg, and he spends the night in their company before resuming his journey at first light. It is thus his sense of things that frames the story as a whole, including any reaction to the inner story told by Ananyev. Ananyev, the narrator of the story within the story, is naturally talkative and has been made more so by the wine he drinks in the hut. His narrative is partly a sentimental reminiscence and partly intended as a moral and philosophical rebuke to the nihilistic ideas of the student; and our reception of it is qualified by the complacency which – in other forms as well – comes out of Ananyev's middle age. But the whole tenor of Ananyev's narration, which though philosophical is never abstract, and the strange mixture of conviviality and compulsion with which he tells of his experience gives his story a greater intensity and concentration than the wider story which encompasses it. In the course of 'Lights' Ananyev wrests our attention right away from the voice and judgments of the main narrator, so that we are left in the curious position of feeling at odds (in sympathy) with the overall teller of the story. Yet we cannot afford to neglect the voice and outlook of that teller, for his further evidence about the world of 'Lights' (including his reaction to Ananyev's story and his later images of Ananyev himself) is no less relevant than the evidence supplied by Ananyev's narrative. Furthermore, the inner story gets a lot of its conviction from the particular circumstances in which it is told, at night; and the most compelling part of the story itself is also set in an atmosphere of night. In both the inner and wider stories the daytime projects a more mundane – in fact a more nihilistic – sense of reality. So that at the end of 'Lights' one has the intriguing sensation of having felt Ananyev's story to contain the truer values and yet of being made aware by the story itself that that feeling has probably to do with its powerful night setting, which has no more claim to being 'real' than the opposite sensations associated with the day.

The story begins with an effect Chekhov had successfully achieved in 'Happiness', of a sense of animal nervousness about the night being registered through the dogs: 'The dog was barking excitedly outside.' There is in fact nothing to bark at, and that fact itself helps establish an atmosphere of superstitious excitement. But immediately, in the way Ananyev speaks to the dog Azorka, there is a reassuring gentleness and familiarity not found amid the landscape of 'Happiness':

'Why are you barking for nothing, creature?' he said in the tone in which good-natured people talk to children and dogs. 'Have you had a bad dream or what? Here, doctor, let me commend to your attention,' he said, turning to me, 'a wonderfully nervous subject! Would you believe it, he can't endure solitude – he is always having terrible dreams and suffering from nightmares; and when you shout at him he has something like an attack of hysterics.'

'Yes, a dog of refined feelings,' the student chimed in.

Azorka must have understood that the conversation was concerning him. He turned his head upwards and grinned plaintively, as though to say, 'Yes, at times I suffer unbearably, but please excuse it!' (XIII.15–16)

The new warmth of narrative tone, the sense of communication between people and of the feeling between people and animals, is a significant difference from 'Happiness'. In 'Lights' the comfort and enjoyment to be had from ordinary human relationships are fully affirmed as a deep instinctual fear in both the doctor and the dog impels them (somewhat shamefacedly) toward the good-humoured and reassuring presence of Ananyev. In the end the story will have made a powerful case (without seeming actually to argue anything) for adopting a stance like Ananyev's – one based in humanist values – even if its own images of the world lead logically in the direction of nihilism. But to follow the stages of that unobtrusive dramatic argument and to recognize the kind of art by which it is managed involves attending first to the whole setting of the story and to the different metaphorical or symbolic constructions which its different characters place upon the lights.

In its setting the story is quite modern in feeling, having some of the surreal quality on which modern literature frequently depends. This surreal quality is particularly evident in the evoked 'chaos' of the railway camp. In the dark the scene is primitive, even grotesque, and the sense of the world it projects is anything but congenial:

It was an August night, there were stars, but it was dark... I was on a railway line which was still in process of construction. The high, half-finished embankment, the mounds of sand, clay, and rubble, the holes, the wheelbarrows standing here and there, the flat tops of the mud huts in which the workmen lived – all this muddle, coloured to one tint by the darkness, gave the earth a strange, wild aspect that suggested the times of chaos. There was so little order in all that lay before me that it was somehow strange in the midst of the hideously excavated, grotesque-looking earth to see the silhouettes of human beings and the slender telegraph posts. Both spoiled the ensemble of the picture, and seemed to belong to a different world. It was still, and the only sound came from the telegraph wire droning its wearisome refrain somewhere very high above our heads.

We climbed up on the embankment and from its height looked down upon the earth. A hundred yards away where the pits, holes, and mounds melted into the darkness of the night, a dim light was twinkling. Beyond it gleamed another light, beyond that a third, then a hundred paces away two red eyes glowed side by side – probably the windows of some hut – and a long series of such lights, growing continually closer and dimmer, stretched along the line to the very horizon, then turned in a semicircle to the left and disappeared in the darkness of the distance. The lights were motionless. There seemed to be something in common between them and the stillness of the night and the disconsolate song of the telegraph wire. It seemed as though some weighty secret were buried under the embankment and only the lights, the night, and the wires knew of it. (XIII.16–17)

The foundations for the nihilistic viewpoint held by Von Schten-berg (and, one suspects, by the narrator of the main story) are clearly established in these images. Although the row of lights stretching into the distance is there through the labours of men, it seems, rather, simply to measure the vastness in which man seems small and irrelevant; and this impression is reinforced by the darkness and the sense of empty space created by the complete stillness. In other words, the railway-camp setting – at least in its predominant imagery – provides a generalized image of something very close to the view of the world against which Ananyev's story will warn. But, as in 'Easter Eve', the transfigured quality of the landscape – through the mysterious, intriguing image of the twinkling lights, and the suggestion of primaeval energies in the 'two red eyes' glowing in the distance or the scene's 'strange, wild aspect that suggested the times of chaos' – retrieves it from feeling bleakly nihilistic. Even its bleak-ness has a heightened property: there is something almost romantic about it. And because of this, human responses to it are easily polarized: Ananyev asserts the value of the human energy and purposiveness which have pushed first the telegraph and now the railway across the land; while Von Schtenberg feels the futility of those forces against the brooding expanse and timelessness of the steppe. Since it is so important to the subsequent development of the story, I shall quote in full the scene where these two 'interpretations' of the lights are made:

'How glorious, O Lord!' sighed Ananyev; 'such space and beauty that one can't tear oneself away! And what an embankment! It's not an embankment, my dear fellow, but a regular Mont Blanc. It's costing millions...'

Going into ecstasies over the lights and the embankment that was costing millions, intoxicated by the wine and his sentimental mood, the engineer slapped Von Schtenberg on the shoulder and went on in a jocose tone:

'Well, Mihail Mihailitch, lost in reveries? No doubt it is pleasant to look at the work of one's own hands, eh? Last year this very spot was bare steppe, not a sign of human life, and now look: life...civilization... And how splendid it all is, upon my soul! You and I are building a railway, and after we are gone, in another century or two, good men will build a factory, a school, a hospital, and things will begin to move! Eh!'

The student stood motionless with his hands thrust in his pockets, and did not take his eyes off the lights. He was not listening to the engineer, but was thinking, and was apparently in the mood in which one does not want to speak or to listen. After a prolonged silence he turned to me and said quietly:

'Do you know what those endless lights are like? They make me think of something long dead, that lived thousands of years ago, something like the camps of the Amalekites or the Philistines. It is as though some people of the Old Testament had pitched their camp and were waiting for morning to fight with Saul or David. All that is wanting to complete the illusion is the blare of trumpets and sentries calling to one another in some Ethiopian language.'

And, as though of design, the wind fluttered over the line and brought a sound like the clank of weapons. (XIII.17–18)

The story is beginning to take a dialectical shape. Ananyev takes the humanist's long-term view of his work as contributing to the future progress of humanity; the even longer view which the student takes – though backward-looking in its span of time – places the unfinished railway in a generalized framework of the brevity of life and the transience of all human energy and effort. As my previous discussions of the stories have suggested, the tension between these two attitudes is basic to Chekhov's temperament. By having Ananyev and Von Schtenberg ascribe such different significances to the lights, each according to his own outlook on life, Chekhov allows the two to reverberate in philosophical conflict.

So far, then, the organization of the story appears clear-cut and even schematic. As in the later 'The Duel', the patterning is at first quite bold, taking the risk of seeming over-obvious in casting its central characters as such direct opposites. Everything about the two men contributes to the impression of their difference, making sense directly in terms of their different outlooks. Take, for example, the doctor's first descriptions of them, beginning with Ananyev:

His movements and his voice were calm, smooth, and self-confident, as they are in a man who is thoroughly well aware that he has got his feet firmly planted on the right road, that he has definite work, a secure living, a settled outlook. . . . His sunburnt, thick-nosed face and muscular neck seemed to say: 'I am well fed, healthy, satisfied with myself, and the time will come when you young people too will be well fed, healthy, and satisfied with yourselves.' (XIII.21–2)

Von Schtenberg is created in deliberate contrast:

His movements and voice were calm, and smooth too, but his calmness was of a different kind from the engineer's. His sunburnt, slightly ironical, dreamy face, his eyes which looked up from under his brows, and his whole figure were expressive of spiritual stagnation – mental sloth. He looked as though it did not matter to him in the least whether the light were burning before him or not, whether the wine were nice or nasty, and whether the accounts he was checking were correct or not . . . And on his intelligent, calm face I read: 'I don't see so far any good in definite work, a secure living, and a settled outlook. It's all nonsense. I was in Petersburg, now I am sitting here in this hut, in the autumn I shall go back to Petersburg, then in the spring here again . . . What sense there is in all that I don't know, and no one knows.' (XIII.22–3)

By placing these two men together in the isolated railway hut, Chekhov has created a virtually ideal situation for dialogue. However, the story actually develops in a quite different way, since Von Schtenberg is never given a chance to answer Ananyev or to argue a case of his own. All the real exploring is done by Chekhov as he relates and juxtaposes (through the complex structure provided by the interaction of the inner and outer stories) the various day and night scenes, the behaviour which occurs in them and the very different senses of reality which they project. The opposite temperaments of the two men and the differences in their personal philosophies make us feel forcefully what is at issue in the telling of the night story and the effect it has (or fails to have) on the listeners. To that extent the contrast between the men is profoundly necessary to the whole conception of the work. But imaginatively the most meaningful opposition in the story is between the heightened intimacy and strange

certainty about human values of the night scenes and the bleak-
ness of the world of work which seems to refute those values by
daylight.

I have already pointed out that the story begins with the
instinctually based fear of night revealing itself in both men and
animals as they seek refuge in the light. The intermittent whining
of the dog outside the hut, breaking across Ananyev's narrative,
reminds us again of that fear. But in the hut itself, where the
comfort of light and warmth are felt the more strongly for the
existence of the engulfing darkness outside, there is an atmosphere of cosiness and special intimacy which makes us feel the
rightness of Ananyev's basic faith in human relationships and the
strength of his humanity. His tale of Kisotchka, framed as a
rebuke to the student's complacent nihilism and yet, it seems,
partly just elicited from him by the intimacy of the situation and
his need to talk, is told in the voice and attitude of middle-aged
experience. Consistent with that, its persuasiveness, as against the
fashionable nihilism of Von Schtenberg, is almost entirely emotional. It is authoritative by virtue of that very quality of *experienced* awareness which the younger man, by definition, cannot
possess. Thus the pattern of the story as it emerges is to assert
the emotional conviction of the older man, the result of his lived
experience, against the strictly intellectual tenets of the student,
whose knowledge of life is largely theoretical. In the supporting
imagery of the story this difference is as between a 'night' sense
of things, when feelings are potent but irrationally based and
therefore are not to be explained by rational argument, and the
rational 'knowledge' on which the world generally operates by
day.

Ananyev's story, then, is a 'night' story – told at night, elicited
by the night. The fact that it exists at all in Chekhov's work is
crucial evidence against the common view of Chekhov as the
'voice of the twilight years', for the story is a sustained critique
of the then-fashionable brand of nihilism with which he himself
has frequently been charged. Here, for example, are some of the
important comments he has Ananyev make:

'Thoughts of the aimlessness of life, of the insignificance and transi-
toriness of the visible world, Solomon's "vanity of vanities" have been,
and are to this day, the highest and final stage in the realm of thought.
The thinker reaches that stage and – comes to a halt! There is nowhere
further to go. The activity of the normal brain is completed with this, and

that is natural and in the order of things. Our misfortune is that we begin thinking at that end. What normal people end with we begin with. From the first start, as soon as the brain begins working independently, we mount to the very topmost, final step and refuse to know anything about the steps below...If we find means of mounting to the topmost step without the help of the lower ones, then the whole long ladder, that is the whole of life, with its colours, sounds, and thoughts, loses all meaning for us...Let us suppose you sit down this minute to read Darwin or Shakespeare, you have scarcely read a page before the poison shows itself; and your long life, and Shakespeare, and Darwin, seem to you nonsense, absurdity, because you know you will die, that Shakespeare and Darwin have died too, that their thoughts have not saved them, nor the earth, nor you, and that if life is deprived of meaning in that way, all science, poetry, and exalted thoughts seem only useless diversions, the idle playthings of grown up people; and you leave off reading at the second page...You must admit that with such a disastrous way of looking at things there can be no progress, no science, no art, nor even thought itself.' (XIII.24–5)

It should be said that this is not actually a philosophical refutation of the nihilistic viewpoint, since Ananyev endorses that viewpoint as the highest form of wisdom for the old. Earlier, too, the doctor who narrates the main story has seemed to hear, in the wind among the wires, the clank of the weapons of lost armies: he, like Von Schtenberg, responds to the lights in terms of life's transience and the momentariness of all its apparent glories. Neither shares Ananyev's humanistic vision of a heroic future. Chekhov, too, is clearly inclined towards a nihilistic understanding of the world – particularly in so far as it involves an acute awareness of the erasing activity of time. The principal images with which the story opens and closes reinforce such a view, so that Ananyev's quite different set of values, his positively humanistic outlook, is framed on either side by a sense of futility and of the world's indifference to specifically human needs. But internally the story resists the possible superficiality of this kind of nihilistic stance, and Chekhov is very far from taking that stance – with the inertia, inaction and lack of moral responsibility which tend to flow from its highly developed sense of transience – as a given basis from which he might work. Rather, he shows, through Ananyev, an analytical awareness of when and how this viewpoint became fashionable in Russia and of its social cost in debilitating the Russian intelligentsia. Moreover, the night story in 'Lights' exists precisely to explore the possible consequences of such a viewpoint (especially when adopted prematurely by the young) for the *moral* life. The example Ananyev gives of the 'poison' preventing a serious reading of Darwin or Shakespeare is followed by another in which, this time, morality is directly involved:

'Now, let us suppose that people come to you as an intelligent man and ask your opinion about war, for instance: whether it is desirable, whether it is morally justifiable or not. In answer to that terrible question you merely shrug your shoulders and confine yourself to some common-place, because for you, with your way of thinking, it makes absolutely no difference whether hundreds of thousands of people die a violent death, or a natural one: the results are the same – ashes and oblivion.' (XIII.25)

Later, and with more relevance to the actual content of the night story, the same question of responsibility is raised in relation to sexual matters:

'The trouble is that youth makes its demands, and our philosophy has nothing in principle against those demands, whether they are good or whether they are loathsome. One who knows that life is aimless and death inevitable is not interested in the struggle against nature or the conception of sin: whether you struggle or whether you don't, you will die and rot just the same…Thirdly, our philosophy denies the significance of each individual personality. It's easy to see that if I deny the personality of some Natalya Stepanovna, it's absolutely nothing to me whether she is insulted or not. To-day one insults her dignity as a human being and pays her *Blutgeld*, and next day thinks no more of her.' (XIII.32)

But these are only theoretics which we may or may not find convincing. Ananyev's objections to the fashionable nihilism of the young are practical and emotional, as indeed they can only be, since intellectually he seems finally to accept such a viewpoint himself: his objections come solely out of practical and emotional experience. His only real argument in the night story is his own experience and how he felt; and it is not surprising that the persuasiveness of the night story comes from those qualities of experience – including the habit of introspection born out of it – represented by, and felt in, the actual narrative, rather than from the surrounding theoretical argument.

In Ananyev's night story, as he recounts his thoughts and behaviour during the nihilistic phase of his youth, it is a daylight scene by the sea which helps elicit and also expresses his nihilistic sense of the world. In the wider story, too, we find the same reversal of our accustomed imagery of night and day, by which the daylight seems to offer less comfort than the dark. But here it is the sea, especially, which Ananyev speaks of as having the power to make a man feel his own littleness and of intensifying his sense of life's transience; and the young Ananyev's reactions to the sea are not far different from Von Schtenberg's feelings about the lights:

'I sat down on the seat, and, bending over the parapet, looked down. A path ran from the summer-house along the steep, almost overhanging cliff, between the lumps of clay and tussocks of burdock. Where it ended, far below on the sandy shore, low waves were languidly foaming and softly purring. The sea was as majestic, as infinite, and as forbidding as seven years before when I left the high school and went from my native town to the capital; in the distance there was a dark streak of smoke – a steamer was passing – and except for this hardly visible and motion-less streak and the sea-swallows that flitted over the water, there was nothing to give life to the monotonous view of sea and sky. To right and left of the summer-house stretched uneven clay cliffs.

'You know that when a man in a melancholy mood is left *tête-à-tête* with the sea, or any landscape which seems to him grandiose, there is always, for some reason, mixed with melancholy, a conviction that he will live and die in obscurity, and he reflectively snatches up a pencil and hastens to write his name on the first thing that comes handy.' (XIII.28)

However, the important difference between this speech, where the older Ananyev recounts his reactions in youth, and Von Schtenberg's speech about the lights (while both are highly evo-cative) is the detached, semi-analytic tone Ananyev adopts. For in recounting his experience Ananyev continuously judges it from the humanized perspective which living through these events has given him. Thus, throughout the whole account of his attempted seduction of Kisotchka – the kittenish beauty he adored in his high-school days, but now a subdued, unhappy, respectable married woman – he combines his new appreciation of Kisotchka's dignity and wistful charm with a blunt account of his own motives. This kind of explicitness about masculine sexual calculation would have been impossible for reputable English writers at that time:

'Though I had little confidence in success, I made up my mind to begin the attack anyway. First of all it was necessary to get into a familiar tone and to change Kisotchka's lyrically earnest mood into a more frivolous one.

'"Let us change the conversation, Natalya Stepanovna," I began. "Let us talk of something amusing. First of all, allow me, for the sake of old times, to call you Kisotchka."

'She allowed me.

'"Tell me, please, Kisotchka," I went on, "what is the matter with all the fair sex here. What has happened to them? In old days they were all so moral and virtuous, and now, upon my word, if one asks about anyone, one is told such things that one is quite shocked at human nature."...

'I spoke in a vulgar, playful tone. If Kisotchka had laughed in response I should have gone on in this style: "You had better look out, Kisotchka, or some officer or actor will be carrying you off!" She would have dropped her eyes and said: "As though anyone would care to carry me off; there are plenty younger and better looking..." And I should have said: "Nonsense, Kisotchka – I for one should be delighted!" And so on in that style, and it would all have gone swimmingly. But Kisotchka did not laugh in response; on the contrary, she looked grave and sighed.

'"All you have been told is true," she said. "My cousin Sonya ran away from her husband with an actor. Of course, it is wrong...Everyone ought to bear the lot that fate has laid on him, but I do not condemn them or blame them...Circumstances are sometimes too strong for anyone!"' (XIII.39–40)

Much of the persuasiveness of the night story is anchored in this acute perception of the psychological realities of masculine and feminine sexuality. These feel so exactly observed – and not just observed, but played out in the tone and tempo of Ananyev's account here – that they make us feel Ananyev's reliability in observation generally. As for Kisotchka herself, I think there are signs of unconscious condescension in Chekhov's conception of her, with the naivety of her 'quiet gravity' tending to work against the suggestion that she is a competent, mature woman who deserves respect in those terms. Later, when she is once again 'kittenish' in the light of the street-lamp, she is made touching and vulnerable at the cost of some reduction in our sense of her personality; and her desperate, romantic gestures of despair during the night scenes in the summer-house feel somewhat weak and unoriginal to anyone who knows those dignified manifestations of emotional pain and despair which Chekhov later created for the women of *Three Sisters*. But there is a genuine insight, as well as delicacy, in Chekhov's suggestion of Kisotchka's unconscious sexual attraction to Ananyev through her unusually voluble expressions of delight at seeing him, which prepares us to accept her desperate flight to the summer-house where she unconsciously hopes to find him again.

It is this night scene within the night story which gives the most intense definition of human feelings in 'Lights' and makes us feel most strongly the power of the night in freeing emotional energies which daylight reality works to suppress. Chekhov is on guard against romanticizing the scene to the point where it becomes unconvincing, and Von Schtenberg's interruption is made – somewhat obviously – to act as one form of check:

'Marvels upon marvels!' said Von Schtenberg with a sigh. 'Black night, the murmur of the sea; she in grief, he with a sensation of world solitude . . . It's too much of a good thing.' (XIII.48)

But Chekhov will not abandon the intensities of the night story, however special and even 'unreal' they may seem to Von Schtenberg or to others who judge by daylight standards, because it is exactly the question of what is real that is at issue. The whole landscape of this night scene within the night story is romantically weird, seeming (like the scenes from Tolstoy and Lawrence with which I began this chapter) both to energize the psyche by the strangeness of the spectacle and to be partially determined in quality by the subjective emotions of the people involved. The best example comes as Ananyev and Kisotchka begin to walk from the summer-house to the town:

'In the end Kisotchka took my arm and we set off. Going out of the gate, we turned to the right and sauntered slowly along the soft dusty road. It was dark. As my eyes grew gradually accustomed to the darkness, I began to distinguish the silhouettes of the old gaunt oaks and lime trees which bordered the road. The jagged, precipitous cliffs, intersected here and there by deep, narrow ravines and creeks, soon showed, indistinctly, a black streak on the right. Low bushes nestled by the hollows, looking like sitting figures. It was uncanny. I looked sideways suspiciously at the cliffs, and the murmur of the sea and the stillness of the country alarmed my imagination. Kisotchka did not speak. She was still trembling, and before she had gone half a mile she was exhausted with walking and was out of breath. I too was silent.' (XIII.50)

It is not, obviously, a moonlight scene; but still it has (in the story's own word) an 'uncanny' intensity. The darkness and the 'gaunt' and 'jagged' forms give the landscape a subtly symbolic relation to our culture's habitual images of death; and yet there is a sense of special intimacy in the pact of silence being maintained by the characters and, as in the Tolstoy night scene, the sense of the characters' physical proximity to one another. At the same time, the penetrating psychological perception is kept up, with Ananyev intermittently aware that for all the romantic strangeness of the moment Kisotchka will later be a problem to him (he will have somehow to dispose of her, which will not be easy), and Kisotchka at one point deciding to turn back, unconsciously seeking reassurance that Ananyev wishes her to go on.

The whole journey across the dark countryside past the deserted flour-mill is felt as a kind of 'night' pilgrimage in which the characters are more and more at the mercy of their emotional impulses and less concerned for the daytime consequences. Thus the climax of the night story occurs as Ananyev is completely possessed by intense (though temporary) feeling, quite unlike his hitherto cool sexual calculation:

'The childish gladness on her face, the tears, the gentle smile, the soft hair, which had escaped from under the kerchief, and the kerchief itself thrown carelessly over her head, in the light of the street lamp reminded me of the old Kisotchka whom one had wanted to stroke like a kitten.

'I could not restrain myself, and began stroking her hair, her shoulders, and her hands...' (xiii.54)

Kisotchka, bewildered, at first protests but then breaks into hysterical tears. For both, it is a sudden release and recognition of what has been inherent in the night scenes, and it culminates in their love-making, although Ananyev is represented as taking Kisotchka half by force.

In any narrative, such a climax is bound to be followed by a decline in intensity and, on the reader's part, a sense of partial disappointment. Here, however, that sense of anticlimax is unusually well suited to the story's purposes: it accords with Ananyev's cynicism in no longer caring for Kisotchka, and it reinforces our sense of the quite different quality of reality by day. In the daylight Ananyev betrays Kisotchka's trust when he packs his bags and leaves the town of N. by train without her. The account then of the torment of his conscience, and of the powerlessness of his nihilistic views to dispel those torments, is a sustained and powerful instance of a generalized argument conducted through intensely personal and particular experience:

'I realized that I was not a thinker, not a philosopher, but simply a dilettante. God had given me a strong healthy Russian brain with promise of talent. And, only fancy, here was that brain at twenty-six, undisciplined, completely free from principles, not weighed down by any stores of knowledge, but only lightly sprinkled with information of a sort in the engineering line; it was young and had a physiological craving for exercise, it was on the look-out for it, when all at once quite casually the fine juicy idea of the aimlessness of life and the darkness beyond the tomb descends upon it. It greedily sucks it in, puts its whole outlook at its disposal and begins playing with it, like a cat with a mouse. There is neither learning nor system in the brain, but that does not matter...

'Our generation has carried this dilettantism, this playing with serious ideas into science, into literature, into politics, and into everything which it is not too lazy to go into, and with its dilettantism has introduced, too, its coldness, its boredom, and its one-sidedness and, as it seems to me, it has already succeeded in developing in the masses a hitherto non-existent attitude to serious ideas.

'I realized and appreciated my abnormality and utter ignorance, thanks to a misfortune. My normal thinking, so it seems to me now, dates from the day when I began again from the A, B, C, when my conscience sent me flying back to N., when with no philosophical subtleties I repented, besought Kisotchka's forgiveness like a naughty boy and wept with her.' (xiii.62–4)

In this resolution of the inner story (and in Ananyev's self-criticism during the telling of the story), the values asserted are moral responsibility, respect and finally also love. But how these values came suddenly to be important to Ananyev, the young nihilist callously prepared to abandon Kisotchka, is a chance fact of his emotional life of which he can only tell. He cannot logically explain it or argue a justification for it: it is simply a fact of his experience. And since it is that experience which underlies his whole objection to Von Schtenberg's nihilism, his objection is really outside the framework of ordinary argument. His position is non-negotiable.

We shall not be surprised, then, if in the main story Ananyev's listeners are represented as unconvinced. Von Schtenberg is feeling uncomfortable, but it is in the nature of the kind of wisdom Ananyev's is – born of experience – that it cannot be transferred simply by explanation (or even by the story – 'Lights' – itself). Chekhov carefully creates an exchange on that subject between the two men:

'You look as though you have really convinced some one this time,' he said irritably.

'Me convince anybody!' said the engineer. 'My dear soul, do you suppose I claim to do that? God bless you! To convince you is impossible. You can reach conviction only by way of personal experience and suffering!' (xiii.64)

It is the special achievement of 'Lights' to convince us of the viewpoint of the older man (whose modes of address to other people, it will be seen, reveal the condescension of middle age) and then to make us aware that what we have been valuing is experience – something which not even 'Lights' can really give and which, in fact, it makes clear that it is not giving. The entire inner story is a warning against trusting other people's theories or, for that matter, other people's experience. And the doctor – who simply comes across Ananyev and his tale one dark night, having no direct experience of the narrated events – significantly remains unmoved. Chekhov offers us the illumination of describing 'those who have been speaking or thinking about God and pessimism, how, and under what circumstances'.[3] He will not propound a truth, because the truth is something separate for each man according to his own experience: that is the extension of his humanism into the very principles of his art.

The night story of 'Lights' shows a moralist's concern for the possible consequences of holding a nihilistic outlook. It is not, however, inevitable that that outlook will produce identical behaviour in all men; and, even if it did, that still would not prove, one way or the other, that the nihilist's philosophy of the world was untrue. Ananyev's tale, as long as it lasts, successfully combats the possible attraction of the nihilistic outlook; but the setting of the railway camp when the doctor awakens at dawn again substantiates it:

It was a cloudy morning. On the line where the lights had been gleaming the night before, the workmen, just roused from sleep, were swarming. There was a sound of voices and the squeaking of wheelbarrows. The working day was beginning. One poor little nag harnessed with cord was already plodding towards the embankment, tugging with its neck, and dragging along a cartful of sand.

I began saying good-bye...A great deal had been said in the night, but I carried away with me no answer to any question, and in the morning, of the whole conversation there remained in my memory, as in a filter,

only the lights and the image of Kisotchka. As I got on the horse, I looked
at the student and Ananyev for the last time, at the hysterical dog with
the lustreless, tipsy-looking eyes, at the workmen flitting to and fro in
the morning fog, at the embankment, at the little nag straining with its
neck, and thought:
'There is no making out anything in this world.' (XIII.70–1)

The dawn light reasserts in the major story the workaday reality
of trivial busy-ness which yet involves suffering and hardship.
The greyness and bleakness of the scene, with the labour and
suffering so well epitomized in the little nag, seem to counter
Ananyev's certainties as they have been felt during the night.
Indeed, not only the landscape but the men themselves are
revealed under a new aspect, both Von Schtenberg and the
humane Ananyev shouting inconsiderately at the tired and
hungry peasants who can't find the person to whom they should
deliver their cauldrons. It is no wonder, then, that the doctor
should leave the scene perplexed about his feelings and wonder-
ing how much weight to give to his own night experience of
getting to know Ananyev through his tale.

The last view of the lights in the story likens them to 'the
thoughts of man', disappearing into the distance of old age
without shedding light on anything. It is on a similar pessimistic
note about the possibility of knowledge that the story ends:

And when I lashed my horse and galloped along the line, and when a
little later I saw nothing before me but the endless gloomy plain and
the cold overcast sky, I recalled the questions which were discussed in
the night. I pondered while the sun-scorched plain, the immense sky,
the oak forest, dark on the horizon and the hazy distance, seemed saying
to me:
  'Yes, there's no understanding anything in this world!'
  The sun began to rise...(XIII.71)

It is significant that Chekhov here has the landscape itself seem
to insist on the unknowability of the truth. It is a steppe landscape: that landscape which, most of all, seems to have fascinated
Chekhov with its ambiguities, with its capacity to influence one's
whole cast of mind by the temporary effects of different lights
across it.

The journey to the steppe in 1887 gave a new philosophical
and psychological profundity to Chekhov's art of 'thinking in
images'. 'Lights' is a classic story which is actively engaged with
epistemological problems and systems of thought which are

seminal to twentieth-century consciousness. The problem of knowledge, which Chekhov appreciates as a man of science, is articulated within the framework of a novelist's accuracy of psychological observation and the humanist's concern about the human consequences of various philosophies of life as they manifest themselves in behaviour. Moreover, since one of the intellectual characteristics of our own age has been the malaise born out of popularized versions of the nihilistic outlook, the existence of such a deeply motivated and carefully executed critique is highly important. While the story does not discount the possible (even probable) truth of such a view of the world and maintains a characteristically modern scepticism about 'ultimate truth', it asserts a moral value in its own sense of responsibility about the way in which one holds particular philosophical views. Importantly for the twentieth-century reader, whose general culture frequently tends to trust visual imagery (as in television and film) as a reaction against the possible deceptions of language, 'Lights' also promotes distrust of the possible deceptions of visual images, too; and it reveals intellectual dilettantism not simply as reproachable laziness but, in some circumstances, as amounting to a moral crime.

Part IV

I know Tolstoy, I feel that I know him well, and that I understand every movement of his brows, – and yet I love him.

Letter to L. A. Avilov (Yalta, 23 March 1899)

7
Chekhov and Tolstoy

Chekhov has often been regarded as suffering from a certain philosophical and imaginative indecisiveness. At the end of 'Lights', for instance, the doctor rides away thinking only 'There is no making out anything in this world'; and in 'The Duel' Laevsky, watching the little boat struggling against the high waves, thinks to himself, 'No one knows the real truth'. Especially in a literary tradition whose towering figure is Tolstoy – considering the resounding certainty with which he brings *his* novellas to a close – the reader's reaction to this may well be adverse. Indeed, it is a mark of what Tolstoy achieved for Russian literature that so many of its expectations are conditioned by his genius, that it should be so relatively intolerant of any divergence from it. Chekhov himself could hardly avoid sharing the general admiration of Tolstoy in his day and the sense of his great authority: 'Oh, that Tolstoy, that Tolstoy! He, at the present time, is not a human being, but a superman, a Jupiter.'[1] No one, I think, would ever have said that of Chekhov. But that is not necessarily to concede to one a greatness denied to the other: it focuses, rather, their radical difference as men. The difference is that Tolstoy fulfilled the role of artistic sage, having the sage's certainty about the truth of his ideas, whereas Chekhov saw himself as having the power to illuminate human predicaments but not as being beyond ordinary men in his grasp of 'the truth'. One has the stubborn pride of a massive genius, seeing himself as a leader of men ('a superman, a Jupiter'), while the other is distinguished by a humble and intense humanity which speaks for, not to, the mass of the people. It is basically a difference of temperament: Tolstoy has the drive and subjective purposiveness characteristic of his particular kind of energetic genius, where Chekhov is more introspective, more careful, and guided by a more objective intelligence. Chekhov's characters are capable of saying 'If only we knew, if only we knew!'; Tolstoy's have resolutions willed onto them. The impulse of Tolstoy's art is towards completeness, and he thinks of that completeness partly in terms of his ability to settle truths. The grand structures of *War and Peace* and *Anna Karenina* are products of that impulse, attempted projections of a complete Tolstoyan vision. And such is his certainty of the general truth of his vision, particularly as it hardens in the later works, that – as Chekhov points out – accuracy of detail, other than in psychological portraiture, is not always important to him. He manages it all with the same air of certainty; and only someone as meticulous as Chekhov would take issue with him for it without losing a basic sense of admiration. The following are some of Chekhov's comments on Tolstoy's 'The Kreutzer Sonata':

On reading it one can hardly refrain from exclaiming: 'This is true!' or 'This is preposterous!' True, it has some very annoying defects. Besides those you mention there is another thing for which one does not feel like forgiving the author, namely, the boldness with which Tolstoy treats that which he does not know and which he refuses to understand, out of sheer stubbornness. Thus, his statements about syphilis, about asylums for children, about women's aversion to copulation, etc., are not only open to dispute, but they actually betray an ignorant man who, in the course of his long life, has not taken the trouble to read two or three pamphlets written by specialists. And yet all these defects scatter like feathers before the wind.[2]

This letter reveals something essential about both men: Tolstoy's overriding faith in his mission which, especially in his later years, made him actually despise 'specialists', and Chekhov's own scrupulous concern for the factual evidence. Of course, the views in 'The Kreutzer Sonata' are propounded by a narrator and not by Tolstoy himself; but I think Chekhov is right in feeling that the narrator is merely a convenience for Tolstoy, partially protecting him from the controversy of his views while allowing him to indulge them. Certainly, 'The Kreutzer Sonata' lacks any of the qualifying perspectives which arise, in Chekhov's work, from his interest in 'how' such views are propounded, by whom, and 'under what circumstances'. Chekhov is preoccupied with what is actually *known* about human life, down to its smallest details. If he maintains an air of reservation in some of his judgments – as in the letter 'Oh, that Tolstoy, that Tolstoy!' where he pronounces him a Jupiter 'at the present time' – it is out of a highly developed sense of the possibility of change in reality itself or in our knowledge of it, which Tolstoy was unable to share.

That is probably one of Chekhov's reasons for preferring the short-story form: that he could express, in a variety of stories, the variety of shapes that life might take. So that, against the partially fragmentary quality of Chekhov's vision (if he may be said to possess anything so encompassing) and the absence of overt force in the way it is articulated, one has to place the flexibility and adaptability of his understanding compared with that of Tolstoy. The cry 'If only we knew!' in Chekhov's work is not an indication of imaginative weakness and indecisiveness but a genuine reflection of the circumstances in which it is usually uttered – not in relation to moral facts, where Chekhov's judgments are unequivocal and firm, but in relation either to an unpredictable future or to questions of metaphysical reality where conclusions cannot reliably be drawn.

The whole question of Chekhov's relation to Tolstoy is a fascinating one. For while the two writers are temperamentally far apart, there can be no doubt that Chekhov's writing was energized in important ways by Tolstoy, sometimes directly and sometimes by reaction. From the first, Chekhov had resisted pressures from critics and from some of his editors to take up an overtly didactic stance, and the principle he formulated for his art was one of 'objectivity'. As late as 1890 he was still protesting to one of his editors:

You abuse me for objectivity, calling it indifference to good and evil, lack of ideals and ideas, and so on. You would have me, when I describe horse-thieves, say: 'Stealing horses is an evil.' But that has been known for ages without my saying so. Let the jury judge them; it's my job simply to show what sort of people they are...Of course it would be pleasant to combine art with a sermon, but for me personally it is extremely difficult and almost impossible, owing to the conditions of technique. You see, to depict horse-thieves in seven hundred lines I must all the time speak and think in their tone and feel in their spirit, otherwise, if I introduce subjectivity, the image becomes blurred and the story will not be as compact as all short stories ought to be. When I write, I reckon entirely upon the reader to add for himself the subjective elements that are lacking in the story.[3]

The terms here are perhaps rather stiff and involve a somewhat unorthodox conception of 'subjectivity', but Chekhov's stubborn unwillingness to be caught in an attitude of literary moralizing is clear. In this respect he never desired to emulate Tolstoy. Sometimes in the early stories there are isolated effects reminis-

cent of Tolstoy, as in 'Sorrow',[4] where Grigory Petrov, lost and
alone after the death of his maltreated wife, is made passionately
to wish 'to live over again!' There, the way in which Chekhov
insists upon Grigory's realizing the waste of his life (with the pain
of the recognition being the moral price of the way he has lived)
does feel Tolstoyan. But there is no more a consistent influence
from Tolstoy in Chekhov's early art than there is from Gogol or
Turgenev. The motivating values, as always, are Chekhov's own
implicitly humanist ones, with the general concern centring on
what becomes of people's lives in relation to the chances open
to them. It was not until 1889, with the challenge to 'The Death
of Ivan Ilych' in Chekhov's 'A Dreary Story',[5] that the Tolstoy
influence became dominant in a very special sense. Chekhov
began to respond directly to – and ultimately to resist – Tolstoy's
dogmatism with his own more provisional sense of things as an
empiricist and humanist. The very complex relationship between
the two writers thus began to emerge.

'The Death of Ivan Ilych' was published in 1886, 'A Dreary
Story' three years later in 1889. Each story offers to confront the
implications of a single death, awaited and experienced more or
less in isolation and agonizing in its physical and psychological
impact. Given that resemblance, it seems distinctly probable that
Chekhov would never have written his short masterpiece without
the stimulation and the provocation of Tolstoy's work before him.
To write about the individual and death is a formidable task for
any author to take on. But if he takes a model, particularly in
late Tolstoy, the areas of contention which Tolstoy has brushed
aside for the sake of his polemical purpose will virtually dictate
a shape to him. For instance, Tolstoy writes of Ivan Ilych in the
third person and in the past tense, reviewing his life from the
perspective of his death and funeral. It is this which gives 'The
Death of Ivan Ilych' – until near the end – a disconcertingly
distant air of resumé:

Things went particularly well at first, before everything was finally
arranged and while something had still to be done: this thing bought,
that thing ordered, another thing moved, and something else adjusted.
Though there were some disputes between husband and wife, they were
both so well satisfied and had so much to do that it all passed off without
any serious quarrels. When nothing was left to arrange it became rather
dull and something seemed to be lacking, but they were then making
acquaintances, forming habits, and life was growing fuller.[6]

If one perceives (as Chekhov presumably did) that what is happening here is a harshly invariable subjugation of all experience to a generalized sense of *process* ('this thing bought, that thing ordered') made possible by the completed perspective on Ivan Ilych's life, it should be easy to see that a quite different view will come out of a first-person narration by a man still experiencing these things as lived realities. The tone will not involve Tolstoy's incipient sarcasm, as in the last sentence where the mocking of Ivan Ilych's own clichés moves into the terrible cruelty of life's 'growing fuller' when Tolstoy already knows that Ivan Ilych is fatally ill. Instead we might expect – as indeed we find in the Chekhov story – a range of tones from nostalgia through regret to present irritation, which registers the way such a life feels as it is actually being lived:

> I gaze at my wife and wonder like a child. . .is it possible that this woman is no other than the slender Varya whom I fell in love with so passionately for her fine, clear intelligence, for her pure soul, her beauty, and, as Othello his Desdemona, for her 'sympathy' for my studies? Could that woman be no other than the Varya who had once borne me a son?
>
> I look with strained attention into the face of this flabby, spiritless, clumsy old woman, seeking in her my Varya, but of her past self nothing is left but her anxiety over my health and her manner of calling my salary 'our salary', and my cap 'our cap'. It is painful for me to look at her, and, to give her what little comfort I can, I let her say what she likes. . .(v.136)

The semi-elegiac tone and the co-existence in Nikolay Stepanovitch of different layers of feeling and awareness deriving from different times in his life are in direct contrast to the flatness of the representation in 'The Death of Ivan Ilych' – at least of Ivan Ilych's life.

In broad terms, then, the difficulty of Chekhov's task is mitigated by the immediate provocation of the Tolstoy, especially since Tolstoy's polemical purpose (in bringing a member of a class he despises to face the reality of death) interferes with the value of his work as a representation of universal experience. 'The Death of Ivan Ilych' made it possible to feel that an *Everyman* might be written for the modern age, while also making it obvious that it was not that itself, since so much of what Tolstoy portrays depends on the particular kind of person Ivan Ilych is. Until he is dying, Ivan Ilych is content to have no 'real' friends and to live amongst blunted people with no sensitivity whatever to others' needs. His position in a bureaucracy makes the reception of the news of his death especially liable to self-interested responses by those of lower rank; and even then Tolstoy apparently cannot resist slyly shifting the sober assertion of a survival instinct in each man – 'it is he who is dead and not I' (which we are probably bound, in all honesty, to recognize) – to a nasty impulse of triumph in 'Well, he's dead, but I'm alive!' Much of the invention is, I think, overtly misanthropic. But, that aside, with all this concentrated in front of him, Chekhov had a shape against which to react and from which to work. Instead of a third-person resumé narration, he has a first-person dramatized account of experience. Instead of a member of a class for whom he does not care, he has a medical professor from the Moscow University, a man who has lived his life according to values which Chekhov himself basically shares. And, most important of all, the subject of the story is not a man who has died but a man who is dying. The story itself dramatically enacts that man's loss of grip on his world and his partial loss of faculties, and it prepares for his loss of the entire fund of sensuous experience – some of it stored in memory and some of it experienced on the day of his death – by which his life has been defined. The result is, I think, a greater work than 'The Death of Ivan Ilych': it is not a partially vindictive account of the unpreparedness of a particular kind of man for the suffering which awaits him, but a penetrating and moving revelation of the fate of the best values of civilization, as embodied in people, when these are beset by the biological crises of old age and approaching death. (For this reason I have reserved 'A Dreary Story' for detailed discussion in the next chapter.)

But as well as emphasizing the importance of the prior achievement of 'The Death of Ivan Ilych' to the actual conception of 'A Dreary Story', any critic of the two works must point to the obvious influence Tolstoy is now beginning to have on Chekhov's prose. 'The Death of Ivan Ilych' contains, as isolated speeches, some of the most moving and direct projections of loneliness and fear any reader will have been asked to bear:

He removed his legs from Gerasim's shoulders, turned sideways onto his arm, and felt sorry for himself. He only waited till Gerasim had gone into the next room and then restrained himself no longer but wept like a child. He wept on account of his helplessness, his terrible loneliness, the cruelty of man, the cruelty of God, and the absence of God.

'Why hast Thou done all this? Why hast Thou brought me here? Why, why dost Thou torment me so terribly?'

He did not expect an answer and yet wept because there was no answer and could be none. The pain again grew more acute, but he did not stir and did not call. He said to himself: 'Go on! Strike me! But what is it for? What have I done to Thee? What is it for?'[7]

The starkness of the physical detail and nakedly direct speech, which co-operate in so complete and terrible a vision of Ivan Ilych's helplessness, have an intensity particular to Tolstoy. In large part the intensity probably has to do with Tolstoy's personal fear (his need, as John Bayley puts it, to 'outface' death),[8] since the cumulative force of the syntax has more weight than the personality of Ivan Ilych could bring to it. Ivan Ilych's moment of capitulation to self-pity is partly generalized by Tolstoy's own foreboding of the dreadful extinction awaiting all men: 'his helplessness, his terrible loneliness' modulates into the impersonal 'the cruelty of man, the cruelty of God, and the absence of God'. Such intensity, where it involves some component of the author's own fears, cannot simply be reproduced as an ordinary influence on another writer. But 'A Dreary Story' comes as close as is practically possible to reproducing that distinctive Tolstoyan intensity, giving us moments of incipient hysteria in Nikolay Stepanovitch which directly bring to mind the Ivan Ilych of the last three days:

In the middle of my lecture tears suddenly rise in my throat, my eyes begin to smart, and I feel a passionate, hysterical desire to stretch out my hands before me and break into loud lamentation. I want to cry out in a loud voice that I, a famous man, have been sentenced by fate to the death penalty, that within some six months another man will be in control here in the lecture-theatre. I want to shriek that I am poisoned; new ideas such as I have not known before have poisoned the last days of my life, and are still stinging my brain like mosquitoes. And at that moment my position seems to me so awful that I want all my listeners to be horrified, to leap up from their seats and to rush in panic terror, with desperate screams, to the exit.

It is not easy to get through such moments. (v.149–50)

The old man in this story does 'get through such moments'. He is given a specific courage and strength which Tolstoy does not give to Ivan Ilych; and, as a doctor diagnosing his own condition and knowing more about himself than Ivan Ilych, he is morally superior, braver and more in control. Yet in this account of his feelings there is the same plaintive quality as in Tolstoy's 'Ivan Ilych' cadences, a similar anguish projected by the accumulating syntax ('And at that moment my position seems to me so awful . . .'), and a Tolstoyan agility of movement between physical and psychological manifestations of the character's condition, by which each gives an appalling force to the other. Only the last sentence could not have been written by Tolstoy, and it brings us, somewhat jarringly, back from a Tolstoy-dominated sensibility in the writing to Chekhov's own. The transition itself enforces a recognition of the basic temperamental differences between the two men. Chekhov is able partially to emulate Tolstoy's powerful directness of statement; but Nikolay Stepanovitch's half-ironic and embarrassed transition out of such a directly confessional moment into an opposite mode of understatement brings him more closely into line with Chekhov's own inclination towards tactful reticence.

'A Dreary Story', then, is a work stimulated by the challenge of Tolstoy, combating Tolstoy's conclusions, but doing so in an art that is more than ever locally receptive to Tolstoy's influence. This is important because it is a sign of Chekhov's developing recognition that art might entail quite direct forms of social and moral responsibility, a recognition which for some years changed the apparent course of his career. As I have argued throughout my accounts of the earlier stories, Chekhov's art nearly always manifests a humane concern for the fate of people's lives, whatever his theoretical commitment to 'objectivity'. In fact, it is possible that he simply meant that word to indicate that he did not wish his art to include any directly stated judgments (though he would of course subtly organize his materials so that his own values might be clear.) But with the publication of 'A Dreary Story' in 1889, followed by the non-fictional enterprise of his journey to and report on the penal island of Sakhalin, there is evidence of a different kind of social conscience stirring in Chekhov from the one which had previously dictated his interest in individuals. *The Island of Sakhalin* was not actually serialized until 1893 and did not appear as a book until 1895, but Chekhov's journey there in 1890 across the primitive wastes of Siberia, and the appalling conditions he found on the island, not only gave him important experience but also gave him a confidence about the range of that experience. If he doubted Tolstoy before, he now felt he had the measure of him; and in September 1891 (the

year in which he produced 'The Duel') came his passionate
outburst to Souvorin after reading the 'Afterword' to 'The
Kreutzer Sonata':

Strike me dead! but it is stupider and stuffier than 'Letters to a Gover-
nor's Wife', which I despise. The devil take the philosophy of the great
ones of this world! All the great sages are as despotic as generals, and
as ignorant and as indelicate as generals, because they feel secure.
Diogenes spat in people's faces, knowing that he would not suffer for
it. Tolstoy abuses doctors as scoundrels, and displays his ignorance in
great questions because he's just such a Diogenes who won't be locked
up or abused in the newspapers.[9]

Chekhov's annoyance and indignation are in proportion to his
sense of Tolstoy as a great man, one with immense power of
influence for good or ill. And the combination of respect and
exasperation in his response to Tolstoy's work made it virtually
inevitable that, for a while at least, his preoccupations would be
dictated by the theories of the older man, and that he would turn
his art more directly towards the form of a critique. His fiction
would for a time implicitly pursue the non-fictional end of
mitigating the influence of Tolstoyanism among Russia's literary
intelligentsia – or at least of those elements of Tolstoyanism
which Chekhov found most misleading. Ultimately, the spirit of
enquiry in which Chekhov created testing situations for Tolstoy's
theories hardened into one of refutation. In 'Peasants' (1897),
we find Chekhov countering Tolstoy's idealized view of the
peasants with a *tour de force* of increasingly sordid detail. At that
point Tolstoy's influence is obviously harmful; and it is then,
significantly, that Chekhov begins to abandon it. But at first,
particularly in 'The Duel' (1891), the challenge of meeting Tolstoy on his own ground and of positing another possibility against
Tolstoy's polemicized 'truth' excited Chekhov's imagination into
new and unexpected insights.

'The Duel' has as its subject one of Tolstoy's own most persistent concerns: the redemption of a human being from a state of
moral squalor to a new and purified mode of life. Its two main
characters undergo not simply a moral reformation but an almost
total change in their personalities which brings new shape and
purpose to their lives – if, however, not complete satisfaction. But
the way Chekhov shows this personal redemption as coming
about – spontaneously and half-mysteriously, through a particular, fortuitous combination of circumstances – amounts in

essence to his challenging the simple Tolstoyan *dicta* of salvation
through Christian kindness and the pain of self-knowledge – that
is, challenging formulae – with a more fully novelistic sense of
the way things may actually happen in life. Christian principles
are represented in practical form in the kindly army doctor,
Samoylenko, and more theoretically in the deacon, Pobyedov.
Samoylenko attends to Laevsky's needs, and Pobyedov saves him
from Von Koren's bullet at the duel. But, as Chekhov represents
it, Samoylenko's Christian kindness is powerless actually to
change Laevsky, and Pobyedov's 'saving' him is physical, not
spiritual. On the night before the duel Laevsky himself painfully
comes to terms with his life; but not even this Tolstoyan self-
accusation saves him. Indeed, it is in that night scene, during the
storm, that one is most aware of Chekhov's great debt to Tolstoy
and yet senses the challenge that is being thrown down:

'What in my past was not vice?' he asked himself, trying to clutch at some
bright memory as a man falling down a precipice clutches at the bushes.
　School? The university? But that was a sham. He had neglected his
work and forgotten what he had learnt. The service of his country? That,
too, was a sham, for he did nothing in the Service, took a salary for doing
nothing, and it was an abominable swindling of the State for which one
was not punished. (II.132)

There are reminders of Tolstoy here both in the cadencing of
Laevsky's thoughts (compare Ivan Ilych's 'Maybe I did not live
as I ought to have done') and in the simile of the falling man
clutching at the bushes, with the suggestion of light as against
darkness in the 'bright memory' which might save him from the
black void of the ravine. But there is something unusually deliberate about the Tolstoyan echoes, as if Chekhov were inten-
tionally making us feel that this is the moment for a Tolstoyan
outcome, if there is to be one, and thus capitalizing on our
surprise when there is no redeeming 'light' to bring the medita-
tion to an end. In 'The Death of Ivan Ilych' there is no difference
between Ivan Ilych's self-knowledge and his redemption of his
past as signalled by the light: they are synonymous because each,
for Tolstoy, centres on the fact of repentance.[10] In 'The Duel'
they are in fact different things, and a self-knowing man is not
necessarily a man on the brink of triumph:

Seek salvation in men? In whom and how? Samoylenko's kindness and
generosity could no more save him than the deacon's laughter or Von

Koren's hatred. He must look for salvation in himself alone, and if there were no finding it, why waste time? He must kill himself, that was all. (II.135)

To have to 'look for salvation in himself alone' is to have to do something distinctively Tolstoyan; but Chekhov's Laevsky does not find it by looking. Instead, at a point of intellectual despair, he finds it 'warmly and impulsively' in a sudden, unexplained resurgence of pity and love for his mistress Nadyezhda. The 'light' for him is a delayed one and a mysterious one: the broad green streaks of light by the river at dawn, which are tantalizingly beautiful but which still do not indicate a particular predisposition of the world towards Laevsky which might allow us to be confident of the outcome of the duel.

The effect of 'The Duel' is to assert, implicitly against the Tolstoyan formulae, life's own power to work in new ways and to shape people's lives into new forms. Working with much the same material, and with a passion for psychological verisimilitude learnt in part from Tolstoy himself,[11] Chekhov concedes an essential human freedom which the Tolstoyan injunctions would deny. He convincingly creates a redemptive transformation in the personalities of two of the major characters, giving us the psychological evidence of that transformation and the spectacle of its effects when Von Koren bids farewell to Laevsky and Nadyezhda in their new and spartan surroundings. Yet, as I shall argue in a fuller account of the story in chapter 9, he dares assert the origins of that redemption to be partly mysterious – simply a benevolence which life itself seems occasionally to manifest in the way things work out. And there may, after all, be something more basically religious about that act of faith in life than about all the prescriptions so powerfully propagated by the Christian Tolstoy.

Chekhov's artistic relationship to Tolstoy at this stage, then, might remind one of a sentence in Shestov's 'Darwin and the Bible': 'Try to admit, if you are capable of it, that in certain cases one can, one must, do without proofs – and look a little at man.'[12] Chekhov's whole impulse is towards freeing our minds from dogmatic interpretations of what life involves. So we find in many of the stories of this phase actual arguments about principles conducted by the major characters – for example, the arguments between Von Koren and Laevsky and Von Koren and the deacon in 'The Duel', between Ragin and Gromov in 'Ward No. 6' and between Poloznev and Dr Blagovo in 'My Life' – and a broader, implicit argument with Tolstoy in the way the art is worked out. 'My Life' (1896) is perhaps the clearest case of this: as in the other stories, its final outcome points to a freer and more complicated understanding of the Tolstoyan dogmas, but here the argument between the characters is also directly about Tolstoyan principles. Poloznev, the son of an architect, is a Tolstoyan committed to manual labour and the principles of human equality and brotherhood. His acquaintance, Dr Blagovo, is a man of learning who sees in peasant life nothing but squalor and a degrading preoccupation simply with food and drink. As the story unfolds, Poloznev seems to lose the argument. The behaviour he encounters in the peasants is ignorant and coarse; the project-school he and Masha try to establish is sabotaged by the peasants themselves; and until he has Masha's fortune to sustain him, he too – while working as a common labourer – thinks only of food and drink. But if Blagovo is factually right, Poloznev is nevertheless the more courageous, and morally the superior, man. Blagovo remains essentially unchanged, while Poloznev (like his sister Kleopatra after him) learns and grows. Blagovo sacrifices other people's happiness to his sacred ideal of learning; Poloznev loses Masha – and therefore he loses his own happiness – but his personality has deepened, and so has his understanding. There is, in fact, a formal imperfection in the story in that the sudden deepening of our sense of Poloznev, about midway through the tale, ought logically not to happen in that way: since the story is first-person *past* narrative, the consequences to Poloznev of living the life he has lived ought to be evident in his thoughts and feelings from the beginning. But what our deepened sense of him does illuminate is a typically Chekhovian irony: that whatever the naivety of his Tolstoyan views and the failure of his Tolstoyan ideal, Poloznev's experience of living through its failure and the failure of his marriage has made him a morally deeper man. Chekhov's aim is not to disprove the arguments advanced by Tolstoy: he does, however, suggest that every end can be the product of many means, and that there is no one end, anyway, to which it is desirable that all men should come.

Yet it was perhaps in the nature of an artistic dialogue with so powerful and respected a writer as Tolstoy that Chekhov himself should begin to feel the urge towards proof; and this happens, I think, in both 'Ward No. 6' (1892) and 'Peasants' (1897). Moreover, the difference between these stories and 'A Dreary Story', 'The Duel' and 'My Life' is that in 'Ward No. 6' and 'Peasants' the area of contention between Chekhov and Tolstoy is less philosophical: it is a question more of fact and of moral practicability. As one who had seen the conditions on Sakhalin Island – where there is said to have been a kindly but criminally negligent administrator not unlike Dr Ragin of 'Ward No. 6' – Chekhov would naturally want to challenge Tolstoy's creed of non-resistance to evil, which enjoined men neither to judge nor to take action against those who do wrong. Further-more, as a man of peasant ancestry, Chekhov could speak with more authority than Tolstoy on the subject of the peasants: as he said, 'I have peasant blood in my veins, and you won't astonish me with peasant virtues.'[13] But the problem is that in these matters of fact and practical responsibility Chekhov answers Tolstoy with a relentless documentation of the relevant detail, relying less than usual on his abundant and complex inventiveness. 'Ward No. 6' is perhaps more genuinely creative in this respect than 'Peasants', since the dialogue of ideas in 'Ward No. 6' is very convincingly grounded in social and psychological factors in the background of each character. Gromov, the son of an overworked government official, has been flogged in his youth, has suffered and has known poverty. Dr Ragin, on the other hand, has never known the physical pain he theorizes about and has always been comfortably off; he even took his medical degree simply to comply with the wishes of his father. Chekhov ensures that Gromov's inclination for protest and Ragin's unwittingly callous passivity are traced back to their origins. But as a total conception 'Ward No. 6' – which was, significantly, one of the Chekhov stories most admired by Tolstoy himself – is a prime example of a story as thesis, a story counter-ing the demonstrative force of Tolstoy's own art in kind.

As I have already suggested, Russian literature, particularly as represented in Dostoevsky and Tolstoy, has a much freer and more inclusive sense of its relationship to the realm of ideas than English or even French literature. An interest in ideas as such is intrinsic to some of Russian literature's greatest achievements: *War and Peace*, *Anna Karenina* and *The Brothers Karamazov* to mention the best. To some extent, therefore, the interest in 'Ward No. 6', in theories about freedom and suffering as argued in the rather static context of Ragin's repeated visits to Gromov in the hospital ward is sanctioned by the story's literary milieu. Again we have the pattern, so frequent in Chekhov, of the theorist in dialogue with a man arguing from the irrefutable evidence of his own sensations, except that this time Chekhov is clearly on one side of the argument:

'There is no real difference between a warm, snug study and this ward,' said Andrey Yefimitch [Ragin]. 'A man's peace and contentment do not lie outside a man, but in himself.'

'What do you mean?'

'The ordinary man looks for good and evil in external things – that is, in carriages, in studies – but a thinking man looks for it in himself.'

'You should go and preach that philosophy in Greece, where it's warm and fragrant with the scent of pomegranates, but here it is not suited to the climate. With whom was it I was talking of Diogenes? Was it with you?'

'Yes, with me yesterday.'

'Diogenes did not need a study or a warm habitation; it's hot there without. You can lie in your tub and eat oranges and olives. But bring him to Russia to live: he'd be begging to be let indoors in May, let alone December. He'd be doubled up with the cold.'

'No. One can be insensible to cold as to every other pain. Marcus Aurelius says: "A pain is a vivid idea of pain; make an effort of will to change that idea, dismiss it, cease to complain, and the pain will disappear." That is true. The wise man, or simply the reflecting, thoughtful man, is distinguished precisely by his contempt for suffering; he is always contented and surprised at nothing.'

'Then I am an idiot, since I suffer and am discontented and surprised at the baseness of mankind.' (x.74–5)

Gromov actually *is* mentally ill. His persecution mania, for which Ragin has committed him to Ward 6, is clearly evident in a number of episodes – the dialogues in the ward as well as the circumstances leading to his first being sent there. Yet he is also frequently very perceptive along lines that one feels to be Chekhov's own, and this is one such occasion. In fact, the relationship between Gromov's madness and his perceptiveness seems not to be fully worked out in the story and the reader tends to alternate between two opposite senses of him according to the differing pressures of narrative necessity at different points. But all the details of the story work to vindicate Gromov's sense of the terrible reality of suffering, as against Ragin's stoical theories; and finally the moralist in Chekhov traps Ragin himself, fatally, in the conditions which he has helped maintain by his passive non-resistance to the squalor and corruption in his hospital.

The important facts about Ragin are that he is a complacent theorist of stoical 'contempt' for suffering (suffering he has not experienced), and that his complacency is mixed up with an element of absurdism in his view of the world, so that Ward 6 seems to him almost a metaphor of the general arbitrariness of things:

'Morality and logic don't come in, it all depends on chance. If anyone is shut up he has to stay, and if anyone is not shut up he can walk about, that's all.'...

'So long as prisons and madhouses exist someone must be shut up in them. If not you, I. If not I, some third person.' (x.66–8)

This abstraction from the actual physicality of the environment of Ward 6 and from the sufferings of its inmates forms the background to Ragin's 'non-resistance to evil'. He is not a Tolstoyan, but for his own reasons he 'resists not' the evil in the system he administers. Throughout the narrative, Chekhov is quite relentlessly demonstrating the actual consequences of this non-resistance for the inmates and ultimately for Ragin himself. To begin with, the patients in Ward 6 are generally passive and uniformly benign, and they are in the ward supposedly for their own welfare. Yet these gentle madmen – in Ragin's view simply the victims of chance – are guarded by the brutal Nikita who defends the doorway with ferocious blows. Nikita's thuggish brutality and the gratuitous suffering he inflicts are what Ragin's philosophy adds up to in practice. The moral logic of the story, then, requires that Ragin himself end up confined in Ward 6 to experience the suffering he claims to despise and that he be killed by a stroke precipitated by Nikita's blows. He realizes the need to resist his hospital environment only when he is powerless to do so. Chekhov is following Tolstoy in having the man come to experience fully the cruelties he has previously inflicted on others; and, like Tolstoy, he is merciless in reminding us of, and having Andrey Yefimitch himself incredulously remember, his former views. Chekhov, in fact, does allow Ragin the dignity of clinging to his views on stoicism for a short time – an effect which I find rather unconvincing in the circumstances. But all the time he is preparing for the final storm of Ragin's pain and self-recognition. So although the work as a whole is given over to disputing one of Tolstoy's central theories, the way the narrative is shaped and the actual pattern of Ragin's coming to terms with his life are still Tolstoyan:

Then all was still, the faint moonlight came through the grating, and a shadow like a net lay on the floor. It was terrible. Andrey Yefimitch lay and held his breath: he was expecting with horror to be struck again. He felt as though someone had taken a sickle, thrust it into him, and turned it round several times in his breast and bowels. He bit the pillow from pain and clenched his teeth, and all at once through the chaos in his brain there flashed the terrible unbearable thought that these people, who seemed now like black shadows in the moonlight, had to endure such pain day by day for years. How could it have happened that for more than twenty years he had not known it and had refused to know it? He knew nothing of pain, had no conception of it, so he was not to blame, but his conscience, as inexorable and as rough as Nikita, made him turn cold from the crown of his head to his heels. He leaped up, tried to cry out with all his might, and to run in haste to kill Nikita, and then Hobotov, the superintendent and the assistant, and then himself; but no sound came from his chest, and his legs would not obey him. Gasping for breath, he tore at the dressing-gown and the shirt on his breast, rent them, and fell senseless on the bed. (x.110–11)

The simile of the sickle being thrust into Andrey Yefimitch, which expresses the intense physicality of his pain, has a boldness Chekhov must have learnt from Tolstoy. From Tolstoy too he seems to have realized, perhaps instinctively, that the starkness of such scenes involves an absence of colour, a stress on darkness and light, black and white, as here with the people in the ward seeming shadows in the moonlight and the shadow of the grating 'like a net...on the floor'. Moreover, the thought-cadences in which Ragin's realization of his culpability is expressed ('How could it have happened that for more than twenty years he had not known it and had refused to know it?') have again the distinctive moral charge of self-accusation which we associate with 'Ivan Ilych'. But the modernity of that image of imprisonment, the shadow of the grating like a net on the floor, is distinctively that of Chekhov. And the ending, too, where Ragin simply falls senseless on the bed, has an unnerving, un-Tolstoyan flatness, a complete absence of any triumph about his self-recognition, which reveals a peculiarly Chekhovian grimness about the fact that some self-awakenings happen too late. The emphasis in Tolstoy is completely individualistic; he puts an absolute value on each man's coming morally to terms with himself, which allows a sense of triumph to pervade even the appalling situation of Ivan Ilych on his death-bed. Chekhov, at this stage, writes from a realist's and a humanist's standpoint, with the stress on general social consequences – something which Ragin's late recognition of guilt, and of the need to resist, has no power to affect.

I have already implied some connection between the details in 'Ward No. 6' and Chekhov's experience on Sakhalin Island; and the very firm factual outline of the work is, I think, both a weakness and a strength. Its weakness is, of course, that the story has little real freedom for invention and that its didacticism is rather harsh. The appalling squalor of the ward environment is captured in graphic detail, and the indignation which the recording of it excites in Chekhov produces a punitive response unusual in him. But within the narrow limits of the story its major achievement, the source of its success in challenging Tolstoy's stance of non-resistance to evil, is the sheer plausibility of the narrative consequences as they are worked out. Gromov is not a completely sane man caught in a nightmarishly improper captivity such as we associate with some modern surrealist literature. He is 'properly' confined in the sense that he is mentally ill; nor could anything be more logical, in a way, than that a doctor given suddenly to spending long hours in serious conversation with a lunatic should himself be thought insane and eventually be confined. This factual plausibility is essential to the story's success and is, indeed, the thing that makes it so frightening. For, while there is a nightmare quality coming from the extreme nature of what happens to the doctor, the whole point of the story is that such things can and do actually occur. When some sections of the story do begin to feel like dream-sequences or surreal fantasy, the power of the work is temporarily lost: the suffering seems unreal and is therefore cushioned from us, and the chain of causation by which Ragin himself is trapped is lost in a floating, irrational progression of images which, because of their dream-like unreality, carry little moral weight. In the following passage, for instance, Ragin's real terror is not captured nearly so successfully in the nightmare images of the first paragraph as in the hard, factual outline of the immovable bars:

The moon and the prison, and the nails on the fence, and the far-away flames at the bone-charring factory were all terrible. Behind him there was the sound of a sigh. Andrey Yefimitch looked round and saw a man with glittering stars and orders on his breast, who was smiling and slily winking. And this, too, seemed terrible.

Andrey Yefimitch assured himself that there was nothing special about the moon or the prison, that even sane persons wear orders, and that everything in time will decay and turn to earth, but he was suddenly overcome with despair; he clutched at the grating with both hands and shook it with all his might. The strong grating did not yield. (x.107)

It is the total physical resistance of the Ward 6 environment to the emotions of men, not the temporary effect of moonlight on the prison wall, that is the real source of terror, and the best instinct guiding Chekhov at this moment recognizes it. Though he is obviously tempted to indulge in the menacing impressionistic possibilities of the visual effects of 'the far-away flames' and the moonlight shining through the grating, some deeper realization of the nature of the dominant power in this story keeps warning him away from it back to the literal harshness of fact. For it is only by this persistent documentation of the ward routines, the soiled and ill-fitting linen and the repetitive habits of the inmates that Chekhov can hope to impress his reader with what Sakhalin no doubt impressed on him: that some nightmares are real.

I think one can feel from 'Ward No. 6' that the most fruitful phase of Chekhov's artistic rebellion against Tolstoy is now past. Chekhov has learnt what he is going to learn from Tolstoy – the set-piece of Ragin's coming to know himself seems somehow easy, without the tension of Laevsky's introspection in 'The Duel' – and the stimulation and provocation of Tolstoy's theories has begun to be replaced with a disagreement that is in danger of becoming merely sour. In fact, Chekhov's basic mood towards Tolstoy by this time is captured well in a famous letter:

Tolstoy's philosophy moved me deeply and possessed me for six or seven years. It was not so much his basic postulates that had an effect on me – I had been familiar with them before – it was his way of expressing himself, his common sense, and probably a sort of hypnotism as well. But now something in me protests. Prudence and justice tell me there is more love for mankind in electricity and steam than in chastity and abstention from meat. War is an evil and the court system is an evil, but it doesn't follow that I should wear bast shoes and sleep on a stove alongside the hired hand and his wife, and so on and so'forth. But that's not the issue: it's not a matter of the pros and cons, the point is that in one way or another Tolstoy has departed from my life, he's no longer in my heart and he's left me, saying, 'Behold, I leave your house empty.' He dwells in me no longer. I'm tired of listening to disquisitions...[14]

'Peasants' (1897), then, is little more than a postscript to the once-powerful engagement of Chekhov's art with Tolstoy's. The enthusiasm with which the story was welcomed in some circles at the time and the disturbance it caused in others is completely understandable, given its sheer stamina in countering the pre-vailing literary image of the peasant with stark and squalid fact. Probably no work better conveys both the squalor and the pathos of peasant life in its poverty, its over-crowding and its terrible ignorance – the brutalizing effects of that life and yet the touch-ing vestiges of humanity that remain. As literary testimony in evidence against Tolstoy, by one who had served the peasants for five years as a doctor, it is a document no social historian of nineteenth-century Russia should ignore. But Chekhov's intolerance of theorizing at this time means that he opposes Tolstoy's view of the peasants by intensely particular reporting which ultimately limits the value of the work as fully creative literature. Though informed, generally, by a special spirit of humane understanding which distinguishes it from any ordinary journalistic report, there is no doubt that it projects only a rather flat image:

Meanwhile Nikolay's father and mother, two gaunt, bent, toothless old people, just of the same height, came back. The women – the sisters-in-law Marya and Fyokla – who had been working on the landowner's estate beyond the river, arrived home, too. Marya, the wife of Nikolay's brother Kiryak, had six children, and Fyokla, the wife of Nikolay's brother Denis – who had gone for a soldier – had two; and when Nik-olay, going into the hut, saw all the family, all those bodies big and little moving about on the lockers, in the hanging cradles and in all the corners, and when he saw the greed with which the old father and the woman ate the black bread, dipping it in the water, he realized he had made a mistake in coming here, sick, penniless, and with a family, too – a great mistake! (vi.282)

There is just sufficient individual characterization thereafter in the story to make us feel that some of the characters might have been really interesting with further development. But it is ob-vious that Chekhov is very distant from this class (though he was only at a second-generation remove from it) and even somewhat frightened by it in some respects. In 'My Life', written a year earlier, he conveys powerfully the mass ignorance and coarseness of the peasants as they defy and defeat Masha's and Poloznev's attempts to live in harmony with them and give them aid. Through the views of the otherwise somewhat untrustworthy Dr Blagovo, Chekhov voices some of his own realistic objections to the Tolstoyan ideal of the peasant, confirming them in the narrative detail. But in 'Peasants' he goes a step further. Here there is no real narrative line to take one's attention into other areas: simply a deliberate, *tour-de-force* rendering of what it means to live that primitive and squalid life. To give a sense of how far from the Tolstoyan ideal his 'real' peasants are, Chekhov alternates his imagery of the extremely sordid conditions inside the hut with picturesque images of the surrounding countryside; and the structure of events through which this is sustained is much too loose, while also exhibiting signs of wilfulness in the sheer accumulation of negative detail. Unlike 'My Life', 'Peasants' feels very much like a reflex creation written in sheer irritation at the then-popularized image of the peasant, the responsibility for which could again be traced (at least in part) to Tolstoy.

As we have seen, Chekhov's art in his longer novellas in the early 1890s owes much to the influence of Tolstoy. We have also seen that influence becoming less beneficial in its effects and ultimately turning sour. But Chekhov himself, in a letter of 1900, gives the best possible general summary of his deep, lasting love for Tolstoy and the reasons for it:

His sickness frightened me and kept me in a state of tension. I fear Tolstoy's death. If he were to die there would be left in my life a great, empty space. In the first place, I love no man as I do him; I am an unbeliever, but among all faiths, I consider that of Tolstoy nearest my heart and most suited to my nature. Secondly, when there is Tolstoy in literature it is easy and pleasant to be a literary worker; even to be aware that you have done and will do nothing is not so terrible, because Tolstoy does enough for all. His activity serves as a justification for those hopes and expectations that are attached to literature. Thirdly, Tolstoy stands unshaken; his authority is tremendous, and while he lives, bad taste in literature, all sorts of vulgarity, insolence, and sentimentality, all kinds of shoddy, irritated ambitions, will remain deep in shadow. His moral authority alone is able to hold to a certain height so-called literary moods and tendencies. Without him, these would be a shepherdless herd or a hodge-podge in which it would be difficult to find anything that rings true.[15]

It was in this sense that Tolstoy, as a predominant force in Chekhov's literary and cultural environment, continued to exert a pressure on Chekhov's work (and to command Chekhov's personal respect and affection) even after he had ceased to be a direct influence.

8

'A Dreary Story'

'A Dreary Story', as I have already suggested, takes up the challenge of Tolstoy's 'The Death of Ivan Ilych'. It gives no less moving an account than Tolstoy's of a man's realization that he is dying and of his confrontation with death, but it views that situation in almost opposite terms. Tolstoy's Ivan Ilych, as a number of critics have pointed out,[1] discovers selfhood in death. It is the experience of facing death which makes him suddenly aware of what life has been about and of his own shortcomings in relation to it: thus it is the fact of death which develops in Ivan Ilych a genuine inner life. Chekhov's Nikolay Stepanovitch, in 'A Dreary Story', discovers virtually the opposite. His selfhood, which has been firmly established during his long life as a doctor and university professor, is profoundly threatened by the approach of death: all that he has seemed to live by and to stand for begins to disintegrate in his personality as old age engulfs it and death draws closer. In 'A Dreary Story', therefore, we are given a quite different sense of the way death encroaches on life from what we find in 'The Death of Ivan Ilych'. Tolstoy gradually brings Ivan Ilych to know himself; Chekhov reveals Nikolay Stepanovitch becoming progressively detached from, and experiencing the slow disintegration of, his hitherto meaningful and dignified life.

'The Death of Ivan Ilych' has an unparalleled power in conveying Ivan Ilych's terror of helplessness, of loneliness, of physical pain – his terror, most of all, of death itself. It gives us one moment of almost unbearable pathos when Ivan Ilych just cannot believe that his particular consciousness, with all its unique memories, especially of events in his childhood, could ever really become extinct. Yet in so far as the days leading up to Ivan Ilych's death witness his discovery of himself and his seeing of the light, there is at least a partial triumph accompanying his death which takes the emphasis away from all that is lost. In Chekhov's story, on the other hand, we are less under the spell of, and less appalled by, Nikolay Stepanovitch's sheer terror, since, as an educated man committed to certain forms of reticence, his declarations of his deepest fears are much more intermittent. But Nikolay Stepanovitch's account of his life in 'A Dreary Story' nevertheless expresses a much wider range of feelings in a wider variety of situations than Tolstoy captures in his account of Ivan Ilych. We seem to know Nikolay Stepanovitch better and feel a deeper sense of his uniqueness as an individual, which in turn allows us to feel more of the pathos of his predicament. For although Nikolay Stepanovitch too has to endure loneliness, helplessness and a degree of pain, he fears these less than the possibility that his old age and the approach of death will lead him into a shattering betrayal of his life. We see this in his speech to Katya:

'For thirty years I have been the favourite professor, I have had splendid comrades, I have enjoyed fame and honour. I have loved, married from passionate love, have had children. In fact, looking back upon it, I see my whole life as a fine composition arranged with talent. Now all that is left to me is not to spoil the end. For that I must die like a man. If death is really a thing to dread, I must meet it as a teacher, a man of science, and a citizen of a Christian country ought to meet it, with courage and untroubled soul. But I am spoiling the end; I am sinking, I fly to you, I beg for help, and you tell me "Sink; that is what you ought to do."' (v.180)

The 'sinking' he fears is the moral erosion of his generally humane standards and attitudes (associated with his being a teacher, a man of science, a citizen of a Christian country) by poisonous thoughts and irrational irritations which go with old age. So, through him, the story is set to look at the general fate of those values which have been most enduring in Western civilization when, in particular individuals, they are confronted with biological decay. For this reason, 'A Dreary Story' has, to my mind, a breadth and depth of reference and ultimate general value which 'The Death of Ivan Ilych', with its very specific class context (and its basic animosity towards that class), for all its power, does not have.

'A Dreary Story' is a monologue 'from the notebook of an old man'. It is Nikolay Stepanovitch's own account of the last months of his life, his stock-taking of his life, while he is yet experiencing it. As such it has not only that fullness and fluidity of response of which I spoke in the last chapter (contrasting it with the uncharitable resumé mode of 'The Death of Ivan Ilych') but also a dramatic dimension by which more is revealed of Nikolay Stepanovitch than he himself consciously knows. Logan Speirs has pointed to this aspect of the story very usefully:

The old scientist is engaged in writing up the last notes on that apparently abortive experiment, his life, carefully selecting what seem to him the salient facts in his existence. We see more in them than he does, for no man ever succeeds in seeing himself objectively. Nikolay Stepanovitch, who suffers from a deep sense of failure, is biased against himself. His most generous feelings are therefore played down in the telling. And this self-discipline gradually becomes more absorbing to contemplate than even the agonies of Ivan Ilych. The courage of the man earns progressively more of one's respect.[2]

Basically, this comment seems to me true; however, Nikolay Stepanovitch is sometimes more and sometimes less than he represents. Moreover, the deepest interest of the story, I think, comes not from the way Nikolay Stepanovitch manages and disciplines his materials, but from the values in relation to which he disciplines them. Nikolay Stepanovitch is a man of specialized abilities, a member of an educated élite, a Moscow medical professor. All his life he has believed in the great value of science and in the ethos of the university generally. But the account he gives of his life shows him to have been capable of prejudice and self-delusion in some matters, though he has been selfless and full of integrity in others; and the way he recounts all this in the present makes us aware that these faults are continuing and not just a thing of the past. Like nearly all people (and, the story suggests, nearly all institutions), Nikolay Stepanovitch partly falsifies the values by which he supposes himself to live. Indeed, were he ideally to embody the humane values theoretically associated with the discipline of medicine, he would be far less convincing a character than he is, and Chekhov would inexplicably have abandoned his usual realism. Yet Nikolay Stepanovitch does embody enough of that ideal for the corrosion of his standards and attitudes by old age to have a direct relevance to the fate of civilized values generally when challenged by encroaching physical and mental decrepitude and death.

When he first introduces himself, Nikolay Stepanovitch appears as one who has achieved an unusually high degree of personal fame and fulfilment; who, though disgruntled about his present life, yet derives some satisfaction from being held in high esteem. The most cherished word in his vocabulary, past and present, is 'science', and about science he shows a passion and excitement quite undampened by age. In fact it is in the speeches about science that the fuller dramatic definition of the kind of person Nikolay Stepanovitch is, on the positive side, begins:

Unfortunately, I am not a philosopher and not a theologian. I know perfectly well that I cannot live more than another six months; it might be supposed that I ought now to be chiefly concerned with the question of the shadowy life beyond the grave, and the visions that will visit my slumbers in the tomb. But for some reason my soul refuses to recognize these questions, though my mind is fully alive to their importance. Just as twenty, thirty years ago, so now, on the threshold of death, I am interested in nothing but science. As I yield up my last breath I shall still believe that science is the most important, the most splendid, the most essential thing in the life of man; that it always has been and will be the highest manifestation of love, and that only by means of it will man conquer himself and nature. This faith is perhaps naive and may rest on false assumptions, but it is not my fault that I believe that and nothing else; I cannot overcome in myself this belief. (v.148–9)

The careful and eloquent structure of the statement, which recognizes both the reader's possible resistance to this view and its own possible naivety, bespeaks an educated man committed to certain values and to certain conventions of utterance. The way Nikolay Stepanovitch speaks of science, in so emphatic a syntax and with a rising inflexion in his voice ('the most important, the most splendid, the most essential thing in the life of man'), convinces us of the depth of his commitment to it; but he is committed to something more than science alone. For although Nikolay Stepanovitch denies that he is a philosopher, he does in fact express a consistent understanding of the world throughout this speech. He observes the conventions of polite academic discourse; he is respectful of the complexity of life's problems, recognizing the possible limitations in his own reasoning; he has selflessly dedicated his life to the pursuit of truths whose benefits to his own life are purely abstract. Above all, his love of science is expressed in terms which reveal also a love of man and desire for his general betterment. In all these things Nikolay Stepanovitch is revealed as instinctively adhering to a consistent core of values – ones recognizably associated with a long tradition of Western humanism.

This humanist outlook on life unfolds itself unconsciously

through most of Nikolay Stepanovitch's descriptions of the disappointing or distasteful things around him. He dislikes the university buildings because they are dismal and dilapidated, whereas, he says, at a university one should be confronted only by 'what is lofty, strong, and elegant' (v.140). He appreciates the porter's love for the institution of the university and the demonstrator's scholarship, but he laments the ignorance of the former and the latter's lack of inspiration, his joylessness. In personal matters, as in his references to Katya and her unfortunate past, he strives to be tactful and delicate (he speaks of Katya's 'having been a mother without being a wife' (v.167), for instance). Implied in all these reactions are values centring on human freedom and dignity of body and spirit. For Nikolay Stepanovitch has an innate sense of justice and an impulse to preserve human dignity at all costs. Even his aesthetic judgments, as for example of Katya's flat, are motivated by these humanistic values:

For the indolent body there are soft lounges, soft stools; for indolent feet soft rugs; for indolent eyes faded, dingy, or flat colours; for the indolent soul the walls are hung with a number of cheap fans and trivial pictures, in which the originality of the execution is more conspicuous than the subject; and the room contains a multitude of little tables and shelves filled with utterly useless articles of no value, and shapeless rags in place of curtains... All this, together with the dread of bright colours, of symmetry, and of empty space, bears witness not only to spiritual indolence, but also to a corruption of natural taste. (v.164)

To Nikolay Stepanovitch, at the ideal level anyway, life is an opportunity for the vigorous exercise of human faculties, for energetic habits of living associated with 'bright colours', 'symmetry' and 'empty space'. He is impatient with purely decorative objects (like the numerous little tables and the shelves full of useless articles of no value) which neither stimulate the spirit nor have a functional use. Katya's 'indolence', therefore, is not simply a characterization of her manner but, obviously, a judgment of her and, implicitly, a recognition that there is a deep unhappiness in her life. Moreover, her indolence, the disorder of her life and the oppressive quality of her flat stand in clear contrast to Nikolay Stepanovitch's educated discrimination of all that is implied by the outer details of Katya's life, and to his own civilized standards which are so deeply instilled that he unconsciously equates them with 'natural taste'.

However, as I suggested earlier, there are also areas in Nikolay

Stepanovitch's life where he fails his own theoretical values. He himself is aware of some of these, especially of those minor compromises he more or less has to make in running his subject within the medical faculty. Chekhov gives us a vividly realistic outline of Nikolay Stepanovitch's customary interviews with young doctors who are looking for a research topic. Always, it seems, Nikolay Stepanovitch finally gives in and dictates a topic, even though he recognizes that, by doing so, he will only increase his students' 'distaste for independence'. But although Nikolay Stepanovitch can recognize such betrayals of his principles as this, and even one or two obvious omissions in his duties toward Katya, he does not see that there are continuing omissions of moral duty in his present life. We now have, of course, Chekhov's letter to this effect: 'one of my hero's chief characteristics is that he cares far too little about the inner life of those who surround him, and while people around him are weeping, making mistakes, telling lies, he calmly talks about the theatre or literature. Were he a different sort of man, Liza and Katya might not have come to grief.'[3] But even without the support of this letter, the language of the story makes it very plain that Nikolay Stepanovitch's instinct for humanist values is often too passive and that he is and has been at his worst in his relations with other people. In his inner self he feels compassion for other people, but he does nothing positive to help them: in terms of action he has remained – and remains – unmoved through the most terrible crises. Before considering those crises, however, it might be useful to look at one instance of the emotional passivity which Nikolay Stepanovitch displays from day to day, noting the habits of language through which it is revealed. The scene is Nikolay Stepanovitch and his family at dinner:

There is none of the gaiety of the old days, the spontaneous talk, the jokes, the laughter; there is nothing of mutual affection and the joy which used to animate the children, my wife, and me when in old days we met together at meals...

To describe our dinner nowadays is as uninteresting as to eat it. My wife's face wears a look of triumph and affected dignity, and her habitual expression of anxiety. She looks at our plates and says, 'I see you don't care for the joint. Tell me; you don't like it, do you?' and I am obliged to answer: 'There is no need for you to trouble, my dear; the meat is very nice.'... And so on in the same style all through dinner. Liza laughs spasmodically and screws up her eyes. I watch them both, and it is only now at dinner that it becomes absolutely evident to me that the inner life of these two has slipped away out of my ken. I have a feeling as though I had once lived at home with a real wife and children and that now I am dining with visitors, in the house of a sham wife who is not the real one, and am looking at a Liza who is not the real Liza. A startling change has taken place in both of them; I have missed the long process by which that change was effected, and it is no wonder that I can make nothing of it. (v.170–1)

The irretrievable drifting apart of Nikolay Stepanovitch and the rest of his family is here movingly documented and encompassed in a tone of sad indignation to which we respond. Also, the images of Varya's and Liza's social affectations, set against the ideal of spontaneity, gaiety and mutual affection to which he holds, and which he has known in the past, dispose us to sympathize entirely with the old man. But against that, Nikolay Stepanovitch's response to his wife's anxiety about the joint is polite but cold: he himself does nothing to recover the spontaneity whose loss he deplores. More tellingly, such passive constructions as 'the inner life of these two *has slipped away* out of my ken' circumvent the moral force which a more direct statement – such as 'I have not kept touch' – would have had, indicating Nikolay Stepanovitch's equal culpability. The 'startling change' that has taken place in his family has in fact been a 'long process' which he has somehow 'missed'. It does not occur to Nikolay Stepanovitch that that might indicate the great moral failure of his life: his neglect of his family duties and of his obligation to keep close to his wife and children, and his damaging passivity about what happens to them. For it is, of course, that same passivity and neglect, extending into the present, which makes him delay in investigating Gnekker's circumstances – a delay which in turn helps to precipitate Liza's ruin.

The person whom Nikolay Stepanovitch has failed most is Katya, the daughter of a deceased colleague and now legally his ward. Katya is a powerful figure in the story, with something of the irrepressibly passionate nature of Masha in *Three Sisters* though she is far more desperate. In the story she appears as a sort of opposite self to Nikolay Stepanovitch in her passionate love of art and the theatre and her propensity for sudden dramatic gestures; but in fact she has more in common with him than his own family, commmitted as she is to a life and an endeavour which will satisfy something larger than herself.

It is she who gives him the loving attentions his own children neglect, she who offers him her money as he has wished Liza would do. But Nikolay Stepanovitch cannot match the depth and generosity of Katya's personal feeling, and he continuously delivers her unconscious rebuffs. So, for example, his manner of refusing her money is open to a misunderstanding which is badly damaging to Katya's self-esteem:

'Will you take it? Yes? Nikolay Stepanovitch darling, yes?'
  She looked greedily into my face and repeated: 'Yes, you will take it?'
  'No, my dear, I won't take it...' I said. 'Thank you.'...
  'I beg your pardon...' she said, dropping her voice a whole octave. 'I understand you...to be indebted to a person like me...a retired actress...But, good-bye...' (v.210)

Nikolay Stepanovitch records Katya's reaction, but he never does anything to erase that false impression of his reasons. Even in talking of Katya's attempted suicide after her unhappy affair he is as vague about it in the present as he was at the time, even though he is officially Katya's guardian: 'I gathered that there had been an attempt at suicide. I believe Katya tried to poison herself' (v.163). Indeed much of the extreme formality of his manner of speaking, when he recounts the growth of Katya's love for the theatre, comes from his unconscious desire to excuse himself for having neglected his responsibility:

I regret that I had not time nor inclination to watch over the rise and development of the passion which took complete possession of Katya when she was fourteen or fifteen. I mean her passionate love for the theatre...
  I had never shared Katya's inclinations for the theatre. To my mind, if a play is good there is no need to trouble the actors in order that it may make the right impression; it is enough to read it. If the play is poor, no acting will make it good. (v.157-8)

The conspicuous stiffness of the opening phrases, and the rapid movement away from the personal situation into the comfortable complacency of Nikolay Stepanovitch's own views on the theatre, indicate the presence of guilt – guilt being distanced defensively through the formal mannerisms of the prose. His admission of 'regret' signals his uneasiness about his role in the past, but such things as the shift from 'passionate love' to 'inclinations' to describe Katya's feeling for the theatre show Nikolay Stepanovitch protecting himself from fully recognizing his culpability. Even in these last months of his life, when he seems to himself to be undertaking a bitterly explicit self-criticism, he rationalizes his failures with regard to Katya and is incapable of perceiving the poignancy of his own images of her. For example, his observation – 'I go on working while Katya sits silent not far from me on the sofa, wrapping herself in her shawl, as though she were cold' (v.165) – conveys to us a basic insight into Katya's state of mind of which Nikolay Stepanovitch himself is apparently unaware. As he goes on working, as Katya sits by silently in desperate insecurity, he fulfils the pattern of unconscious moral compromise of which, one way and another, he has been guilty throughout his adult life.

In Nikolay Stepanovitch, then, Chekhov has given us a very complex figure (quite unlike Ivan Ilych's stereotyped personality before he is changed by facing up to death). The first challenge of the story is thus to perceive the kind of person Nikolay Stepanovitch actually is and to see that that is sometimes more and sometimes less than what he represents as himself. But as Nikolay Stepanovitch's account of himself becomes more deeply introspective and as the story moves forward in time towards his death, Chekhov goes on to dramatize Nikolay Stepanovitch's gradual but perceptible and painful loss of comfort from the things he previously has genuinely valued. What has been and is good in him – what might be summarized as his educated refinement and his basic humanity – is now under threat both from his dawning intellectual disbelief in what he once so strongly valued, as oncoming death makes the polite academic rituals seem pointless and absurd, and from uncontrollable, irrational elements in his behaviour which seem biological in origin. Where Tolstoy's Ivan Ilych moves towards self-discovery in the cruel circumstances of his death, Nikolay Stepanovitch moves towards a complete collapse of his confidence in the values by which he has lived, until finally he is in despair about the absence of a 'general idea' to govern and make sense of his disparate thoughts.

Already in the first paragraph of the story Nikolay Stepanovitch's references to himself are semi-ironic in a peculiar and significant way. He already recognizes the discrepancy which exists between his public image ('what is called my "name"') and the private reality of his physical and mental decay; and the recognition seems partly to have undermined his confidence that his fame is of any importance. We perceive this from his tone:

That is my name as known to the public. In Russia it is known to every educated man, and abroad it is mentioned in the lecture-room with the addition 'honoured and distinguished'. It is one of those fortunate names to abuse which or to take which in vain, in public or in print, is considered a sign of bad taste. And that is as it should be. You see, my name is closely associated with the conception of a highly distinguished man of great gifts and unquestionable usefulness. (v.131–2)

It is easy to feel Nikolay Stepanovitch's detachment from this public conception of himself. Particularly in such formulations as 'And that is as it should be' and 'a man of great gifts and unquestionable usefulness' there is a highly precarious balance between a sense of satisfaction and a sense of absurdity, between conviction and irony. This academic self is also the subject of many later and more overt ironies as Nikolay Stepanovitch loses his sense of belonging to the academic world and becomes increasingly absorbed in the physical and psychological realities of his private being. For example, as early as the beginning of Part II, there is a striking increase in Nikolay Stepanovitch's detachment from academic life in the account Chekhov has him give of a visit from a colleague:

To begin with, we both try to show each other that we are extraordinarily polite and highly delighted to see each other. I make him sit down in an easy-chair, and he makes me sit down; as we do so, we cautiously pat each other on the back, touch each other's buttons, and it looks as though we were feeling each other and afraid of scorching our fingers. Both of us laugh, though we say nothing amusing. When we are seated we bow our heads towards each other and begin talking in subdued voices. However affectionately disposed we may be to one another, we cannot help adorning our conversation with all sorts of Chinese mannerisms, such as 'As you so justly observed', or 'I have already had the honour to inform you'; we cannot help laughing if one of us makes a joke, however unsuccessfully. When we have finished with business my colleague gets up impulsively and, waving his hat in the direction of my work, begins to say good-bye. Again we paw one another and laugh. I see him into the hall; then I assist my colleague to put on his coat, while he does all he can to decline this high honour. Then when Yegor opens the door my colleague declares that I shall catch cold, while I make a show of being ready to go even into the street with him. And when at last I go back into my study my face still goes on smiling, I suppose from inertia. (v.150–1)

The mannerisms and gestures are caught accurately enough to be immediately recognized, which only heightens the comedy of the imagery. But this meeting of academics is viewed by Nikolay Stepanovitch as if wholly from the outside. Although the courteous rituals referred to are in reality often over-eager and somewhat tense, Nikolay Stepanovitch exaggerates them to the point of parody and seems to regard even the usual polite habits of speech as something alien ('Chinese mannerisms'). Indeed, it is significant that Chekhov has Nikolay Stepanovitch describe a large part of the meeting through lightly sketched animal imagery ('we cautiously pat each other on the back, touch each other's buttons...Again we paw one another...'), for that imagery reduces the civilized rituals to primitive and instinctive forms of behaviour which have no other meaning beyond their own ritual qualities. The very things, the very values, which should sustain a civilized man during his old age by preserving at least his outward dignity evaporate into absurdity for the man looking upon death.

Nor is Nikolay Stepanovitch simply becoming more and more intellectually detached from the life around him: he is also prone to quite irrational forms of irritation (the 'poison' in his thoughts of which he is afraid), which to the reader feel almost compulsively produced by some reaction of his body chemistry. Nikolay Stepanovitch's former attempts at dignity and forbearance in his home life give way at times to outright contempt and childish loss of temper. His always rather condescending view of women hardens into a conviction of their inferiority; and he gradually abandons his restraint over his feelings of outright hatred for Gnekker. Always in his account of himself he deplores these outbursts, seeing how he is betraying his former values. Yet the self-analysis does not fully succeed in ridding his prose of traces of the same annoyance and impatience:

Carried away by evil feeling, I often say things that are simply stupid, and I don't know why I say them. So on one occasion it happened that I stared a long time at Gnekker, and *à propos* of nothing, I fired off:

> 'An eagle may perchance swoop down below a cock,
> But never will the fowl soar upwards to the clouds...'

And the most vexatious thing is that the fowl Gnekker shows himself much cleverer than the eagle professor. Knowing that my wife and daughter are on his side, he takes up the line of meeting my gibes with condescending silence, as though to say:

'The old chap is in his dotage; what's the use of talking to him?'

Or he makes fun of me good-naturedly. It is wonderful how petty a man may become! I am capable of dreaming all dinner-time of how Gnekker will turn out to be an adventurer, how my wife and Liza will come to see their mistake, and how I will taunt them – and such absurd thoughts at the time when I am standing with one foot in the grave! (v.198–9)

Here, Nikolay Stepanovitch's basic tone of reasonableness does not prevent him from keeping to his categories of 'fowl' and 'eagle', from regarding his relationship to Gnekker in terms of opposing 'sides', or even from unconsciously entertaining still the hope that Gnekker will turn out to be an adventurer. It is the same with his opinions on modern students, where his overall defence of them as being no worse than the students of the past sometimes lapses into generalized complaint about their unusual ignorance: 'They don't know modern languages, and they don't express themselves correctly in Russian; no longer ago than yesterday my colleague, the professor of hygiene, complained to me that he had to give twice as many lectures...' (v.186). Indeed, in general in Parts II and III there is a loss of the former restraint of the narrative voice, a sudden shrillness or sudden insistences issuing in cadences like 'I cannot tolerate...'. And every instance of prejudice, every loss of temper and lapse into slander, marks the tragic loss of some aspect of that civilized self which has previously seemed innate to Nikolay Stepanovitch's personality.

This collapse of Nikolay Stepanovitch's personality and of the civilized values to which he once so strongly adhered is, I think, more movingly relevant to most of our lives than Ivan Ilych's opposite and unusually climactic process of coming to see, near death, the values by which he ought to have lived. But in attempting actually to dramatize that collapse through a first-person narrative, Chekhov was bound to come up against one inherent and probably irremediable difficulty. For the very fact that Nikolay Stepanovitch's mental world is so lively, so interested in things, makes it hard for us to feel the reality of his extreme physical deterioration – and it is on that that Chekhov's power to convince us of the imminence of Nikolay Stepanovitch's death depends. Chekhov is caught between the need to keep the story told by the old professor energetic and evocative and his need somehow to convey the decline of the professor's physical and mental powers. Tolstoy's third-person syntax can quite easily make us sustainedly aware of Ivan Ilych's hysterical fear, because there is no need for the actual prose to enact the disruption of Ivan Ilych's powers of expression. Writing in the third person, Tolstoy commands the resources of interpretative imagery, metaphor and simile. Thus we can even witness the appalling terror of Ivan Ilych's death scene, for Tolstoy is there to describe sensations of which Ivan Ilych cannot really be conscious:[4]

For three whole days, during which time did not exist for him, he struggled in that black sack into which he was being thrust by an invisible, resistless force. He struggled as a man condemned to death struggles in the hands of the executioner, knowing that he cannot save himself.[5]

Chekhov's story, significantly, does not actually include the immediate scene of Nikolay Stepanovitch's death but ends with the moment of his psychological renunciation of life – his cry of farewell to Katya. One of the differences between the two stories is Chekhov's interest in the psychological changes which themselves signify the approach of death, where Tolstoy conveys his character's psychological reactions specifically to the physical facts of pain and decay. But if we take even Nikolay Stepanovitch's moments of sudden fear – which, as I argued in the last chapter, are often directly imitative of passages in late Tolstoy – we can see clearly that Chekhov is having difficulty accommodating such moments into the general and necessary self-command of the first-person prose. Any outbursts of panicked reaction must necessarily be short-lived and therefore cannot be powerfully cumulative as Tolstoy's are; and the ordered narration never really lets us feel that Nikolay Stepanovitch is as close to death as his own commentary says he is. For example, Nikolay Stepanovitch gives us an account of the breakdown of his lecturing, of his inability to order his thoughts, and of his sudden impulse to cry out to his audience for help; but he does so in an eloquently constructed verbal essay – in effect a lecture – on what an ideal lecture might be. Either, then, Chekhov means us to see that Nikolay Stepanovitch has more resilience than he thinks he has, or he is trapped by his need to create a coherent and moving story out of what is supposed to be the incoherence of an old man. Given these examples, I am inclined to think it is the latter, especially since some of the most memorably alert and acutely perceived of all the professor's images in fact come very near the end of the story.

It is perhaps because he recognized this difficulty that after Part IV, when Nikolay Stepanovitch has abandoned the university altogether and removed to a summer villa, Chekhov supplements Nikolay Stepanovitch's dramatic self-revelation with poetic imagery of a very deliberate kind:

I read French books, and I look out of the window which is open; I can see the spikes of my garden-fence, two or three scraggy trees, and beyond the fence the road, the fields, and beyond them a broad stretch of pine-wood. (v.195)

This scene is calculated to act as a kind of metaphor. Nikolay Stepanovitch has already said that he reads French literature because of the sense it projects of personal freedom. Likewise, the pine-wood now on the distant horizon has been his private emblem of 'what is lofty, strong and elegant' – the human attributes he has most appreciated in the course of his lifetime. But, as later with the spiked fence around Anna's house in 'The Lady with the Dog', the fence carries a suggestion of Nikolay Stepanovitch's imprisonment in his condition; and his condition is reflected in the diminished landscape of 'scraggy trees' by the villa itself. Here he receives the visits of the 'carthorse', Pyotr Ignatyevitch, and of a tongue-tied Nikolay whose inadequacies complete the dreariness of his new surroundings. And although Katya comes to take him for drives in the lofty pine-wood, even that has an altered significance for him:

At first we drive through the open country, then through the pine-wood which is visible from my window. Nature seems to me as beautiful as it always has been, though some evil spirit whispers to me that these pines and fir trees, birds, and white clouds on the sky, will not notice my absence when in three or four months I am dead. (v.200–1)

Like Ivan Ilych, Nikolay Stepanovitch is deprived of some comforts which Chekhov could have given him: the presence of intellectually equal companions, the love of his wife or of someone else of his own age who might more fully understand his fears, or even the paradoxical comfort of a mental decline so great that it might help blur and mask death's approach. In this sense Nikolay Stepanovitch's situation is not necessarily typical; nor is Chekhov really seeking to create in Nikolay Stepanovitch a modern-day Everyman. Like Tolstoy, he perhaps feared to give his character any of these comforts, lest, in softening the starkness of Nikolay Stepanovitch's predicament, he should unconsciously evade the horror of the facts. Both 'The Death of Ivan Ilych' and 'A Dreary Story' manifest this anxiety to the extent that they equate a true confrontation of death with a situation in which their central characters are completely isolated and comfortless (although Tolstoy's portrayal of this is more extreme and thus more painful than Chekhov's). But whereas Tolstoy's attention is centred wholly on Ivan Ilych, so that those around him seem to need no form of sympathy at all, Part IV of 'A Dreary Story' begins to widen the range of the story's compassion and to take account of the fact that some people are as vulnerable all through life as Nikolay Stepanovitch is just before his death. Nikolay Stepanovitch himself, after his irritation at Pyotr Ignatyevitch's visit, suddenly feels compassion for this 'carthorse' – dutiful and mediocre man that he is – as his grey felt hat appears behind the garden fence. The image has sufficient poignancy for the reader to feel that sudden compassion too. And, more importantly of course, there is Katya – Katya, who pleads with Nikolay Stepanovitch in the pine-forest to advise her of some direction she might take to escape the negativity of her life.

Katya has been the victim of Nikolay Stepanovitch's moral passivity in the past. She is the living embodiment of the major area of failure in his life, and it is dramatically right that as he nears death Katya's demands upon him finally to rescue her should intensify. Significantly, it is not Nikolay Stepanovitch's conscience that dictates the sense of urgency about Katya's fate, but Katya's own need to have him finally show that concern for her and give her that positive direction which he failed to do at the appropriate time. She first approaches him, with this new openness about her predicament, in the forest:

'Nikolay Stepanovitch, I am a negative phenomenon! Yes?'

'Yes,' I answer.

'H'm! what am I to do?'

What answer was I to make her? It is easy to say 'work', or 'give your possessions to the poor', or 'know yourself', and because it is so easy to say that, I don't know what to answer.

My colleagues when they teach therapeutics advise 'the individual study of each separate case'. One has but to obey this advice to gain the conviction that the methods recommended in the textbooks as the best and as providing a safe basis for treatment turn out to be quite unsuitable in individual cases. It is just the same in moral ailments. (v.201)

In this scene both characters are comparatively calm, and Nikolay Stepanovitch's avoidance of moral cliché and his tone of conviction about 'individual cases' give further evidence of his educated humanism. Chekhov could almost himself be tendering that speech against the simple formulae of late Tolstoy. But although the old professor earns our admiration for his refusal to simplify, what he actually replies to Katya – that perhaps she might consider returning to the theatre – is pitifully misjudged and only makes her seem the more vulnerable for – as we later learn – she has no talent.

This is the first of three final encounters between Katya and Nikolay Stepanovitch, which have an almost symbolic value in marking the stages of the old man's gradual disengagement from life. They also have a terrible pathos in that each of Katya's attempts to move closer to Nikolay Stepanovitch, to derive some kind of protection from him before he dies, results in their being more estranged, stranded further apart. I think Chekhov concentrates so much on this relationship because Nikolay Stepanovitch and Katya both have a stature in their expectations of living which none of the other characters has. Their vulnerability – dissimilar as their two cases are – is qualitatively different from, and more potentially tragic than, that of Liza, of Pyotr Ignatyevitch or even of the touching Mihail Fyodorovitch who so obviously loves Katya. But the fact that Chekhov does recognize the quite different kinds of vulnerability and loneliness felt by these other characters ensures a balance in his representation of Nikolay Stepanovitch's predicament, a balance which Tolstoy does not achieve in 'Ivan Ilych'.

At this point I want to include an unusually long quotation from a passage which I consider to be extraordinarily good:

There are terrible nights with thunder, lightning, rain, and wind, such as are called among the people 'sparrow nights.' There has been one such night in my personal life...

I woke up after midnight and leaped suddenly out of bed. It seemed to me for some reason that I was just immediately going to die. Why did it seem so? I had no sensation in my body that suggested my immediate death, but my soul was oppressed with terror, as though I had suddenly seen a vast menacing glow of fire.

I rapidly struck a light, drank some water straight out of the decanter, then hurried to the open window. The weather outside was magnificent. There was a smell of hay and some other very sweet scent. I could see the spikes of the fence, the gaunt, drowsy trees by the window, the road, the dark streak of woodland; there was a serene, very bright moon in the sky and not a single cloud, perfect stillness, not one leaf stirring. I felt that everything was looking at me and waiting for me to die...

It was uncanny. I closed the window and ran to my bed. I felt for my pulse, and not finding it in my wrist, tried to find it in my temple, then in my chin, and again in my wrist, and everything I touched was cold and clammy with sweat. My breathing came more and more rapidly, my body was shivering, all my inside was in commotion; I had a sensation on my face and on my bald head as though they were covered with spiders' webs.

What should I do? Call my family? No; it would be no use. I could not imagine what my wife and Liza would do when they came in to me.

I hid my head under the pillow, closed my eyes, and waited and waited ...My spine was cold; it seemed to be drawn inwards, and I felt as though death were coming upon me stealthily from behind...

'Kee-vee! kee-vee!' I heard a sudden shriek in the night's stillness, and did not know where it was – in my breast or in the street. 'Kee-vee! kee-vee!'

'My God, how terrible!' I would have drunk some more water, but by then it was fearful to open my eyes and I was afraid to raise my head. I was possessed by unaccountable animal terror, and I cannot understand why I was so frightened: was it that I wanted to live, or that some new unknown pain was in store for me?

Upstairs, overhead, someone moaned or laughed...I listened. Soon afterwards there was a sound of footsteps on the stairs. Someone came hurriedly down, then went up again. A minute later there was a sound of steps downstairs again; someone stopped near my door and listened.

'Who is there?' I cried.

The door opened. I boldly opened my eyes, and saw my wife. Her face was pale and her eyes were tear-stained.

'You are not asleep, Nikolay Stepanovitch?' she asked.

'What is it?'

'For God's sake, go up and have a look at Liza; there is something the matter with her...' (v.204–6)

This is the opening of Part V, where the dramatized process of Nikolay Stepanovitch's collapse from his previous demeanour and values stabilizes into this poetically created state of heightened and fearful intuition of death. With it the whole world of the story perceptibly darkens and becomes emotionally more volatile, and the factual world and the world of the psyche seem virtually identified. The scene will of course remind us again of Natasha by the window in *War and Peace* and that strange intensity of night experience which Tolstoy created and by which Chekhov was so compelled. There is stillness, blackness and yet almost preternaturally intense moonlight (as in the scenes which I discussed in chapter 6), with such details as the 'smell of hay' assuring us that this night takes place in nature, though it does seem a night of supernatural portent. Here it evokes strong romantic associations of symbolic death, which is reinforced by the bird-cry 'Kee-vee! kee-vee!' – Chekhov's distinctive contribution to such nightscapes which in Tolstoy are usually strangely hushed. There is also a Tolstoyan concentration of attention upon the physical sensations of the dying man, the physical manifestations of his panic as he feverishly feels for his pulse and finds his body 'cold and clammy with sweat' and his strange but vivid sensation of feeling his spine drawn inwards. But just as the maximum power coalesces around the image of Nikolay Stepanovitch lying with his eyes shut, waiting to see if death will come, Chekhov turns the waiting to listening: and thus it is *through* Nikolay Stepanovitch that our attention is concentrated on another situation as well as his own. As in the scene in *War and Peace*, much depends upon the sense of there being an upper and a lower floor, with people having their consciousness of themselves intruded upon by lives going on above. Tolstoy has the simpler effect of Andrey listening throughout Natasha's sleepless exclamations, whereas Chekhov (as usual) manages his effects through an instinctively appropriate timing. Nikolay Stepanovitch is totally alone throughout his panic, and the rest of the house seems to be asleep. Only at the point where his fear is liable to subside into anticlimax, since death has not come, is he made to hear the moan or laughter (he is not sure which it is) above and then to begin consciously listening to the footsteps up and down the stairs. The moan and then the hurried footsteps seem both a confirmation of his own feelings – almost as if the footsteps were coming to him – and a distraction from them. And when Varya comes in and says 'For God's sake, go up and have a look at Liza; there is something the matter with her', there is a strange compounding of one character's experience with that of another. Nikolay Stepanovitch, who has seemed about to die, becomes the centre of appeal for other people who are intuitively drawn to him in their distress. The comfort he can give is the closeness of sympathy made possible by a common suffering:

'Liza, my child,' I said, 'what is it?'

Seeing me, she began crying out, and flung herself on my neck.

'My kind papa!...' she sobbed – 'my dear, good, papa...my darling, my pet, I don't know what is the matter with me...I am miserable!'

She hugged me, kissed me, and babbled fond words I used to hear from her when she was a child.

'Calm yourself, my child. God be with you,' I said. 'There is no need to cry. I am miserable, too.' (v.207)

In this moment of distress we feel most poignantly – and for the first and last time, explicitly, in the story – what a family is. It is a flickering assertion of what Nikolay Stepanovitch has already partly lost and stands to lose altogether in death. The same is true of the encounter with Katya which follows, where Katya herself first appears as a symbolical figure of death:

There was a deathlike stillness, such a stillness, as some author has expressed it, 'it rang in one's ears'. Time passed slowly; the streaks of moonlight on the window-sill did not shift their position, but seemed as though frozen...It was still some time before dawn.

But the gate in the fence creaked, someone stole in and, breaking a twig from one of those scraggy trees, cautiously tapped on the window with it.

'Nikolay Stepanovitch,' I heard a whisper. 'Nikolay Stepanovitch.'

I opened the window, and fancied I was dreaming: under the window, huddled against the wall, stood a woman in a black dress, with the moonlight bright upon her, looking at me with great eyes. Her face was pale, stern, and weird-looking in the moonlight, like marble, her chin was quivering.

'It is I,' she said – 'I...Katya.' (v.208–9)

The pale, stern face like marble and the black dress make Katya seem an emanation out of the landscape, and her summons feels like the summons of death. But again instead of death there is a call for comfort from Nikolay Stepanovitch ('I couldn't stand it, so came here'); and, in Katya's offer of her money, there is a last assertion of all that he has meant to her as a father. So Part V, with its intensified and volatile atmosphere, while giving a sustained premonition of Nikolay Stepanovitch's death also indirectly asserts what he has still to lose in losing life.

However, it is important to notice that Nikolay Stepanovitch is actually helpless in those scenes and really helps neither the pregnant Liza nor Katya. This, indeed, is one of the faults of this section: its highly romantic conception may temporarily relieve our impression of the professor's diminished energies, his more physically based sense of desperation and his nervous irritability. For the sake of the potency of the composite scene, the delivery here is slowed, the prose voice restrained and oddly quiet in tone. We have lost the dramatic disclosure of Nikolay Stepanovitch's breakdown which was previously felt in sudden shrillnesses and inconsistencies in the narrative. Furthermore, the eerie beauty of the scene and even of Katya's sombre figure, the formal symmetry of first one summons to Nikolay Stepanovitch and then another, and Katya's romantic gesture, tapping on the window with a twig, all make this a highly romanticized foreboding of death which makes death seem somehow attractive. But at Harkov, in Part VI, this imbalance is redressed by the sobering realism of the image of Nikolay Stepanovitch sitting apathetically in a cheap hotel room by a tin wash-stand and whirring clock, no longer even perplexed about where he is or how he will fill in the hours. As Logan Speirs says, 'This rail journey has transported him out of life, and the end is to be very soon.'[6] He is no more wretchedly ill, physically, than he has apparently been all along; but his detachment from life is now such that he greets even Katya with a shrug and asks 'What have you come for?' (v.217). Chekhov is an acute psychologist.

It is at Harkov, then, that Nikolay Stepanovitch is really a broken man, and it is important that it is there – and not earlier – that Chekhov has him make his often-quoted speech:

And now I examine myself: what do I want?

I want our wives, our children, our friends, our pupils, to love in us, not our fame, not the brand and not the label, but to love us as ordinary men. Anything else? I should like to have had helpers and successors. Anything else? I should like to wake up in a hundred years' time and to have just a peep out of one eye at what is happening in science. I should have liked to have lived another ten years... What further? Why, nothing further. I think and think, and can think of nothing more. And however much I might think, and however far my thoughts might travel, it is clear to me that there is nothing vital, nothing of great importance in my desires. In my passion for science, in my desire to live, in this sitting on a strange bed, and in this striving to know myself – in all the thoughts, feelings, and ideas I form about everything, there is no common bond to connect it all into one whole. Every feeling and every thought exists apart in me: and in all my criticisms of science, the theatre, literature, my pupils, and in all the pictures my imagination draws, even the most skilful analyst could not find what is called a general idea, or the god of a living man.

And if there is not that, then there is nothing. (v.214–15)

This speech is followed by the statement 'I am vanquished' and then by the final interview with Katya, when she coldly turns her back on Nikolay Stepanovitch because he cannot give her a formula – 'one word' – to save her life. Consequently, there has been a tendency for readers to regard this as Nikolay Stepanovitch's realization of the great lack in his life (a self-realization in Tolstoyan terms), through which, implicitly, Chekhov is expounding the need for such an 'idea'. But in the light of all that has preceded it, it is surely much more likely that this is the dramatic moment in which the old professor feels the collapse of faith in his own principles and opinions which has been subtly enacted throughout the narrative. It is the point at which he formulates to himself the erosion of his wholeness of personality by old age. But, though old age has in one way reduced him to this sense of collapse, again the narrative tells us more than he himself does. He fails to comfort either Katya or himself, but a part of that failure derives from his appreciation, enduring to the end, that life simply cannot be incapsulated in formulae. And when he asks himself what he wants, the answers movingly declare some remnant of his old humanism, which he is not aware that he still has: love of people as people, continuity in his life's work, the progress of science and, finally, life for life's sake.

Nikolay Stepanovitch is basically a good and civilized man, but his best qualities are more and more tenuous in his personality as he nears death. In this respect the story is 'dreary', as its title suggests. But it would be misleading to think of the work as negative or pessimistic in any final sense. Nikolay Stepanovitch's basic goodness does seem to survive as far as his death (his last word is for Katya – 'Farewell, my treasure!'); and there is a great deal of evidence in the story of broadly humanist values held by Chekhov himself. Indeed, the whole impulse of the work is to assert those values, to feel saddened by their loss when they are lost, but – in their name – to be objective about their fate in old age and to extend to old age itself an appropriate sympathy. Death is 'what no man knoweth'. As such, it must provide great authors like Chekhov and Tolstoy with a challenge which lesser authors might be loath to take. But to Tolstoy, the powerful commandment to be learnt from death was 'Know thyself'; whereas to Chekhov's more complex understanding, at this stage in the two authors' careers, the most tragic fact about death was exactly that it could never truly be prepared for by any man. Nikolay Stepanovitch's self-examination yields only one unequivocal truth:

'Know thyself' is excellent and useful advice; it is only a pity that the ancients never thought to indicate the means of following this precept. (v.214)

9

'The Duel'

> But life is never a material, a substance to be moulded. If you
> want to know, life is the principle of self-renewal, it is constantly
> renewing and remaking and changing and transfiguring itself,
> it is infinitely beyond your or my inept theories about it.
>
> (Boris Pasternak, *Doctor Zhivago*, chapter 10 (London: Collins, 1958),
> p. 373).

The second great work to emerge from Chekhov's highly complex reaction to Tolstoy is 'The Duel' (1891). In his letters
Chekhov calls it a 'novel', and it is indeed one of the most
novelistic of his works. To begin with, it has, for a novella, an
unusually wide range of fully developed characters. Apart from
Von Koren and Laevsky, there are three other characters –
Nadyezhda, the deacon and Samoylenko – who are created in
some psychological depth, and there are a number of minor
figures as well. The interaction of these characters is also
unusually volatile: their temperaments and their particular
situations interact to cause decisive changes in one another's
lives, although at all times throughout the story we are made to
feel the unpredictability of the result. Finally, the very motion
of the narrative in 'The Duel' might be described as novelistic,
since its situations develop in a fluid way, not returning upon
themselves as they tend to do in the more static settings of the
early stories, including even 'Easter Eve' and 'Lights'. Chekhov
now seems to be letting his understanding move through a range
of situations and characters with a sense of confidence that an
order in his art will spontaneously emerge. I do not mean that
the development is not (in one way) planned: the basic conception
of the duel itself ensures that Chekhov will have a firm line of
conflict to develop and resolve, between Von Koren and Laevsky.
But as if in reaction to that highly programmed quality increasingly evident in Tolstoy's work, whereby both 'The Death of Ivan
Ilych' and 'The Kreutzer Sonata' begin with an outcome and

move backward through a rigid line of causes, Chekhov seems more and more impelled to immerse himself in his materials and to direct them gently from point to point to test where they might go. In 'The Duel' he has developed a special milieu for the narrative events: the highly sensuous and yet also lethargic environment of a Black Sea port, with its leisurely sense of time, which itself seems to encourage an unusual fluidity in human relationships and events. But the unusual spirit of the story derives less from these effects of its setting than from the new sense of freedom and confidence, and a cautious optimism about life, which have now entered Chekhov's work. Of course, the conditions in the story are special, and no general deductions can be made from them; but in tracing the process of Laevsky's salvation from its unlikely beginning through to the point where he adopts his 'new life' at the end, Chekhov has affirmed his faith in a crucial human possibility. He has let his art do what he envisages life as having done in Laevsky's case: put itself at the service of just a chance – almost, it seems, of a miracle – and then gently nurtured that chance until it slowly assumes a life and probability amid circumstances which seemed initially hostile to it. Moreover, in affirming this possibility of life conspiring, as it were, on its own behalf, Chekhov traces the events in Laevsky's life with such ease that the reader is readily convinced that, at least within the story's special circumstances, events could just as easily take this benevolent direction as not.

Behind at least some elements of 'The Duel' is Chekhov's reaction to Tolstoy's 'The Kreutzer Sonata'. Chekhov's letter, quoted on p. 136, says that he found 'The Kreutzer Sonata' stimulating while obviously marred by prejudice.[1] Pozdnyshev is Tolstoy's conception of a reformed man; Laevsky is Chekhov's. Pozdnyshev's reformation seems to have come about through some cathartic effect of his violence in killing his unfaithful wife. Laevsky is saved (such is Chekhov's basic faith in life) by his suddenly renewed love for Nadyezhda when he discovers her infidelity and sees in it the reflection of his own ruin, and by the experience of facing the violence of the duel from which he is rescued by the deacon's impetuous shout. Tolstoy's case seems to have interested Chekhov sufficiently for him to wish to take up similar interests in his own art, an art which inevitably modified or even transformed them. I think, for example, that the disproportionate space devoted to Nadyezhda's thoughts and feelings in 'The Duel' comes from Chekhov's concern for what was omitted from Tolstoy's account of Pozdnyshev's wife: the account of her state of mind when she reaches out from an apparently barren and even hostile relationship to some new form of romantic love. Tolstoy, at this stage, was beyond a sympathetic appreciation of individual psychologies: in 'The Death of Ivan Ilych' and 'The Kreutzer Sonata' his moral purpose is such that his characters' fates, and even their supposedly private thoughts and feelings, are ultimately less personal than exemplary. Perhaps understandably, then, Chekhov's reaction seems to have been to determine to understand his characters more warmly and individually, and to do so at least partly for understanding's sake. Nadyezhda is actually less directly instrumental in bringing about Laevsky's salvation than Von Koren or the deacon or Samoylenko – though what brings about his salvation is larger than any of them. Nadyezhda's essential passivity in the major events means that she does not earn the amount of interest Chekhov shows in her; but in the context of Chekhov's reaction to 'The Kreutzer Sonata', the careful and sustained realism with which he accounts for her reactions is explicable and probably even called for.

More generally, Nadyezhda's presence in the story and the account of her response to the 'soft waves' and the warm air show Chekhov's valuing of sensual experience, which is again in contrast to Tolstoy's withering asceticism in his artistic old age. 'The Duel' sets out, first of all, to capture the particular atmosphere of a Black Sea port in the Caucasus, with its sultry heat and anaemic palms and its changing sensual stimuli at different times of day. As evocation of a hot climate it surely equals – if it does not actually surpass – Conrad's much-praised descriptions of Sulaco in *Nostromo*. And as in *Nostromo* the portrayal of the landscape is inseparable from the definition of the author's major preoccupations, as in this description of Nadyezhda's state of feeling:

The long, insufferably hot, wearisome days, beautiful languorous evenings and stifling nights, and the whole manner of living, when from morning to night one is at a loss to fill up the useless hours, and the persistent thought that she was the prettiest young woman in the town, and that her youth was passing and being wasted, and Laevsky himself, though honest and idealistic, always the same, always lounging about in his slippers, biting his nails, and wearying her with his caprices, led by degrees to her becoming possessed by desire, and as though she were mad, she thought of nothing else day and night. Breathing, looking, walking, she felt nothing but desire. The sound of the sea told her she must love; the darkness of evening – the same; the mountains – the same...And when Kirilin began paying her attentions, she had neither the power nor the wish to resist, and surrendered to him...

Now the foreign steamers and the men in white reminded her for some reason of a huge hall; together with the shouts of French she heard the strains of a waltz, and her bosom heaved with unaccountable delight. She longed to dance and talk French. (II.42–3)

The warm, close nights and the murmur of the sea make the setting potently romantic, well suited to Chekhov's interest here in portraying sexual desire and a desire for romantic love. Similarly, the sultriness, and the pace of life so different from that in Petersburg, are associated with listlessness and possible boredom, thus intensifying the essential inertia of Laevsky's and Nadyezhda's life, which Chekhov portrays as typifying the situation of certain intellectuals in his day and of certain members of the privileged class. The long, fluid first sentence of the quotation – 'The long, insufferably hot, wearisome days, beautiful languorous evenings...' – with its leisurely syntax, is simultaneously defining a quality of the climate and the quality of Nadyezhda's life; and her desire is so intimately bound up with the special atmosphere of the landscape, the foreign steamers and the shouts of French which suggest the freedom and adventure of faraway places, that it is impossible to say which is putting a particular interpretation on which. The warm air and soft waves ensure that bodily sensations have an unusual force, but it is the psychology of her general relationship with Laevsky which directs her desire towards Kirilin and the imagined men at the ball. So although the story as a whole is critical of such a romantic conception of love – we remember Samoylenko's speech to Laevsky about the great thing in marriage being patience and duty, and the quite unromantic final image of Laevsky's and Nadyezhda's renewed love – this definition of Nadyezhda's state of mind has a certain warmth of understanding.

This drawing-out of qualities inherent in the characters' personal lives by setting them in an environment which intensifies them is an essential part of the story's method – except that with Laevsky himself the understanding is initially much less willing. In his case, the atmosphere of the resort intensifies our sense of

his idleness and lack of energy or purpose, but it does not
explain his disposition even to the extent that the romantic
elements of the landscape explain Nadyezhda's. He has left
Petersburg in the hope of a better life in the South, and now he
wishes to leave the South for a better life in Petersburg. In fact,
he is suffering from an acute form of that spiritual malaise, so
common in the characters of the later drama, which expresses
itself as alienation from one's immediate environment. In that
sense there is little real interaction between Laevsky's feelings and
the created setting, except that his physical reaction to the heat
gives some credibility to Chekhov's physical portrait of him,
which otherwise might seem too contrived. His perspiring face
and the signs of his insomnia of course help to define his
psychological state:

Laevsky grew pensive. Looking at his stooping figure, at his eyes fixed
dreamily on one spot, at his pale, perspiring face and sunken temples,
at his bitten nails, at the slipper which had dropped off his heel,
displaying a badly darned sock, Samoylenko was moved to pity. (II.11)

As the images somewhat single-mindedly suggest, Laevsky is
caught in a self-perpetuating lethargy, the physical and mental
conditions of which are at most reinforced by the sultriness of
the environment. Frequently, in fact, the climate, with the sticky
closeness of the heat, acts simply as a correlative for his debilitating self-absorption: never does it actually elicit an imaginative
response from him. His relation to it is entirely negative, while
against it his imagination asserts a counter-image of the cold
North:

Hurrah for freedom! One station after another would flash by, the air
would keep growing colder and keener, then the birches and the fir-trees,
then Kursk, Moscow... In the restaurants cabbage soup, mutton with
kasha, sturgeon, beer, no more Asiaticism, but Russia, real Russia. The
passengers in the train would talk about trade, new singers, the Franco-
Russian *entente*; on all sides there would be the feeling of keen, cultured,
intellectual, eager life... Hasten on, on! At last Nevsky Prospect, and
Great Morskaya Street, and then Kovensky Place, where he used to live
at one time when he was a student, the dear grey sky, the drizzling rain,
the drenched cabmen... (II.17–18)

But while Chekhov himself obviously has a feeling for the North
and a patriotic love of the emblems of the national life, the
implication here is directly critical, in a way that the description

of Nadyezhda's response to the waves, the warm air and the snatches of French from the men in white on the foreign steamer is not. Here the environment is obviously idealized and (despite the particularity of some of the detail) has something of the quality of an intellectual construct, rather than of an actual place. Furthermore, if the lives in this story are to have a positive outcome (the story progressively makes us feel), the attraction of that landscape in Laevsky's mind must be gradually negated by positive forces – forces he initially resists and resents – which are unique to his particular environment in the South.

'The Duel', then, anticipates *Three Sisters* in imaging Laevsky's escapism in geographical terms – first his flight to the South and then his wanting nothing but to return to the pure life in Petersburg. Laevsky himself is also a type of the 'superfluous man' whom Chekhov had portrayed in *Ivanov* and whom many writers see as the dominant type, though in more subtle form, in the late plays. It is true that in this story one can feel, in embryo, some of the basic conceptual elements of those plays. But, as I have said, the development of character in 'The Duel' is essentially novelistic; and, in contrast to the situations of the characters in *Ivanov* or the later *Three Sisters*, the closing-in of the immediate environment around Laevsky is in fact what saves him. Laevsky, like Ivanov, is conceived quite deliberately as a 'type'. He might even be a stereotype, were it not for the fact that he *knows* that the part he is acting is stereotyped and uses even that knowledge to rationalize and confirm what he is and does. He does not merely evade but continuously rationalizes his evasion of the difficulties and responsibilities of living a different kind of life. For example:

'I know very well you can't help me,' he said. 'But I tell you, because unsuccessful and superfluous people like me find their salvation in talking. I have to generalize about everything I do. I'm bound to look for an explanation and justification of my absurd existence in somebody else's theories, in literary types – in the idea that we, upper-class Russians, are degenerating, for instance, and so on. Last night, for example, I comforted myself by thinking all the time: "Ah, how true Tolstoy is, how mercilessly true!" And that did me good. Yes, really, brother, he is a great writer, say what you like!' (II.6)

The supposed self-analysis here simply lets us know the characteristics of the type we are dealing with, confirming them in the act of enumerating them. Laevsky's explanation of why he is talking quite shamelessly of his private life to Samoylenko is an excuse for going on doing so; and just as he reaches the telling near-sarcasm of his recounted reaction to Tolstoy – where the analysis might really begin to take effect – he instinctively retreats into direct praise of Tolstoy, presumably for so 'mercilessly' capturing his type. Such literature 'justifies' his existence by making him feel that such types as he are fated to be, that his symptoms are those of the age, and therefore that there is no point in trying to rectify them.

It is clear, then, that Laevsky can be of no real help to himself. His efforts at self-analysis ('knowing himself') come to nothing until the night before the duel, because until then he analyses only what he can afford to analyse – past, not present, self-deceptions:

'My God!' sighed Laevsky; 'how distorted we all are by civilization! I fell in love with a married woman and she with me...To begin with, we had kisses, and calm evenings, and vows, and Spencer, and ideals, and interests in common...What a deception! We really ran away from her husband, but we lied to ourselves and made out that we ran away from the emptiness of the life of the educated class...Alien people, an alien country, a wretched form of civilization – all that is not so easy, brother, as walking on the Nevsky Prospect in one's fur coat, arm-in-arm with Nadyezhda Fyodorovna, dreaming of the sunny South. What is needed here is a life and death struggle, and I'm not a fighting man. A wretched neurasthenic, an idle gentleman...From the first day I knew that my dreams of a life of labour and of a vineyard were worthless.' (II.7–8)

Apart from the obvious point that Laevsky is now really running away from Nadyezhda and not from the collapse of his ideal, there is the self-deception and futility of his running anywhere if he cannot escape himself. And escaping himself would mean escaping that facile and debilitating conception of himself as 'a wretched neurasthenic, an idle gentleman' which allows him to remain so purposeless and irresponsible and thus gradually to slip into a mire of laziness and deceit. For there are signs that Laevsky actually could be better than he is, that unconsciously his indolence and irresponsibility are a strain even to him. Not only is he self-critical within limits (though the limits, as we have seen, are severe), but his nerves seem to be continually frayed – and not, as he thinks, from the frustration of his attempts to get away, but actually from inner self-dissatisfaction and half-recognized feelings of guilt. This exacerbation of Laevsky's nervous state culminates in his fit of hysterics and then, more overtly, in his fit of temper at Samoylenko's, which leads to the challenge and the duel. In both scenes it is the shame of feeling his moral shabbiness exposed that motivates the nervous reaction, rather than any simple feeling that he is physically trapped into remaining with Nadyezhda. In any case, his dissatisfaction with Nadyezhda is really also dissatisfaction with himself – which is one of the reasons why she can do nothing to bring about the needed change in him. Now and then in the relationship between Nadyezhda and Laevsky Chekhov makes us feel parallels with Anna and Karenin; he cannot resist such Tolstoyan effects as Laevsky's irritation at the carefully arranged curls on the back of Nadyezhda's neck and at the angle of her head when she reads. But the emotional situation which Chekhov develops between them is actually a further and possibly even stronger development out of that intense Tolstoyan realism. For one of the important insights of the story concerns the way Chekhov has Laevsky's developing self-hatred express itself as an aversion to the woman who shares his mode of life. Disliking himself, Laevsky feels irrationally annoyed that Nadyezhda continues to accept him, and his aggression is thus directed against what is specifically sexual about her – that is, specifically feminine things like her curl-papers, her powders and medicines, and the fevers she suffers because of her 'female complaint'. The effect is to make us newly aware of the irrational (but, in retrospect, fairly common?) process by which personal dissatisfaction and self-dislike may express themselves as aversion to one who is sexually close, and aversion specifically to the small indicators of his or her different sex.

How, then, is such a man as Laevsky to be redeemed? In considering this, 'The Duel' becomes directly involved with differing theories of morality – particularly the Christian as against the Darwinian conceptions of the appropriate relationship between strong and weak. So as well as the basic temperamental opposition between Laevsky and Von Koren, the puritanical zoologist (an opposition which can at times seem over-schematic), there is a wider philosophical dispute embodied in the story, between the Christian and scientific theories. Significantly, the theories are not in pure form: they are shown as particular characters hold them and are therefore complicated by factors of temperament. Chekhov is not arbitrating between the two

views but testing their viability in terms of the kinds of temperaments they attract and the kinds of behaviour to which they may
give rise. This is so even during the open argument between Von
Koren and the deacon in Part 16:

'The moral law, let us suppose, demands that you love your neighbour.
Well? Love ought to show itself in the removal of everything which in
one way or another is injurious to men and threatens them with danger
in the present or in the future. Our knowledge and the evidence tells
us that the morally and physically abnormal are a menace to humanity.
If so you must struggle against the abnormal; if you are not able to raise
them to the normal standard, you must have strength and ability to
render them harmless – that is, to destroy them.'

'So love consists in the strong overcoming the weak.'

'Undoubtedly.'

'But you know the strong crucified our Lord Jesus Christ,' said the
deacon hotly. (II.123)

The deacon obviously is not strong in argument and expresses
his convictions only by the emotional way he reacts. Intellectually,
he relinquishes the argument to the more intelligent Von Koren
by uncritically accepting Von Koren's basic terms and definitions,
and his persuasiveness as a theoretician is not enhanced by his
infantile sense of humour which can suddenly distract him at
almost any point. Moments later Von Koren (and Chekhov too,
fleetingly) will react with a sense of comic delight to the deacon's
refusal to attend the duel because he is in a 'state of grace' – he
who so delights in calling Laevsky and Nadyezhda the 'Japanese
monkeys' and whose laughter explodes in the hall after seeing
the scene of the challenge to the duel. Von Koren, on the other
hand, speaks consistently with a callous deliberation which makes
nonsense of his supposed 'love' of the race. His acceptance of
the notion of some innate moral law, according to which some
species must be systematically destroyed, also runs directly counter to the true Darwinian conception of natural selection. In
effect, he has incorporated into Darwinian theory elements from
Spencer and Nietzsche which accord with his arrogant, puritanical and somewhat sinister temperament and with what seems
to be a natural bent for destruction. His argument thus depends
on the fallacies that physical and moral strength are synonymous
and that the process by which natural and unconscious organisms
are physically perfected is analogous to that by which human
beings might attain moral perfection. The story, in its entire

development leading up to Laevsky's reformation, exposes these fallacies; but the deacon is not sharp enough to perceive them, and at the theoretical level the argument for the destruction of Laevsky seems to carry the day.

Considering what Chekhov valued in 'The Kreutzer Sonata', he too seems to want his work to be a stimulus to thought. The fact that the theories are complicated or even altered in presentation by aspects of character does not hinder the reader's intellectual excitement in engaging with them, especially in the urgency of the story's created circumstances. In any case, they give a theoretical framework to our understanding of why some things in the narrative are as they are – for example, why Samoylenko is, apart from being delightful, of such importance. It is the novelist in Chekhov who has created Samoylenko so lovingly and in such detail as a good-natured, self-satisfied man with an inoffensive love of ceremony:

When, bulky and majestic, with a stern expression on his face, he walked along the boulevard in his snow-white tunic and superbly polished boots, squaring his chest, decorated with the Vladimir cross on a ribbon, he was very much pleased with himself, and it seemed as though the whole world were looking at him with pleasure. Without turning his head, he looked to each side and thought that the boulevard was extremely well laid out; that the young cypress-trees, the eucalyptuses, and the ugly, anaemic palm-trees were very handsome and would in time give abundant shade; that the Circassians were an honest and hospitable people.

'It's strange that Laevsky does not like the Caucasus,' he thought, 'very strange.' (II.14)

Without entering into the depths of Samoylenko's personality, Chekhov immediately creates a warmly affectionate sense of him – enhanced, if anything, by the faint touch of the ridiculous in his self-consciously dignified bearing. His self-satisfaction so generously expands into a basic good will towards the world at large that he makes a very positive contribution to the general morale of those around him and in a way to that of the reader, who finds in him a source of hope and a centre of well-being in what initially seems to be a somewhat blighted context. He also compares more than favourably with those much-celebrated, genial, middle-aged figures in Conrad. But through him Chekhov is also investigating the efficacy of practical and instinctive Christian good will in helping to redeem Laevsky, and in this respect Samoylenko is finally found wanting. His love for his neighbour is too simplistic to cope with the psychological complexities of Laevsky's situation, and he is too intimidated by Laevsky's intellectual pretensions to be appropriately stringent with him. He vastly overrates Laevsky to begin with because he cannot quite separate his sense of people's morality from his sense of their intelligence. And the reason why he cannot really *help* Laevsky is that his love is of a passive and serving kind, which has not sufficient force to combat the kind of psychological deterioration from which Laevsky is suffering.

It might seem at first a very negative thing that the most powerful force immediately evident in the story is Von Koren's hatred and unremitting self-will. In every respect Von Koren emerges as anti-sensuous and anti-life. For example, look at what happens even to the big flowers on his shirt in the opening description of him:

Von Koren was usually the first to appear. He sat down in the drawing-room in silence, and taking an album from the table, began attentively scrutinizing the faded photographs of unknown men in full trousers and top-hats, and ladies in crinolines and caps. Samoylenko only remembered a few of them by name, and of those whom he had forgotten he said with a sigh: 'A very fine fellow, remarkably intelligent!' When he had finished with the album, Von Koren took a pistol from the whatnot, and screwing up his left eye, took deliberate aim at the portrait of Prince Vorontsov, or stood still at the looking-glass and gazed a long time at his swarthy face, his big forehead, and his black hair, which curled like a negro's, and his shirt of dull-coloured cotton with big flowers on it like a Persian rug, and the broad leather belt he wore instead of a waistcoat. The contemplation of his own image seemed to afford him almost more satisfaction than looking at photographs or playing with the pistols. He was very well satisfied with his face, and his becomingly clipped beard, and the broad shoulders, which were unmistakable evidence of his excellent health and physical strength. He was satisfied, too, with his stylish get-up, from the cravat, which matched the colour of his shirt, down to his brown boots. (II.23–4)

The dull-coloured shirt with big flowers 'like a Persian rug' gives the effect of something blatant and self-assertive, yet without sensuous appeal and unassociated with liveliness or spontaneity. Moreover, the scrupulously matching cravat, broad leather belt and brown boots give his appearance a Prussian harshness which makes even his physical strength seem slightly sinister. Beyond that, the attitudes in which he is cast are highly stylized, having

both the force and the partial crudity of similar kinds of stylization in the conception of Solyony in *Three Sisters*: the strange
self-absorption in his contemplation of his own image, the fascinated playing with the pistols and the masterly effect of his silent
scrutiny of the old photographs. Such stances are the means by
which Chekhov anticipates the cruelty of both characters, in both
of whom potentially gregarious energies are tensely indrawn and
thus perverted, so that their natures seem to be turned in on
themselves, poised for some future explosion of aggression. But
Von Koren is potentially even more dangerous than Solyony,
because unlike Solyony he is convinced of his infallibility. Part
of what is disturbing in his looking at the old photographs is the
feeling that he is scrutinizing blemishes, somehow judging with
the evolution of the race in mind. And the linearity of his
posture and the deliberateness of his aim provide assurance –
necessary for the remarkable tension of the later duel scene – that
he is not an amateur with his pistols. Even his scientific research
is done, Laevsky tells us, in this spirit of defiant self-will and
personal arrogance:

'What does he want here?'
    'He is studying the marine fauna.'
    'No, no, brother, no!' Laevsky sighed. 'A scientific man who was on
the steamer told me the Black Sea was poor in animal life, and that in
its depths, thanks to the abundance of sulphuric hydrogen, organic life
was impossible. All the serious zoologists work at the biological station
at Naples or Villefranche. But Von Koren is independent and obstinate:
he works on the Black Sea because nobody else is working there; he is
at loggerheads with the university, does not care to know his comrades
and other scientific men because he is first of all a despot and only
secondly a zoologist.' (II.72)

This information comes effectively from Chekhov himself, and
we believe it easily because we have already watched Von Koren
emphasizing discipline to the deacon, subordinating people to
grandiose abstractions in the course of argument, and holding
his opinions with a dangerous self-certainty and fixity.

It is important to stress, then, that it is not Von Koren's hatred
that reforms Laevsky, either – that his hatred would actually
have killed Laevsky had the deacon not distracted him with his
horrified cry. Chekhov gives the credit of physically saving
this now-valuable life to the Christian ethic of brotherly love
represented nominally – and at last actually – by the deacon.

Von Koren's hatred is a catalyst to Laevsky's reformation – but his reformation itself is something in which every one of his acquaintances, each event, and even the physical nature of the village where he lives, all mysteriously play a co-operative part. This is where the great originality of 'The Duel' lies. For we have been used to Chekhov's realism revealing the frustration of people's lives, the cruelty of chance in operating against their hopes, the misunderstandings which rob them of one another's comfort, and so on. His portrayal of these circumstances and reactions as people pursue their separate and conflicting ends may indeed make us feel that realism and pessimism are much the same thing. But it is Chekhov's consistency to his own principles that makes him recognize in 'The Duel', and to some extent in the later 'The Lady with the Dog', that the same element of chance, the same intersection of people's conflicting personalities and needs, might work the other way around – that is, actually to give fulfilment where one would not expect it. So the unexpectedly optimistic outcome of 'The Duel' is not the result of Chekhov's suddenly abandoning his usual realism but a natural corollary of it and of his highly developed sense of life's unpredictability. 'The Duel' offers no guarantee that life will work this way even once in a thousand times; but it could do so, and to acknowledge that possibility matters quite as much as defining a general sense that life habitually does resolve itself less happily. Given all the prerequisites for a pessimistic tale – Laevsky's discontent with his mistress, her infidelity to him, and Von Koren's hatred of them both – Chekhov places his psychological perception and capacity for constructing organically inter-connected events at the service of that occasional benevolence in life itself which somehow survives through, and despite, the more general tragedy of the human condition. Life is seen acting on its own behalf, at least this once, to replenish and in a sense to perfect itself.

The first element in this psychologically significant combination of circumstances and events by which Laevsky is reformed is the very isolation and sense of claustrophobia of the village from which he wishes to escape. The town is not named in the story, and Laevsky says it is not even on the map: there is, therefore, a certain likeness to the constricting self-enclosure of the provincial estates in the plays (one remembers especially the ludicrous irrelevance of Vanya's map of Africa in his study, in

Uncle Vanya). But though this constriction is unpleasant for Laevsky, particularly since it means that he comes inexorably up against Von Koren's hatred wherever he goes, it does force him eventually to face himself and thus has a positive effect on his life. Laevsky must have none of the comforts of a big city: he cannot simply choose whom to avoid, nor seek the companionship solely of his own kind. He must feel himself to be alone; he must meet Von Koren on nearly every social occasion he attends, must share the same acquaintance and must even depend on him, indirectly, for the money he needs to get away. Only in such uncomfortable – but, as it turns out, propitious – circumstances will Von Koren's hatred, working together with Samoylenko's innocent betrayal of confidences and Nadyezhda's unfaithfulness, act as a catalyst in the reformation of Laevsky's life. The fullness with which the atmosphere of the seaport is evoked and the sense of greater Russia stretching beyond the Caucasus ensure that the environment feels convincingly real. But it is important for the optimistic outcome of the story that life in the town be virtually self-contained. Samoylenko simply must go to Von Koren to get money for Laevsky: had he anyone else to go to he might help Laevsky leave his obligations behind and so fail him in a deeper sense. Von Koren is able to taunt Laevsky at the party, to make him shame himself by his fit of hysterics and thus indirectly to prepare for the challenge to the duel, because he has special information from Samoylenko. Likewise, Laevsky is made to see the extent of his own ruin by having it objectified in the sight of Nadyezhda lying beside Kirilin, because Atchmianov knows both men and is jealous of Nadyezhda himself. All the lines of people's lives in this self-enclosed society converge unconsciously towards Laevsky's being brought to recognize, and come to terms with, his life and himself.

I have said that 'The Duel' is one of the most novelistic of Chekhov's stories. At the same time it anticipates the major drama in many respects. Chekhov's dramatic skills maximize tension through conversations that otherwise proceed with a novelistic sense of leisure and novelistic length:

Von Koren opened a box and took out a hundred-rouble note.

'The mole has a powerful thorax, just like the bat,' he went on, shutting the box; 'the bones and muscles are tremendously developed, the mouth is extraordinarily powerfully furnished. If it had the proportions of an elephant, it would be an all-destructive, invincible animal. It is interesting when two moles meet underground; they begin at once as though by agreement digging a little platform; they need the platform in order to have a battle more conveniently. When they have made it they enter upon a ferocious struggle and fight till the weaker one falls. Take the hundred roubles,' said Von Koren, dropping his voice, 'but only on condition that you're not borrowing it for Laevsky.' (II.87–8)

The concentration of feeling in the lower voice and terse utterance at the end, the significant and tense postponement of action, and the oblique (but in this case somewhat crude) reference of the monologue to the later duel, are clearly preparatory to recurrent effects in the dramatic work. But, even more importantly, the psychological sequence by which the mental duel between Von Koren and Laevsky becomes a physical one and the tightening of tension which accompanies it clearly anticipate the development (say) between Acts I and III of *Uncle Vanya* or, less directly, the subtle and completely plausible sequence of events in *Three Sisters* by which Natasha eventually takes control of the house.

After the first five parts, in which we meet each character more or less on his or her own terms, all the people in 'The Duel' are collected together at the mountain picnic. The scene of the picnic will later be the scene of the duel; and, as in the late plays, the change in the dramatic and psychological situation from one occasion to the other is felt through the changed appearance of the scene. However, in this case Chekhov seems over-interested in the directly symbolic properties of this essentially static locale. So apart from conveying a quite legitimate sense of geographical claustrophobia, as the mountains close around the people and the night closes around both, the picnic scenery reveals Chekhov trying to combine literal details and an opportunistic symbolism:

When in the rapidly falling darkness the trees began to melt into the mountains and the horses into the carriages, and a light gleamed in the windows of the *duhan*, she climbed up the mountain by the little path which zigzagged between stones and thorn-bushes and sat on a stone. Down below, the camp-fire was burning. Near the fire, with his sleeves tucked up, the deacon was moving to and fro, and his long black shadow kept describing a circle round it; he put on wood, and with a spoon tied to a long stick he stirred the cauldron. Samoylenko, with a copper-red face, was fussing round the fire just as though he were in his own kitchen, shouting furiously:

'Where's the salt, gentlemen? I bet you've forgotten it. Why are you all sitting about like lords while I do all the work?'...

On the further bank some unknown persons made their appearance near the drying-shed. The flickering light and the smoke from the camp-fire puffing in that direction made it impossible to get a full view of them all at once, but glimpses were caught now of a shaggy hat and a grey beard, now of a blue shirt, now of a figure, ragged from shoulder to knee, with a dagger across the body; then a swarthy young face with black eyebrows, as thick and bold as though they had been drawn in charcoal. (ii.56–7)

Such writing is powerfully 'atmospheric'. One feels the characters doubly displaced – from Russia, and then from their village in the Caucasus – as they are drawn into the uncannily enclosed atmosphere of the ravine, amid natural forms made partly menacing by the darkness and among people whom the firelight reveals only as flickering shapes. The familiarity preserved with those we do know – the superb management of Samoylenko's outburst, for instance – almost allows Chekhov to get away with his superfluous 'atmosphere'. But there is a problem of exactly what to make of the surreal effects of the figures on the other bank – the dagger across the body, the thick charcoal eyebrows – and indeed of the heathen overtones of the deacon's ritual round the cauldron. The effects are conspicuous as such, while their meanings are vague. From the fact that there is some incongruous joke lingering around the deacon making fish soup for the multitude, and that his dream of the time when he will be a bishop involves a hierarchically organized religious procession quite opposite from the disorder of the present scene, it can be deduced that this occasion epitomizes something more violent and elemental. On the way to the picnic the carriages have passed the junction of the Black River with the Yellow River, where 'the water black as ink stains the yellow and struggles with it' (ii.52); and we will later be given that image of Laevsky feeling the heat of the camp-fire on his back and the heat of Von Koren's hatred beating on his breast. The occasion both epitomizes and intensifies the animosity between the two men, preparing the way for their later violence. But the meeting of the Black and Yellow rivers also ambiguously suggests reconciliation, as does the Tartar *duhan* flying the Russian flag; and in that sense the imagery seems to look forward to an end to conflict and thus implicitly to some resolution of the developing confrontation between Laevsky and Von Koren. Furthermore, Chekhov is attending equally to all who are present at the scene, and for all those – like Marya Konstantinovna, Nikodim Alexandritch, Katya, Kostya, the deacon and Samoylenko – who have peace of mind, much of this suggestive 'atmosphere' feels and is irrelevant. As a whole it is an impressive episode, particularly in the definition it gives to Von Koren's aggression and Laevsky's discomfort and developing self-hatred; but its imagery is too strained and ambitious for it to rival the more specific dramatic realism of the later episode at Kostya's birthday party.

From the picnic to Kostya's party where Laevsky has his fit of hysterics to the scene at Samoylenko's house when Laevsky first abuses Samoylenko and then challenges Von Koren to the duel, Chekhov is accumulating tension both within Laevsky himself and between Laevsky and others. The outright challenge comes as a relief both to Laevsky and in the story as a whole; and the storm which follows, that night, seems both to underline that partial sense of release and to anticipate the greater release of aggression and anxiety in the duel the next day. Chekhov makes the storm brilliantly ambiguous in significance: it objectifies the turbulence in men's minds, yet it diminishes our sense of the importance of such emotional storms by its own superior display of might. It forces people apart, as they seek the refuge of their own homes; but in that it seems god-like, directing each to face himself and the implications of what is to happen at dawn:

Behind them on the sea, there was a flash of lightning, which for an instant lighted up the roofs of the houses and the mountains. The friends parted near the boulevard. When the doctor disappeared in the darkness and his steps had died away, Von Koren shouted to him:
'I only hope the weather won't interfere with us tomorrow!'
'Very likely it will! Please God it may!'
'Good-night!'
'What about the night? What do you say?'
In the roar of the wind and the sea and the crashes of thunder, it was difficult to hear.
'It's nothing,' shouted the zoologist, and hurried home. (II.129–30)

The roar of the wind interposes itself in the spaces between people, but though the storm feels mighty it does not feel malevolent. To Laevsky, alone in his study after the shock of having Nadyezhda's infidelity revealed to him, it brings a sudden new sense of life as an active agency larger than himself, and a sudden impulse to worship – 'Dear storm!' Under its impetus he under-

takes that exhaustive Tolstoyan examination of his life which I
have already discussed (p. 144). The existence of the storm, with
its impersonal drive to cleanse the world by its release of energy,
and Laevsky's self-cleansing release of all the suppressed areas
of his guilt, in a way both communicate hope. They feel too
momentous simply to go to waste in Laevsky's death at the duel
– and yet we cannot be sure. By the time the rain has stopped
Laevsky has faced fully the consequences of the life he has led,
but there is no sign of triumph either in himself or in the world
outside:

Laevsky put on his overcoat and cap, put some cigarettes in his pocket,
and stood still hesitating. He felt as though there was something else
he must do. In the street the seconds talked in low voices and the horses
snorted, and this sound in the damp, early morning, when everybody
was asleep and light was hardly dawning in the sky, filled Laevsky's soul
with a disconsolate feeling which was like a presentiment of evil.
(II.135–6)

One feels here the advantages for Chekhov of a mode of directly
interpretative commentary learnt, at least partially, from Tolstoy.
Laevsky's feelings are expounded for us and not simply left
implicit between the lines, as are Tusenbach's feelings in similar
circumstances in *Three Sisters*. Tusenbach's speech about the dead
tree swaying in the wind is a profoundly moving moment of
poetic expansion in the play and is certainly very impressive in
combining a strong apprehension of human mortality with an
impulse for worship. But the dramatic form of the episode, being
restricted to dialogue and external gesture, does not allow a full
entering into Tusenbach's state of mind, leaving us to speculate
quite what that state is and so, in a way, allowing us to have a more
accepting sense that he is fated to die. In 'The Duel', where we
have interpretative access to Laevsky's state of mind, his consciousness seems so full – of dread anticipation, guilt, memories
of the past and of his childhood – that it seems, as it seems with
Petya Rostov in *War and Peace*, that such fullness could not
suddenly die: hence the shock when Petya's consciousness does
suddenly cease. The death of Tusenbach does not carry quite that
kind of shock, because we do not know him so well. Although
there is, then, obviously a danger for an author in attempting
to give interpretative definition to such highly complex and
untypical states of mind as those before the two duels, it does
seem to me that the interpretative narrative in 'The Duel' is

potentially capable of projecting a more genuine, more unbearable pathos in the circumstances than the dramatic scene in
Three Sisters can manage through speech and gesture alone.

In comparing these two scenes, which have in common the
situation of an impending duel, with the seeming certainty of his
imminent death weighing on each man's mind, we will also be
aware once again of the importance Chekhov ascribes to love
as giving value and meaning to life. For whereas Laevsky's
despair of finding comfort from any source inside or outside
himself is suddenly relieved by his impulsive love for Nadyezhda,
and Laevsky lives, Tusenbach pleads unsuccessfully for one word
of love from Irena and dies. I think it highly probable, in fact,
that Chekhov is far more critical of Irena in that scene in *Three
Sisters* than most commentators make out. But the upsurge of love
which Laevsky feels and the self-knowledge he has achieved do
not, of course, guarantee that he will live. His immediate feeling
is still that there is no alternative but death, and he is, at least
consciously, resigned to being shot.

Yet in the greyness of this first light Chekhov begins, at first
tentatively and then more boldly, to sound a new note of hope
for Laevsky's life. It begins with Laevsky's hesitation – his feeling
that there is something left to do before he must die. He has not
quite taken leave of life, because he has not yet taken leave of
Nadyezhda; and in going to take leave of her he actually has his
hold on life intensified, first by his pity for the wretched figure
as she lies hunched up on the bed, and then by his sudden
renewal of love as she speaks of her shame. Something is working
mysteriously to preserve and redeem Laevsky, through these
perfectly plausible new reactions in new circumstances. So later,
when (after we have followed the deacon making his way in secret
up the river) Von Koren arrives exclaiming about the sudden
peculiar beauty of the dawn light, that too seems obliquely
reassuring:

'It's the first time in my life I've seen it! How glorious!' said Von Koren,
pointing to the glade and stretching out his hands to the east. 'Look:
green rays!'
   In the east behind the mountains rose two green streaks of light,
and it really was beautiful. The sun was rising. (II.143)

After the turbulence of the night of storm there is the calm of
renewal and regeneration in the natural world which seems to

prophesy a similar outcome in the human events. Yet this is far from being a facile optimism expressed through the hackneyed dawn symbolism that is part of the stock-in-trade of any writer. The strangely beautiful and sudden apparition of the shafts of light does feel like an impersonal event in nature, with the unexpectedness of such an event: it has not been anticipated by what has gone before, though it seems so in retrospect. It is characteristic of the story as a whole that the pre-conditions for this moment have been carefully laid to make it completely plausible, but there is no sense (as in Tolstoy) of effects being mapped out in the process of preparation. The direction of events always feels fluid, and only on looking back does one see the organic connection between one event and another which makes it almost inevitable that things should happen as they have done. Even the apparition of the light assumes a sure significance only after the duel has been fought without mishap, and it has to wait for its full significance until Chekhov gives us images of a reformed Laevsky at the very end of the story. At the time, Von Koren's response to the rays seems ostentatious, a way of covering nervousness and an indirect manifestation of aggression in the calm he wishes to display before Laevsky. Also, the strangely beautiful colour of the light is ambiguous in suggestion, connected somehow with a sense of imminent catharsis but removed in significance from the blinding white light of revelation. And the spectacle of the light, in Laevsky's immediate response to it, produces only an odd apathy:

Laevsky felt the exhaustion and awkwardness of a man who is soon perhaps to die, and is for that reason an object of general attention. He wanted to be killed as soon as possible or taken home. He saw the sunrise now for the first time in his life; the early morning, the green rays of light, the dampness, and the men in wet boots, seemed to him to have nothing to do with his life, to be superfluous and embarrassing. All this had no connection with the night he had been through, with his thoughts and his feeling of guilt, and so he would have gladly gone away without waiting for the duel. (II.143–4)

Laevsky's perception of the brightness of the natural world for the first time just when he thinks he has lost it is in essence a Tolstoyan effect, albeit one Chekhov manages again triumphantly with Tusenbach in *Three Sisters*. But Laevsky's feeling that nature's vividness is 'superfluous and embarrassing' is something quite different from what we would find in Tolstoy, an aspect of Chekhov's bleaker psychological realism. It is also impossible that Tolstoy in his late phase could have imagined a light dawning which, at least as the character himself feels it, 'had no connection with the night he had been through, with his thoughts and his feeling of guilt'.

The duel itself is the objective expression of a psychological duel which has reached a point of absolute crisis. It is the occasion of total release of aggression, tension and frustration which have had preliminary release in Laevsky's humiliating fit of hysterics at Kostya's party; and it takes place on the same site as that of the picnic, with most of the same characters assembled. There is no escaping a comparison with the construction of the late plays – where, as Chekhov himself said, his dramatic tensions still seem to want to resolve themselves in a pistol-shot. But the anticlimax of the characters' returning to their carriages, after Laevsky has deliberately missed Von Koren and the deacon has distracted Von Koren from his aim, is accompanied by a sudden relief and expansion in the writing, with the comedy of the deacon's breakfast with the Tartar Kerbalay. The trial of seeing whether a vision that is both realistic and optimistic will work is over. From the whole nature of this new episode it is clear that Chekhov knows that that possibility has been successfully realized in his art; and the sense of triumph communicates itself through the good-humoured exuberance of this comic interlude within the more generally serious framework of the story. Just temporarily, the main concerns of the achievement of human understanding and the reconciliation of differences are translated into the lighter vein of the deacon's misjudged idiom to a man who speaks perfect Russian ('Come to the *duhan*, drink tea...Me wants to eat') and their subsequent muddled discussion of their different conceptions of God. The interlude also tactfully provides a space before we turn to Laevsky again.

The images of the redeemed state itself are deliberately few. They are sufficient to make us feel that Laevsky is indeed a reformed man and to suggest the rather bleak mode of life that that reformation actually adds up to. Certainly they make nonsense of the view that Chekhov is a faint-hearted writer who could not go beyond commiseration with doomed, 'superfluous' men: Laevsky is lifted right out of that syndrome by which Chekhov is said to have been so fascinated. But it is a sign of Chekhov's primary interest in the strange *process* of Laevsky's reformation, rather than in the polemics of what constitutes a 'good life', that he does not linger too long with Laevsky and Nadyezhda in their new mode of life. After the picnic, when Laevsky is suffering from a sense of claustrophobia about Von Koren's hatred of him (and, though he does not realize it, from his own self-contempt), he passes on the way to Samoylenko's a lighted passenger ship in the harbour, with the red light of the little Customs boat going out to it. As we read of it, it seems a completely natural and unobtrusive part of the scene, and Laevsky merely envies the passengers their apparent peace of mind. But again, in retrospect, the timing of the ship's coming in is just right (this is the point at which most of the pre-conditions for the duel have been set); and it gives significance to the ship's departure, carrying Von Koren away, at the end, where there is an explicit symbolism attaching to the little boat heading out to join the steamer through the rough waves:

The boat turned briskly out of the harbour into the open sea. It vanished in the waves, but at once from a deep hollow glided up on to a high breaker, so that they could distinguish the men and even the oars. The boat moved three yards forward and was sucked two yards back.

'Write!' shouted Samoylenko; 'it's devilish weather for you to go in.'

'Yes, no one knows the real truth . . .' thought Laevsky, looking wearily at the dark, restless sea.

'It flings the boat back,' he thought; 'she makes two steps forward and one step back; but the boatmen are stubborn, they work the oars unceasingly, and are not afraid of the high waves. The boat goes on and on. Now she is out of sight, but in half an hour the boatmen will see the steamer lights distinctly, and within an hour they will be by the steamer ladder. So it is in life . . . In the search for truth man makes two steps forward and one step back. Suffering, mistakes, and weariness of life thrust them back, but the thirst for truth and stubborn will drive them on and on. And who knows? Perhaps they will reach the real truth at last.'

'Go-o-od-by-e,' shouted Samoylenko.

'There's no sight or sound of them,' said the deacon. 'Good luck on the journey!'

It began to spot with rain. (II.161)

This is more open symbolism than most English writers would risk, a more open exposition of Laevsky's feelings which here seem to bear the burden of Chekhov's feelings also. The story as a whole has worked to ensure that the imagery of the boat's

struggle does not feel trite, that the journey metaphor has appropriate weight, and that the cautiously tendered optimism about
the boat's reaching the steamer has been dramatically substantiated in the events of Laevsky's life. What exactly it is within the
events of 'The Duel' and the accumulation of tension between
Laevsky and Von Koren that is redemptive is never actually said;
and the partial mystery of such processes, and the sense that
redemption itself is not so much a state as a continuing process,
lie behind Laevsky's repetition of the words 'no one knows the
real truth'. But by the very nature of its organization the story
is optimistic in implying that life can in some cases be self-
redeeming – even if the redemption is never quite final – and
that it will be so regardless of the various theories of perfectibility
advanced by both religion and science.

A note on 'Three Years'

'The Duel', as I have already suggested, is one of the most
important of all Chekhov's works in alerting us to the true nature
of Chekhovian realism. It also helps explain the new mellowness
which began to enter Chekhov's work at about this time, a
peculiar confidence in life itself which persists through all his
compassionate portrayal of the troubles and disappointments of
people's lives. Chekhov's realism is neither a strict naturalism
about detail nor a working towards conventionally probable
results in the narrative events, but rather a respect accorded the
active, shaping power of reality itself. That is, at its deepest level,
Chekhov's realism is a reflection of the fact that no choice in life
is positively final and no situation absolutely fixed. He recognizes
that reality is always re-constituting itself in and around people's
lives and that, as long as this is so, there must always be a chance
of unanticipated happiness or unexpected salvation, just as
tragedies may always suddenly arise. And he sees this ultimate
unpredictability of life, on the positive side, as making always for
a kind of freedom beyond what people seem to have determined
for their lives, happily or unhappily, by conscious choice.

In 'The Duel', where this sense of life is first explored in
Chekhov's work, Laevsky's situation is unusually critical: he must
either be saved or be prepared to die. Moreover, in that story
the whole question of life's own power to change people is seen
in moral terms, centring on the process of Laevsky's reformation.

Chekhov is expressing, in the face of more rigid sets of beliefs about human nature, a tentative optimism about people's capacities for positive moral change. But these unpredictable changes in people's lives may take a number of forms, quite outside the dominantly moral terms in which they are represented in 'The Duel'. So the next step in Chekhov's exploration of this fluidity and unpredictability of reality was almost inevitably to examine the more ordinary and apparently less momentous changes accomplished in more average lives simply through the process of time. And it is this which he has done in the more fully naturalistic and longer narrative called, simply, 'Three Years'.

In *Tolstoy and Chekhov*, Logan Speirs gives an account of 'Three Years' under the heading 'Chekhov as novelist'.[2] It is true that 'Three Years' (published in 1895) was apparently begun as a novel, and it gives probably the best sense of what a mature Chekhovian novel would have been like. Certainly, it would not have been at all like the classic novels of the last century with which we are familiar, since, unlike most of the great nineteenth-century novelists, Chekhov is sceptical of – and in 'Three Years' actively questions – the apparent decisiveness of particular moments of choice. In 'Three Years' the characters' feelings that they are making fixed choices 'for life' are set against the reality of what actually becomes of their lives in even the relatively short space of three years. For, as I have suggested, time for Chekhov is not merely a passive medium through which the consequences of human choices and actions are gradually unfolded (as it tends to be for (say) George Eliot): it is an active force in bringing new friendships, new feelings, new realities into people's lives, to the point where it is hard to perceive the causal relationship between 'choices' and 'consequences' and therefore more than usually difficult to evaluate them. Both Laptev and Yulia, when they embark on their loveless marriage, feel that they are forfeiting forever the romantic hopes which both have held for their lives. On the morning after their marriage both are painfully aware of their 'mistake'. Yet was it or wasn't it a mistake? In the course of a mere three years Yulia grows to love Laptev as he could never have dared hope, and her own life is immeasurably enriched by the life she leads in Moscow, by the people she meets and finally of course by her love. On the other hand, three years have also seen the death of Yulia's baby, and – such is Chekhov's sense of life's peculiar irony – those years have gradually lost Yulia

Laptev's love. Laptev, at the end of three years, no longer values the fulfilment of what was once his dearest wish; while Yulia, so much more attractive now in her new womanliness, must suffer the cruelty of knowing herself to be the person whose love is unreturned. Also, although Yulia herself has been changed and enriched by her Moscow life, these sadder aspects of her private world are already beginning to make her retreat from society and all its benefits. Such are the changes in Yulia's and Laptev's lives over three years: it is difficult to decide, on balance, whether either has gained or lost by the decisions they have made, especially as their lives – even at the end of the story – are, of course, still incomplete. But one thing is sure: that life, in the event, is and will be a hundred times more complex, variable and indeterminate in shape than it seemed to either Yulia or Laptev when they made their choice to marry and then repented of their 'mistake'.

Much of the specific social detail in 'Three Years' derives from Chekhov's own boyhood experience and his knowledge of Gavrilov's warehouse where his cousin Misha, and later his own father, worked. There is a great deal of power in his descriptions of conditions in the warehouse and of the psychology of the merchants and clerks dictated by those conditions. But this kind of social realism in the story is only the context for Chekhov's larger and in some ways more impersonal interest in the freedoms (or in the lack of freedom) which characters think they have, as against those which they actually have. This is one of the reasons why we are continually invited to compare Laptev with his brother Fyodor. Laptev and Fyodor have had the same upbringing; they have been to the university together, and there both met Yartsev. Yet Fyodor is the older of the two and temperamentally the less flexible. He is less able to avail himself of the chances which come to him, yet apparently also incapable of facing the reality of his own lack of status and of the lying and cheating going on all around him in the warehouse. Fyodor's only escape is into madness. Laptev, therefore, is a much more fortunate and freer man than he thinks. Although he is inhibited from enjoying a truly fulfilled life by his limited assumptions about himself, he is psychologically emancipated from his family to a considerable degree, and all sorts of opportunities are given him by his wealth, by his chance acquaintance with Yartsev and so with Polina, and by his marriage with Yulia. Reality – though

Laptev only begins to glimpse the fact at the very end – is often mysterious and always fluid.

The story is careful to make us realize that life is not working actively *for* Laptev, that the chances he is given are, in the deepest sense, impersonal. One notices the stress which Chekhov puts on the impenetrable, intractable nature of the physical world around the characters, where, despite all the changes that have taken place, the cherry-tree continues to blossom as it did when Laptev was a child, where the dark is so dark coming back from Sokolniki that Yartsev and Kostya almost lose their way, and where the sun glistening on the train windows in the distance is blinding to the eyes. In fact, one of the great strengths of 'Three Years' is in capturing the sheer objectivity of objects and yet the intense (and sympathetically conveyed) subjectivity with which people react to them. It is high summer when Laptev goes to be near his sister Nina in the provincial town. Chekhov carefully documents the heat, the scent of hay, the blustery wind and the holiday atmosphere. The summer is simply true to its nature. But to Laptev, away from Moscow and the familiarity of his mistress Polina, this summer atmosphere with its scent of lime-trees, smothered laughter and distant music is a form of prompting to the romantic love he begins to feel for Yulia. Likewise, Yulia's changing her mind about Laptev's offer is conditioned by the storm which happens to break out that night, the creaking of the house around her which emphasizes to her her own isolation and loneliness. These are impersonal events, but they have personal psychological significance to the characters. Thus they strangely impel the characters into particular decisions and unusual forms of behaviour which puzzle even themselves. Both Laptev and Yulia ask themselves in a hurt, bewildered way, of their marriage 'why this had happened'. Yet this partial mystery of the way things come about is revealed in a number of positive forms during the three recorded years of Yulia's and Laptev's married life. The love which Yulia comes to feel for Laptev is perhaps the most important instance of it: but some of the others are the unexpectedly easy way in which Yulia is accepted by Laptev's family, Polina's unanticipated relinquishing of her claims on Laptev, and Polina's giving and finding comfort and security with Yartsev. Life's accidents are often cruel: Laptev's sister dies, his father grows old and blind and his brother goes mad. These things seem designed to trap Laptev into the 'grey half-life', as he calls it, of being the new warehouse manager. But that very principle of chance also gives Laptev friends like Yartsev and Polina, who enrich his life and teach him important things; and it gives him Yulia and, ultimately, the love he once so desired. This is what Chekhov – rather too abruptly, and therefore not altogether convincingly – has Laptev himself begin to see when, after hearing at last (but with relative indifference) that his wife loves him, he ponders the changes that have taken place in three years:

'And what changes in these three years...But one may have to live another thirteen years, another thirty years...What is there in store for us in the future? If we live, we shall see.' (I.311)

This is less optimistic, in context, than Laevsky's 'no one knows the real truth' in 'The Duel', but it faces life with the same – at least semi-optimistic – conviction about its unpredictability. Though there are more stoical tones in Laptev's voice than in Laevsky's ('But one may have to live another thirteen years, another thirty years...'), this has partly to do with Laptev's misunderstanding of himself and of the potentialities of his life. Laptev thinks in stereotypes: when he has to take over the family business he is sure that he is destined to become a 'complete slave', just as when he loses his romantic feelings for Yulia he decides to have no further thoughts of happiness at all. The closing sections of the story are imbued with Chekhov's regret at the spectacle of a man so stubbornly blind to the things which life is actually holding out to him, so tragically resolved to be imprisoned in the conditions he has largely defined for himself. But even Laptev, having said '*If* we live...' (my italics) must later say instead '*Let us* live...and we shall see.'

It will be clear that, although this vision of reality entails a very active awareness of the changes time brings about, it can be pursued only through very small spans of time. It is too chaotic to assume anything like the shape of a history. Logan Speirs has compared this relatively limited sense in Chekhov's work of no more than the immediate pasts and immediate futures of his characters' lives with Tolstoy's much wider sense of the historical and ancestral past.[3] As he says, Tolstoy has a sense of history, and he perceives his characters' lives as unities: he can 'shape great masses'. For Chekhov, reality is too uncertain. So, in place of Tolstoy's massive pursuit of the themes of war and peace through a span of historical (re-created as novelistic) time, Chekhov the novelist simply takes a unit of time – three years – and tries to reproduce the abundance and unexpectedness of experience *per se* that it might be likely to contain. This may explain why Chekhov never wrote a work of what we would usually consider the length or scope of a novel. Lacking a specific vision in the Tolstoyan sense, seeing life as constantly producing new situations and opportunities even before the consequences of previous ones are fully realized, he has no ready sense of order in which to hold 'great masses'. His fidelity to his own sense of realism precluded him from ever having a Tolstoyan grandeur and sweep. He has, as Speirs says, an uncertain voice. But his intelligent uncertainty about what reality is like is also one of the marks of his modernity. It gave us some of his most remarkable novellas – and it deprived us of the Chekhovian novel.

Part V

Lenotchka liked dukes and counts in novels, not ordinary persons. She loved the chapters in which there is love, pure and ideal, not sensual. Descriptions of nature she did not like. She preferred conversations to descriptions. While reading the beginning she would glance impatiently at the end. She did not know the names of authors. She wrote with a pencil in the margins: 'Wonderful!' 'Beautiful!' or 'Serve him right!' Lenotchka sang without opening her mouth.

(Notebooks 1892–1904)

Chekhov's women

As early as 1883, when Chekhov was still a student of medicine at Moscow University, he wrote a letter to his brother Alexander in which he proposed that they work jointly on a 'scientific' thesis to be known as 'The History of Sex Authority':

Do you want to occupy yourself with science? I am now working and shall work in the future over a little problem: the Woman problem. First of all, do not laugh. I put the question on the naturalistic basis, and thus arrive at 'The History of Sex Authority.' (Prestige, Superiority.) Turning to natural history you will see oscillations of this authority.[1]

Not unpredictably, given the rather adolescent solemnity of the proposal, this project as such was never undertaken. But it is evidence of Chekhov's very early and serious interest in the subject of women, in their domination by men and in something primitive, as he saw it, in their psychological impulses which both fascinated and frightened him as being alien to the psychological life of men. This interest can probably be traced to that same empirical and humanistic emphasis in Chekhov's thinking to which I have pointed throughout this book: a concern with the facts about human life as they are there to be observed, an interest in the conditioning influences in people's lives (with an oblique view to what might be done about them) and a sense of life's ultimate value as inhering in human understanding itself and the love which ought to follow from that. The special interest in women, which is observable from his earliest work, derives from his recognition of the differences of outlook and under-standing which arise from differences of sex. As a humanist, too, he extends his sympathy to specific aspects of sexual inequality, inequalities in the way the two sexes are treated; while, in an effort to understand the feelings of women in situations quite foreign to his own experience, he begins gradually to adjust the perspec-tives of his stories to enable him to see – and perhaps even to feel – some of those situations in the way a woman might her-self. But even beyond this commitment to understanding women, their predicaments and their particular outlooks on experience, Chekhov was artistically interested in them as part of his wider concern, again as a humanist, with the possible fulfilment of people's lives (or, alternatively, their lack of fulfil-ment) through sexual love. For if his experience as a doctor was one of the things which drew him away from a religious view of life, it no doubt also alerted him to the central importance of sexuality in determining personal happiness. Furthermore, Russia seems to have allowed Chekhov much more freedom in expressing that preoccupation than was available in England at the time; consider, for example, the difficulties Hardy experienced in trying to publish *Tess of the D'Urbervilles* and the later fuss over the novels of Lawrence.

Chekhov approaches the controversial subject of sexual rela-tionships with an explicitness which neither sacrifices force-fulness nor abandons tact. He apparently does not feel obliged, as Hardy obviously did, to make desire, as such, simply a passive and latent force in his female figures – like Tess's unconscious sensuality waiting to be acted upon. On the contrary, Chekhov imputes active desire more frequently to his women characters than to his men. And in view of the tendency in English criticism to applaud Lawrence for defiantly proclaiming facts about sexuality which no other respectable novelist dared proclaim, it might be helpful to quote Chekhov and Lawrence side by side. The passages I have chosen are necessarily fairly short, and I will begin with the more familiar one, from Lawrence:

Then she was afraid. She wanted him. When he was oblivious of her, she almost went mad with fear. For she had become so vulnerable, so exposed. She was in touch so intimately. All things about her had become intimate, and she had known them near and lovely, like presences hovering upon her. What if they should all go hard and separate again, standing back from her terrible and distinct, and she, having known them, should be at their mercy?

This frightened her. Always, her husband was to her the unknown to which she was delivered up. She was a flower that has been tempted forth into blossom, and has no retreat. He had her nakedness in his power. And who was he, what was he? A blind thing, a dark force, without knowledge. She wanted to preserve herself.[2]

Here, now, is a passage of comparable length from Chekhov's much earlier work 'A Misfortune':

Her conscience whispered to her that she had behaved badly, foolishly, that evening, like some madcap girl – that she had just been embraced on the verandah, and still had an uneasy feeling in her waist and her elbow. There was not a soul in the drawing-room; there was only one candle burning. Madame Lubyantsev sat on the round stool before the piano, motionless, as though expecting something. And as though taking advantage of the darkness and her extreme lassitude, an oppressive, overpowering desire began to assail her. Like a boa-constrictor it gripped her limbs and her soul, and grew stronger every second, and no longer menaced her as it had done, but stood clear before her in all its nakedness. (IV.289)[3]

I have no wish to denigrate either passage by reference to the other. Lawrence seems to me, in this instance, to capture well the woman's ambivalent feeling of pleasure and fear and the particularly feminine quality of savoured intimacy which we so often miss in his more 'advanced' women figures. But even here the staccato rhythm coming from the short sentences and emphatic syntax seems to insist on the pattern of the relationship, which is itself a slightly mechanical one of approach and retreat. And as in Lawrence generally, I think, there is something finally unreal and non-sensual in the physical life he presents: the man becomes not a compellingly sexual presence, but an abstraction ('the unknown'); and sentences like 'She was in touch so intimately', having no syntactical object, can give only the vague impression of a sensation, without specificity. In the Chekhov passage, by contrast, the movement through the phases of Sofya Petrovna's feelings is confident and easy, as if there is no need to insist; and the detail is highly specific – both about Sofya Petrovna's sensations and about the kind of environment in which they occur. I cannot see that Chekhov lacks anything here in comparison with Lawrence: there is, in fact, a Lawrentian force about Chekhov's final image of desire gripping the woman like a boa-constrictor, which actually gains something by coming so unexpectedly in the drawing room setting and emerging out of the generally non-figurative writing which surrounds it. Furthermore, there are memorable non-Lawrentian effects like the reference to Sofya Petrovna's 'uneasy feeling in her waist and elbow', which gives some physicality even to sexual conscience.

In this chapter I shall try to trace the development in Chekhov's art of the related concerns of human love and sexuality, particularly in the context of his developing inwardness with the psychology of women. For, from the small story 'Anyuta' (1886) to *Three Sisters* (1900), Chekhov's conviction about the suppressed potentialities of women seems to take ever more certain shape. There are, of course, a number of unsympathetic female figures in Chekhov's fiction – Aksinya of 'In the Ravine', Natasha of *Three Sisters*, even Olga Ivanovna of 'The Grasshopper' – and one recent study, by Virginia Llewellyn Smith, has argued that Chekhov in many ways feared women and rarely, if ever, created in his fiction images of fulfilled sexual relationships. But while Virginia Llewellyn Smith has presented some interesting biographical material in her book, I find myself mistrustful of many of her judgments.[4] Even in the early stories, it seems to me, there are many situations in which we feel Chekhov's sympathy for women who are bullied and oppressed; and in general he is painfully aware of the under-utilization of the talents of very fine women, for what it means both to their own lives and to society at large. Above all, it is important to realize that Chekhov's understanding of women is something that develops. It grows out of a theoretical commitment to human rights, which at first produced women of emblematic or intellectualized significance, women who are conspicuously 'representatives' of their sex. Few of the female characters in the early stories are developed as individual persons. It grows into the magnificently realized, full and distinctively feminine personalities of the sisters in *Three Sisters*.

In the early stories (1885–6), Chekhov's interest in the predicaments of women and the sexual determinants in their behaviour is inclined to take either of two mutually exclusive and limited forms. Either he takes up the issue of feminine submissiveness, making us feel the pathos of that component of female sexual psychology, or he concentrates on the physicality of sex in a semi-humorous, exaggerated way – as, for example, in 'The Witch'. A very few stories – among which are 'Agafya' and 'A Misfortune' – do bring together the physical and psychological components of sexual situations and thus achieve a serious, if fairly limited, insight. But mostly in the early stories we find the physical and psychological aspects of sexuality treated quite

separately, with obvious consequences for Chekhov's usual realism. In fact, even when Chekhov's motives are humane in the
early stories and he is making a plea on women's behalf, still he
tends to work with very limited psychological models which
deprive his case of its potential force. For example, in 'The
Huntsman' – that very early story which I have discussed already
but which is again pertinent here – what we are given is not a
personal but rather an emblematic situation: the man, confronted by the woman who loves him, faithlessly repudiates her
dependent love. The man's life and that of the woman embody
opposite principles: he is mobile and carefree, while she is bound,
by work and domesticity, to the place where she was brought up.
In this case, the pathos of the woman's situation is intensified by
the fact that the marriage was always merely nominal and that
she is Yegor's inferior in class. But the pity evoked for Pelagea
as she puts her hand over her smiling mouth or stands, pale and
statuesque, watching the man she loves depart, is won at the
expense of her seeming to possess any form of womanly strength
or of her seeming likely ever to attain a mature awareness about
herself.

One sees Chekhov's problem: what is pitiable about such
women is their helplessness and their innocent liability to exploitation. They have therefore to be depicted as subject and gentle
creatures, conditioned by upbringing and even by economic
circumstances to expect little of life. But since Chekhov seems
to want us to feel the suppressed potentiality of women, he needs
also to indicate the existence in them of latent strengths and
talents – and this is what the women in the early stories lack.
Another story, 'Anyuta', takes the sexually symbolic situation of
a young woman being used first by a medical student and then
by his artist friend as the model for their work. Anyuta undresses
first to have her anatomy traced by the student preparing for his
exam and then to be the subject of the artist's picture. Her
shivering is psychologically as well as physically suggestive as she
stands in the winter cold. Yet while the story is implicitly a
criticism of the way Anyuta is regarded as an object by these
future 'gentlemen', she emerges in Chekhov's writing with little
more than the submissive dumbness of a gentle beast:

'Look here, my good girl...sit down and listen. We must part! The fact
is, I don't want to live with you any longer.'

Anyuta had come back from the artist's worn out and exhausted.

Standing so long as a model made her face look thin and sunken, and her chin sharper than ever. She said nothing in answer to the student's words, only her lips began to tremble.

'You know we should have to part sooner or later, anyway,' said the student. 'You're a nice, good girl, and not a fool; you'll understand...'

Anyuta put on her coat again, in silence wrapped up her embroidery in paper, gathered together her needles and thread: she found the screw of paper with the four lumps of sugar in the window, and laid it on the table by the books.

'That's...your sugar...' she said softly, and turned away to conceal her tears. (I.88).

Anyuta's meekness and the strictly domestic terms through which the pathos of her situation is conveyed (through her gathering up her sewing and giving the student the sugar she has earned for him) make her a much less resourceful figure than Chekhov needs if his criticism is to have a proper point in this context. After five lovers, she still meets such a situation with meek acceptance; she is not presented as having any personal initiative of her own. Of course, she is real enough: there actually are women like Anyuta, and she behaves quite convincingly and consistently within the terms in which Chekhov has created her. But it is dangerously easy for Chekhov to elicit pity for such a character; and while the actual example of her offering the sugar is quite understated in its way, it is a sign of the relatively sentimental direction in which the story is headed. By working with such a limited model, Chekhov is, I think, unconsciously condescending to women in the very act of sympathizing with their plight. Though he clearly depicts – and judges – the student's condescension in the terms on which he lets Anyuta stay, Chekhov, in presenting Anyuta as so starkly vulnerable and without resource, is falling into a perhaps habitual male assumption about women's helplessness, which makes even his defence of her something one feels instinctively on guard against.

At the same time (in 1885–6), Chekhov also adopts a comic mode of writing about sexual situations in which we find a rather more conscious attitude of disrespect. It was Grigorovich, in 1886, who complained to Chekhov, 'Why is it that you often have motifs with pornographical nuances at the basis of your tales?' And although none of the stories is pornographic in the modern sense, it is true that 'The Witch' and 'Mire', for example, depend in an obviously limited way on the titillation of sexual intrigue.

In 'The Witch' Chekhov captures the pathos of the sexton's growing sense of his wife's attractiveness as her mysterious powers slowly remove her from his reach; and in 'Mire' he gives an intriguing, if distasteful, account of Susanna, pronouncing a moral judgment upon her, especially at the end. But in both instances the narrative stance is aligned more with the male figures, leaving the women half-mysterious; and there is a playing-about with mysterious 'atmospheres' in which some near-realization of the force and irrationality of sexual desire is mixed up with an impulse to entertain. Thus 'The Witch':

She was still sitting motionless, staring at the visitor. Her cheeks were pale and her eyes were glowing with a strange fire. The sexton cleared his throat, crawled on his stomach off the bed, and going up to the postman, put a handkerchief over his face.
'What's that for?' asked his wife.
'To keep the light out of his eyes.'
'Then put out the light!'
Savély looked distrustfully at his wife, put out his lips towards the lamp, but at once thought better of it and clasped his hands. (vi.15).

On the whole, the insight struggling to realize itself through such details as Raïssa's eyes 'glowing with a strange fire' is subordinated to the comedy of the battle of wits and instincts between husband and wife. Also, the comic conception of the witch commanding the demons of bad weather to bring her a man from out of the cold is too exaggerated to convey any very serious understanding of sexuality itself.

Yet in other ways 'The Witch' is quite an important early story. The differences in manner and appearance between Raïssa and her uncouth husband make us feel the class element in her revulsion from him and her impulse to direct her sexual energies elsewhere. As in 'Agafya', there is a sense of energies unappeased in the woman by a restrictive – and in this case coarse and primitive – way of life. Furthermore, the externalization and amplification of the woman's potent sexuality so that it pervades the whole environment through the roaring storm, is, though exaggerated, a recognition of sexuality as a positive force – a re-cognition notable for that time. It is like the ever-present heavy jasmine scent in Susanna's house in 'Mire', or Hardy's association of Tess's unconscious but active sensuality with the brimming abundance of natural life at Talbothays: the author's imagination instinctively connects human sexuality with something more disturbing and ambivalent in the natural world than the calm cycle of renewal and rebirth. The storm is violent and howling; the jasmine scent sweet but oppressive; the atmosphere of Talbothays rich to the point of over-richness, a sense of calm being first induced but then threatened by the relentless pulse of it all. In fact, in Chekhov's case this sense of partial perturbation about sexuality does seem unusually highly developed and can at times be a problem in his writing. For as well as being sympathetically disposed towards women, Chekhov is occasionally amused and sometimes deeply frightened by them, in particular by their capacity to utilize their sexual natures in the pursuit of power. Von Koren and Solyony are frightening Chekhovian men whose sexual energies, conversely, are strangely indrawn. The destructive elements in their natures are conveyed (and simultaneously distanced, to some extent) through mannerisms which are highly stylized. It is only when contemplating feminine destructiveness that Chekhov very obviously recoils from his own creations, as we can feel from the sudden extremes of animal imagery:

Her eyes stared at the lieutenant without blinking, her lips parted and showed clenched teeth. Her whole face, her throat, and even her bosom, seemed quivering with a spiteful, catlike expression. Still keeping her eyes fixed on her visitor, she rapidly bent to one side, and swiftly, like a cat, snatched something from the table. ('Mire', II.195)

This sinister imagery, like that of Raïssa pacing to and fro, eyes ablaze, a tormented tigress, is only half-sanctioned by the exaggerated drama of the story. Fourteen years later, in 'In the Ravine', Aksinya too is imaged as slender and unblinking, this time like 'a viper among young rye'. It seems that Chekhov was more or less persistently disturbed by something he felt to be untamed and uncivilized in the female psyche, some conquering impulse which is instinctive rather than calculating but which is merciless in attaining its ends. In fact, it is interesting that the imagery in these instances does nothing to interpret the components of the impulse, that it remains mysterious; whereas when the whole context of a story is such that this feminine self-assertion can be placed in a wider framework of social or psychological understanding, when Chekhov can see feminine defiance as frustration with lack of opportunity, he can often cope with it more composedly and much more realistically. The latter, I think, is the case in 'Agafya', where so much of Agafya's self lies unextended in her limited duties as a wife:

There was an instant when, seeming to come to herself, she drew herself up to get upon her feet, but then some invincible and implacable force seemed to push her whole body, and she sank down beside Savka again.

'Bother him!' she said, with a wild, guttural laugh, and reckless determination, impotence, and pain could be heard in that laugh. (VI.131)

The 'wild, guttural laugh' comes from the same anarchic component of the female personality to which the animal imagery in the other stories refers. Here, though, Chekhov has the facts which enable him to interpret it: Agafya's dissatisfaction with her marriage, her sense of luxury in lying beside Savka, while the train carrying her husband back home bears relentlessly down on the small time available to her. Thus he analyses the components of that feeling – 'reckless determination, impotence, and pain' – whereas in the other stories, without the same situational explanations behind him, he simply gives *images* of a behaviour which, to him and to us, stays enshrouded in mystery.

'Agafya' is, in its small way, a fine story. The woman in the story is portrayed as having complex and specific feelings about her responsibility as a wife; and, unlike Anyuta or Pelagea, she is seen as taking quite reckless initiatives. Chekhov still seems more interested in the abstract situation than in individual personalities, but the story is forceful enough in feeling to give real significance to the woman's fearful walk back across the fields from Savka's hut to the erect, waiting figure of her husband. Here Chekhov avoids falling into too pitying a condescension:

Agafya stepped upon the bank and went across the fields to the village. At first she walked fairly boldly, but soon terror and excitement got the upper hand; she turned round fearfully, stopped and took breath.

'Yes, you are frightened!' Savka laughed mournfully, looking at the bright green streak left by Agafya in the dewy grass. 'She doesn't want to go! Her husband's been standing waiting for her for a good hour... Did you see him?'

Savka said the last words with a smile, but they sent a chill to my heart. In the village, near the furthest hut, Yakov was standing in the road, gazing fixedly at his returning wife. (VI.133)

The scene (for it is deliberately cast in a highly visual way, with Agafya leaving a bright green trail between the two men) epitomizes the fearful subjugation of the woman's needs and basic personality to the stern authority of her husband, while her lover is granted an enviable masculine immunity. Savka's callous lightheartedness and Yakov's threatening austerity are two kinds of masculine tyranny, between which Agafya is trapped. Chekhov has, in his own terms, 'correctly stat[ed the] problem' of two quite different forms of male domination. Yet the narrator (as both a passive figure in the landscape and the voice of the narrative) is queerly unable to do more than to sympathize with Agafya's plight. There is no real sense of protest; and the woman's feelings are shown only by default, through Chekhov's concentrating on the threatening or callous attitudes of the two men. Having avoided condescension in the obvious form to be found in 'Anyuta', he is still not directly inward, in any way, with the psychology of women.

Ernest Simmons, in his biography, stresses Chekhov's instinctive fear of the volatile temperament of Lika Mizinova – his sister Masha's friend, who loved him and whom he teasingly, never quite seriously, seems to have toyed with the idea of marrying. When he did marry the actress Olga Knipper, he seems to have welcomed the relief from domesticity provided by her months of residence in Moscow while she worked for the Art Theatre, though he certainly missed her over long stretches. In his notebooks 1892–1904, too, his comments about women are frequently disparaging; and, from the evidence of the stories themselves, sexual energies displaced from love or desire into ambition or crime seem to have disturbed him unusually. There is evidence, then, some of which Virginia Llewellyn Smith has collected, to suggest, that Chekhov was indeed repulsed by some aspects of femininity though in my view this should be restricted to two broad areas: first, the bourgeois immersion of married women in trivial domesticity (it may be relevant to remember that Chekhov seems to have mistrusted bourgeois values generally), and second, the primitive sexual aggression of uneducated, and again often bourgeois, women engaged in some quest for power. In a later chapter I shall discuss Chekhov's tendency to focus through these bourgeois women his misgivings about particular aspects of social change. But there are also women of course who exist outside these categories, whom Chekhov in fact depicts particularly well. And these sympathetically portrayed women predominate in Chekhov's later fiction. They are generally upper-middle- or upper-class women, usually but not always educated, who are themselves discontented with the apparent triviality of their daily duties and whose sexuality is expressed within civilised conventions which divorce it from its possible associations with aggression. Perhaps the first to appear in Chekhov's work is Sofya Petrovna of 'A Misfortune', the finest undoubtedly Olga Mihalovna of 'The Party'. For there is, in fact, a continuing line of development in Chekhov's portrayal of women from 'A Misfortune' (1886) to 'The Party' (1888), and thereafter a change in the nature of his interest in them signalled by 'The Lady with the Dog' (1899). This accumulated understanding of women, in turn, underlies the great but unobtrusive success of Chekhov's portrayal of the sisters in *Three Sisters*. In any case, it is this development, particularly between 'A Misfortune' and 'The Party' that I shall trace in the next few pages.

In 'A Misfortune', the story of a young married woman's attempts to resist, and her final surrender to, her love for another man, the tone and detail are respectfully serious, and Sofya Petrovna, as a gentlewoman very aware of her responsibilities, has Chekhov's sympathetic attention. Right from the initial setting, we are made to feel the strain on Sofya Petrovna of a situation which she herself does not yet feel as a strain, but which will rapidly begin to determine the future shape of her life:

Sofya Petrovna, the wife of Lubyantsev the notary, a handsome young woman of five-and-twenty, was walking slowly along a track that had been cleared in the wood, with Ilyin, a lawyer who was spending the summer in the neighbourhood. It was five o'clock in the evening. Feathery-white masses of cloud stood overhead; patches of bright blue sky peeped out between them. The clouds stood motionless, as though they had caught in the tops of the tall old pine-trees. It was still and sultry.

Further on, the track was crossed by a low railway embankment on which a sentinel with a gun was for some reason pacing up and down. Just beyond the embankment there was a large white church with six domes and a rusty roof.

'I did not expect to meet you here,' said Sofya Petrovna, looking at the ground and prodding at the last year's leaves with the tip of her parasol, 'and now I am glad we have met. I want to speak to you seriously and once for all.' (IV.273)

The still and sultry weather, the tall trees and motionless clouds and the circumscribed perspectives provided by the railway embankment and domed church co-operate to give a sense of the enclosed and static nature of Sofya Petrovna's life, reinforced here by the presence of the sentinel and 'last year's leaves' which she prods with her parasol. Though the details have a cumulative poetic effect, they are not overtly symbolic: Chekhov creates a precise environment which is both provincial and noticeably genteel. It is plainly quite attractive. Yet the only thing to give life to the scene (and, by implication, to Sofya Petrovna's own life) is the emotional drama being acted out with Ilyin, which – the syntax of the story subtly suggests – gives Sofya Petrovna unconscious relief. As that drama proceeds, Sofya Petrovna is shown to be as genuine in her protestations as Ilyin is in his love, but such phrases as 'Sofya Petrovna *stole a glance* at her companion' (my italics) prepare us dramatically for the revelation that she is not being quite honest with herself. She is actually gratified by the attentions of this lover and by his histrionics, and that gratification is slowly becoming the main interest of her life. Unlike Lawrence, who tends to convey his characters' emotional states through similes and metaphors of a solipsistic kind ('He was a spectre, divorced from life. He had no fullness, he was just a flat shape'[5] and so on), Chekhov conveys by dialogue and dramatic suggestion feelings of whose existence the woman herself is not yet consciously aware.

Both 'Agafya' and 'A Misfortune' (and later, of course, 'Lights') place their female protagonists in a carefully mapped, and constricting, provincial environment. In each story, a special significance is attached to the husband's being on his way back to the village on the train. In fact, there is an almost symbolic quality about the railway in these stories, since it circumscribes the woman's environment and opens up that of the man. The sense of confinement in the woman's life is epitomized by her fear at the sound of the returning train, which feels as if it were physically bearing in on the freedom available to her:

They heard the hoarse, discordant whistle of the train. This cold, irrelevant sound from the everyday world of prose made Sofya Petrovna rouse herself.

'I can't stay...it's time I was at home,' she said, getting up quickly. 'The train is coming in...Andrey is coming by it! He will want his dinner.' (IV.280–1).

This coming-in of the train makes us feel the moral as well as the domestic demands the marriage makes of Sofya Petrovna, but it is neutral enough in suggestion to convey both her sense of confinement by those demands and the real force of her husband's claims upon a wife who is in serious danger of betraying him. So it is consistent with at least one of these suggestions attaching to the train that Sofya Petrovna should resort to it in her plan to escape Ilyin by going on a holiday with her husband; just as it is predictable that, in the event, her departure will actually be with Ilyin. For Chekhov makes it clear from the first with whom Sofya Petrovna's departure is to be: from the moment that Ilyin falls on his knees in the forest, he has a hold on her romantic and sexual imagination which her routine life with her husband, poignantly, can do nothing to dispel. Chekhov conveys this brilliantly through the way he has such domestic irritations as the buzzing of a trapped bee behind a blind begin to colour Sofya Petrovna's feeling about her husband and her married life, and the association he suggests between that and her romantic infatuation with Ilyin as she transfers the buzzing sound, in day-dream, to the sound of the train carrying her away:

Behind the blind a bumble-bee was beating itself against the window-pane and buzzing. Sofya Petrovna looked at the threads on the socks, listened to the bee, and pictured how she would set off... *Vis-à-vis* Ilyin would sit, day and night, never taking his eyes off her, wrathful at his own weakness and pale with spiritual agony. He would call himself an immoral schoolboy, would abuse her, tear his hair, but when darkness came on and the passengers were asleep or got out at the station, he would seize the opportunity to kneel before her and embrace her knees as he had at the seat in the wood...

She caught herself indulging in this day-dream. (IV.284–5).

This is a very convincing portrayal of wayward instincts triumphing over a conscious attempt at self-control; and if we are aware of Tolstoy's influence in the detail of Sofya Petrovna's annoyance at the little threads hanging from the ends of Lubyantsev's socks, we will also be aware that this is an area of human experience quite foreign to Tolstoy and one which we do not get in quite this form anywhere else. For a young writer of twenty-six, Chekhov was already writing with unexpected authority about the collision between conscience and instinct in the sexual life, about the romantic overtones of feminine sexual desire, and the self-delusions by which women in particular avoid recognizing sexual impulses in themselves. In the final pages of 'A Misfortune', he succeeds in capturing perfectly a distinctively feminine form of sexual tension, emotional self-delusion and semi-dishonesty:

She recognized all this clearly till it made her heart ache, and if at that moment she had gone up to him and said to him, 'No', there would have been a force in her voice hard to disobey. But she did not go up to him and did not speak – indeed, never thought of doing so. The pettiness and egoism of youth had never been more patent in her than that evening...

Sofya Petrovna sang nervously, with defiant recklessness as though half intoxicated, and she chose sad, mournful songs which dealt with wasted hopes, the past, old age, as though in mockery of another's grief. '"And old age comes nearer and nearer"...' she sang. And what was old age to her? (VI.286–7)

This is someone of George Eliot's sanity and observational powers writing of the subject which interested Lawrence: there is no parallel for it in the English tradition nor, so far as I can see, elsewhere. Though Chekhov is not 'judging' Sofya Petrovna in a moralistic way, he is clearly outside her in wisdom and maturity – able to isolate that 'pettiness and egoism' of her youth and implicitly to perceive it again, in a different form, when she decides to leave with Ilyin. In fact, his attitude is suggested by the title, 'A Misfortune'. Entering into the subjective intensity of Sofya Petrovna's feelings, he recognizes the inevitability of her succumbing. Sofya Petrovna is still young, and the romanticism of Ilyin's love, as against the routine of marriage, is highly – even overwhelmingly – appealing. Yet, looking beyond her, he also recognizes the illusion to which she commits herself by envisaging the future with Ilyin as always romantic, and the sad powerlessness of Sofya Petrovna's husband to invest their marriage (precisely because it *is* a marriage, entailing familiarity) with an equivalent sense of romantic possibilities. Chekhov's portrayal of Sofya Petrovna's thoughts and feelings is detailed and sympathetic, but it is also one of the most 'objective' representations of distinctively feminine behaviour in all his fiction.

One is aware in 'A Misfortune', then, that the voice of the prose is a masculine one, unavoidably detached from Sofya Petrovna's own sense of her actions:

Then she found her daughter Varya, picked her up in her arms and hugged her warmly; the child seemed to her cold and heavy, but she was unwilling to acknowledge this to herself, and she began explaining to the child how good, kind, and honourable her papa was. (IV.282–3)

Sentences like this are the work of a shrewd observer, but their past-tense narrative structure makes the motive force of the actions seem very cold, as if there were more direct calculation in them than there surely would have been. This is the difficulty of a male writer whose own prose presence, in this story, is quite strong. It is probably a difficulty inherent in any attempt actually to interpret the feelings of a character whose motives are only half-conscious and who does not have a completely honest sense of his or her own feelings. But Chekhov was by no means always confined by this problem, for in both 'Lights' and 'The Party' – both written two years later, in 1888 – he has given us women who are subtly emancipated from direct commentary by the author and hence from his stance of deliberate 'understanding'.

In 'Lights' this happens in a quite intriguing way through an aspect of the story's structure: we are told of Kisotchka not by the author but by another character, and it is part of that character's self-criticism that he admits to not understanding Kisotchka during their recounted meetings. What is more, during the time that he was with Kisotchka, and now for other reasons, he is intent upon his own state of mind, so that he does not speculate much about hers. What we know about Kisotchka, then, is only a brief outline of her circumstances and her actions, together with the dramatic content of what she herself says. She is encompassed by the narrative, dramatically presented in it, but in no way interpreted by it. And through what we see of her dramatically, she emerges as superior to the sexual objectives on which Ananyev represents himself as having been intent, though we do not know how conscious or otherwise she is of them. It is a useful narrative procedure, and the passage bears quoting again:

'I spoke in a vulgar, playful tone. If Kisotchka had laughed in response I should have gone on in this style: "You had better look out, Kisotchka, or some officer or actor will be carrying you off!" She would have dropped her eyes and said: "As though anyone would care to carry me off; there are plenty younger and better looking..." And I should have said: "Nonsense, Kisotchka – I for one should be delighted!" And so on in that style, and it would all have gone swimmingly. But Kisotchka did not laugh in response; on the contrary, she looked grave and sighed.

'"All you have been told is true," she said. "My cousin Sonya ran away from her husband with an actor. Of course, it is wrong...Everyone ought to bear the lot that fate has laid on him, but I do not condemn them or blame them...Circumstances are sometimes too strong for anyone!"

'"That is so, Kisotchka, but what circumstances can produce a regular epidemic?"

'"It's very simple and easy to understand," replied Kisotchka, raising her eyebrows. "There is absolutely nothing for us educated girls and women to do with ourselves. Not everyone is able to go to the University, to become a teacher, to live for ideas, in fact as men do. They have to be married...And whom would you have them marry? You boys leave the high school and go away to the University, never to return to your native town again, and you marry in Petersburg or Moscow, while the girls remain..."' (XIII.40–1)

The fact that a man, who is not the author, is telling the story of Kisotchka allows Chekhov dramatically to contrast the primitive and insulting assumptions about women which Ananyev held at the time with Kisotchka's unexpected and genuine gravity. Kisotchka, though she does not realise that she is being cheapened and condescended to, makes us realize it very strongly as she instinctively maintains her seriousness, strength of understanding and dignity. By seriously analysing the predicament of educated provincial women, she gives the rationale for her later actions in a context where no immediate self-rationalizing is involved, so that we have an explanation of her behaviour in which we can fully believe. The narrative as a whole is thus structured to win respect and sympathy for her, while keeping her independent of any direct masculine 'interpretation' of her actions or her states of mind.

Still, as I argued on p. 126, in the descriptions of Kisotchka's appearance and the kind of response commanded for her in that way, there is a weakening change at the point where she is about to become Ananyev's mistress. Earlier, she has been shown to have a kind of maturity and autonomy, an air of matronliness:

'It was not that her features looked old or faded, but they had somehow lost their brilliance and looked sterner, her hair seemed shorter, she looked taller, and her shoulders were quite twice as broad, and what was most striking, there was already in her face the expression of motherliness and resignation commonly seen in respectable women of her age, and this, of course, I had never seen in her before...' (XIII.35)

The description beautifully balances Kisotchka's loss of youthful vibrancy against a new solidity about her figure and an implied gain of inner, spiritual strength. But when she has fled her home with Ananyev, she is suddenly represented as once again the vulnerable, kittenish girl she previously was:

'She muttered, "Ah, how splendid it is!" The childish gladness on her face, the tears, the gentle smile, the soft hair, which had escaped from under the kerchief, and the kerchief itself thrown carelessly over her head, in the light of the street lamp reminded me of the old Kisotchka whom one had wanted to stroke like a kitten.' (XIII.54)

Tender as the feeling may be, the sudden reversion to the romantic Kisotchka of the past (to prepare for the sexual scene that is to follow) is a disappointment. It makes the imagining of the seduction so much easier and so much less moving than it might have been had Kisotchka been kept a mature woman. Indeed, it seems to me a problem in Chekhov generally that in sexually direct situations his women characters tend to lose their strength as fully realized women. His best portrayals of women occur in conditions of frustration or of fulfilment, on either side of any directly recognizable sexual situation – which brings me to Chekhov's finest single portrait of a woman, his representation of Olga Mihalovna's feelings and sensations in late pregnancy in 'The Party'.

'The Party' is so important a story that it deserves a separate discussion, and I have, in fact, devoted the next chapter to it. But some things about it need to be mentioned here, because it is the first of Chekhov's stories to give real factual density to the oppressive domestic necessities of a woman's life (in one way relieved and in another intensified by the giving of the party), and to the influence of physiological factors in determining her capacity to cope with them. Olga Mihalovna is in an untypical situation. She is a woman in advanced pregnancy obliged, while feeling physically wretched, to perform all the duties of a hostess at her husband's nameday party. Of all subjects for a male author this must surely be one of the most difficult and exacting, not only because the sensations of pregnancy must for him be largely a matter of speculation, but also because it requires an unusual appreciation of the pressures of domesticity on a woman in the role of hostess. Yet the sheer detail Chekhov provides of Olga's duties at the party is astonishing, and so is his inwardness with a woman's reactions and feelings at such a time. The precise weighting of different pressures and anxieties on Olga's consciousness is only one part of this, but it is enough to give a glimpse of what I mean:

'I shall have to suggest a walk in the birch-wood before tea, or else a row in the boats,' thought Olga Mihalovna, hurrying to the croquet ground, from which came the sounds of voices and laughter. 'And sit the old people down to *vint*...' She met Grigory the footman coming from the croquet ground with empty bottles.

'Where are the ladies?' she asked.

'Among the raspberry-bushes. The master's there, too.' (iv.20).

It is through such documentation of the behind-the-scenes activity of keeping the party a success that Chekhov gives Olga Mihalovna such a substantial presence, quite unlike the increasingly romantic and etherealized conception of Kisotchka. Though Olga is actually highly vulnerable in her present condition, Chekhov avoids any incipiently condescending *images* of that vulnerability, but creates sympathy for Olga by virtually aligning his narrative tone and position with her thoughts. Even when the pressures of the party intensify and her feelings of insecurity about her husband move into resentment and outright jealousy, he still maintains his closeness to Olga, conveying her feelings in all the vividness with which she feels them and capturing, also, her acute fatigue. So there is throughout the story a near-identification of Chekhov's voice with Olga's, even when her emotions are – viewed from the outside – unreasonably extreme:

She made up her mind to find her husband at once and tell him all about it: it was disgusting, absolutely disgusting, that he was so attractive to other women and sought their admiration as though it were some heavenly manna; it was unjust and dishonourable that he should give to others what belonged by right to his wife, that he should hide his soul and his conscience from his wife to reveal them to the first pretty face he came across. What harm had his wife done him? (iv.11)

The prose, as it continues in this vein, contains no ironic distancing of the author from his character. By the construction of the overall scene we feel Olga's reaction as one of insecurity, out of all proportion to anything her husband has (objectively) done; but the prose candidly assimilates Olga's own sensibility to itself, giving her thoughts and feelings full authority in the circumstances and weighting them with complete conviction. Moreover, while reproducing and recognizing the peculiar extremity of Olga's reactions where, in her condition, even the most trivial aspects of other people's behaviour elicit resentment or irritation, Chekhov still convinces his reader that Olga Mihalovna is both a profoundly normal and profoundly agreeable woman.

'The Party' seems to me the culmination of Chekhov's deliberate effort to imagine and enter into feelings and sensations belonging distinctively to women, ones bound up with their biological differences from men. For that, the situation of a woman in pregnancy was the most natural and the most difficult challenge for him; and the fact that he could draw on what he had witnessed as a doctor perhaps helps explain his achievement, so far ahead of Lawrence in this respect. In biological–psychological terms I doubt whether Chekhov was ever again so profound about women, partly because of his own tact in not attempting to repeat the achievement, having written so finely about that situation once. After 'The Party', women in Chekhov's stories tend to occupy only a part of a wider scheme of meaning, as in 'The Duel'; or else, in short tales like 'The Grasshopper' and 'The Darling', they are rather flatly presented to embody one particular aspect of feminine behaviour which, by comparison, feels one-dimensional and light-weight. But the later stories do engage more specifically and delicately with the actual nature of feminine sexual desire, and they give us a fuller and more particular delineation of actual relationships. Furthermore, in portraying feminine desire they develop an association between that desire and climate and scenic contour which in the earlier stories was simply latent.

I have already suggested that different physical landscapes in Russia seem to have elicited different kinds of energy and pre-occupation from Chekhov's imagination. His narratives about the intellectual life, including 'A Dreary Story', are set in the clean, crisp air and snow of the northern region, among the towering firs. In 1888 the landscape of his stories was the steppe, which seems to have stimulated him to write tales of myth and to engage with the mysterious, instinctual elements of the psyche. His response to the geographically varying regions of Russia was to take up artistically the different senses of life they conveyed to him and the changed priorities they gave to particular human qualities. So that when he turns to the Black Sea ports in 'The Duel' and later in 'The Lady with the Dog', one is not surprised that they too focus a new set of pre-occupations – or at least give a new quality and intensity to old ones.

In retrospect, we see that even the earliest stories projecting some sense of feminine desire tend by intuition to be set in warm climates, and only one – 'The Witch' – is set in the cold. The association of sexuality with warm climates is for most of us both instinctual and cultural (formalized in earlier times in spring rituals), and Chekhov does not seem initially to have been very self-conscious about it, the warm atmospheres simply being present in the stories as background. In 'A Misfortune' and 'Lights' we are only just aware that the warm weather, particularly nighttime warmth, is allowing a freedom of movement in and out of doors, and a certain luxury of sensation, which multiply the possibilities of sudden or secret encounters and generally intensify the emotional atmosphere. Of course 'The Party' is a special case, since there the moisture-impregnated skies, sultry warmth and scent of moist hay become objective correlatives of Olga's glad but sluggish state of pregnancy. But it is after 'The Party', especially where the interest of the stories is explicitly sexual, that Chekhov seems consciously to have realized this conjunction between warm climates and a heightening of sexual instincts and to have begun to think more, artistically, about its implications. Gradually, then, he portrays the actual arousal of feminine desire amid summer atmospheres which he has deliberately depicted as lyrically intense.

I mentioned something of this in discussing 'The Duel' and the figure of Nadyezhda Fyodorovna in that story. Nadyezhda is not an altogether successful character, largely because Chekhov has so much else in action that he seems to lose interest in her, and he denies her much autonomy by having her 'redemption' passively follow upon that of Laevsky. She is supposedly an educated woman of some depth and we first meet her in a refined attitude, drinking coffee and reading Herbert Spencer. But there is a change in Chekhov's conception of her about midway through the story, once Laevsky's irresponsibility in attempting to abandon her has been demonstrated and once Chekhov's interest has turned to *her* self-degradation in her affairs with Kirilin and Atchmianov. In the scene at the picnic, for example, she is flighty, flirtatious and feather-headed; she seems to herself butterfly-like in her swift movements, with her cotton dress with the pansies, red shoes and straw hat. She is not the mature and dignified person with whom the story opened but much more of a stereotype. Furthermore, in the later scenes where she is privately becoming more and more burdened by guilt, Chekhov has her react in images natural neither to her first self in the story nor to the stereotype (nor, I suggest, to any woman):

And it seemed to her that all the evil memories in her head had taken shape and were walking beside her in the darkness, breathing heavily, while she, like a fly that had fallen into the inkpot, was crawling painfully along the pavement and smirching Laevsky's side and arm with blackness. (II.105).

I think one could be forgiven for simply asserting that this is not a feminine way of thinking or reacting but a masculine, authoritarian moral construction imposed on the woman's supposed feelings. Were it a moment of actual self-examination we might allow that such literary terms and objectifying images could be called in; but as a supposedly private and spontaneous womanly reaction it is surely unconvincing. The images are too abstracted from the persons involved, too much bound up with a metaphysical interpretation of moral law (like Tolstoy's, on which they are obviously based) to have a womanly feel to them. So we have neither a proper entering into the woman's consciousness, such as we have had in 'The Party', nor even that stable sense of her which would be necessary for us to be fully convinced by her 'new life' at the end. Sometimes the inner resources necessary to sustain that kind of new life seem to be potential in her, but most often they do not.

Still, there is some insight involved in the way Nadyezhda is made to rationalize her infidelity to Laevsky with the proposition that her 'soul' is always his, and in her defence of herself against the disrespect of the other women by defiant, boastful aggression. Chekhov also creates an utterly convincing sense of how the sensation of floating in the water, with the warm air all around and objects vividly visible, helps to provoke a longing for life in immediately sexual terms:

Nadyezhda Fyodorovna put on her straw hat and dashed out into the open sea. She swam some thirty feet and then turned on her back. She could see the sea to the horizon, the steamers, the people on the sea-front, the town; and all this, together with the sultry heat and the soft, transparent waves, excited her and whispered that she must live, live . . . A sailing-boat darted by her rapidly and vigorously, cleaving the waves and the air; the man sitting at the helm looked at her, and she liked being looked at. (II.46)

The detail is offered as literal and sensuous: it is not in any way allegorical. But Nadyezhda's turning on her back, and then the vigorous, cleaving motion of the gay sailboat amid the waves, are precisely the kinds of detail needed to convey the sexual overtones of this awakening of a desire to 'live'. They are reinforced, obviously, by the man 'looking at her' and her 'lik[ing] being looked at'. In Nadyezhda Fyodorovna, as in Olga Ivanovna of 'The Grasshopper' on that July night of clear moonshine on the Volga, and in Anna Sergeyevna ('The Lady with the Dog') among the romantic rituals of the summer season at Yalta, the warmth of the air and the enticing patterns of light and shade on the water liberate desire in an instinctual way:

The sound of the sea told her she must love; the darkness of evening – the same; the mountains – the same . . . And when Kirilin began paying her attentions, she had neither the power nor the wish to resist, and surrendered to him. (II.43).

The women in these stories have, at least initially, the leisure to indulge their bodily sensations, which are themselves intensified by the mild, caressing air of the southern summer. But, in the event, the true reality of love in each story turns out to be something quite distinct from this romantic desire. Having achieved such a convincing portrayal of the arousal of desire, Chekhov then places it in a more everyday context of moral responsibility and social consequence. For it is part of the ironic shape of these stories, of 'The Grasshopper' in particular and in a sadder way of 'The Lady with the Dog', that such casual desire should use up the time and space that might have been devoted to real love – which, when it is recognized, has tragically little or no time left to it.

'The Grasshopper' (1892) and 'The Darling' (1899) are among the better-known of Chekhov's stories. As products of his later career they are highly polished, and they do offer insights into particular aspects of feminine psychology; but neither, I would say, really advances Chekhov's understanding of women as it has been achieved up to this point. I think Tolstoy was right when he said of Chekhov and 'The Darling', 'He, like Balaam, intended to curse, but the god of poetry forbade him, and commanded him to bless.' (I.26–7)[6] The ending of the story, where the little boy upon whom 'the darling' now concentrates her love cries out in his sleep – 'I'll give it you! Get away! Shut up!' (I.21)

– certainly suggests an intention to judge; and so does the ironic exaggeration throughout of Olenka's own emptiness of opinions and total transference of interests along with her transferences of affection. But the source of the irony also becomes a source of delight and the comedy gradually outweighs the judgment:

It was evident that she could not live a year without some attachment, and had found new happiness in the lodge. In anyone else this would have been censured, but no one could think ill of Olenka; everything she did was so natural. Neither she nor the veterinary surgeon said anything to other people of the change in their relations, and tried, indeed, to conceal it, but without success, for Olenka could not keep a secret. When he had visitors, men serving in his regiment, and she poured out tea or served the supper, she would begin talking of the cattle plague, of the foot and mouth disease, and of the municipal slaughter-houses. (I.13–14).

In the context – after so many easy transferences of love – the 'everything she did was so natural' is obviously uneasy in its sympathies. Yet its sarcastic echo cannot survive the humour of Olenka's talking of the foot and mouth disease, a humour which immediately expands the reader's tolerance. Without going so far as to say, as Tolstoy does, that Olenka emerges as an ideal of devoted womanhood, one can surely agree with the outline of his response:

In spite of its exquisite gay humour, I at least cannot read without tears some passages of this wonderful story. I am touched by the description of her complete devotion and love for Kukin and all that he cares for, and for the timber merchant and for the veterinary surgeon, and even more of her sufferings when she is left alone and has no one to love; and finally the account of how with all the strength of womanly, motherly feelings (of which she has no experience in her own life) she devotes herself with boundless love to the future man, the schoolboy in the big cap. (I.24)[7]

It is indeed a 'wonderful' story in the sense that that word expresses one's affection for it. Yet the sources of its pathos are relatively facile, and it does not really advance our understanding of women beyond the understanding reached in the earlier stories. The reason for this is not that what Chekhov embodies in Olenka is unpalatable as a psychological truth – we probably recognize some truth in the portrait, at least in relation to some women – but that Olenka is an embodiment of a proposition rather than a real character. She embodies one possible aspect of womanhood, singled out and exaggerated; if we recognize her and respond to her, it is still, I think, not with complete belief.

The same is true, in my view, of Olga Ivanovna in the opening sections of 'The Grasshopper'. Olga Ivanovna is depicted so perilously near the brink of total satire that she too is a one-dimensional figure, embodying one possible mode of feminine behaviour but initially in an unrealistic extreme. Her 'At Homes', her constant concern with new 'celebrities', and her arty decoration of her house (with its bedroom that looks like a cavern) are all elements of the life-style of a certain kind of woman, and Olga herself has a stereotyped personality to go with them:

There were no ladies, for Olga Ivanovna considered all ladies wearisome and vulgar except actresses and her dressmaker. Not one of these entertainments passed without the hostess starting at every ring at the bell, and saying, with a triumphant expression, 'It is he', meaning by 'he', of course, some new celebrity. (v.95)

Chekhov is here a shrewd, though slightly cruel, observer of certain feminine social mannerisms, but mannerisms which may have any number of inner psychological concomitants. We do not, as yet, know much about Olga Ivanovna the actual person. In any case the shape of the story is basically moral, since the irony is directed at Olga Ivanovna's neglect of the one real celebrity and truly good man among her acquaintances – her husband, Dymov. Dymov in effect dies from that neglect, for it is because of it that he so immerses himself in his work and is so careless about what happens to him in the course of it. So the story has, in fact, a very conventional moral shape – unlike that of (say) 'The Party' or 'The Duel' – and it is more interested in that moral shape than in delineating Olga's womanliness. But the connection Chekhov makes between Olga's public self-display through her possession of 'celebrities' (given the possessive inflexion of 'It is he') and her sexual possessiveness about Dymov and Ryabovsky is, though undeveloped, inherently interesting; and, despite Olga's being overall a rather flat creation in comparison with Olga Mihalovna or the three sisters, two things in particular stand out as important facets of feminine nature being newly taken up in Chekhov's art. The first is Olga's completely sincere oscillation between absolute disregard of Dymov and delighted love for him, an oscillation that can take place in a matter of seconds, according to whatever area of self-gratification is uppermost in her mind:

'To-morrow?' asked Olga Ivanovna, and she looked at him surprised. 'You won't have time to-morrow. The first train goes to-morrow at nine, and the wedding's at eleven. No, darling, it must be to-day; it absolutely must be to-day. If you won't be able to come to-morrow, send them by a messenger. Come, you must run along . . . The passenger train will be in directly; don't miss it, darling.'
  'Very well.'
  'Oh, how sorry I am to let you go!' said Olga Ivanovna, and tears came into her eyes. 'And why did I promise that telegraph clerk, like a silly?' (v.101).

This paradox of a superficial nature which is yet convinced of its feelings from moment to moment and genuinely intense about them is well represented, and it may make us confront an un-palatable truth about one propensity of the female psyche quite distinct from any of the forms of superficiality we are used to associating with men. Certainly, the sheer sustainedness of this tendency in Olga throughout the story makes us feel that Che-khov is convinced of it as a possible feminine characteristic, and it seems related also to that strange absence of moral and emo-tional memory he dramatises with such ambiguous feeling in Olenka in 'The Darling'.

The second feature worth noting in Chekhov's portrayal of sexual and emotional relationships in 'The Grasshopper' is his representation of Olga's and Ryabovsky's deteriorated relations:

If she did not find him at his studio she left a letter in which she swore that if he did not come to see her that day she would poison herself. He was scared, came to see her, and stayed to dinner. Regardless of her husband's presence, he would say rude things to her, and she would answer him in the same way. Both felt they were a burden to each other, that they were tyrants and enemies, and were wrathful, and in their wrath did not notice that their behaviour was unseemly, and that even Korostelev, with his close-cropped head, saw it all. (v.114)

Again, Olga is trapped in the emotional duality of her nature – this time almost hating Ryabovsky but being suicidally unable to relinquish him. She coerces both men, husband and lover, while she actually possesses less and less of them. But here, with Ryabovsky, Chekhov has given us intimacy in its inverted form – the intimacy of rudeness, wrath, even hatred, such as is not possible with one who is or has been simply an acquaintance. The remarkable thing is that that negative intimacy is made so real, and that, by concentrating on Olga's and Ryabovsky's reactions, Chekhov creates so sympathetic a sense of Dymov's unspoken sorrow and shame. The overall structure of Chekhov's sympathies in the story is like the structure of that last sentence: the detailed recounting gives us Olga's feelings, but the emphasis goes to the sadness and humiliation of Dymov's, and even Korostelev's, '[seeing] it all'.

These last stories were written when Chekhov also had larger works in hand. He had, anyway, already attempted his most complete definition of a distinctively feminine personality in 'The Party'. What remained for him to do was to come more fully to terms with the highly complex social and cultural pressures which impinge on, and to some extent ensnare, women's lives – as he did in 'A Woman's Kingdom' (1894) and later and most triumphantly in *Three Sisters*. Or alternatively he could take the relationship between a woman and a man as a way of focusing a more general sense of life itself, as happens in 'The Lady with the Dog'. In the concluding chapters I shall discuss each of these three works in its own terms. However, 'The Lady with the Dog' belongs naturally as the finale to, and culmination of, this chapter on Chekhov's portrayal of women and of feminine sexuality, since in that story he actually traces the conversion of desire into love, and the conditions which life then places upon it. The story is structured in such a way as to give more access to Gurov's feelings in each episode than to Anna's; yet we have a strong sense of Anna, of Chekhov's basic affection for her and of his intense sympathy for her in her eventual predicament. Furthermore, this portrayal of casual sexual adventure turning to love, the story's appreciation of the worth of that love and, simultaneously, its sad awareness of its great difficulties, is such that – psychologically and philosophically – it marks a point of rest for one kind of preoccupation in Chekhov's art. It has the most particularly and intensely evoked summer atmosphere of all the warm-climate stories, and it is the most deft in managing that atmosphere. It also makes the same strong connection between warmth, the sound of the sea and sexual desire as was made in 'The Duel', compounding it with the leisureliness and picturesque social life of Yalta at the height of the season:

And often in the square or gardens, when there was no one near them, he suddenly drew her to him and kissed her passionately. Complete idleness, these kisses in broad daylight while he looked round in dread of someone's seeing them, the heat, the smell of the sea, and the continual passing to and fro before him of idle, well-dressed, well-fed people, made a new man of him; he told Anna Sergeyevna how beautiful she was, how fascinating. (III.13)

But the reason why 'The Lady with the Dog' is so much more important in conveying Chekhov's understanding of sexual desire and love than (say) 'The Grasshopper' or the Nadyezhda sections of 'The Duel' is that in 'The Lady with the Dog' this summer landscape of romance becomes profoundly enmeshed in time. In the later stages of Anna's and Gurov's love the Yalta landscape takes on the poignancy of a lost dream, as the fate of sexual desire in the story becomes the fate of a love, and the fate of that love the fate of two lives:

And only now when his head was grey he had fallen properly, really in love – for the first time in his life.

Anna Sergeyevna and he loved each other like people very close and akin, like husband and wife, like tender friends; it seemed to them that fate itself had meant them for one another, and they could not understand why he had a wife and she a husband; and it was as though they were a pair of birds of passage, caught and forced to live in different cages. (III.27)

The pacing of these final clauses gives a lingering, prolonged, even savoured quality to the ambiguous affirmation of Anna's and Gurov's love. The voice of the prose, emerging through such cadences as 'And only now...', conveys both the pleasure and the pain, deeply interfused, which Gurov himself must obviously feel. And through such details as Gurov's greying hair at this moment of discovering himself and the meaning of his life, and through the description of Anna's and Gurov's mutual tenderness, Chekhov conveys time both as the tragic condition of their love (so little time, in one sense, is left to them) and as a component of it, giving it that special sense of cherishing. It is here that Chekhov's interest in women and in the whole subject of sexuality ceases to be itself, as the time-saturated landscapes of 'The Lady with the Dog' merge that preoccupation with a more general feeling about love and mortality. As I will attempt to show more fully in the chapter actually devoted to 'The Lady with the Dog', the preoccupation with feminine sexuality at this point resumes its place in Chekhov's more general portrayal of the conditions which govern all life.

'*The Party*'

'The Party' makes a very special kind of claim on the reader's attention. It is quite unlike (say) 'Lights' or 'The Duel' with their unconventional and challenging imaginative structures, but has rather more in common with the narrative mode in Tolstoy. By this I do not mean simply that it reproduces certain prose effects or draws upon Tolstoyan formulations in describing moments of physical or psychological pain (as, of course, a number of the stories do), but that, in addition, it displays an intense naturalism and projects a sense of the actual duration of events such as one usually associates with Tolstoy. An unusually intense observation seems to have replaced vivid imagining, and the mode of one's response is not so much to feel the power of a work of art as such, as to want to exclaim (as one does with Tolstoy's own work) in the light of one's own experience, 'how true!' or 'how false!' The ladies of Chekhov's acquaintance pronounced the descriptions in 'The Party' true, to which he says in a letter: 'It really isn't bad to be a doctor and to understand what one is writing about.'[1]

Inevitably, so private a subject as a woman's sensations during the biological and emotional crisis of pregnancy will command quite different personal reactions; and it will be hard to convince anyone who disputes the typicality of Olga Mihalovna's experience that there is any deep truth to be derived from the portrait. But the psychological reporting here of various aspects of Olga Mihalovna's feelings is certainly outstandingly sensitive, and it reveals Chekhov as inward with kinds of feminine sensation which one would have thought inaccessible to the understanding of any man. The sense of duration created through the party, with all its trying social and domestic demands, is also impressively done, preparing for the ultimate crisis of Olga's premature confinement and her dislocated time-sense during labour. In this way the story gives us some insight into the social roles which women are required to play and the social demands made of them, as well as into the heightened or altered patterns of feminine reaction during pregnancy. But outside that, and most impressive, is the way Chekhov, in capturing Olga's distinctively feminine perspective on the party and what happens at it – including her strained relations with her husband – deepens that perspective, without losing it, into a general *human* insight into the tension between the social and private nature of people's personalities. Olga Mihalovna's sense that she and all those around her are acting out social roles which project mere stereotypes of their true selves becomes the means for Chekhov to focus the inner isolation and private loneliness which probably beset each person's real and essential self, whatever his sex. Through this insight the story attains a depth of human reference which could never be achieved by a more specialized account simply of a woman's reactions and behaviour in the special circumstances of her pregnancy and premature confinement.

Olga Mihalovna's party for her husband takes place both inside and outside her apparently stately house, and the story traces Olga's sensations from immediately after the formal dinner, through the hours spent in the garden, on the island, at supper in the drawing-room, and with her husband after the guests finally leave. The opening atmosphere of after-dinner languor is important in giving the party a semi-purposeless air which encourages our sympathy with Olga's detachment, and that sense of languor is reinforced by the highly evocative description of the sultry heat. But there is also a sense in which the ripeness of the fruit and flowers, the sultry weather and even the inescapability of her guests objectify Olga's condition as a woman biologically fulfilled but also, at this late stage of her pregnancy, biologically oppressed:

Olga Mihalovna was sitting on the nearest side of the hurdle near the shanty. The sun was hidden behind the clouds. The trees and the air were overcast as before rain, but in spite of that it was hot and stifling. The hay cut under the trees on the previous day was lying ungathered, looking melancholy, with here and there a patch of colour from the faded flowers, and from it came a heavy sickly scent. It was still. The other side of the hurdle there was a monotonous hum of bees...

Suddenly she heard footsteps and voices; someone was coming along the path towards the bee-house.

'How stifling it is!' said a feminine voice. 'What do you think – is it going to rain, or not?'

'It is going to rain, my charmer, but not before night,' a very familiar male voice answered languidly. 'There will be a good rain.' (IV.5)

The overcast sky with its burden of moisture quite palpable in the air, the ripe hay with its 'heavy, sickly scent' and the monotonous hum of the bees all suggest Olga's subjective state. The stress on heaviness and weightiness has reference to that same quality and its associated sluggishness in Olga's body, which, like the season, is mature with its fruit. At the same time, the odd listlessness engendered by the heat, and evident in the conversation she has overheard, epitomizes Olga's mental state, since it is clear that, on this particular day, she cannot even concentrate her mind with her usual calm and contentedness upon 'the little creature'. In place of the child whom she wants just to 'think about' come, one after another, distracting images of those to whom she has had to attend at the party.

It is, I suppose, unfashionable today to applaud a work which gives so much attention to feminine states of mind whose basis is clearly represented as biological. Virginia Llewellyn Smith, in the paragraph which she devotes to 'The Party',[2] is clearly uneasy about it and inclined to dismiss the story as a whole. But this representation of the interaction between the biological and psychological factors in Olga Mihalovna's personality seems to me, in fact, an important aspect of what 'The Party' finally achieves. The changed relations between Pyotr Dmitritch and his wife, for instance, clearly do have to do with the biological fact of Olga's pregnancy, in ways which I think the reader can recognize. Pyotr Dmitritch seems to feel that Olga, now that she is pregnant, is somehow remote from him – someone to respect and protect, but at this stage not someone to whom he feels particularly close. Olga Mihalovna, for her part, has her inner life intensified in a way that seems to discredit the reality of outside things, at the same time as her fears and insecurity magnify her sense of threat from without. She feels at a disadvantage beside the radiant purity of the seventeen-year-old Lubotchka, and it is Olga Mihalovna's own sense of the discrepancy between Lubotchka's prettiness and freshness and her own sluggishness which is captured in Chekhov's prose:

He was probably thinking as he looked at her, of his farm, of solitude, and – who knows? – perhaps he was even thinking how snug and cosy life would be at the farm if his wife had been this girl – young, pure, fresh, not corrupted by higher education, not with child . . . (IV.10)

The emphasis here on the last phrase gives it an almost sum-marizing power for Olga's own sense of disadvantage beside the young girl's simple prettiness and sexual purity. What is more, Pyotr Dmitritch's body has undergone no change, and he is still attractive to women; that too seems a betrayal of Olga and the child. In all this Chekhov displays an unusually fine understand-ing of a feminine way of feeling things in the complex and trying circumstances of pregnancy. The one moment of relief Olga feels from the tension of jealousy and the strain of sustaining her role at the party is when she comes upon Varvara, the gardener's wife, who is also expecting a baby:

Varvara, too, was with child and expecting to be confined on Elijah's Day. After greeting her, Olga Mihalovna looked at her and the children in silence and asked:
'Well, how do you feel?'
'Oh, all right...'
A silence followed. The two women seemed to understand each other without words. (IV.27)

Chekhov admitted that this very fine moment came, creatively, from the influence of Tolstoy. It emerges as the most 'real' thing that happens in the course of the day – real in that, for a brief space, silence and genuine understanding replace Olga's nervous social chatter. The distinctively Chekhovian feature of this Tols-toyan moment is, however, that the comfort Varvara gives is not complete. Olga does not feel able to confess her anxieties to Varvara, for she does not wish to seem naive: she is intimidated by the older woman's calm composure and by her much longer and more substantial experience of motherhood. Being thus inhibited about confiding her fears, she is unable to find in Var-vara's companionship the deeper relief she so desperately needs.

These, then, are some of the things of which Chekhov is sensitively aware – and which he tactfully communicates – about feminine psychological reactions in pregnancy. But as I have said, the way in which this is done – the careful attention given to physical sensations as they contribute to feminine psychology – makes this portrayal significant for an understanding of women generally. Here, for example, the physical illness, irritability and propensity for tears are captured as a recognizable compound which immediately suggests a feminine biological basis:

None of them understood that these trifles were agonizing to their hostess, and, indeed, it was hard to understand it, as Olga Mihalovna went on all the time smiling affably and talking nonsense.

But she felt ill...She was irritated by the crowd of people, the laughter, the questions, the jocular young man, the footmen harassed and run off their legs, the children who hung round the table; she was irritated at Vata's being like Nata, at Kolya's being like Mitya, so that one could not tell which of them had had tea and which of them had not. She felt that her smile of forced affability was passing into an expression of anger, and she felt every minute as though she would burst into tears. (IV.35)

The illness manifesting itself as irritability and fatigue, and the lack of psychological resilience, are common states emerging, in a quite distinctive combination, from feminine sexuality. Chekhov has reproduced them with a precision of weighting (sensing the exact pressure of the physical fatigue, for example, as it joins with emotional strain) which I have not seen elsewhere. What is more, he has made their context a distinctively feminine one – Olga's having to play hostess to a large and demanding crowd, which is a quite different thing from playing host – and the irritation is rendered in peculiarly feminine terms: 'she was irritated at Vata's being like Nata, at Kolya's being like Mitya, so that one could not tell which of them had had tea and which of them had not'. It is, I think, an extraordinary act of imaginative empathy.

In Olga Mihalovna's condition, in which she wants simply to be at rest and alone, the small obligations of social pretence made necessary by the party, and normally accepted every day, suddenly become a terrible burden. Her resentment of them and her reluctance to comply with them lead to her becoming more and more aware of social life itself as a kind of role-playing in which everyone is forced to assume a part. She herself is forced into a role, and the fact that she is at present unhappy in it intensifies her sense that others are adopting roles too:

Coming out into the big avenue, Olga Mihalovna assumed an expression of face as though she had just gone away to look after some domestic matter. In the verandah the gentlemen were drinking liqueur and eating strawberries: one of them, the Examining Magistrate – a stout elderly man, *blagueur* and wit – must have been telling some rather free anecdote, for, seeing their hostess, he suddenly clapped his hands over his fat lips, rolled his eyes, and sat down. Olga Mihalovna did not like the local officials. She did not care for their clumsy, ceremonious wives, their scandal-mongering, their frequent visits, their flattery of her husband, whom they all hated. Now, when they were drinking, were replete with food and showed no signs of going away, she felt their presence an agonizing weariness; but not to appear impolite, she smiled cordially to the Magistrate, and shook her finger at him. She walked across the dining-room and drawing-room smiling, and looking as though she had gone to give some order and make some arrangement. 'God grant no one stops me,' she thought, but she forced herself to stop in the drawing-room to listen from politeness to a young man who was sitting at the piano playing: after standing for a minute, she cried, 'Bravo, bravo, M. Georges!' and clapping her hands twice, she went on. (IV.12–13)

The Magistrate clapping his hand over his mouth is no more genuine in his performance than Olga Mihalovna is in shaking her finger back at him. Everything being acted out is hollow and unreal. But the purpose of this description is not to make us feel simply that reality is only a matter of appearances or that social gestures such as these are disconcertingly stylized: it is to define Olga's disorientating sense of the party's irrelevance to her. The care with which the details of the party are given and the general absence of irony in the description of the people there should assure us that social occasions are not being devalued as such. Even Olga Mihalovna, whose detachment from the party is extreme, recognizes the need to be polite and endears herself to the reader through the consideration for others implied by her effort. It is just that her real self, at this important time in her life, has a quite different set of needs from those which are supposedly being satisfied at her husband's nameday party.

What upsets Olga Mihalovna in her husband's behaviour is of course her intensified awareness that he too is playing a role, even to her. Moreover, in some ways he seems to be playing that role to her especially, for she has overheard him confiding more private fears to the pretty Lubotchka. But it is the special achievement of the story to give us sympathy for Pyotr Dmitritch's own predicament, even while conveying a perfect understanding of Olga Mihalovna's jealousy. For in fact there are clear parallels between his experience and Olga's own: he too has his social role to play, while being unable to escape his less secure, more vulnerable and anxious, inner self. His anxiety about the impending law-suit is not unlike Olga's anxiety about having the baby, except that it holds no prospect of joy. His feigned nonchalance and his boasting about his conservative opinions, like his harsh manner in the District Court, represent simply the face-saving adoption of seemingly confident masks. He now presents them to Olga Mihalovna too, partly to save her the worry of the trial, and partly, one assumes, because of his sense of isolation from her, since her present experience is something he cannot really share. So although at first we are inclined to dislike Pyotr Dmitritch as a result of our sympathetic involvement with his wife, this feeling changes as the story goes on. In fact, it is by giving us a compassionate understanding of Pyotr Dmitritch, as well as of Olga, that the story goes on to deepen significantly what are already important insights.

The deepening happens quite suddenly when Olga Mihalovna seeks out her husband in his study:

She found her husband in his study. He was sitting at the table, thinking of something. His face looked stern, thoughtful, and guilty. This was not the same Pyotr Dmitritch who had been arguing at dinner and whom his guests knew, but a different man – wearied, feeling guilty and dis-satisfied with himself, whom nobody knew but his wife. He must have come to the study to get cigarettes. Before him lay an open cigarette-case full of cigarettes, and one of his hands was in the table drawer; he had paused and sunk into thought as he was taking the cigarettes.

Olga Mihalovna felt sorry for him. It was as clear as day that this man was harassed, could find no rest, and was perhaps struggling with himself. (IV.13)

This view of Pyotr Dmitritch, strikingly different from the one conveyed in the party scenes, has a more sudden dramatic impact than any of the insights we have into Olga. Up to this point we have more or less the public view of him, which is then suddenly displaced by this private self caught unawares in a moment of solitude. Moreover, in this weary and dissatisfied inner frame of mind Pyotr Dmitritch is seen to be poignantly resourceless even by comparison with Olga herself, having nothing inwardly con-soling to set against his sense of the falsity of his role in outward things. Olga at least has the 'little creature' to think about; Pyotr Dmitritch seems more than ever alone, reaching for the lonely, inadequate consolation of a cigarette. Chekhov makes sure that we feel the intensity of this masculine isolation at the time when the carrying of a baby gives a special, private fulfilment to the wife. He makes us aware of the discrepancy between the re-sources available, respectively, to men and to women in these circumstances, in meeting the anxiety which both feel about the

apparent insubstantiality and seeming hypocrisy of the larger
social world around them. Pyotr Dmitritch is 'himself' at his
Poltava property and for the brief time at the party when he takes
up his scythe. It is not that self but rather the self-protective public
figure of the man which struts in such an apparently self-satisfied
way through the house and garden, showing off to the guests at
his party. He, too, has an inner and an outer self; and by
showing us this Chekhov has enlarged his very sensitive understanding of a particular feminine state into a moving general
apprehension of an area of essential human loneliness.

The sad irony of 'The Party' is that Olga's mounting distress
at what she interprets as her husband's 'falsity' should be a
reaction to that same necessity of adopting a public personality
which she feels as such a burden on herself. She doesn't see why
he might find it necessary, at this stage of their relations, to act
a role even to her; while he, for his part, cannot see the anxieties
concealed behind Olga's confidence. So once Olga has overheard
Pyotr Dmitritch being more open with Lubotchka about his fears
than he is to her, Olga's suspicions and anxieties are bound to
become worse and worse. In following those developing anxieties
Chekhov is not taking sides – in fact we have a more and more
sympathetic sense of Pyotr Dmitritch, along with our sympathetic understanding of Olga. He is recognizing both that it is
the woman's intensifying sensations in such circumstances which
will precipitate the destructive climax, and that they deserve
intense sympathy.

I have already pointed, in the last chapter, to the near-
identification of Chekhov's prose with Olga's thoughts and feelings. Even when the commentary seems to be Chekhov's there
is so much sympathy for Olga that we cannot, I think, be dogmatic
about which is which. The third-person narration merges into
first-person introspection with no ironic placing. Always the most
vivid thing before us is Olga's state of mind:

She went out and glanced at her watch: it was five minutes to six. And
she wondered that the time had gone so slowly, and thought with horror
that there were six more hours before midnight, when the party would
break up. How could she get through those six hours? What phrases
could she utter? How should she behave to her husband? (IV.20)

At least the construction here, if not the content, is Tolstoyan
in the kind of continuous access it gives us to Olga's psychological

life. And the mode of the short story itself facilitates this immersion of the narrative details in the woman's subjectivity, for it is far more possible in a short story than it is in a novel to keep the reader held within the subjective orbit of one character – in this case, projecting Olga Mihalovna's own sustained sense of her husband's party as a mere charade. Even in James Joyce or Virginia Woolf, where we are also given access to characters' inner consciousnesses, the sheer duration of the novel makes some objectification of its situations virtually inevitable, whether through the existence of multiple perspectives which check and balance one another or through a structurally co-ordinated irony. The overall shaping of the novel, as it counterpoints one consciousness against another, provides us with a perspective outside any one given personality, allowing us to some extent to feel detached from, and therefore to judge, the reactions of individuals, however privately recorded. The short story, on the other hand, may exist simply as a mimesis of one character's state of mind. Concentrating as it customarily does on only one or two episodes, it has no need to move out beyond the terms in which those episodes are felt. So there is no formal necessity for 'The Party' to balance Olga's sense of the unreality of the party with another sense of it, since the story stops with her sickness and the baby's death. It can take advantage of its own formal freedom to depict Olga's feelings with an unusually concentrated sympathy, not having to project the party itself with any objective truth. In fact, it can rely on our feeling the comparative intensity of Olga's inner sensations and the insubstantiality of the party to reflect Olga's own sense of the discrepancy between the social life in which she is obliged to engage and the more pressing needs of her private self.

We also find in 'The Party' a Tolstoyan sense of psychological suffering perpetuated through time. Instead of the rapid dramatic transitions and jumps in time to which we are accustomed in the major novellas and plays, 'The Party' follows a consecutive time-scheme, relying heavily on the accumulative power of the reporting. So in following Olga Mihalovna and Pyotr Dmitritch through the long hours after the formal dinner, through the scenes in the garden and then at the boating picnic, it reproduces that sense of the actual physical duration of the party which Olga finds so painful – a duration felt almost as a physical burden on Olga Mihalovna, gradually depleting her energies. To begin with,

Olga is simply seeking refuge from the constant demands of her guests, wanting to be alone to think about 'the little creature'. Her hyper-nervousness extends only to her being 'vexed and frightened and pleased that she could listen to' Lubotchka and Pyotr Dmitritch when they come along. But what she hears about the coming trial, along with her sense that her husband has been hiding something from her, is the beginning of that extreme alertness to adopted (and in that sense 'false') mannerisms and poses which disorientates and distresses her more and more. At the same time, as I have said, Pyotr Dmitritch's own distress, and his attempts to mask it from Olga and from the rest of the company, make it clear that each is bound to intensify the other's trouble, whatever their actual inner feelings for one another may be. Time and again Chekhov shows us the chances they have for mutual reassurance, which, always, they miss:

Olga Mihalovna went up to the table in silence: wanting to show that she had forgotten the argument at dinner and was not cross, she shut the cigarette-case and put it in her husband's coat pocket.

'What should I say to him?' she wondered: 'I shall say that lying is like a forest – the further one goes into it the more difficult it is to get out of it. I will say to him, "You have been carried away by the false part you are playing; you have insulted people who were attached to you and have done you no harm. Go and apologize to them, laugh at yourself, and you will feel better. And if you want peace and solitude, let us go away together."'

Meeting his wife's gaze, Pyotr Dmitritch's face immediately assumed the expression it had worn at dinner and in the garden – indifferent and slightly ironical. He yawned and got up.

'It's past five,' he said, looking at his watch. 'If our visitors are merciful and leave us at eleven, even then we have another six hours of it. It's a cheerful prospect, there's no denying!'

And whistling something, he walked slowly out of the study with his usual dignified gait. (IV.13–14)

I think we feel here the careful timing in the way each utterance and each gesture is paced. Pyotr Dmitritch does not immediately walk nonchalantly away: he 'meets his wife's gaze' and then deftly evades what she might have been going to say. This is what gives time in the story so strong an air of being *humanly* significant time, time as tension, suspense in the characters' feelings. And, given the difficulty of those feelings, the duration of the party is felt, for Olga, in terms of emotional attrition and near-collapse from physical and emotional fatigue:

'He did that to please the ladies,' thought Olga Mihalovna; 'he knows it's charming.' Her hands and feet began trembling, as she supposed, from boredom, vexation from the strain of smiling and the discomfort she felt all over her body. And to conceal this trembling from her guests, she tried to talk more loudly, to laugh, to move.

'If I suddenly begin to cry,' she thought, 'I shall say I have tooth-ache...' (IV.33)

Beginning with this scene on the way to the island picnic, Olga's detachment from the party is attributed more and more to causes that are physiological; and, from sensation to sensation, the prose is sympathetically mimetic. Though there are some forms of compression, there are no summarizing statements or large gaps in time, because the conviction and credibility of Olga's feelings depend on our feeling, precisely, that they are a response to an accumulation of things. Then, just before the crisis of Olga's hurling an insult at her husband, which in turn is followed by intense self-recrimination, Chekhov creates one last opportunity for Olga and Pyotr which again is missed:

Olga Mihalovna looked at his handsome profile for five minutes in silence. It seemed to her for some reason that if her husband were suddenly to turn facing her, and to say, 'Olya, I am unhappy,' she would cry or laugh, and she would be at ease. She fancied that her legs were aching and her body was uncomfortable all over because of the strain on her feelings.

'Pyotr, what are you thinking of?' she said.

'Oh, nothing...' her husband answered. (IV.40)

The effect of this is to make some form of outburst feel as necessary to the formal structure of the story as it does to Olga Mihalovna's feelings. The surge of sympathy has been turned back each time; so Olga's hysterical protest, when it comes, has been imaginatively prepared for and, in a sense, justified.

In these late scenes, Olga is represented as tense and excited yet wretched and fatigued, and it is her husband's very coolness, when she begins to cite her grievances, that leads to her becoming completely overwrought. Her reaction when Pyotr Dmitritch simply leaves the room provides us with one of the great moments of Chekhov's unusual understanding of the psychology of women:

Olga Mihalovna jumped out of bed. To her mind there was only one thing left for her to do now; to dress with all possible haste and to leave the house forever. The house was her own, but so much the worse for Pyotr Dmitritch. Without pausing to consider whether this was necessary or not, she went quickly to the study to inform her husband of her intention ('Feminine logic!' flashed through her mind), and to say something wounding and sarcastic at parting. (IV.42–3)

Chekhov can afford Olga's reflection 'Feminine logic!' because, for whatever reason, that female reflex which demands a ceremonious leave-taking in such circumstances is indeed a largely inexplicable one and almost universally common. The prose of this whole section is adapted to Olga Mihalovna's thoughts, giving us their sequence and their rather feverish pacing, together with the curiously emphatic imperatives of action in which they result. Her insult to Pyotr Dmitritch is a release of a whole complex of anxieties about herself which have no strictly rational cause, seeking a pretext in comparatively trivial domestic facts and an old worry about whether Pyotr Dmitritch may have married her for her money. But the truly remarkable thing about the scene as Chekhov creates it is the intense emotional conviction that is given to the outburst, followed immediately by an equally intense awareness that it is sadly and stupidly unnecessary. Pyotr Dimitritch's one sentence – 'Olya, how could you say it?' – is so gentle and plaintive that it reasserts the continuing, untouched reality of their love and makes all the preceding anxieties seem like nonsense. It is in scenes such as these that one either assents to or rejects the dense reporting of Chekhov's art. Chekhov seems to me to have captured here a distinctive truth about the emotional life of women, and he makes us feel the pathos of deep love obscured by the trivial hurts and frustrations of daily married life.

The psychological climax of Olga Mihalovna's outburst is the structural climax of the story. Her feverish explanation to Pyotr Dmitritch – 'Understand! . . . You were lying, I was lying . . .' – is an extreme way of putting it, and perhaps it is not very clear to him; but the story has ensured that the reader understands what she means in terms of what we have seen of their subordination of their private selves to public roles ill suited to them. Pyotr Dmitritch replies with touching tenderness and honesty:

'I understand . . . Come, come, that's enough! I understand,' said Pyotr Dmitritch tenderly, sitting down on her bed. 'You said that in anger; I quite understand. I swear to God I love you beyond anything on earth, and when I married you I never once thought of your being rich. I loved you immensely, and that's all . . . And that I have been deceitful in little things, that . . . of course, is true. (IV.46)

But the cost of this belated understanding is the child's life, and in the immediate context of the story that loss outweighs whatever understanding may have been achieved. The death of their child is the price Chekhov (with deep regret and complete sympathy) sees Olga Mihalovna and Pyotr Dmitritch as having to pay for failing to recognize and respond in time to one another's needs.

Olga's illness is impressively rendered, from the first stab of pain through the course of an indeterminate number of nights and days when Olga simply notices a different kind of light at the window, to the final numbness of chloroform. Imaginatively, its duration seems to be determined by Chekhov's need to wind down the hysterical pitch of Olga's feelings completely but gradually. There is thus a counterbalancing effect to the increase of tension in the first half of the story, which means that the scene of her illness must be fairly long. Chekhov can, therefore, give a quite detailed account of Olga's delirium, not merely telling us of it but dramatically enacting it through the distortion of the dialogue Olga thinks she hears, when Varvara's instruction to the maid to unlock a box becomes blurred into an instruction to unlock a casket and to send word to the priest to 'unlock the holy gates'. Throughout the delirious phase of her illness, too, her attention is occupied by the drawers beside her bed rather than by the people attending her. These, presumably, are details coming to us from Chekhov's first-hand experience as a doctor; they show, once again, the areas of specifically medical interest which strongly distinguish such scenes in Chekhov from comparable ones in Tolstoy. Yet Chekhov cannot resist the occasional Tolstoyan set-piece, as where he extends Olga's sense of the duration of her pain to some time even before childhood:

The pain and the constant screaming and moaning stupefied her. She heard, saw, and sometimes spoke, but hardly understood anything, and was only conscious that she was in pain or was just going to be in pain. It seemed to her that the nameday party had been long, long ago – not yesterday, but a year ago perhaps; and that her new life of agony had lasted longer than her childhood, her school-days, her time at the University, and her marriage, and would go on for a long, long time, endlessly. (IV.50)

The whole conception here, together with the emphatic cast of the syntax ('was in pain or was just going to be in pain'; 'would go on for a long, long time, endlessly'), is obviously borrowed

from late Tolstoy. But Olga, unlike Tolstoy's late characters, has
nothing to learn from her pain. Chekhov is not interested in
having her undergo a moral self-examination, nor is her predicament such that moral decisions can help it. The attention of
the writing is simply directed to the oddly disembodied and
passive quality of her consciousness and to her stupefied sense
of being engulfed by a pain that feels infinite. Only in *alternation*
with this, as it were, are moments when the past asserts its
emotional authority over Olga Mihalovna to bring about some
new indirect display of her love:

> She remembered how in the spring he had meant to buy himself some
> harriers, and she, thinking it a cruel and dangerous sport, had prevented
> him from doing it.
> 'Pyotr, buy yourself harriers,' she moaned. (IV.49)

The irony and pathos of such moments can hardly be missed
when we reflect that to save Olga this illness and to save the life
of the child needed only some earlier, open manifestation of such
understanding and love.

The final section of 'The Party' seems to me quite as finely
constructed and precisely timed for its emotional effect as the
final paragraphs of 'The Lady with the Dog'. Beginning with
Olga's realization 'I am not dead...', it moves deftly but
significantly from her awareness of the chattering birds and the
bright summer sunshine at the window to her noticing the cold
order of the room, the motionless figure of her husband and the
fact that no child is crying. In this indirect way Chekhov makes
us feel the meaning – the sense of loss – of the child's death. The
reason 'The Party' does not stop with that recognition is not that
it is not important – the whole story has implicitly founded its
faith on the importance of the child – but that the real subject
is Olga Mihalovna and her particular state of mind:

> But nothing mattered to Olga Mihalovna now, there was a mistiness
> in her brain from the chloroform, an emptiness in her soul...The dull
> indifference to life which had overcome her when the two doctors were
> performing the operation still had possession of her. (IV.52)

It is the short story's privilege to be able to end at such a point
and on such a note, where the novel would be obliged to resume.
Like the beginning, the ending too is concerned with Olga's
psychological state, with reference – past or present – to her pregnancy. The story has described a kind of arc from discomfiture

through mounting tension and a climax back simply to discomfiture again. Both emotionally and formally a *proportionate* resolution has been found, one in which the energies of the first half of the narrative are fully and completely counterbalanced. The difference between the beginning and the ending – the source of the desolation which I think we do feel – is that beyond the ending there is a void (formally, and emotionally with the death of the child) which any other literary form would have been obliged to fill.

'The Lady with the Dog'

'The Lady with the Dog' is a tale of adultery which again seems to have the influence of Tolstoy behind it, although this time the Tolstoy of *Anna Karenina*. It is Chekhov's response to the challenge of a subject which *Anna Karenina* had made an occasion for compassion, psychological understanding and tolerance quite unlike anything we find before it in the literature of adultery;[1] and it is, again, a testing extension of sympathies beyond even the point at which Tolstoy's sympathies end. For although Tolstoy presents Anna's predicament with unprecedented compassion, he nevertheless sees her as offending against a social and moral law, and for this there is a price to be paid. He may admire Anna, he may present her death as determined within her as an inevitable consequence of her guilt; but in fact he pursues her, determined that she shall die for what she has done: the moralist in him never quite gives rest to his instinctive sympathies. Chekhov, on the other hand, read *Anna Karenina* time and time again and knew it familiarly as 'dear *Anna*'; and the warmth of his response to Anna herself suggests that she would not have suffered the same eventual fate at his hands. His sense of the preciousness of life itself and of its unpredictability in moral terms would make it unlikely that he should feel impelled to sacrifice her for anything. So it is perhaps not surprising that his own Anna – although she is, within the much-contracted scale of 'The Lady with the Dog', less sympathetic, less mature and altogether less splendid than Tolstoy's – is given as much satisfaction and fulfilment as the restricted terms of her situation can possibly offer. Her life as one man's wife – while she loves another – is simply that sad, bitter-sweet combination which Chekhov himself, at this stage, seems to sense and accept as the reality of things.

In all art that reflects upon the sadness of life and is burdened with the sense of its limitations, there is yet perhaps an impulse to serve life and even sometimes to celebrate its persistence and its tragically incomplete satisfactions. It is an impulse that seems to win through especially in the final phase of a great artist's work – for example, in Shakespeare, Rembrandt, Mozart and Beethoven – after earlier phases, first of exuberant discovery of sheer technical power (power exercised over a range of materials and maintaining a certain factual objectivity) and then of deepening psychological understanding and an intense confrontation of the great moral and philosophical issues of existence. That is, in the creative lives of some of our greatest artists (and Chekhov among them) we can observe three distinct phases, the third of which seems to involve a mysterious transcendence of those issues by which it has, in its second phase, been darkened and perplexed. As one would expect, it is a pattern that usually emerges from a long creative life. But there is a small group of artists whose own lives were tragically shortened and who lived in the expectation of an early death, whose apparently instinctive sensitivity to that fact seems to have caused a compression of all three phases into a span of time normally occupied by one. When Chekhov wrote 'The Lady with the Dog' he had known for some time that he was dying, and the mellowness and tolerance in the story indirectly reflect his awareness of the fact. And we find in Chekhov, as we find in Mozart, a new and quiet confidence emerging strangely but distinctly from among the tragic nuances of the art: a confidence (of which we have had some premonition in 'The Duel') that life, though often sad, can never be worthless and that it may even be self-enhancing – a confidence substantiated by the existence of the creative faculty itself.

The love between Gurov and Anna Sergeyevna, as it eventuates in 'The Lady with the Dog', is a love maintained in secrecy and constricted circumstances, and as such it has something of that 'quiet desperation' which Thoreau ascribed to most modern lives. But desperation is not the dominant note of the story, nor is its outcome really tragic, because the hardship of Anna's and Gurov's love cannot be separated from the *fact* of that love and from the fact that it brings each a degree of fulfilment not known before. Anna's and Gurov's position is a willing one, it gives a rationale to their lives, and it retains a strong element of indeterminacy as part of its condition. The story seems deliberately to be presenting us with the ambiguity of their position. Throughout, the tone and detail of the writing are peculiarly balanced between celebration and sympathy – hence the lyricism together with the consciousness of pain. It is a similar sort of ambiguity to that which characterized Chekhov's own life at this time. The pattern of his last years was one both of great promise and of its painful curtailment: his talent was continually expanding, his mind crowded with stories, just as tuberculosis was leaving him less able to write and hastening his end. So it is a triumph, both within the story and outside it, that Chekhov's art should transcend in spirit the ambiguities it portrays in its characters' lives. For if the ambiguity of Anna's and Gurov's position is, in a way, the story's subject, it is important to see that it is not the final quality of the story itself. Over and above it is an unusual formal serenity and a peculiar poise in the narrative voice which encompass even the sad elements in Anna's and Gurov's predicament in a larger – yet cautious – spirit of trust in the residual value of life.

From the beginning, Anna's and Gurov's relationship is treated sympathetically, even though the explanatory sections about each, and about Gurov's background in particular, are not flattering to them. There is nothing specific about their initial attachment and nothing particularly intense: they have come to Yalta separately, aimlessly, in the vague hope of finding some casual amusement in a holiday-resort relationship. But the fact that Anna is a gentlewoman and therefore that Gurov's pursuit of her must observe certain conventions, together with the stylization of life at the resort itself, masks the vulgarity of their motives in an aura of rather attractive gentility. The lady with the little dog appearing on the sea-front – amid the elderly ladies and generals, in a world of hats, bouquets and parasols, and leisurely evening walks down to meet the steamer – is a figure to catch a civilized imagination and impress it with the warmth of desire from out of a picturesquely rarefied atmosphere. In this sense, the Yalta setting itself is probably the first element in the sympathy which Chekhov extends to Anna and Gurov, before there is any suggestion of love between them at all. It has something of the aura of dream, of a fantasy-state where encounters take place and desires are fulfilled without the usual moral complications; and as such it relieves the situation from seeming sordid, though the motives of both characters are indicated bluntly enough:

He beckoned coaxingly to the Pomeranian, and when the dog came up to him he shook his finger at it. The Pomeranian growled: Gurov shook his finger at it again.

The lady looked at him and at once dropped her eyes.

'He doesn't bite,' she said, and blushed.

'May I give him a bone?' he asked; and when she nodded he asked courteously, 'Have you been long in Yalta?'

'Five days.'

'And I have already dragged out a fortnight here.'

There was a brief silence.

'Time goes fast, and yet it is so dull here!' she said, not looking at him.

'That's only the fashion to say it is dull here. A provincial will live in Belyov or Zhidra and not be dull, and when he comes here it's "Oh, the dullness! Oh, the dust!" One would think he came from Grenada.'

She laughed. Then both continued eating in silence, like strangers, but after dinner they walked side by side; and there sprang up between them the light jesting conversation of people who are free and satisfied, to whom it does not matter where they go or what they talk about. They walked and talked of the strange light on the sea: the water was of a soft warm lilac hue, and there was a golden streak from the moon upon it. They talked of how sultry it was after a hot day. Gurov told her that he came from Moscow, that he had taken his degree in Arts, but had a post in a bank; that he had trained as an opera-singer, but had given it up, that he owned two houses in Moscow...And from her he learnt that she had grown up in Petersburg, but had lived in S— since her marriage two years before, that she was staying another month in Yalta, and that her husband, who needed a holiday too, might perhaps come and fetch her. She was not sure whether her husband had a post in a Crown Department or under the Provincial Council – and was amused by her own ignorance. And Gurov learnt, too, that she was called Anna Sergeyevna. (III.5–7)

The subjects and the strategies of conversation here are those of any seduction which has the compliance of the woman as well as of the man, and Chekhov does not spare his characters the ordinary cheapness of Gurov's coaxing the dog and Anna Serge-yevna's amusement at her ignorance about her husband. There is nothing in the situation that he decides to evade. But the superficial decorum of the conversation, and then the soft lights on the water that seem to release a fuller communion between the two, take away the harshness of the sexual facts, blending them with our sense of the freedom and aimlessness of the place. The lazy days and warm evenings encourage a drifting and delicious but superficial engagement in a world of sensations, which the prose of the Yalta scenes acts out in its unhurried pace. Thus 'They walked and talked of the strange light on the sea:

the water was of a soft warm lilac hue, and there was a golden streak from the moon upon it. They talked of how sultry it was after a hot day' has a leisurely peripatetic rhythm which will later contrast with the winter bustle of the scenes in Moscow. There is no pressure about time, and time seems strangely expanded, not only because of the passivity induced by the sea but also because of the almost ritual spectacle of people moving along the Yalta promenades.

I have spoken already of the connection that seems to exist in Chekhov's imagination between warm, sensuous climates and an intensified awareness of human sexuality. Anna Sergeyevna experiences in Yalta a feeling of sensual luxury and liberation similar to that felt by Nadyezhda Fyodorovna in the superbly evoked Black-Sea-port atmosphere of 'The Duel'. But 'The Lady with the Dog', being set at the actual port of Yalta, has additionally potent elements in its setting on which Chekhov can depend. One is the highly stylized sense of fashionable life at the resort, of which Anna's promenading with a 'little dog' is a part, which establishes a genteel atmosphere quite different from the lethargy of life in 'The Duel'. The other is that elusive quality of reality about a particular place which allows it a whole range of moods which are still characteristically its own. The port in 'The Duel' is a fictive construct out of any number of places, and it has a certain symbolic quality in that its atmosphere is unchangeable so long as nothing changes in the lives of its people. It is stiflingly hot until the storm suddenly breaks out on the night before the duel. Yalta, on the other hand, can be blustery without reason, simply because it is Yalta:

A week had passed since they had made acquaintance. It was a holiday. It was sultry indoors, while in the street the wind whirled the dust round and round, and blew people's hats off. It was a thirsty day, and Gurov often went into the pavilion, and pressed Anna Sergeyevna to have syrup and water or an ice. One did not know what to do with oneself. (III.7)

This intense particularity about the actual place is important: for by keeping Yalta so convincingly itself, unable to be duplicated by any other place because it is so caught up in its own history and its mythology of permissive romance, Chekhov is able to make what happens there seem, by rights, something that does not have to impinge on either Gurov's or Anna's later life. We therefore feel it, as Chekhov I think intends us to do, as a peculiar irony that neither character can actually relegate it simply to memory – that it does remain so durable an influence throughout the rest of their lives.

Of course, not all the landscape images in the story are well managed, and one of the most important – the view from Oreanda with Yalta barely visible in the distance – is probably the most flawed. Along with the particular and quite moving detail describing the scenery, there is too much generalized teleological speculation about our 'unceasing progress towards perfection', which comes with disastrous heaviness in a story that is otherwise so delicate. But the dusty day that precedes Anna's and Gurov's first lovemaking, and then the grand panoramic views they later enjoy high above the mists of Yalta, do have the effect of encompassing their passion, literally, in a special Yalta air. The mode of the story is predominantly naturalistic in the way it represents both the people and the place: Yalta itself is almost lovingly documented. But it is in the nature of the place, as of Anna's youthful inexperience, to have some timeless and emblematic properties. In Anna's case, there is her reaction to her 'fall':

> The attitude of Anna Sergeyevna – 'the lady with the dog' – to what had happened was somehow peculiar, very grave, as though it were her fall so it seemed, and it was strange and inappropriate. Her face drooped and faded, and on both sides of it her long hair hung down mournfully; she mused in a dejected attitude like 'the woman who was a sinner' in an old-fashioned picture.
> 'It's wrong,' she said. 'You will be the first to despise me now.' (III.9–10)

Gurov finds her attitude alternately boring, irritating and ludicrous, and the story implicitly concedes its unexpectedness. But her unconsciously reproduced posture of a classical Magdalen is made to express a genuine shame and humility which give Anna a new depth in our eyes; and it is undeniable that this classical posture and all that it expresses, however apparently incongruous in the story's particular circumstances, is partly why she haunts Gurov's (and in a way the story's own) memory after she has gone.

The case of Yalta is in some ways similar. By the time Anna Sergeyevna leaves for home, Yalta already breathes a 'scent of autumn', and the weather is turning cold. Then, to Gurov, it ceases to seem real at all amid the crisp busy-ness of Moscow to which he returns:

At home in Moscow everything was in its winter routine; the stoves were heated, and in the morning it was still dark when the children were having breakfast and getting ready for school, and the nurse would light the lamp for a short time. The frosts had begun already. When the first snow has fallen, on the first day of sledge-driving it is pleasant to see the white earth, the white roofs, to draw soft, delicious breath, and the season brings back the days of one's youth. The old limes and birches, white with hoar-frost, have a good-natured expression; they are nearer to one's heart than cypresses and palms, and near them one doesn't want to be thinking of the sea and the mountains.

Gurov was Moscow born; he arrived in Moscow on a fine frosty day, and when he put on his fur coat and warm gloves, and walked along Petrovka, and when on Saturday evening he heard the ringing of the bells, his recent trip and the places he had seen lost all charm for him. (III.15)

oth the imagery and the pacing of the prose create the new sense . activity, the new sharpness and clarity, which belong to the northern city. The movement, particularly in the last sentences of the passage, is energetic and purposive, to contrast with the aimless superfluity of time in Yalta. But the Yalta landscape, as it turns out, will not allow itself to be forgotten: with its summer ripeness and its ritualized spaciousness of time, it slowly assumes, in retrospect, a dream reality and an archetypal character as a place of freedom and romance. As such, it, too, haunts Gurov more and more as Moscow presses itself upon him as a set of mundane obligations and responsibilities.

'The Lady with the Dog' was, of course, written at a time when Chekhov's major energies were going into his plays, and it is noticeable that during this period his stories contain more straightforward situations and fewer characters than the longer stories of the middle years. It is this which enables the story to concentrate so intensely on Anna and Gurov and their developing love, while making us feel, at the same time, a certain thinness of substance in comparison with the earlier works. Compared with 'The Party', for example, where the documentation of Olga Mihalovna's domestic environment and her duties at the party is impressively dense, 'The Lady with the Dog' – while highly appealing in visual terms, delicate and deft – does feel only lightly impressionistic. The swift time-transitions and the definition of the stages of Anna's and Gurov's relationship through the way places are imaged remind us of the plays rather than of the novelistic elements of 'The Party' or 'The Duel'; and, in this sort of impressionistic construction, it is much easier for Chekhov to evade or omit aspects of the situation which a fuller and more inclusive account would have faced. I am thinking particularly of the way in which Chekhov represents Anna's husband and Gurov's wife. The shortness of the story and its high dependence on visual imagery allow him to under-create these people and, in doing so, to under-present their claims to consideration and sympathy. Take, for example, the following description of Von Diderits:

And there really was in his long figure, his side-whiskers, and the small bald patch on his head, something of the flunkey's obsequiousness; his smile was sugary, and in his buttonhole there was some badge of distinction like the number on a waiter. (III.21)

Here Chekhov is co-operating with Gurov's wish to find Anna's husband unappealing: from the non-Russian name to the endorsing syntax ('And there really was...') and the unsympathetic adjectives and similes, everything works against our being able to feel the sort of sympathy which, for example, Tolstoy accorded Karenin. Chekhov is thus directing our sympathies more simply than is arguably required by the difficult and delicate nature of the problem. But the gain associated with that failing is, of course, the sheer intensity of the story's feeling; and the story projects so refined an essence of Anna's and Gurov's feelings, whether of pleasure or of pain, that we are ultimately, perhaps, disinclined to press for greater inclusiveness at the cost of its unusual potency and haunting lyricism.

Like the plays, the story has four parts, and each deftly captures a different phase of Anna's and Gurov's love. The first deals with their meeting and becoming acquainted in Yalta; the second, still in Yalta, tells of their adultery and then their separation; the third gives us Gurov living out the winter in Moscow, finding himself unable to forget Anna and finally seeking her out in a stuffy theatre in a dreary province; and the fourth captures one of their many meetings, years later, in a Moscow hotel. In this highly visual story, each change of scenery reflects significant changes in the emotional atmosphere. In Yalta there is warmth and space, with panoramic vistas for Anna and Gurov to look down on and horizons that seem to sparkle with promise. Even the initial

Moscow impressions retain an agreeable sharpness and vivacity. But in Moscow, as the winter sets in and Gurov gradually discovers himself to be a man in love, the imagery of the story begins to project a sense of the difficulties awaiting Anna and Gurov, which will inevitably restrict the promise contained in their love. At S—, the town to which Gurov goes to find Anna again, his hotel room is grey and unattractive; and Anna's house, when he finds it, is sealed off, in effect, by 'a long grey fence adorned with nails'. This is the beginning of a whole sequence of images of hardness, constriction and enclosure whose symbolic purport is clear: we are now to see the difficulty and the sadness of a love begun so carelessly in the summer world of Yalta. But at least there *is* love; and the fullness of that feeling, together with the pitifulness of its context – not contending with one another, but reconciled in a rush of acceptance – are caught as Anna Sergeyevna enters the stalls of the provincial theatre:

> Anna Sergeyevna, too, came in. She sat down in the third row, and when Gurov looked at her his heart contracted, and he understood clearly that for him there was in the whole world no creature so near, so precious, and so important to him; she, this little woman, in no way remarkable, lost in a provincial crowd, with a vulgar lorgnette in her hand, filled his whole life now, was his sorrow and his joy, the one happiness that he now desired for himself, and to the sounds of the inferior orchestra, of the wretched provincial violins, he thought how lovely she was. He thought and dreamed. (III.21)

Over and above the provincial setting, the difficulty of their position and the sorrow in store for them (things of which the story is most obviously and painfully aware), Chekhov still captures the contraction of Gurov's heart, the sudden new understanding which is to give meaning to the remainder of his life. Anna is to be 'his sorrow *and* his joy': neither is to be thought of as cancelling out the other.

There is, of course, a tragic contrast to their life together in Yalta – alone and free, with time to spend and no real love to spend it on – in the scene which takes place on the crowded theatre staircase. The same movement of retreat which led them up to the mountains high above Yalta now leads them deeper and deeper into the heart of the theatre, where there is a claustrophobic sense of the presence of other people and a pervasive tension and fear. The movement is in each case an upward one towards light and life, but in the theatre it ends on the gloomy and narrow stairway leading to the amphitheatre, which is, in effect, a trap – a dead end. The visual perspectives, instead of opening out to reveal Yalta mistily enshrouded in the lower distance, close in to oppress Anna and Gurov with the narrowness of the staircase and the inescapability of people. As I have said, there is an irony in the fact that this stuffy little theatre should prove the setting of their love, after the enticing but wasted atmosphere of Yalta. But the imagery of this theatre scene is more specifically directed towards reflecting Anna's and Gurov's immediate emotional turmoil, and towards giving, above all, a symbolic embodiment to the restrictions lying in the future of that love. The figures around Anna and Gurov flit by, as if themselves hurrying away to some secret purpose of time-ridden urgency. The air on the staircase is stale with the smell of tobacco; and in place of the picturesque old ladies and generals of the seaport, there are only strangely indeterminate figures clad in civil-service uniforms. Anna's fear of being caught by her husband or seen by her friends intensifies the urgency about time which is spatially represented by the closing-in of people coming up and down the stairs:

On the landing above them two schoolboys were smoking and looking down, but that was nothing to Gurov; he drew Anna Sergeyevna to him, and began kissing her face, her cheeks, and her hands.
'What are you doing, what are you doing!' she cried in horror, pushing him away. 'We are mad. Go away to-day; go away at once... I beseech you by all that is sacred, I implore you...There are people coming this way!'
Someone was coming up the stairs. (III.23)

This physical compression of time, in which there is space only for self-absorbed initial reactions, and in which any potential happiness is felt only as painful anguish, is a premonition of the broad terms of Anna's and Gurov's later meetings in Moscow. But the staircase also symbolically affirms the continuation of Anna's and Gurov's relationship, whatever the pain and sense of constriction fated to be theirs. As they mount the stairs towards their gloomy heights and Gurov remembers their parting at the train, Chekhov surely intends us to perceive the difference between the train's horizontal line of separation and this new struggle, together, to make of their lives the most that can be made:

...figures in legal, scholastic and civil service uniforms, all wearing badges, flitted before their eyes. They caught glimpses of ladies, of fur coats hanging on pegs; the draughts blew on them, bringing a smell of stale tobacco. And Gurov, whose heart was beating violently, thought: 'Oh, heavens! Why are these people here and this orchestra!...'

And at that instant he recalled how when he had seen Anna Serge-yevna off at the station he had thought that everything was over and they would never meet again. But how far they were still from the end!

On the narrow, gloomy staircase over which was written 'To the Amphitheatre', she stopped. (III.22)

Anna and Gurov declaring their love midway between landings on this gloomy little staircase epitomizes their general fate. Their lives are not happy; and in the last section, the impersonal hotel room and Anna's appearance, pale and tired in her grey dress, reflect the misery of their struggle to gratify an unsanctioned love. The signs of age, like Gurov's greying hair, make us feel the pathos of how little time, in the scheme of things, is offered to them: all that seems to await them is continuing secrecy, continuing difficulty and, ultimately, death. But it is a triumph of Chekhov's spirit and of his art that these things do not overwhelm the story with pessimism. The intensity of that inner life of which no one knows but Anna and Gurov, the tenderness and compassion that Gurov displays toward Anna in her misery, and their love itself, are not sufficient to make the story optimistic, but they do prevent it from seeming quite tragic. Without that painful secret in his life, Gurov would be merely empty: in his own almost feminine metaphor, he would be the sheath without the kernel. Anna is now more heroic, more able to endure; and Gurov is softer, no longer cynical. As in 'The Duel', Chekhov again rejects any view of people which would hold them to rigidly fixed natures or even fixed fates. Indeed, the possibility of people's changing, of their learning to love or to live a better life, is the small flame of hope that Chekhov, at this stage in his life, is committed to defend. Thus, even at the very end of the story, where the image of Anna and Gurov impresses us as very sad, still we feel a resilience, a refusal to give in – not only in the characters but in the author, who in keeping up a spatial metaphor ('they still had a long, long way to go') keeps a *future* – however difficult – open for them:

And it seemed as though in a little while the solution would be found, and then a new and splendid life would begin; and it was clear to both of them that they still had a long, long way to go, and that the most complicated and difficult part of it was only just beginning. (III.28)

'The Lady with the Dog' is not one of Chekhov's most complex stories, nor by any means his greatest. But, within the limitations of the task it sets itself, it is a moving and memorable story and one which could only have come towards the end of his career. It is, like many of his works, a testimony to his belief in the worth of human love, which, in this case, is affirmed even in the most adverse and difficult circumstances; but few of his stories manifest such mellowness and so lingering and lyrical an effect of tone. One does not wish to speak of a 'balance' in the portrayal of the joys and sorrows of Anna's and Gurov's love: rather, the story has a strange capacity – felt in the very voice of the prose – to behold the sad and bitter elements of life, to accept them for what they are, and yet to perceive even those as having a value in deepening and giving a more savoured quality to whatever is most valuable in people's lives. And it is because of this, and because of the strong sense of the pressures of time on the characters' lives, that one wants to affirm that in 'The Lady with the Dog', Chekhov's portrayal of the mingled joy and pain of Anna's and Gurov's love is inseparable from what was, at this stage, his sense of life itself.

Part VI

The more refined the more unhappy.

(Notebooks 1892–1904)

13
'A Woman's Kingdom'

It is a sign of Chekhov's willingness to concern himself with a great variety of the problems, theories and conditions of his time that, in one place or another, his stories reach out to practically every class in late-nineteenth-century Russia. It would be difficult, and perhaps not very fruitful, to list all the classes and occupations represented throughout his work. Edward Garnett has given a preliminary list in his Introduction to the first volume of the Garnett edition,[1] and W. H. Bruford gives a more expansive account in his unsystematic but useful *Chekhov and His Russia: A Sociological Study*. In fact, of all the features of Chekhov's art discussed by his biographers and critics, his attitudes to the various classes of Russian society are probably the most frequently stressed – and least illuminating of the art itself. I do not propose, therefore, to duplicate this kind of discussion or even fully to discuss the terms in which Chekhov perceives and imagines class structures, which does seem to me a more interesting line of investigation. Instead, I want to concentrate on Chekhov's appraisal of class situations and predicaments as expressed through his portrayal of women, and (related to that) on the way a particular kind of woman, represented by Aksinya of 'In the Ravine' and Natasha of *Three Sisters*, seems to epitomize what he most feared about social change.

As in life itself, the settings and situations of all Chekhov's works are inevitably class settings and situations to some degree. Anyuta's vulnerability, Ragin's complacency and Laevsky's idleness all at least partially reflect class attitudes and conditions, and it is part of Chekhov's acuteness as a psychologist that he is interested in the role these play in determining his characters' lives. But although *Three Sisters* and *The Cherry Orchard* demonstrate how closely class psychology is related to the social fate of classes, there is a difference between Chekhov's early interest in the class-conditioned elements of personal psychology and his later direct interest in the conditions of particular social groups, an interest which post-dates his journey to Sakhalin Island. It is only after his journey to Sakhalin that he draws on a wide range of non-fictional, sometimes autobiographically based, material for directly social purposes – for instance, to counter the Tolstoyan view of the peasants (in 'My Life' and 'Peasants') or to project the degrading and enslaving conditions of the mercantile warehouse (in 'Three Years').

'Peasants' is, of these stories, the one most limited to a purely sociological interest. Both 'My Life' and 'Three Years' gain a further dimension by involving us quite deeply with the thoughts and feelings of a central character and in particular with what he learns of life through his experience of love. Chekhov is apparently able to enter more fully and sympathetically into the experience of the dissatisfied gentleman Misail Polozniev of 'My Life', or of the merchant Laptev of 'Three Years', than into the psychology of the peasants, who are more alien to him and who (while they command a certain sympathy) inspire him partly with fear. In general, he writes best about people whose sensibilities in some way approximate his own: that is to say, about people who have an urge for freedom, about sensitive or educated people whose instincts are refined, and particularly about educated women like the sisters in *Three Sisters* who possess some tact and delicacy of awareness. Furthermore, when Chekhov sets out to portray whole categories of people (as in 'Peasants', or in 'The Horse-Stealers' where, he said, his aim was to 'show what sort of people they are'),[2] he is never quite as good as when he is sympathetically involved with individuals. But more importantly, both 'My Life' and 'Three Years' give us characters in relatively mobile class situations, whereas the condition of the peasants in 'Peasants' is completely static. Misail Polozniev is a young gentleman who deliberately renounces upper-class life and chooses to move down: he begins life again in Tolstoyan terms. Alexei Laptev is the grandson of a serf and the son of a merchant, and, however painfully limited the ultimate terms of his life, he has had a university education and is a very rich man. Though neither succeeds in fully adapting himself to the changed conditions of his life, each has, at least, the opportunity to change his life and to exercise his right of choice. That is why the lives of both of these characters are so interesting. For it is in mobile class contexts that Chekhov really excels in testing how much actual freedom particular sorts of people have; or, in the plays, in exploring those sub-surface tensions and subtle shifts of power by which the fates of individuals and of whole classes are decided. Containing no apparent inner momentum of change and unattractive enough to be secure from outside threat, the peasant way of life (as in 'Peasants') seems to have offered no challenge to the dramatic basis of Chekhov's creative temperament.

The proposition with which I want to begin the main part of this discussion is, then, that Chekhov's most productive involvement with class problems is in the area of class mobility, in situations where persons are actually supplanting one another in positions of power or where unstable class mixes are germinating change. Conditions of change stimulate him into creativity where static, perennial class realities fail; and in this he is again very different from Tolstoy. In Tolstoy a sense of process emerges only on the grand scale, in the great repeated patterns of nature and of Russian history. Human truths are as apparently unchangeable as the stable classes of people to whom they apply. Tolstoy's sense of class is virtually an organic one: one that could never conceive of Karataev of *War and Peace*, for example, as ever even wanting a cherry orchard, let alone coming to possess one. Chekhov, on the other hand, takes a shorter-term, more dramatic, view of process as something involving individual persons and the sectional groups to which they belong – the process of one class yielding power to another in the span of a single lifetime. Thus the great plays commence just as the power-structures of households or of societies are about to change – as, for example, when Andrey Prozorov begins to love the vulgar, petty-bourgeois Natasha, or when the cherry orchard is under mortgage and about to be sold. In both situations a way of life is both under pressure from hostile outside influences and subject to inner collapse. And, whether Chekhov needed repeatedly to come to terms with the pain of that situation, or whether he saw it simply as providing him with valuable dramatic opportunities, these situations of class conflict and of wider social and cultural threat to an established way of life recur noticeably throughout his late work.

The stories, of course, cannot convey these losses or transferences of power with the same dramatic impact as do the plays: the narrative mode of the stories cannot make us feel class tensions so dramatically and immediately. But two of the late stories – 'A Woman's Kingdom' (1894) and 'In the Ravine' (1900) – are like the plays in being shaped around social tensions, products of recent or in-process shifts of status and/or of economic power. Chekhov's stories have always recognized categories of rich and poor, some people gaining and others losing. But from about the mid-nineties he seems aware of these categories in a new way and is fascinated by what he perceives to be the power of money. Anna Akimovna, the rich heroine of 'A Woman's Kingdom', finds that it makes her position awkward and unhappy. Aksinya in 'In the Ravine' dispenses glittering but counterfeit heaps of it to the unpaid workmen, until her father-in-law cannot tell real money from false and has to hand his business over to her. Moreover, Chekhov seems to have felt – as did Lawrence after him – that women were the best characters through whom to focus the moral and psychological consequences of social change. In both these stories, the men who initially make the money on which the new status is based continue to hold their old positions (as workmen or merchants) in the social scheme. Because their identities are in some sense bound up with these continuing occupations, the impact of social change is not strongly felt through them. But they do have ambitions for their wives and children – that is, for those in their families who, while they benefit financially from the occupations of the men, are not directly involved in those occupations and thus partly escape the stigmas attached to them. Furthermore, this ambition in the men is met by an impulse in the women which Chekhov (again like Lawrence, if we think of Mrs Morel in *Sons and Lovers* or of the Brangwen women in *The Rainbow*) seems to suggest is integral to a certain kind of feminine temperament: the impulse of wives to maintain a clean, respectable, orderly atmosphere in their own households, as part of their more general aspiration towards bourgeois acceptance and respectability. We remember Varvara Nikolaevna, old Tsybukin's wife in 'In the Ravine', whose snow-white tablecloths, gay geraniums and separate bowls at table present so respectable a façade to the lying and swindling, and the sheer grime, of the business on which their prosperity is based. But more important than Varvara Nikolaevna are those women whom Chekhov depicts as directly enmeshed in the world of work, whose femininity is felt as operating through that situation to reveal very forcefully the effects of social mobility on the personal life. Anna Akimovna, displaced from her class of origin by her education and her gentlewoman's dress, and Aksinya, climbing to power through her skill in her father-in-law's business, embody, in a heightened form associated with their femininity, opposite fates within the newly monied class: in the first case loneliness and isolation, and in the second case brutalization of the personality by greed for money. Anna Akimovna is a moving figure with whom Chekhov's personal sympathies are strongly engaged. What he represents in Aksinya, on the other hand, is something of which he has the deepest fear; and the extremity of the violence he associates with her seems a creative over-reaction on Chekhov's part to the threat posed by such women, which may also explain the confused, unstructured quality of that story's emphases.

'A Woman's Kingdom' is Chekhov's account of the difficulties felt by a young, generous and potentially loving woman whose life is consumed by the anxieties of running a business and whose chances of ordinary happiness are frustrated by her peculiar social position *vis-à-vis* men of both the working class and the upper class. At the opening of the story Anna Akimovna is twenty-six years old, perplexed at the difference between her life and that of other women, and instinctively longing for the warmth and comfort of a husband to release her into a more ordinary womanly life. It is then that she meets the workman Pimenov, in whom she briefly centres that hope, before relinquishing it in the face of the sheer difficulty of making any kind of approach to him and her own recognition of the vast differences of expectation and of sensibility which divide them. This interest in the predicament of the socially superior woman attracted to a lower-class man is again one which brings Lawrence to mind. Both Alvina Houghton in *The Lost Girl* and Louisa Lindley in 'Daughters of the Vicar' experience the external difficulties and the internal anxieties and feelings of ambivalence associated with their taking sexual initiatives across otherwise fixed class boundaries. They, too, do so in the context of a certain desperation about their fates, as they feel themselves destined for spinsterhood, largely because of the peculiarity of the financial positions of their families. Alvina and Louisa come of good families but are poor; Anna Akimovna is of working-class origin but is now a millionairess. For different reasons, each is likely to be spurned by upper-class men but unnoticed, because considered out of reach, by those below them. However, there are important differences between Chekhov's portrayal of this particular situation in 'A Woman's Kingdom' and Lawrence's portrayal of it twenty years later. For Lawrence is temperamentally incapable of maintaining anything like Chekhov's spirit of objectivity; he approaches this kind of situation through a particular framework of belief – belief in working-class energy, in the authenticity of whatever is primitive and unadorned, and in the primacy of the sexual impulse over socially imposed and subsequently internalized forms of inhibition. In Lawrence's novels and novellas the attraction which his women feel towards lower-class men is felt as a recognition of something animal and intense within the woman's own psyche, which Lawrence himself celebrates as primal and especially real. To Lawrence, it is the triumph of authentic energies of being over the more conditioned and educated areas of the civilized personality. The very syntax in which he embodies their desire urges his characters towards an overthrow of inhibition and convention – so much so, in fact, that the class implications of this feeling for a working-class man are lost amid a more general sense of the super-ego being overruled by the id:

The water in which his arms were plunged was quite black, the soap-froth was darkish. She could scarcely conceive him as human. Mechanically, under the influence of habit, he groped in the black water, fished out soap and flannel, and handed them backward to Louisa. Then he remained rigid and submissive, his two arms thrust straight in the panchion, supporting the weight of his shoulders. His skin was beautifully white and unblemished, of an opaque, solid whiteness. Gradually Louisa saw it: this also was what he was. It fascinated her. Her feeling of separateness passed away: she ceased to draw back from contact with him and his mother. There was this living centre. Her heart ran hot. She had reached some goal in this beautiful, clear, male body. She loved him in a white, impersonal heat.[3]

Now, this may be all very well as an impressionistic account of intense psychological experience, but it does not properly keep in mind the complexities of the particular facts of class and of class-consciousness with which the story is supposedly dealing. For example, Lawrence's account of Louisa's predicament captures nothing of the sheer difficulty which Chekhov's Anna Akimovna has simply in finding opportunities to meet Pimenov (and hence to make him notice her), because the fact that Alfred's mother is dying creates its own special circumstances and even dispenses with some of the embarrassment which Louisa and Alfred might ordinarily feel. Moreover, our sense of Louisa's hesitations and of the awkwardness of her position is significantly reduced by the knowledge Lawrence gives us of Alfred's unarticulated feelings and the suggestion, all through, that there is a sort of inevitability about their love – an inevitability which Lawrence helps to build up by transforming actual social landscapes into psychologically impregnated, semi-symbolic ones at crucial psychological turning points in the narrative. In the Chekhov story, on the other hand, both the internal and external circumstances of Anna's predicament are kept densely realistic. Anna is kept within a factually documented environment of men and machines, faced with the sweat and dirt of their labour – seeing Pimenov actually at work, having him defer to her as his employer and having to bear the sense of what others are thinking, or will think, of her choice. Nor is any single element of her predicament isolated for special emphasis. Thus, although Anna is plainly attracted to Pimenov, her consciousness of the implications of choosing such a man and her rational understanding of her position complicate the simple flow of her feelings. And Chekhov ensures that we feel the extreme awkwardness of her position in that neither we nor Anna have any sense of how Pimenov himself feels: we do not know whether he has, or could have, any affection for her or not. But the most important difference between the Lawrence and the Chekhov is that Chekhov is not prepared to say that Anna's emotional and sexual attraction to Pimenov is what is *real* in her, at the cost of other elements of her personality and sensibility. He does not share Lawrence's sense of people as unstable egos whose complex individuality may suddenly give way to a so-called primal self. Anna Akimovna, though she is swayed first by one impulse and then by another, is her whole, complex self at all times. That is why she cannot suddenly love Pimenov in a 'white, impersonal heat'. To Chekhov, to have been educated or brought up in a civilized way is to have had the very nature of one's impulses modified and civilized. His characters carry their personal histories with them, thoroughly internalized, as unalterable factors within their private sensibilities. It is this which gives his portrayal of a dilemma like Anna Akimovna's its realistic complexity and its profundity. Nothing could be more tempting than to simplify the issues and give Anna Akimovna some kind of satisfaction. But it is

Chekhov's superiority over Lawrence in this area that he should so resolutely refuse to simplify. However much Anna Akimovna longs for that ideal of family life which she centres in Pimenov, she cannot escape recognizing the insurmountable differences between them. It is not just a difference of manners, or a case of socially inculcated inhibition: it is a difference of sensibility which extends to the deepest areas of the self:

> ...what seemed to her most vexatious and stupid of all was that her dreams that day about Pimenov had been right, lofty, honourable, but at the same time she felt that Lysevitch and even Krylin were nearer to her than Pimenov and all the workpeople taken together. (IV.137)

In having Anna recognize this, Chekhov is not gratuitously denying satisfaction to her; nor is he pronouncing judgment on either way of life. He is simply being realistic about the unlikelihood of a successful marriage across so vast a social gap, when all the complex facts of Anna's and Pimenov's different expectations of the world and the different perspectives they have on life are taken into account.

In these late stories, Chekhov is taking account also of new social environments in Russia – industrialized environments of factories, pollution, steam. In defining these new environments and the exploitative human situations that go with them, he depends on social occasions like weddings or seasonal ceremonies to bring the diverse elements of his represented communities together. In 'A Woman's Kingdom' the occasion is Christmas, with its long procession of workers and recipients of Anna Akimovna's charity calling at the big house to greet her. There is nothing personal about this visiting: it is a mere convention which becomes, in effect, a parade of Anna Akimovna's burdensome responsibilities, behind which is her inner loneliness. Thus the civil councillor will greet her not as a person but as a figurehead:

> 'I used to respect your uncle...and your father, and enjoyed the privilege of their friendship. Now I feel it an agreeable duty, as you see, to present my Christmas wishes to their honoured heiress.' (IV.110)

Indeed, so bound up is this Christmas visiting with a system of financial patronage that it is impossible to tell who genuinely likes Anna Akimovna and who simply takes advantage of her. In a story beginning 'Here was a thick roll of notes', nearly every social fact is a financial fact; and because she cannot manage the finances of a business she does not understand (hers is about the least feminine kind of factory one could own – a steel factory, left her by her father), she cannot manage the social side of her life either. There is one particularly memorable passage making this point; and the pathos of Anna Akimovna's helpless good will within that situation is very clear:

She felt depressed again, and was no longer glad that she had come, and the thought of the lucky man upon whom fifteen hundred roubles would drop from heaven no longer struck her as original and amusing. To go to some Tchalikov or other, when at home a business worth a million was gradually going to pieces and being ruined, and the work-people in the barracks were living worse than convicts, meant doing something silly and cheating her conscience. Along the highroad and across the fields near it, workpeople from the neighbouring cotton and paper factories were walking towards the lights of the town. There was the sound of talk and laughter in the frosty air. Anna Akimovna looked at the women and young people, and she suddenly felt a longing for a plain rough life among a crowd. She recalled vividly that far-away time when she used to be called Anyutka, when she was a little girl and used to lie under the same quilt with her mother, while a washerwoman who lodged with them used to wash clothes in the next room; while through the thin walls there came from the neighbouring flats sounds of laughter, swearing, children's crying, the accordion, and the whirr of carpenter's lathes and sewing-machines. (IV.82–3)

Throughout the story we find this sympathetic inwardness with Anna Akimovna's guilt and confusion and her longing for the old communality of working-class life still shared by the working people, including those employed by her. Chekhov creates an image of that life which is remarkable for its detail and its sense of solidity, while the opening sequence of the visit to Tchalikov's lodgings serves to remind us of the sordid side of working-class life and thus balances out the nostalgic elements in this later evocation of it. The laughter through the frosty air and the remembered whirr of the sewing-machines and lathes have a homely quality of reassurance, a relaxed and congenial ordinariness, from which Anna Akimovna is now cut off, but which seems the most natural and proper environment to nourish her womanliness. And in the story as a whole Anna's womanly warmth in longing for a true life with a husband and child is bound up with this atmosphere, against which is set her uneasiness in her role as head of the factory where people are either

10

genuinely in awe of her or, if they are like the lawyer and the councillor, simultaneously obsequious and condescending.

The cost of Anna's rise from the working to the employing class is evident even within the place she occupies in her own house. Her house – like the merchant's house in 'In the Ravine', though on a grander scale – expresses in its upper and lower floors two quite different senses of class:

The upper storey of the house was called the best or visitors' half, while the name of the business part – old people's or simply women's part – was given to the rooms of the lower storey where Aunt Tatyana Ivanovna kept house. In the upper part the gentry and educated visitors were entertained; in the lower storey simpler folk and the aunt's personal friends. (iv.97)

These demarcations of different areas of the house reflect the structures of Slavic society rather than our own, but that fact should not obscure the general feeling that the downstairs area is where the most vital life and convivial atmosphere is – hence the pathos of Anna Akimovna's loneliness in the upper storey and sense that she is queerly out of place downstairs. In the lower storey such an exception is made of her that she never quite relaxes: indeed, she envies the aunt with whom the workmen behave so familiarly and playfully. Upstairs, she is even less secure with the lawyer and the civil councillor, whom Chekhov presents as quite distasteful in the superior but wheedling way they behave:

He laid his cheek on her hand and said in the tone commonly used in coaxing little children:
   'My precious, why have you punished me?'
   'How? When?'
   'I have had no Christmas present from you.' (iv.122)

Anna Akimovna is too genuine and honest to be able to manage this: she lacks the wit or gentle birth to command the necessary respect, yet she is too well educated and too well dressed to be accepted on her own terms among the working people.

Like 'The Lady with the Dog' (and of course the plays), the story is in four parts. Its different 'acts' take place at different times of day during twenty-four hours – from night to morning to evening and back to night again. It would be hard to miss the implication of this (given the similar calculation of light effects in the major plays) as a movement out of the loneliness and dreariness of Anna Akimovna's life to her hope centred on Pimenov and then back to her loneliness and dreariness again. Indeed, 'A Woman's Kingdom' is quite like *Three Sisters* in a number of ways, since desirable things resolutely refuse to happen and personal possibilities are unobtrusively, but none the less definitively, lost. Anna Akimovna simply receives a long line of Christmas guests in a ritual that either means nothing or means actual hardship for those taking part in it. This ritual is implicitly set in contrast to the spontaneous communal life of the working people, walking in groups through the frosty air towards the lights of the town. Anna's one chance of escape is her attraction towards the workman Pimenov, whom she meets at Tchalikov's lodgings. But though she even goes so far as to agree to Stinging Beetle's percipient suggestion of a match with Pimenov, it is clear that Anna Akimovna cannot escape the loneliness of her life. The indoor settings of all but the first part of the story, suggesting a kind of claustrophobia, and the sense we are given of the upstairs and downstairs environments as fixed alternatives to one another, ensure that we perceive that Anna Akimovna is trapped between two irreconcilable worlds. A change has taken place in the person she genuinely is, as well as in the person she is deemed to be. She is not *really* of the working class and simply *thought to be* the factory-owner: she actually is, in a curious but completely believable way, both:

When the men were preparing to go, Anna Akimovna put out her hand to Pimenov. She wanted to ask him to come in sometimes to see her, without ceremony, but she did not know how to – her tongue would not obey her; and that they might not think she was attracted by Pimenov, she shook hands with his companions, too. (IV.104)

Anna's 'not know[ing] how' to invite Pimenov and her shame that she should be thought to be attracted to him are as real as her longing for the companionship and support of his honest strength. They are not aspects of a superficial self, contending with something more primary, as Lawrence would have made them: they are as integral to Anna Akimovna's personality as her longing for Pimenov's love, and in Chekhov's syntax they are given equal weight with that longing. It is, as Chekhov has Anna say at the end, 'impossible to go back' and, implicitly, just as impossible for her to go forward. Anna Akimovna is fated to have her loneliness simply exacerbated by the common crowd whom (in a sense) she owns but with whom she does not belong. Through these painful frustrations of the most womanly and loving instincts of Anna Akimovna's nature, Chekhov movingly suggests the hardship – the personal cost – that may attend economic good fortune.

I have implied in this discussion that Chekhov's awareness of class problems and class facts is not simply intuitive but is actually made explicit through his representation of the storey divisions within Anna Akimovna's house. Those divisions are, up to a point, natural ones; but they are so firmly maintained and quietly insisted upon in 'A Woman's Kingdom' that it is clear that they are serving a broad emblematic purpose. In 'In the Ravine' we find again that same near-symbolism in Chekhov's description of the upper and lower storeys of Tsybukin's house, together with the broader impressionism of his descriptions of the factory and town enclosed within the murky and sinister ravine. For, where he could accept with equanimity and even sympathy Anna Akimovna's passive and lawful inheritance of a fortune made through physical work, Chekhov does seem actually to panic before the merchant ethos of 'In the Ravine', according to which fortune, morality and life itself are defined in terms of – and may also, in the reader's terms, be disposed of by – corrupt power. Aksinya, like Natasha in *Three Sisters*, accumulates not only wealth but immense power; and it is the blind instinct to do this, at whatever cost to other people's lives, which disturbs Chekhov more than anything else.

It is commonly observed that, of the two lower-class representatives in the last two plays, Lopahin – the male representative – is conspicuously the more sympathetic. His role in *The Cherry Orchard* – which is to destroy the orchard and displace the cherry-orchard people – is an understandable one from the point of view of his class and is consistent with his own ideals (however limited those ideals may be). Natasha in *Three Sisters*, on the other hand, seems to have no ideals at all. She acts in a blind, instinctive and purely selfish way which does seem more probable in her than it would be in a man. We should not forget, of course, that many of Chekhov's finest people are women, and that he is frequently ironic about the ideals which his male characters supposedly uphold. But Chekhov does seem to find some forms of feminine behaviour, at the basest level, more truly destructive of life than any of the destructive behaviour he associates with men. Furthermore, it is the kind of behaviour which virtually guarantees success in any struggle for power such as Chekhov was interested in in the late stories and plays. Both Aksinya and Natasha, for example, exercise a tyranny of tears over their associates which ensures that they will always ultimately have their way: they see that the easiest and surest way of reversing potentially frustrating situations is not to argue or reason (for that might leave their cases open to objection), but simply to coerce other people emotionally by throwing tantrums. In fact, what is so dangerous about them is that they relentlessly exploit every special licence and respect extended to them as wives or mothers, or simply as women, to the point where they annihilate everything in the world around them which is not of immediate service to themselves. The murderously violent Aksinya is the prototype of this kind of feminine destructiveness, a prototype from which the more subtly destructive Natasha was later derived. Significantly, Aksinya is not merely a murderess but the murderess of a baby. In an extreme way, that fact focuses two things. First, and most conventionally, it suggests the sacrifice of innocence which Aksinya (and those who cover up for her) is prepared to make to the world of commerce. Second, and more suggestively, it makes us feel the extent to which Aksinya's very drive for power is bound up with some distortion or perversion of the maternal instinct. Aksinya has no child of her own, and she kills Lipa's. Emotionally, the child's place in her life – the place of a dependant towards whom she might direct all her energy and extraordinary possessiveness – is occupied by her father-in-law's business. Later, in Natasha, we find another variant of this suggestion. Natasha does have children; but she suffocates all other forms of life through her obsessive preoccupation with them, and it is through them that she gradually extends her influence throughout the sisters' house. The sheer blindness of the destruction which both Aksinya and Natasha bring about feels as if it must relate to some primitive biological drive; and through it Chekhov images the depth of personal assertion (and the cost to others) which may unconsciously be involved in the drive for power.

If, as I remarked earlier, Chekhov's best characters are those who share some temperamental affinity with him, it follows that he may have some difficulty in making such figures as Aksinya and Natasha convincing. There is, I think, a difficulty of this kind

with both, although it takes rather different forms. In Natasha's
case it appears as a sudden element of caricature when
Chekhov cannot cope with her bourgeois thinking in any
other way. With Aksinya it is a problem at the very point of
conception. That is, Chekhov immediately imputes violence to
Aksinya by imagining her in a whole series of near-Gothic images
which work against her assuming, as a character, a continuous
and humanly credible life. She makes the single horrifically
violent gesture of throwing boiling water over the innocent baby
– the kind of violent action which, when we read of it, numbs
reaction in the act of provoking it. All her power, as a dramatized
presence, hinges on that moment. Natasha, on the other hand,
is both a more believable figure and more insidiously and continuously destructive. Compare, for example, the following two
extracts:

Aksinya had naive grey eyes which rarely blinked, and a naive smile
played continually on her face. And in those unblinking eyes, and in
that little head on the long neck, and in her slenderness there was
something snake-like; all in green but for the yellow on her bosom, she
looked with a smile on her face as a viper looks out of the young rye
in the spring at the passers-by, stretching itself and lifting its head.
(VI.198–9)

NATASHA. So to-morrow I shall be all alone here (*sighs*). First of all I
shall have this avenue of fir-trees cut down, and then that maple...It
looks so ugly in the evening...(*To* IRINA) My dear, that sash does not
suit you at all...It's in bad taste. You want something light. And then
I shall have flowers, flowers planted everywhere, and there will be such
a scent...(*Severely*) Why is there a fork lying about on that seat? (*Going
into the house, to the maid*) Why is there a fork lying about on this seat,
I ask you? (*Shouts*) Hold your tongue.[4]

There is of course something sinisterly sexual about the imagery
defining Aksinya, the viper stretching itself amid the young
spring rye; and it is not easy to dismiss the vividness of her green
and yellow, which again compounds a suggestion of natural
growth and ripeness with a sense of perturbation. But the imagery is over-explicit and dehumanizing, and it makes Aksinya
more a nightmare figure (like Geraldine in Coleridge's 'Chris-
tabel') than a truly credible character. By contrast, Natasha –
until the defensive parody elements at the end in the outburst
about the fork – is all too believable as the self-absorbed, vulgar,
petty-bourgeois housewife that she is. Her suffocating self-

preoccupation is dramatically revealed in those speeches which never pause for a response; and the loose transitions between the different areas of domestic preoccupation as those trivial preoccupations take up every last corner of her mind signal a particular kind of feminine lack of intelligence with which it is frighteningly difficult for intelligent people to cope. It is as if Chekhov realized, over the intervening nine months between his creation of Aksinya and his conception of Natasha, that it is because such people actually are persons – blind, destructive persons not even conscious of their own destructiveness – that they are as frightening as they are. We may be sceptical of the violence Chekhov wants us to feel in Aksinya, thinking it too extreme; we can hardly doubt the reality of that more familiar kind of violence which Natasha embodies.

Yet even with Natasha Chekhov is obviously creatively ill at ease. The rather strained 'comic' elements in his dramatization of her seem designed simply to dismiss what he finds to be too intractable a psychology to enter in any sympathetic depth. He also seems to feel some strain in having to render the kinds of environments from which these characters come. Unlike Tolstoy or Lawrence, Chekhov had a strong belief in scientific and material progress as promoting the greater welfare of mankind.[5] The factory he creates in 'A Woman's Kingdom', with its attached workmen's barracks and the sense of community among the workpeople, has a strong physical connection with the family owning it, quite different from the impersonality of the factory monstrosities in *Sons and Lovers* or *The Rainbow*. The difference can of course be explained partly by the relative under-development of Russian industry compared with that in England and by the fact that Lawrence was anyway writing at a later time. Yet when he is actually confronted with imagining the interior of the smelting-works, Chekhov, like Lawrence, does seem temperamentally to recoil. He preserves a surface objectivity, compared with Lawrence's obvious emotionality, but his perturbation is clearly registered underneath.

The high ceilings with iron girders; the multitude of huge, rapidly turning wheels, connecting straps and levers; the shrill hissing; the clank of steel; the rattle of the trolleys; the harsh puffing of steam; the faces – pale, crimson or black with coal-dust; the shirts soaked with sweat; the gleam of steel, of copper, and of fire; the smell of oil and coal; and the draught, at times very hot and at times very cold – gave her an impres-

sion of hell. It seemed to her as though the wheels, the levers, and the
hot hissing cylinders were trying to tear themselves away from their
fastenings to crush the men, while the men, not hearing one another,
ran about with anxious faces, and busied themselves about the machines,
trying to stop their terrible movement. (IV.80–1)

The implicit terror of the response and the vagueness of actual
detail have presumably to do with the fact that the person seeing
this is a woman: the scene is perceived very much as Anna
Akimovna would perceive it herself. Yet the fact that Chekhov's
response is undifferentiated from Anna's is itself significant, and
this passionate impressionistic writing contrasts with Chekhov's
calm particularity elsewhere. Chekhov seems at once repulsed
and oddly fascinated by the brute energy of the factory, and this
gives a noticeable energy to the writing, even while the near-
surreal images make the scene less solid and substantial than it
ought to be. The same happens, at least partially, with the dirt
and moral pollution emanating from the fabric-works in 'In the
Ravine'. It is as if the responsible realist in Chekhov were impelling him to take account of these environments, increasingly
important in his Russia, while his aesthetic reaction toward them
is one of hostility. It is only in such special contexts as 'Lights',
where the emphasis is clearly elsewhere, that he presents a
modern technological environment unperturbedly; and even in
'Lights' the railway-camp is made to suggest at one point the
primaeval disorder of 'the times of chaos'. So it is perhaps
fortunate that the overall development of Chekhov's stories and
plays moves not further and further into modernist landscapes
but ultimately back to a lyrical appreciation of the precariousness
of a threatened upper class. That class, the untitled aristocracy,
was the one with which (despite his origins) he had, temperamentally, most in common. But, having confronted the new
environments in 'A Woman's Kingdom' and 'In the Ravine',
Chekhov was now aware to a heightened degree of class dynamics
and of the complex processes of social change. The dramatic
tensions of the last two plays are social and cultural in their
represented origins, as those of *The Seagull* and *Uncle Vanya*
were not. There is now a more conscious weighing-up of the
benefits and costs of social change, and, under the pressure of the
changes visibly taking place in Russian society, a deeper and
more questioning assessment of the precise state and standard of
Russian civilization at that time. Not unnaturally, that assessment

is done through Chekhov's always sympathetic, but increasingly critical (and, in *The Cherry Orchard*, quite sceptical), representation of those who ought ideally to embody and transmit the best values of their culture: the educated members of what had been a conspicuously privileged upper class.

14

'Three Sisters'

D. S. Mirsky defined something of the essential character of Chekhov's art when he said, in the course of an otherwise hostile account, 'Chekhov...must appeal to Classicist and Romanticist alike: the former will admire the balance and measure of his art and mind; the latter the naturalness of the balance, which in its very harmony remains true to self, and imposes no constraint on spontaneous experience.'[1] The satisfaction with which one reads the best Chekhov stories has undoubtedly to do with this peculiar quality of his art: the measure and clarity with which it balances one aspect of a situation against another, seeking a tentative result, and yet at the same time its unusual feeling for the spontaneous and unpredictable elements in people's behaviour. But it is in the late plays that we feel this quality of the art issuing into a distinctive tension, as the drama conveys both the provisional, chaotic and unpredictable nature of each moment of life and yet the peculiar consistency with which those moments add up to a given fate. And nowhere, perhaps, is this tension more evident or more fruitfully exploited than in the living and varied drama of *Three Sisters*. *Three Sisters* is, in my view, the consummate product of Chekhov's art – tactful, sensitive and deeply understanding in its representation of the Prozorov women; suggestive about the relationship between aspiration and suffering in people's lives; analytical about why it might be that even the best civilizations seem doomed to fail; and above all dramatically alive and challenging through all the shifting moods and changing situations of its fully imagined characters. It is Chekhov's true '*chef d'oeuvre*'; and in capturing the residue of humour, energy and purposiveness and, at the same time, the larger sadness, debilitation and suffering of the sisters' lives, he finally and triumphantly relates – within the quite specific social world of the play – the obvious ambivalences in his own more general response to life.

Considered as a whole, *Three Sisters* is a profoundly sad play

(Lionel Trilling rightly calls it one of the saddest works in all literature). It knows what it is for people to yearn for self-realization and self-fulfilment, those two essentially Romantic ideals; and it knows the negative side of those ideals, where yearning produces only continuing frustration and pain. A century after the initial euphoria of the English Romantics about the possibilities open to the individual, Chekhov surrounds those possibilities with a pervasive sense of irony and even tragedy. Yet whatever the overall sadness of the sisters' situation, Chekhov will not allow it to subdue the moment-to-moment life of his characters, which has often an attractive, and even occasionally comic, buoyancy. Whether, as is often debated by both students and critics, that buoyancy is an effect of Russian manners in general or a particular Chekhovian heightening of the ordinary conventions (or, as is most likely, a combination of the two), there can be no doubt of the air of spontaneity and self-abandon pervading the characters' actions. The presence of such qualities in their behaviour ensures that we never lose sight of life's more exuberant and positive qualities:

FEDOTIK. You may move, Irina Sergeyevna, you may move (*taking a photograph*). You look charming to-day (*taking a top out of his pocket*). Here is a top, by the way...It has a wonderful note...
IRINA. How lovely!
MASHA. By the sea-shore an oak-tree green...Upon that oak a chain of gold...(*Complainingly*) Why do I keep saying that? That phrase has been haunting me all day...
KULIGIN. Thirteen at table!
RODDEY (*loudly*). Surely you do not attach importance to such superstitions? (*laughter*).
KULIGIN. If there are thirteen at table, it means that someone present is in love. It's not you, Ivan Romanovitch, by any chance? (*laughter*).[2]

The intimacy and exuberance here are peculiar for so large a group and give the scene its unusual energy. There is no room for privacy or dejection. Each person responds to the situation in his or her way, but each responds with a sense of being part of a community. So, whatever the deficiencies in these characters' lives, there is something positive which they share. We are aware of feelings and impulses cutting across one another, and thus of the distances between people, but also of the unusual volatility and abundance of reaction in this scene. Moreover, the art itself, while 'impos[ing] no constraint on spontaneous experience', ensures that there is nothing random about these reactions or about the sequence in which they occur. The 'wonderful note' of Fedotik's top, for example, is not just an isolated effect designed to project a surface realism: at a deeper level it merges with Masha's fascination with the mysterious lines from Pushkin and with Kuligin's talk of love, so that together they suggest, beneath the laughing and the teasing, the romantic richness of Masha's personality, presaging her impending love affair with Vershinin.

Much of the effect of *Three Sisters* depends on this multiplicity of response. Manners in the play appear to be spontaneous and yet are subtly stylized; the overall sadness of the sisters' predicament does not preclude some memorably comic moments. Moreover, the characters' own senses of life, conditioned by their predicament as cultured people living in a period of social transition and geographically isolated in the provinces, hold in tension various social and philosophic possibilities. The sisters are frustrated with their lives, and their frustration is the source of their eloquent lyricism. Never finding true happiness, they create images to embody their sense of an ideal life – lovely clean images of birds and snow, blossoms and spring warmth. Their sensitivity to the passing things in nature is splendidly preserved:

TUSENBACH. ...Not only in two or three hundred years but in a million years life will be just the same; it does not change, it remains stationary, following its own laws which we have nothing to do with or which, anyway, we shall never find out. Migratory birds, cranes for instance, fly backwards and forwards...They fly and will continue to fly, however philosophic they may become; and it doesn't matter how philosophical they are so long as they go on flying...

MASHA. But still there is a meaning?

TUSENBACH. Meaning...Here it is snowing. What meaning is there in that? (*a pause*).

MASHA. I think man ought to have faith or ought to seek a faith, or else his life is empty, empty...To live and not to understand why cranes fly; why children are born; why there are stars in the sky...One must know what one is living for or else it is all nonsense and waste (*a pause*).[3]

But as this dialogue shows (and again it is not simply naturalistic, but poetically stylized to deepen the feeling of the scene), the sisters' aspirations and longings emerge always against a back- ground of doubt. The waste of their lives as they go on living, themselves unfulfilled and unable properly to exercise their talents for the sake of others, prompts them to ask questions of

life's meaning which deepen and diversify the dominantly social
and cultural interests of the play. Thus Tusenbach, in answer to
Masha's question, expresses his agnostic sense that life exists
purely and simply for itself – 'Here it is snowing. What meaning
is there in that?' – words which capture something of our response to the sisters' own lives, dignified as they are and yet
apparently without purpose. But it is Masha who takes up that
other call which Chekhov seems equally to have felt – the call to
find a purpose (socially, and in a sense metaphysically) if life itself
lacks one – which lies behind the play's half-convinced idealism
about work and about the happier future of man. This is another
of the play's sources of tension. It is unlikely that the sisters will
find any real fulfilment in their lives: the play dramatizes with
great insight and subtlety the consistency with which even the
most apparently random events work to disadvantage them, and
suggests the complex factors involved in their defeat. But while
Three Sisters suggests the bleakness of the future awaiting the
sisters, it also contains a counterbalancing movement towards a
peculiar variety of optimism about the general future of man.
The 'Man must work...' speeches contain a certain amount of
irony, especially when one sees what happens to Olga and Irina
when they do work. But the faith in eventual human progress
so often adumbrated by the characters, though placed in context
by the near-tragic circumstances of the sisters, is just as essential
to the play as Chekhov's other, more publicized, tendency towards scepticism.

As *The Cherry Orchard* shows, Chekhov is not a dramatist of the
traditional kind. In *Three Sisters* the fire and the duel, which might
seem the most likely dramatic climaxes, happen off-stage, and the
characters seem to interact too obliquely for there to be any open
conflict. But *Three Sisters* does have its own particular kind of
tension, the tension of social change. It concerns a society – or,
rather, an educated class – in a state of crisis, slowly disintegrating
from within and without. That is, its social context is of that
unstable kind which I have suggested as being particularly stimulating to Chekhov's dramatic imagination; and the conflict it
dramatizes between two opposing ways of life is as fundamental
as it is instinctive in the participants:

IRINA. You say life is beautiful...Yes, but what if it only seems so! Life
for us three sisters has not been beautiful yet, we have been stifled by

it as plants are choked by weeds...I am shedding tears...I mustn't do
that (*hurriedly wipes her eyes and smiles*). I must work, I must work! The
reason we are depressed and take such a gloomy view of life is that we
know nothing of work. We come of people who despised work...
(*Enter* NATALYA IVANOVNA; *she is wearing a pink dress with a green
sash.*)
NATASHA. They are sitting down to lunch already...I am late...
(*Steals a glance at herself in the glass and sets herself to rights*) I think my
hair is all right. (*Seeing* IRINA) Dear Irina Sergeyevna, I congratulate
you! (*gives her a vigorous and prolonged kiss*) You have a lot of visitors,
I really feel shy...Good day, Baron![4]

Natasha and her way of life are set against the sisters and theirs.
Irina is sensitive and well-bred, and her way of expressing herself
has a smooth and attractive lyricism. Natasha, obviously, is vulgar,
affected and incorrigibly vain. Her staccato phrases and jerky
movements, along with her pink dress and green sash, reveal by
contrast with Irina a complete lack of taste. Yet, as most audiences
realize, Natasha's gaudiness and clumsy energy also signify a
rough vitality in her which contrasts with the lack of energy of
the sisters. Irina is educated and refined but also exceptionally
vulnerable, and behind her tears there is a dangerous passivity
to life. Her lyricism gives her predicament real pathos: '...we
have been stifled by [life] as plants are choked by weeds...'; but
it is a lyricism which comes from an unusual quality of submission.
Irina lacks real will, perhaps from the very nature of her upper-
class education and what is hidden in it – what W. H. Bruford,
in his 'sociological study' of Chekhov's Russia, calls 'a concealed
fear of life'.[5] As Natasha enters, Irina makes the very important
observation, 'We come of people who despised work'; and that
is just where Natasha is different. Natasha feigns – she may
actually feel – a sense of her social inferiority when she proclaims
that she is shy; but in fact she has all the self-assertive energy
of one who feels herself rising in the world. She does not seem
actually to calculate her effects: she does not need to. With the
steely, self-enclosed will of a person who, all her life, has had to
'know [something] of work', she is bound to triumph over the
superior delicacy of the sisters.

  Yet it is important that *Three Sisters* not be seen simply as a
drama of class conflict, with Natasha the representative of the
bourgeoisie. It appeals to us in terms quite different from those
of *The Cherry Orchard*, with its more directly social emphases.

For one thing, there is no simple choice to be made between one class and another, since Andrey, in actually marrying Natasha, creates something in between. Also, as I have suggested elsewhere, Natasha herself too often borders on caricature to occupy such an important role. Though she is frighteningly destructive as she gradually takes over the sisters' house, she remains an individual figure rather than a representative one, and she is less subtly and less interestingly developed than any other major character in the play. Her purpose in the drama is as the agent of the sisters' defeat; but the way she defeats them – personal as it is – simply focuses more intently the vulnerability of the sisters' fineness and refined aspiration to the coarser and more primitively energetic elements of life.

Three Sisters, then, is less concerned with the outside threat to civilized standards represented by Natasha than with the paradoxical – and tragic – vulnerability of civilization to weaknesses within itself. The sisters, it is true, are caught in an environment peculiar to late-nineteenth-century Russia; but the social and psychological aspects of their predicament, as Chekhov portrays them, have the utmost relevance to other cultures as well. As civilized people surrounded by, and in some ways embodying, an almost defunct culture, the sisters make us aware of the dilemma which later preoccupied Yeats in 'Ancestral Houses', that of cultural refinement working unconsciously towards its own defeat. So although Natasha is necessary to the bolder dramatic outlines of the play, Chekhov I think puts proportionately much more stress on the *internal* nature of the sisters' world and its inbuilt momentum towards destruction. He is intensely sympathetic to the sisters, whose fineness and sensitivity is contrasted with Natasha's coarseness and bluntness; but he is likewise aware of their lack of energy and purpose (again by contrast with Natasha), which signals the decline of a previous phase of Russian civilization.

All three sisters are very attractive, I think, and from moment to moment they behave with a spontaneous – if rather brittle – gaiety:

MASHA (*strikes her plate with her fork*). Ladies and gentlemen, I want to make a speech!
KULIGIN. You deserve three bad marks for conduct.[6]

But beneath the liveliness and humour of these momentary

outbursts there is in the sisters a deep-rooted and tragic inability to act. Beyond their openness – even spiritedness – in daily conversation there is an element of defeatism in their psychological make-up which makes them unusually vulnerable to the frustrating conditions of their lives. Masha exemplifies it least: in her manner – her whistling, her recitations from Pushkin and her occasional bluntness of speech – there is a sensuousness of a distinctly sexual kind. She does find fulfilment, with Vershinin, and her tragedy is that she has to forfeit it. But in Olga particularly, despite her dignity and gentleness, there is finally a damaging lack of flexibility – a deep inability to adapt and to make something positive of life. Olga is the most responsible of the sisters, the one with the most developed sense of duty. At times she acts towards Irina and Masha with the strength and stabilizing force which compensate for the loss of their mother. Yet her strength and stability at some points are matched by complete exhaustion at others, as we see in Act III on the night of the fire. Being the eldest, she has the longest memory, and the sheer strength of her memory of Moscow seems to leave her oddly disabled and unfitted for the present. She feels old, although she is only twenty-eight; and at twenty-eight her life does seem already in the past. Of her personal life she speaks with resignation, and in an implied past tense:

It's all quite right, it's all from God, but it seems to me that if I were married and sitting at home all day, it would be better (*a pause*). I should be fond of my husband.[7]

Olga's gentleness and reserve give her an air of assurance, but she is in an intangible way prematurely aged. She cannot really conceive of a different future: her opportunities all seem to have been missed. She seems, on the surface, the very opposite of Irina; but while Irina, as the youngest, does have innocence and hope – her whole personality suspended towards that mythical future in Moscow – she too shares Olga's passivity. She waits for the happier future to happen to her, rather than taking initiatives of her own. In Act III, in fact, her passivity becomes almost a kind of living death:

You are so pale and lovely and fascinating...It seems to me as though your paleness sheds a light through the dark air...You are melancholy; you are dissatisfied with life...[8]

So, attractive as Irina certainly is, her very refinement seems to shut out those more vigorous energies on which personal happiness often depends. Throughout *Three Sisters* her vitality remains conspicuously chaste, and her adolescence seems rather painfully extended. The fulfilment she awaits does not come. Like her sisters, she has not the psychological resources to seek it out. The sisters, as a group, have much to offer, but they are caught in circumstances that have very little to offer them. Worse, in this situation, where Olga and Irina find no real opportunity for fulfilment and Masha's is only fleeting, the sisters' very differentness from the provincial life around them seems to turn back on them to disable them. Their psychological disabilities, as they emerge to us, stem directly from their embodiment of certain standards of civilization in a world upon which such civilization has no hold. It is on this that the tragedy turns.

The sisters, of course, are as vulnerable as they are because they lack a sustaining environment. What is vulnerable within them has already been defeated in the world outside; or perhaps it never existed at all in the provinces. But it is clear that their predicament is not something they suffer alone, since there is a widespread *malaise* around them in their society. Very few of the characters who come in contact with the sisters show, for example, any sign of positive or virile energy, and they share a common propensity to philosophize as a way of passing time. Apart from the sisters themselves, only Tusenbach and Vershinin have anything like complete personalities – one attached to the future, the other to the past. But Tusenbach and his idealism cannot survive in the world of the play any more than Vershinin can persist in it. Vershinin, by a quiet calculation on Chekhov's part, comes from the world of the sisters' *father* – the former world of Moscow, in which Vershinin played the part of the 'lovesick major'. Vershinin has not had life all his own way, and he can be weak and ineffectual; yet he embodies some of the energy of an earlier age (presumably of the time when the civilization which the sisters reflect was stronger), and he brings that energy, positively, into the world of the play. It is with his entry that the two groups of characters finally come together in Act I, and it is as a result of his optimistic consolation that Masha takes heart and decides to stay for Irina's party. His whole presence – though he can occasionally seem sentimental and is sometimes

a bit foolish – is pervaded by an energetic resilience to life which
finds a contrast in nearly everyone else. At the end of *Three
Sisters*, however, he departs and takes that energy with him. And
his leaving with the battery (together with Tusenbach's death)
marks the symbolic end of whatever energy has still remained
in the sisters' refined society at the time when the play began.

The contrast between Vershinin and Kuligin, and between the
roles they play in Masha's life, tells us much about the inability
of the sisters' provincial environment to offer them fulfilment.
For if Vershinin manifests something of an earlier and more
energetic style of Moscow life, Masha's husband Kuligin is a
relatively harmless but comically ineffectual, parochial and un-
inspired figure of the provincial present:

Now I have always been successful, I am fortunate, I have even got the
order of the Stanislav of the second degree and I am teaching others
that *ut consecutivum*. Of course, I am clever, cleverer than very many
people, but happiness does not lie in that. . .(*a pause*).[9]

Kuligin's stilted, comically pedagogical manner makes us feel
at almost every point a truncated and limited personality. It is
perhaps a fault of the play that he so often borders on mere
caricature, a relation of the provincial types in Gogol (although
there is, in fact, an undercurrent of sadness and self-doubt in
this particular speech). He is a man of no stature; and to live with
him involves living a life whose possibilities are painfully reduced.
Masha's marriage with this provincial schoolteacher thus suggests, in itself, the narrowness and limitation of the sisters' acquaintance. Yet it is important, in the context of the others who
surround the sisters, that Kuligin is nevertheless a character with
whom we can sympathize. For, along with the absurdity of his
exaggerated gestures, his air of nervous confidence and his
quoting and copying the school director, he does have a certain
pathos. As Irina says, he is 'the kindest of men, but he is not the
cleverest',[10] and there is something touching – as well as something irritating – about his refusal to know what has happened to
his own domestic happiness. Chekhov's sympathies are too fully
engaged by Masha for him not to feel a certain malice towards
her limited husband; besides, Kuligin embodies some of the more
tedious aspects of Russian bureaucracy. But Kuligin's presence
around the sisters is no worse than limiting, and Olga in particular regards him with some sympathy. He lacks the capacity,

so prevalent elsewhere in the sisters' society, to bring about actual destruction.

Few characters in the play can be described simply as victors or victims. As I have suggested earlier, there are factors operating both internally and externally to defeat its most civilized characters; and it is one of the play's saddest ironies that Andrey, himself weak and therefore Natasha's victim, should participate so actively in bringing about the downfall of his sisters. Through Andrey, Chekhov focuses the dissipation of the robust energies of an older generation of Prozorovs, while relating the social vulnerability of the present generation back to certain aspects of their family upbringing. We first hear Andrey in Act I playing his violin, deliberately secluded from company. When he appears, he seems somehow oppressed by the superior vitality of the sisters and by their large expectations of him. He is the only son of the Prozorov family and as such has an intolerable burden to bear. We note the bitterness with which Masha will later speak of him:

Here is our Andrey...All our hopes are shattered. Thousands of people raised the bell, a lot of money and of labour was spent on it, and it suddenly fell and smashed. All at once, for no reason whatever. That's just how it is with Andrey...[11]

But Andrey's failure is not as unpredictable as the image would have us think, for to an even greater degree than his sisters he has been overshadowed psychologically by the imposing and austere figure of his father:

Yes. Our father, the kingdom of heaven be his, oppressed us with education. It's absurd and silly, but it must be confessed I began to get fatter after his death, and I have grown too fat in one year, as though a weight had been taken off my body.[12]

After their father's death, Andrey and the sisters, while educated and refined, have been left without the stern direction he had given to their lives. They cannot find the energy and the discipline to continue on their own: Andrey's career, Masha's music and the sisters' knowledge of languages move backwards rather than forwards. The effort that has been made for them is one they cannot make for themselves, and it is this that makes them all so vulnerable to Natasha's energy. Though the sisters disapprove of Natasha they take delight in the infectious proximity of Andrey's love for her, and by their teasing they directly, though inadvertently, forward their and Andrey's defeat. And Andrey himself, in proposing to Natasha, shows a weakness that has fundamentally to do with the psychological predicament of his family, and perhaps even of his class. Lacking any vitality of his own, he crucially mistakes Natasha's instinctive, yet half-calculated, flight from the table (her genuine, yet exploited, gaucherie) for a pure sign of innocence and youth: 'Oh youth, lovely, marvellous youth!'[13] It is a symptomatic mistake from which we feel the unhappiness and destruction to come. By his own defeat, expressed (as we come to feel) in the kiss that ends Act I, Andrey will subsequently co-operate with Natasha in bringing about the future defeat of his sisters. He will be unable to resist her as she assumes a day-to-day control over the house, and he will actually mortgage the house to Natasha's lover, Protopopov, when he takes to gambling as an escape from his unhappiness.

Yet the principal destroyers of life in *Three Sisters* who make us feel the destructive forces at work in society at large are the two extreme figures, Solyony and Tchebutykin. In one way they are opposites – Solyony with his psychopathic aggression, Tchebutykin indifferent and idle amid his self-absorbed nihilism: '"Tarara-boom-de-ay!" (*reads his paper*). It doesn't matter, it doesn't matter.'[14] But while Solyony cultivates the melodramatic postures of the European Romantic hero and Tchebutykin the postures of the fashionable nihilist, both are obsessively caught in the circular traces of riddles and recitations, and both represent principles totally hostile to civilization. By the fourth act, each is prototypically extreme – so much so that doubts arise as to the credibility of both characters. They contract from what they have been into something almost de-humanized – Solyony to a pair of scented hands from which nothing can remove the smell of a corpse, Tchebutykin to a set of disembodied jingles. But whatever their precise believability in the last act (and it is helped by the more rounded sense of them the play has given earlier), they provide a macabre and fatal combination. The sisters, intuiting the explosive violence of his temperament, are actually afraid of Solyony, but it is part of their predicament that they cannot keep him from the house:

IRINA. No; please go, Vassily Vassilyitch. You can't stay here.
SOLYONY. How is it the baron can be here and I can't?[15]

There is no answer they can give consistent with civilized manners. But with Tchebutykin the destruction is more insidious. He is tender towards Irina, and in Act IV he can still give Andrey a piece of honest advice. But his nihilism, his escape-route from responsibility, leaves him indifferent to any situation of moral consequence. Thus it is Tchebutykin who sets Andrey gambling in Act II; he who doesn't pay his rent when the sisters' house is mortgaged; he who breaks the treasured clock in Act III, having become drunk on the night of the fire; and he who attends – and so makes possible – the duel in the final scene.

From the evidence of the characters, then (even minor ones like Vershinin's bohemian wife, with her attempted suicide), the society in the play is a society in a state of crisis. In fact, the play itself is dominated by a prophecy of change:

TUSENBACH. The yearning for work, oh dear, how well I understand it! I have never worked in my life. I was born in cold, idle Petersburg, in a family that had known nothing of work or cares of any kind. I remember, when I came home from the school of cadets, a footman used to pull off my boots...But I doubt if they have succeeded in guarding me completely, I doubt it! The time is at hand, an avalanche is moving down upon us, a mighty clearing storm which is coming, is already near and will soon blow the laziness, the indifference, the distaste for work, the rotten boredom out of our society.[16]

Tusenbach's image of the storm broods symbolically over the whole play: it is both his, and Chekhov's, way of articulating a sense of social crisis. Yet in context the image is not unequivocal: it is, precisely, a characteristic of Tusenbach's class that it reaches for large and unspecific images, rather than seeking specific social reforms. The storm certainly seems inevitable, and perhaps even necessary, but it may or may not take place. So the more relevant metaphor for the actual state of things in *Three Sisters* is, in fact, the one contained in the words of the old porter Ferapont, to whom Chekhov gives his classic image of cultural tension:

And the same contractor says – maybe it's not true – that there's a rope stretched right across Moscow.[17]

This is not unlike the string that actually does snap at the end of *The Cherry Orchard*, releasing the old society into the new. But in *Three Sisters* the string does not snap, and the play remains taut to the very end. The tension is equally social and psychological, with a fastidious correspondence between outer and inner worlds.

Three Sisters has, at points, a strange, sometimes strained, exuberance; but its predominant mood is, I think, one of sadness – that peculiar lyrical sadness epitomized for many people by the emblem of the seagull on the curtains of the Moscow Art Theatre. The central image of the play is the sisters' Moscow, for which they yearn over a geographical and psychological distance they cannot cross. Indeed, as it is invoked from beyond the play's own horizon, the city of Moscow comes gradually to have a near-symbolic force. It is not just a city, nor completely a symbol, but something in between: a kind of metaphor for that unattainable condition of life to which the sisters aspire without success. Along with so many other images from Chekhov's drama, it has for too long been wrongly described as a symbol. In the first place, the reference of the image is not metaphysical, expressing a sense of all life as crucially unfulfilled, but psychological with respect to the sisters and their past. Most important of all, Moscow – unlike the actual symbols in Ibsen's work (one thinks of the famous white horses of *Rosmersholm*) – is poetically defined, qualified and criticized by the varying perspectives of the play in such a way as to limit its resonance. I do not mean simply that *Three Sisters* contains images of Moscow very different from the one held by the sisters. It does do that, of course; and a number of critics have pointed to Vershinin's speech in Act I about the 'gloomy bridge' and to Ferapont's snatches of information that two thousand people have frozen to death or that a businessman died eating forty pancakes in a vulgar competition. But beyond this fairly obvious kind of checking and placing of the sisters' view of Moscow, the sisters' speeches themselves reveal the true intricacy of the psychological affinity they feel with that city. The image of Moscow is not left to stand vaguely, sentimentally, as an expression of unfulfilled aspiration in one of those 'lyrical gestures' of which Raymond Williams complains. Rather, the image is quite specific – and implicitly critical – in the emotions it conveys:

(BARON TUSENBACH, TCHEBUTYKIN *and* SOLYONY *appear near the table in the dining-room, beyond the columns.*)

OLGA. It is warm to-day, we can have the windows open, but the birches are not in leaf yet. Father was given his brigade and came here with us from Moscow eleven years ago and I remember distinctly that in Moscow at this time, at the beginning of May, everything was already in flower; it was warm, and everything was bathed in sunshine. It's eleven years ago, and yet I remember it all as though we had left it yesterday. Oh, dear! I woke up this morning, I saw a blaze of sunshine. I saw the spring, and joy stirred in my heart. I had a passionate longing to be back at home again!

TCHEBUTYKIN. The devil it is!

TUSENBACH. Of course, it's nonsense.[18]

Since the sisters' refinement is essentially urban in origin, their longing for the city has a well-founded psychological basis, and their expression of it is moving and lyrical. The images of blossoms, sunlight and warmth are finely evocative, touching on our sense of the peculiar freshness and warmth of early spring sunshine. But the effect is more than simply aesthetic: it captures a longing for security, a sudden rush of nostalgia, caught up in the phrase 'to be back *at home* again!' (my italics). With its longing and its nostalgia projected through the same speech rhythms, the whole feeling of Olga's speech suggests a deep-rooted longing for the past, for the irrecoverable (and now idealized) world of her childhood. And while this gives it its pathos, it also highlights the unreal and escapist nature of her dream of the city. The very way in which Olga conceives of Moscow represents Chekhov's sympathetic but critical appraisal of her failure to confront the present.

Tchebutykin's and Tusenbach's voices, intruding bluntly across the stage at the end of Olga's speech, provide of course another kind of critical check. The background stage suddenly and unnaturalistically asserts its action and its sounds over those of the foreground, to interrupt Olga's reverie at a carefully judged point. She has just so much space in which to amplify her feeling before the passive and past quality of it is placed by Tchebutykin's outburst – 'The devil it is!' – which is not, of course, literally a response to Olga's speech but certainly feels as if it were. In fact the checking process at this point is fairly crude, cruder than at any later moment in the play; but it does show Chekhov combining certain effects of poetry with the methods of drama to define and place the image of Moscow, right from the beginning, in terms of a clearly formed psychological perception. As Olga goes on, we feel the superior intensity of her feelings, the pathos of her youth ebbing away drop by drop as the sunlight floods through the window. But we feel, too, the complexities which surround the image of Moscow she projects, complexities incompatible with the simple functions of what we recognize as symbol. Moscow epitomizes, poetically, a disabling backward-looking tendency in the sisters' psychology which affects their present lives. The provinces, certainly, give only limited opportunities to personalities with as much potential as theirs; but, then (as Tchebutykin announces in Act III, although the point of his remark is not immediately apparent, even to himself), even Balzac found happiness in the provinces – at Berdichev. As for Moscow, Chekhov subtly suggests the disillusionment that awaits the sisters there: the journey which they plan, beginning in the autumn, would bring them to Moscow for the winter freeze, and not for those delicate, balmy days of blossoms, sunlight and warmth.

The whole play, then, works in a much more complex way than is ordinarily suggested by the term 'symbolism'. It has no symbols as such. But it is, on the other hand, a highly stylized work which never quite asks to be accepted as a piece of naturalism. As my colleague Mr Robin Grove pointed out some years ago,[19] its meaning has a great deal to do with the way the action is paced and with the way Chekhov organizes the space on the stage. Verbal and visual details in *Three Sisters* are co-ordinated to an unusual degree, where even the conflict between Natasha and the sisters seems indirect and partly stylized. There is little in the way of overt climax: more, rather, of the subtle drama of finely wrought composition. The details are arranged visually and metaphorically to externalize the hidden tensions of the sisters' predicament and to create drama from that. So the opening scene, for example, while it is in a much lower key than the high-spirited dinner conversation towards the end of Act I, generates a peculiar visual and poetic drama of its own:

In the house of the PROZOROVS. *A drawing-room with columns beyond which a large room is visible. Mid-day; [outside] it is bright and sunny. The table in the further room is being laid for lunch.*
OLGA, *in the dark blue uniform of a high-school teacher, is correcting exercise books, at times standing still and then walking up and down;* MASHA, *in a black dress, with her hat on her knee, is reading a book;* IRINA, *in a white dress, is standing plunged in thought.*
OLGA. Father died just a year ago, on this very day – the fifth of May, your name-day, Irina. It was very cold, snow was falling. I felt as though

I should not live through it; you lay fainting as though you were dead. But now a year has passed and we can think of it calmly; you are already in a white dress, your face is radiant. (*The clock strikes twelve*). The clock was striking then too (*a pause*). I remember the band playing and the firing at the cemetery as they carried the coffin. Though he was a general in command of a brigade, yet there weren't many people there. It was raining, though. Heavy rain and snow.[20]

For the beginning of a drama, the pacing of this is unusually slow, with very little sense of urgency. In fact, it is positively retarded by the chiming of the clock and the stage direction 'a pause', as if Chekhov were consciously slowing the action and at the same time giving his audience time to reflect on the stage-image before them. For the visual details here are as important to the overall effect as is the measured cadencing of Olga's speech. Outside it is 'mid-day', and 'it is bright and sunny'; but the action is set indoors where the light is less intense. The house itself, with its drawing-room and ballroom, is aristocratically proportioned, though homely enough with Olga correcting her pupils' work and the table being laid for lunch; and we find the sisters in postures which are relaxed but significantly different – Olga walking up and down, Masha reading and Irina 'plunged in thought'. These different postures immediately suggest both the sisters' separateness and their unself-conscious intimacy. But most important of all, the sisters, in the relative gloom of indoors, are in navy blue, black and white – colours which, while they suggest well-bred gentility and reserve, nonetheless also suggest a certain suppression of sexuality. Natasha, when she enters, is vulgar but sensuous in her flamboyant combinations of yellow and red, pink and green. So that visually, through the subdued light and the sisters' ascetic dress, Chekhov begins to convey an element of disquiet in his sense of their world. It is a sense of a peculiar pastness in their lives which the elegiac rhythms of Olga's speech confirm. Although the spring sunlight is streaming in through the window, Olga's mind is somehow fixed back in the cold, the rain and the snow of her father's funeral. Things *seem* to her to have changed, but Irina's name-day party, particularly at the beginning, adheres more to the past than to the present. Indeed, the painful weight of the past is felt with a peculiar tangibility in those twelve chimes of the clock which break across the first note of hope in Olga's speech. With a psychological delicacy we could expect only at this late stage in the development of his understanding of women, Chekhov is both sympathetic and implicitly critical. The sisters' lives go on, but there is something static in Olga's psychology, something that will not allow her to act freely in the present. Some part of her spirit is left behind, just as some part of Irina's remains unreleased. The sisters, that is, share a propensity (though in Masha it is more complicated) to project intense feeling backwards to the past or forwards to the future – rarely to release it, fully and spontaneously, in the present. Their consciousness, as sensitive and civilized people, of time-schemes outside the present and of all that life once contained or might contain – while it remains one of the most attractive things about them – has become sadly debilitating. Whether that over-consciousness, particularly of the past, is a result of the inadequacies of the sisters' present context or is itself a symptom of decadence, it makes the disintegration of their way of life – confronted with something less reflective and more energetic in the person of Natasha – virtually inevitable.

Throughout *Three Sisters* the past and its presences echo throughout the present in this peculiar way, and life seems, in the end, simply to retrace the tragic patterns of the past. Natasha, of course, moves forward all the time; and things do happen to the sisters – Masha falls in love, and Irina decides to marry. But the deepest poetic points in the play are pervaded by a strong and tragic feeling of recurrence, as in the remarkable exchange between Masha and Vershinin in Act II:

VERSHININ...Strange, it's only to you I complain (*kisses her hand*). Don't be angry with me...Except for you I have no-one – no-one...(*a pause*).
MASHA. What a noise in the stove! Before father died there was howling in the chimney. There, just like that.
VERSHININ. Are you superstitious?
MASHA. Yes.
VERSHININ. That's strange (*kisses her hand*). You are a splendid, wonderful woman. Splendid! Wonderful! It's dark, but I see the light in your eyes.[21]

As a moment of love, the atmosphere of this is both intense and strangely other-worldly; and the wind in the stove, evoking the past, has also the force of an omen. Vershinin's presence, like so much else in the play, is surrounded by a peculiar fatality. He will have to leave the sisters at the end, and he will do so – as their father did – to the strains of a military band. Even the fire in Act III will prompt a memory from the old Ferapont:

In 1812 Moscow was burnt too...Mercy on us! The French marvelled.[22]

Everything, it seems, has its counterpart in the past – everything, that is, except Natasha. In fact, it will be her exploitation of the present, along with the weight of the past which inhibits the sisters, that will cause them not only to remain unfulfilled and unhappy but also to lose the small consolations they do have.

Act I sets in motion the limited *action* of the play. We learn of Tusenbach's love for Irina, a love that is unreturned – and this provides one area of dramatic tension. Masha is unhappily married to Kuligin (while Kuligin's speeches reassuring everyone how happy *he* is show us, less directly, that he is unhappy too); and Act I introduces Masha to Vershinin, whose will to live reassures her and slowly becomes the basis of her dawning love for him. On the more obviously negative side, there is the disturbing fact of Solyony, with his strangely indrawn personality and his explosive aggression; and there is Andrey's 'love' for Natasha, the attraction which her energy has for a man consumed by inertia – an attraction fatal for the play's civilized world. All these things emerge in Act I in an oddly unstable mixture: no single element in the sisters' situation is allowed to predominate. In the first few moments we find Olga tearful, Irina joyful, Masha irritated: the sisters share the same life, the same fate, but each feels it somewhat differently, and they react to those differences in one another. Furthermore, after Vershinin's entry and during the actual evening of the party their spirits seem to mount towards real gaiety. We feel very strongly that the house we are in is the sisters' house and that, whatever the shortcomings in their lives, they have space in which to move with a certain amount of freedom.

Act II, however, is set in the same house twelve months later, and it takes only the contrast of the scene on which the curtain now rises to make us feel what kind of twelve months they have been. For although the setting of Act II is the same as that for Act I, the imaginative effect is deliberately reversed: it is inverted to provide, visually, an image of the sisters' worsened situation. From the effect of space and the outside sunshine of Act I, the stage in Act II has darkened and contracted: it is unlit, with the larger perspective of the ballroom lost. It is eight o'clock at night, and there is no sign of life: only the sounds of a concertina come in, significantly, from the street. So, with the light, noise, colour and high spirits of the party in Act I still lingering in our minds, we understand that the darkness and silence now reigning in the sisters' house signals a darkening in the whole mood of the play. When someone does enter, it is Natasha – alone. She carries a candle, which makes her seem symbolically in control of the situation and implicitly in possession of the sisters' house. That again is a deliberate contrast to the situation in Act I. Act I began with the sisters grouped together, and they were central to every conversation and every scene. Natasha, however noticeable she was by virtue of her abrupt manners and colourful dress, was on the periphery of the action, at least until the very end. But Act II begins with Natasha, and now it is the sisters who are pushed aside. They enter only belatedly, and then one after another; they are never all three grouped together as they were before. Faced with Natasha's absorbed domesticity, Andrey is beaten; and even the sense of community which has sustained the sisters is on the brink of collapse. They are dispersed from their quite intimate grouping in Act I into new and separate relationships. Masha is with Vershinin, Irina with Tusenbach, and Olga comes back with Kuligin from the school. The cause of the dispersal is clear. Natasha, now rapidly taking the reins of power, is instinctively afraid of upper-class social life. During the party in Act I, she was bewildered and confused; by the time of Act II, she is in a position to have such parties stopped. Nor is that all: in cancelling the carnival party, Natasha determines the sisters' fate in a single stroke. Andrey and Tchebutykin go off to gamble, and it is Andrey's gambling losses that will cause him to mortgage the house; Irina is left alone for that confrontation with Solyony which will precipitate the death of Tusenbach; and Natasha, to complete her triumph, goes off – she says – for a 'drive' with Protopopov.

One notices in Act II, even more than in the other acts, how the destructive characters in *Three Sisters* unconsciously but infallibly reinforce one another's destructiveness. At the end of that act, after Irina has just been through the psychic assault of first a proposal and then a threat from the sinister Solyony, Natasha takes advantage of Irina's momentary weakness to propose that she yield her room to Bobik. So although there may be little overt conflict between Natasha and the sisters, there is nevertheless a taut dramatic logic operating through events, always to the sisters' disadvantage. Their gradual loss of power in their own house is externalized in the visual details of Chekhov's stage settings, while the sisters themselves are grouped in finely managed postures and attitudes to manifest their psychological relationship to that loss. Thus throughout the first three acts, as the situation becomes more and more desperate, the scenes are set further into the night and the visual impressions become much more sombre. The climax, quite clearly, is Act III, where the night drags on into the early hours of the morning and the background is filled with the glow of fire and the ringing of alarms. It is also the point at which the sisters' longing for Moscow – produced by, and yet counterpointing, the general sense of loss – is at its most intense.

At the beginning of Act III, then, the setting is a bedroom shared by Olga and Irina, and the space on the stage seems almost cramped. It is past two o'clock in the morning, but instead of darkness and sleep there is the ominous glow of fire and an atmosphere of combined tension and exhaustion, panic and fatigue. When the action begins, Olga moves between feverish activity and complete collapse; and in the course of the act the waning of energy through the night hours is felt as a progressive draining-away of the sources of the sisters' vitality. Around them, Tchebutykin has broken his oath of two years and has become hopelessly drunk, while the old Nanny, Anfisa, intuiting some crisis in the air, suddenly pleads not to be sent away. Emotionally, Act III is the play's real turning-point. That, in a way, is the significance of the fire: raging off-stage in the distance, it gives imaginative definition to the explosive domestic situation inside. It is, as I have said, not exactly symbolism, but that subtle extension of literal situations of which Chekhov was capable at his best. For amid the incipient hysteria of Olga's confrontation with Natasha over Anfisa and the many other direct conflicts unleashed in this act, there is an extremely sure timing of effect to give each moment a wider and decisive resonance:

OLGA. Well, let her sit still.
NATASHA (*surprised*). How, sit still? Why, she is a servant. (*Through tears*) I don't understand you, Olya. I have a nurse to look after the children as well as a wet nurse for baby, and we have a housemaid and a cook, what do we want that old woman for? What's the use of her?
    (*The alarm bell rings behind the scenes.*)
OLGA. This night has made me ten years older.[23]

It is not only that the alarm signals a crisis in Natasha's mounting fury and Olga's sad defeat: it penetrates deeper to the sisters' fate generally, giving something like a premonition of their future. As long as Natasha values people according to their utility – 'What's the use of her?' – it is not only Anfisa, but the sisters too, who must eventually go. It is the same kind of thing that happens with Tchebutykin's famous breaking of the clock. His dropping it is, of course, a drunken accident, but it happens at exactly the point when the news that the battery is to be transferred shatters the growing tensions of the scene. Furthermore, Irina has just announced that the sisters will go away too: in that sense the breaking of the clock seems like the shattering of their dream. And the fact that it was the sisters' mother's clock and so has a sentimental value makes the accident upsetting in its own right. One loss – the anticipated departure of the brigade which gives the town its only social life – generates another which both externalizes the first and adds its own upset to it. Such incidents are not isolated, nor part of a loose chain of crises, but moments in which the major drama reaches a special kind of symbolic epiphany.

It is this kind of thing, which we have seen throughout Chekhov's work, which makes the charge of looseness or lack of control so difficult to accept. If anything, Chekhov's meaning in *Three Sisters* can be disconcertingly contrived, as with the reference to Balzac finding happiness at Berdichev, or the development of the association between Solyony and Lermontov. But for the most part Chekhov's effects are both highly dramatic and unobtrusive, with subtle but clear consistency. Under the crisis conditions of Act III, for example, there is a further change in the way the sisters are brought together on the stage. Emotionally and psychologically, the sisters are fatigued; they need one another's protection. In the face of this, they reaffirm their indissoluble relationship as sisters in meeting one another's needs. Masha can now confess her love for Vershinin, though Olga (who already knows about it) refuses to hear it spoken of. On Olga's advice, Irina decides to marry Tusenbach; and Olga herself confronts Andrey over his having mortgaged the house. Psychologically they are close to one another again. As if to emphasize this, and gently stylizing their physical behaviour, Chekhov groups and re-groups the sisters physically around one another more obviously than ever before. They move continuously closer until, at the end of Act IV, they are, as the play directs, literally 'huddled' together to face their future.

I do not myself consider the ending of *Three Sisters* a very hopeful one. Up to a point, Act IV gives a feeling of relief: it is midday again, and the outdoor setting gives a sense of space after the rather claustrophobic setting of Act III. But the brightness and crispness of the scene – it is autumn, and not (as in the first act) spring – and the receding perspectives of the long avenue of firs, the river and the forest give more the feeling of a crisis being over than of anything being solved. Natasha now has all of the house: she and her children appear at the windows, and the house is filled (Chekhov's irony against her is relentless) with the sounds of her 'Maiden's Prayer'. Moreover, any brightness suggested by the sunlight is overhung with shadow. The departure of the battery, in the play's own discreet symbolism, will leave the town 'extinguished' like a candle, and there is still something to be settled between Solyony and Tusenbach. The most moving moment of Act IV, certainly the one to which it gives most attention, is the farewell between Masha and Vershinin. Yet while that farewell is sad, and even tragic, there is something that is both more neglected by the other characters and, finally, more disturbing: the death of Tusenbach and its reception (or lack of reception) among those he loves.

Tusenbach is an idealist, his idealism coloured by his love. But he is also, unlike most of the other characters in the play, a man capable of action. He does leave the militia in order to work; and it is telling that none of the other characters is much interested when he does. But he does it, and – what is more – he is generous-hearted and able to respond deeply to the things around him. One of the finest speeches in the play belongs to him, and it is spoken immediately before his death:

I feel as though I were seeing these pines, these maples, these birch-trees for the first time in my life, and they all seem to be looking at me with curiosity and waiting. What beautiful trees, and, really, how beautiful life ought to be under them!...See, that tree is dead, but it waves in the wind with the others. And so it seems to me that if I die I shall still have a part in life, one way or another. Good-bye, my darling...[24]

This speech reveals, with almost unbearable sadness, the real depth of Tusenbach's character. It manifests the special pressure

of awareness and deliberation of response of a person seeing the
world for the last time, and therefore in a sense for the first; but
it also expands from that into an almost religious worship of life
for its own sake, for its simple beauty and for sensations as simple
as swaying in the wind. So when Tusenbach does die – killed by
Solyony in a duel – his death is the death of a crucial possibility
from the world of the play. It is the death of the possibility of
life being lived for both work and love, or of life being felt as
enough of a value in itself.

Of course, like all Chekhov's characters, Tusenbach does not
simply embody a 'possibility': he is a complete character, and
one with obvious social limitations. His mannerisms in company
are frequently stiff (even bordering on the comic in his mild
paranoia about his German name), and he shows a mixture of
naivety and literal-mindedness both in his speeches about
happiness and in his decision to fulfil his ideal of work and social
usefulness by taking employment in a brickworks. Irina does
seem to be compromising her life when, at that moment of
despair in Act III, she agrees to marry him. But it is still a
symptom of the state of provincial (and, by implication, of Russian) society, as it is represented in the play, that a man as
purposive and sensitive as Tusenbach should fit into no one's
world. Tusenbach has the loyalty of Irina, and yet in a way he
dies that her innocence might be preserved. For, when we
remember Irina's earlier speeches –

IRINA. Tell me, why is it I am so happy to-day? As though I were
sailing with the great blue sky above me and big white birds flying over
it. Why is it? Why?
TCHEBUTYKIN (*kissing both her hands, tenderly*). My white bird . . .[25]

– it seems impossible that such expansiveness and such lovely
cleanness, much less such chastity and fragility, should ever be
immured in Tusenbach's brickworks. The standard of feminine
refinement embodied in the sisters could not survive the robust
masculinity of Tusenbach's 'new life'. But the tragedy is that the
passivity to certain kinds of situations associated with that
refinement unintentionally co-operates with Solyony's aggressive
destructiveness in killing Tusenbach. Tusenbach tries to understand Solyony and be kind to him, and he dies for it. Yet Solyony's
success depends on the fact that everyone – even, in a sense,
Irina – unconsciously acquiesces in the possibility of his death.

Even after a reference as obvious as the one to the 'dead tree', Irina cannot bring herself to intervene, and she cannot say those words of love which might mysteriously have rescued Tusenbach (as Laevsky was rescued in 'The Duel') by giving him new purpose.

Tusenbach's death amounts, from one point of view, to a defeat of the play's own values; but it is the way in which his death is received by the other characters which really consolidates the defeat. In Act IV the play's time-scale is relatively contracted: moments become precious in such a way as to give urgency to Vershinin's departure in particular. Tusenbach, however, attracts none of this sense of urgency. He makes his final plea to Irina in a calm, significantly measured tone. Then he goes off to the duel, to be virtually forgotten amid the more immediately pressing drama of Masha's and Vershinin's farewell. The news of his death hardly ruffles the surface of the play. It may of course be a fault, from the critic's point of view, that the shot which kills him goes almost unnoticed, at least by the characters on stage; but it is more likely that Chekhov meant it to indicate something sinister and disturbing. Tusenbach – able, youthful and ideal-istic, for all his minor faults – dies virtually unlamented by the sisters, and even before his death has been announced Natasha is busily destroying his last claim on life by planning to cut down the firs and maples, his 'beautiful trees', to replace them with the colourful and highly scented flowers which answer to her own spirit. Tusenbach's death is accepted with a sinister lack of protest by everyone in the play: that lack of protest is ominous in what it suggests not only about Natasha's values but about what has happened to the sisters' own, more civilized, world.

The ending of *Three Sisters*, then, looks very bleak indeed, with Tusenbach dead, Vershinin gone and the sisters grouped to-gether in postures of mutual protection. Yet at that very point, when practically everything that has sustained their lives seems lost, the sisters visibly draw strength from their attempt to identify their condition. They find the courage to go on:

MASHA. Oh, listen to that band! They are going away from us; one has gone altogether, gone forever. We are left alone to begin our life over again...We've got to live...we've got to live...
IRINA (*lays her head on* OLGA's *bosom*). A time will come when everyone will know what all this is for, why there is this misery; there will be no mysteries and, meanwhile, we have got to live...we have got to work,

only to work! Tomorrow I shall go alone; I shall teach in the school, and I will give all my life to those to whom it may be of use. Now it's autumn; soon winter will come and cover us with snow, and I will work, I will work.

OLGA (*embraces both her sisters*). The music is so gay, so confident, and one longs for life! O my God! Time will pass, and we shall go away for ever, and we shall be forgotten, our voices, and how many there were of us; but our sufferings will pass into joy for those who live after us, happiness and peace will be established upon earth, and they will remember kindly and bless those who have lived before. Oh, dear sisters, our life is not ended yet. We shall live! The music is so gay, so joyful, and it seems as though a little more and we shall know what we are living for, why we are suffering...If only we knew – if only we knew![26]

This is one of the few points in *Three Sisters* when the sisters' verbalizing of feeling and their introspection about their own states of mind have the effect of strengthening, rather than debilitating, them. As their voices take over from one another they assume, and build upon, one another's feelings, consolidating and forwarding them – from Masha's suffering assertion 'we've got to *live*' to Irina's 'we've got to *work*' to Olga's more positive '*longing*' for life. Masha, true to her usual character, takes the most difficult and energetic initiative; Irina takes up Tusenbach's call for a life made meaningful through work; and Olga looks into the distance for comfort and justification in the joys of others. Then, with Tchebutykin softly humming his nihilistic chant – '"Tarara-boom-dee-ay!"'...It doesn't matter, it doesn't matter' – and Olga calling across the stage 'If only we knew, if only we knew!', the range of the drama itself may seem to have been extended into the metaphysical, as if Chekhov were embodying something of his own general reaction to life (quite independently of the sisters) in the finale of the play. But it is important to recognize that these are sentiments uttered in a particular context by characters who have been carefully individualized and to some extent (albeit sympathetically) criticized. The persuasiveness of the sisters' final speeches is almost entirely emotional, their content dictated by the sheer intensity of the sisters' needs; for if those speeches affirm the sisters' continuing and heroic aspiration to make something of their lives, and to do so on new terms, they are also a way of softening, or warding off, final defeat. To Chekhov, no fate is complete this side of death: the very fact that the sisters' lives are now so reduced that their last reserves of strength are needed merely to survive makes a new beginning conceivable. But, watching this scene, and even while one is drawn into the intensity of the sisters' feelings, it is impossible not to recognize how much has been lost both personally and socially in the world of the play, and to see the sisters' hopes for a new future in relation to the wider facts which the rest of the play has revealed. The sisters do go on living, but living has become virtually synonymous with suffering. They cannot, in fact, 'begin their lives over again', because the whole play has shown their past to be inescapable. And if they seem to draw strength from one another in this final scene, we cannot forget that they are about to go their separate ways, alone. They have abandoned their dream of Moscow which, according to at least one understanding of the play, ought to release them to live more realistically and fully in the present; but the opportunities which were embodied in their present – in Vershinin and Tusen-bach – have already gone. There are, of course, those notes of hope of which I have already spoken. The sisters assert their will to go on living, and Olga in particular is roused by the strains of the military band:

'Oh, dear sisters, our life is not ended yet. We shall live! The music is so gay, so joyful...'

But even as she says it the band grows fainter and fainter in the distance. Winter is coming and the snow will cover everything: that much is certain. Irina, though, may or may not go on working. The stoical determination to live, to survive, and the optimistic determination to work are the two poles between which the feeling runs. Only life itself will decide. But it is characteristic of Chekhov's genius and the subtle tensions it holds in balance – the tensions, essentially, of a temperament both agnostic and humanist – that the doubt and the hope, in his greatest single work, are there as one.

15

Chekhov's modernity

Many of the central elements in Chekhov's temperament, a temperament conditioned by a scientific training in medicine and by the realistic temper of the best Russian literature of his time, were succinctly outlined some years ago by Henry Gifford in *The Novel in Russia*.[1] Like the present study, Professor Gifford's account found that temperament to be pre-eminently a humanist one, classical rather than romantic. Chekhov, it is commonly agreed, was committed less to a given view of life than to a particular means of approaching it – a means disciplined along almost scientific lines, involving detachment, lucidity and respect for the facts, and always keeping in mind the possible biases of any given perspective. He was neither a prophet nor a system-builder like his great predecessors, but (as Gifford says) a diagnostician working unobtrusively but with great care and delicacy through the materials which life itself presented to him. He had no religion, which meant that at one level his sense of the world was comfortless, the world disturbing in its ultimate impersonality. But Chekhov was also capable, as a writer, of great sympathy and warmth. His non-religious outlook did not lead him to insist on the absurdity of people or the meaninglessness of existence, but led him, conversely, to place a great value on those qualities in life itself which give it its meaning: 'the human body, health, intelligence, talent, inspiration, love, and the most absolute freedom – freedom from violence and lying, whatever forms they may take'.[2] On the one hand, then, this humanistic emphasis in Chekhov's work causes him, as Gifford remarks, to deplore and be pained by waste 'whether of talent or emotion or opportunity'.[3] But of course it also indicates that Chekhov is a more positive writer than even his strongest supporters often contend. He positively values people, knowledge and experience. He is anything but that precursor of 'the absurd' which some commentators, responding to the superficial texture of the late plays, have too readily taken him to be. In fact, if one thinks of the central characters in prose fiction and drama generally from about 1890 on, there are few – apart from Joyce's Bloom in *Ulysses* – who manifest such a strong, central, normative humanity as (say) Chekhov's Olga Mihalovna in 'The Party', Nikolay Stepanovitch in 'A Dreary Story' or the sisters in *Three Sisters*. No doubt, if we compare Chekhov's characters with earlier figures in Russian or European fiction, such as Natasha and Pierre in *War and Peace*, we will notice that many of Chekhov's people display psychological debility in some form, but they are by no means negative people in their modern fictional context. The symptoms they reveal have often to do with the changing social terms on which Chekhov represents people as having to live: unlike the central characters in Tolstoy's major fiction, Chekhov's people are not members of a secure aristocracy. But Chekhov intuitively resists the tendency of many twentieth-century novelists to see such characters as totally alienated from their society, inhabiting private worlds of belief and fantasy which may mean, for the writer, a short route to the surreal. He is not tempted (as are some modern writers) to equate the portrayal of psychological disturbance with the attainment of psychological realism and depth; nor, on the other hand, does he feel obliged to lend authorial support to a stance adopted by his alienated characters towards constituted society. Though he does portray psychological disturbance – as in 'The Black Monk' – he also creates characters who convincingly embody, even in situations of great difficulty, the living reality of a sane, decent and finally even composed humanity.

The same positive commitment to enlightened values underlies Chekhov's approach to knowledge and experience. He did not, of course, have Tolstoy's constructional power, Tolstoy's power to range over so great a span of time and through so many inter-related lives. But Chekhov was more aware than was Tolstoy of what we may now think of as the problem of knowledge, the relativity principle inherent in the very perception of reality, which so occupied physicists and philosophers in the twenties of this century. It was the formal extension of his belief that 'Everything in this world is changing, mutable, approximate and relative',[4] and his finest fictional demonstration of this problem occurs in 'Lights', where the truth of what the world is really like seems to shift from one understanding to its opposite according to the experience and temperament of the various speakers and listeners and the contexts of darkness or daylight around them. Typically, then, there is not so much a total vision in Chekhov as an illuminating play of perspectives through which truths, though they are implied by the reactions of characters and the sequences of narrative events and effects, are necessarily provisional. Compared with Tolstoy's power and what Chekhov himself called 'a kind of hypnotism' in Tolstoy's writing, Chekhov displays an undogmatic yet almost specialist intelligence and scrupulosity about experience which are informed by a distinctively modern consciousness of the world. In his letters he constantly stressed the importance of psychology: he wished to extend his medical studies formally into that area. His stories include a penetrating account of feminine sexual psychology, comparable with Henry James's or Virginia Woolf's in its combination of sympathy and detachment, but more frank and comprehensive than theirs about the biological factors in feminine behaviour, and finally less willed and more convincing than that of Lawrence. He was absorbed, as a writer, in the scientific theories of the latter part of the nineteenth century; in fact many of his longer stories, as we have seen, set those theories against more traditional views of the world and man and explore the discrepancies between them. Yet his deepest personal belief was in the integrity of each person's unique and private experience. For although his stories are often energized by arguments about philosophical and scientific ideas, they pursue their own course of testing, and thereby demonstrating, the varieties of reality in different men's lives. They have, therefore, the somewhat paradoxical (and distinctively modern) function of asserting, through our vicarious experience of their narratives, that reality can only really be known through practical experience itself, and that even then it is only one's *own* reality. For the men in 'Happiness', the world is a confusing, mysterious place, and somewhere in their lives there is a kind of emptiness. For Yegorushka in 'The Steppe', it is a hostile place when one is not protected by adults, and even adults (as Yegorushka comes to see) cannot protect one from death. Ananyev in 'Lights' has learnt from experience the destructiveness of thinking along nihilistic lines; but his nihilistic listeners in the story (like Chekhov himself, in so far as he qualifies our complete acceptance of Ananyev's narrative) have a different kind of experience and so remain unconvinced. For Laevsky in 'The Duel' and Laptev in 'Three Years', on the other hand, reality turns out to be a kinder and more various reality than either character predicts.

This, then, is the nature of Chekhov's humanism and of the distinctive realism which embodies it. It is essentially different from – though it obviously grew out of – the Russian realism of Gogol, Turgenev, Dostoevsky and Tolstoy. Chekhov is more tentative than they, but also – and even allowing for some of the prophetically modern elements in Dostoevsky – more modern. Furthermore, as Logan Speirs has pointed out,[5] it was Chekhov's special task to bring Russian drama to the level of achievement and sophistication of Russia's great nineteenth-century prose tradition. Turgenev's *A Month in the Country* is the only nineteenth-century Russian play which in any sense anticipates Chekhov, and Chekhov almost certainly learnt from certain of its elements. Turgenev's opening in particular seems, with hindsight, to anticipate Chekhov as it sets two groups of figures apart on the stage and yet subtly relates them to one another through correspondences of mood and calculated ambiguities of reference within the dialogue. However, Turgenev came to agree with his contemporaries that his play was 'undramatic' and he subsequently abandoned the dramatic form. So it fell to Chekhov to develop the new possibilities of relaxed stage action which Turgenev had left largely unrealized. Yet Chekhov's most important contribution to the theatre (and the basis, ultimately, of his difference from Turgenev) lay not so much in his achieving a more relaxed form and a greater realism of detail in his plays, but in his successfully carrying over to the stage the emotional realism born out of his long experience of the short story. (It may be relevant to remark that this is an experience shared by neither of the other two most important nineteenth-century dramatic naturalists, Ibsen and Strindberg.) For it is another of the semi-paradoxes that we find in Chekhov's work that, despite the structural stringency of his stories and their detachment from the perspectives of individual persons, he can (and does at certain moments) enter fully – even passionately – into the local and subjective intensities of his characters' feelings. One remembers the moment in 'Three Years' when Laptev renounces his hopes of a passionate, idealistic love. Laptev's naively romantic conception of love is partly what the story is criticizing, yet the moment when he seems to himself to be renouncing all hope of it is conveyed with great pathos: he reasons that he can busy himself with other things, devote his life to others, and so on, but still the tears spring uncontrollably into his eyes. Whatever Chekhov's reservations about Laptev's conception of love, he captures the complexity and volatility of Laptev's feelings from a position of real emotional closeness to him. But to transfer such an intensity and complexity of feeling to the stage was not easy. In 1887, when *Ivanov* appeared, Chekhov had already written the stories 'Enemies' and 'Easter Eve'; 'The Party' was to appear in the following year. In 1896, the year of the first performance of *The Seagull*, he had behind him the masterpieces 'Lights', 'A Dreary Story' and 'The Duel'. There is, as a number of writers have pointed out, a large discrepancy between Chekhov's achievement as a writer of fiction and the relatively amateurish nature of his first really serious works for the theatre.

Chekhov had been interested in theatre all his life. Both as a child and as a young artist he devised short one-act sketches, of which perhaps the most successful – certainly the most popular – was *The Bear*. Yet, fertile as his imagination was with ideas for such sketches, they presented him with little sense of challenge. Instinctively, one might say, he recognized that the one-act play was not the appropriate form for him: even as early as *Platonov*[6] he was drawn to the drama in four acts as the one most natural for the expression of his more serious interests. With hindsight, it appears that there were very good reasons for this. Apart from the obvious advantage of allowing greater space for the development of character and for a deepening of the audience's understanding, the drama in four acts allowed Chekhov a new range in capturing the variety of ingredients which make up any situation and a new scope to pursue the effects of that situation through time. Both of these things are integral to the dramatic realism which we find in his late plays; and they underlie that distinctive tension which I have already described in relation to *Three Sisters* between the apparent indeterminacy of each complex moment of dramatized reality and the fate to which those moments add up. But it took some time before Chekhov developed the full potentialities of the form. *Ivanov*, in which he attempts a new portrayal of the already popular – even hackneyed – Russian literary type of the 'superfluous man' is genuinely insightful in its portrayal of Ivanov's self-disgust and yet his terrible powerlessness to escape his condition other than through suicide. It also displays that dialectical quality and balanced distribution of sympathies which we find in so many of the stories: Ivanov is weak and callous, Lvov morally upright; but Ivanov does suffer from guilt and is conscious of not understanding himself, while Lvov lacks understanding and behaves with a dangerous self-certainty. But, for all this, there are no characters in the play who come fully to life, and the play itself is burdened with theatrical paraphernalia of an archaic sort. Its entries and exits have an almost ritualistic quality, while many of its effects, like the screeching of the owl, are conventional and over-obvious. Moreover, it contains open soliloquies in which the characters have to state their feelings, since they are not otherwise adequately dramatized. Even *The Seagull*, which has such importance to Chekhov's long and historic association with the Moscow Art Theatre, is over-ambitious and marred by intense self-consciousness. Like *Ivanov*, it reveals a playwright drawing as much on literary models as on his own experience of life; and, since the play is actually about art and a range of possible relationships to it, its interests are necessarily rather specialized. So, although the relationship developed between Arkadina and Treplev is interesting and although it is hard to resist the poetic appeal of the play's setting, its interest is, I think, limited. While there is a freer movement, both physically and in the dialogue, than in *Ivanov*, there is still not the sense, as there is in the later plays, of a situation developing on the stage with its own momentum – one which, consequently, feels natural to it. The pattern of Nina's life is fixed in advance by her association with the slain seagull and by Trigorin's outline of her story: in fact, the seagull-symbol is intrusive throughout the play, at the same time as it is, I suspect, quite confused in significance. And this sense one has of a pattern being imposed on the play is intensified when the most significant changes in the characters occur between the third and fourth acts. Chekhov gives us no sense of the process by which these changes came about and only the most sketchy explanations of them: the resolution of the drama thus depends on changes in the characters which we have simply to take on trust.

It is only in *Uncle Vanya* (1897) that Chekhov moves perceptibly towards that sustained presentation of powerful undercurrents and cross-currents of feeling, determining people's fates, which constitutes the mastery of *Three Sisters*. His first step towards this was to dispense with the obviously 'dramatic' ending, transferring the shooting episode back from the end (where it had been in *The Wood Demon, Ivanov* and *The Seagull*) to Act III and converting it into anticlimax when Vanya misses his intended victim and delivers a sublimely comic–pathetic speech. One of the problems with the play, of course, centres on the relationship between its comic and its more serious elements, since its comedy is more blatant than that of the later plays and less well-timed (I, for one, can never watch that famous climax of Act III without momentarily withdrawing from the play in a confusion of reaction and disbelief). But *Uncle Vanya* does capture the actual rhythms of its characters' lives, respecting at the same time Vanya's sense of urgency when, at forty-seven, he comes to perceive the terrible monotony of his life; and it is the first of Chekhov's plays to make us feel time passing, and the effects of time passing, through the gradual turn of the season through the four acts. Moreover, Act II is a splendid example of Chekhov's special feeling for those sleepless occasions when people are both restless and exhausted, such as we later find at the climax of *Three Sisters*. As so often in the context of night in Chekhov's stories, people's feelings in this act are both unusually exposed and unusually volatile: the airlessness before the storm intensifies the psychological oppression they feel in one another's company, and their mounting tension is paralleled by the strengthening wind and the sky flickering with lightning. It is this sub-surface complexity of changing emotions, shifts of initiative and power, and the quick instinctive glances of communication between people, and so on, which Chekhov captures in his plays, that comprises what I have called his 'emotional realism', and it is best demonstrated by an example from *Three Sisters*:

MASHA. By the sea-strand an oak-tree green...upon that oak a chain of gold...upon that oak a chain of gold (*gets up, humming softly*).
OLGA. You are not very cheerful today, Masha.
 (MASHA, *humming, puts on her hat.*)
OLGA. Where are you going?
MASHA. Home.
IRINA. How queer!...
TUSENBACH. To go away from a name-day party!
MASHA. Never mind...I'll come in the evening. Good-bye, my darling...(*kisses* IRINA). Once again I wish you, be well and happy. In old days, when father was alive, we always had thirty or forty officers here

on name-days; it was noisy, but today there is only a man and a half, and it is as still as the desert...

IRINA (*discontentedly*). Oh, how tiresome you are...

OLGA (*with tears*). I understand you, Masha.

SOLYONY. If a man philosophizes, there will be philosophy or sophistry, anyway, but if a woman philosophizes, or two do it, then you may just snap your fingers!

MASHA. What do you mean to say by that, you terrible person?

SOLYONY. Nothing. He had not time to say 'alack', before the bear was on his back (*a pause*).

MASHA (*to* OLGA, *angrily*). Don't blubber!⁷

Stylized as this necessarily is, it does capture something essential about the way in which people actually interact and the frequent disjunctions in their conversational responses as patterns of attention are determined by the moods, preoccupations, perceptions and needs of each individual. Chekhov's characters choose not only what they themselves say, but what, of other people's speech, they consciously hear and react to – just as they also choose, in a sense, *not* to hear the things which are difficult or embarrassing for them. This is not a symptom of their so-called 'inability to communicate', but a reflection of the way in which most communication actually occurs. Even more important, though, is the fluidity of feeling which Chekhov captures both in individual characters and in the emotions generated when they interact. From the moment in this passage when Masha quotes aloud the lines from Pushkin and then begins to sing under her breath, there is an air of emotional tension about her which makes her seem very much alive and interesting. She hums to mask, but also partially to cope with, her depression; and even when she directly admits the reason for her depression, she is still half-humorous about it ('to-day there is only a man and a half') and is cross at Olga's maudlin effort to be sympathetic. Her feelings emerge as not only complex in themselves but also fluid through the drama, ranging from depressed dissatisfaction to a resilient half-humour to irritation.

This is a quality of Chekhov's drama which has no parallel in that other classic naturalist, Ibsen. It is partly because Chekhov has a greater number and range of more or less equally important characters, but also because Chekhov is not single-mindedly bent on exposing the one truth or fact which will shatter the complacency of his characters' lives. By comparison with Chekhov,

Ibsen is a moralist with designs on both his characters and his audience. The possibilities and consequences of action for his characters narrow down throughout his plays until a confrontation occurs in which they are made to face the truth. Everything converges, morally and psychologically, on that moment. Chekhov, on the other hand, recognizes the fluidity and changeability of reality even within apparently fixed and predictable situations, so that the drama can change, from moment to moment, from near-tragedy to comedy and from an atmosphere charged with consequence to a sudden irrational effusiveness. There is no one truth, nor any one dilemma, for the characters to confront: the drama consists in the movement of feeling and the pattern of reaction as subtle changes occur in the characters' situations. It is this, for example, which is developed around and through the characters' reactions to the orchard in *The Cherry Orchard*.

Chekhov's Russia had seen the rise of realism simultaneously on many fronts: in the novel, in drama, in stagecraft (with the coming into being of the Moscow Art Theatre under the co-direction of Konstantin Stanislavsky and Vladimir Nemirovich-Danchenko) and in early experiments in the art of photography. It has also been argued by Ronald Gaskell[8] that the rise of naturalism in Western Europe had to do with a new conception of man born out of new tendencies of nineteenth-century thought and the changing nature of socal reality on a broad scale – in particular, the triumph of scientific explanations of human behaviour, the empirical stress which became evident in much contemporary philosophy, and the consolidation of the middle class, the virtual overthrow of aristocracy. In these terms Chekhov seems clearly to belong among the realists and naturalists of the latter part of the last century and, in some sense, to share their preoccupations; but there are certain crucial respects in which he was different. In the first place, Chekhov's characters, though they are frequently challenged by the bourgeoisie, are not – most of them, anyway – themselves of that class. His best and most fully developed characters in the late stories and in the plays are, with a few exceptions, people of upper-class origin whose way of life embodies some of the more civilized and refined values of the Russian past. Because of this, Chekhov's characters have more to gain or lose than prestige, position and money. Indeed, his situations are constructed almost deliberately to suppress the possibility of characters being able to buy their way out of difficulty – always a possibility in bourgeois drama, however apparently deterministic its general atmosphere. Even in *The Cherry Orchard*, where that solution seems most available, Lyubov Andreyevna's extravagance ensures that the estate-owners will never have the money to pay off their debts; and the solution which Lopahin proposes – though it, too, is a financial one – involves a sacrifice of their sensibilities, their identities and the whole sum of their past. Secondly, unlike Ibsen and later Brecht, Chekhov was in no way didactic. If, as Gaskell suggests, the scientific orientation of modern society and society's sense of itself encouraged the view that both men and societies could be altered since they could be explained, Chekhov did not avail himself of the opportunity for moralizing which was a concomitant of that view. The string stretched across Moscow in *Three Sisters* and the breaking string in *The Cherry Orchard* suggest situations of cultural tension and collapse which the characters are powerless to affect: they themselves, while embodying some of the values Chekhov held dear from the past, are the victims of that collapse. Lopahin is Lopahin and Gaev is Gaev: there is no hope of converting one into the other, or even of getting them to see life in one another's terms. The impulse to instruct, and ultimately to reform, which one finds in (say) *A Doll's House* or *Mother Courage* is therefore conspicuously absent from Chekhov. Thirdly, and most importantly, Chekhov's drama escapes that constriction which comes in much naturalistic drama from its urban and bourgeois context, whereby the earthy, the physical and the natural give way to sterility and mere material comfort. For it is Chekhov's point of connection with the great dramas of the past, and, in the kind of emphasis he gives to it, the substance of his very modern consciousness of the world, that he so strikingly relates his characters' situations not only to their social and psychological origins but also to forces within and around them which are non-social and impersonal in kind.

Naturalistic drama, it has been said, either tends to insulate its characters from the wider physical context of existence, by confining its attention to the psychological and moral terms of an action taking place within the closed space of four walls, or else (as in Brecht) tends to stress those physical aspects of life in a drama involving lower-class characters, at the cost of any complexity in the portrayal of their emotional, intellectual or even cultural life. Thus, in general, naturalistic drama entails a contraction in scope from the drama of the Greeks or of Shakespeare, in which both the earthiness and the higher spiritual and intellectual reaches of man's existence were given profound force. This contraction in the scope of later drama has undoubtedly to do with the post-Renaissance change from a broadly religious to a broadly scientific understanding of man's relationship to his world, and with the diminishing possibilities, associated with that scientific understanding, for a richly metaphoric language such as the greatest early dramatists used to identify mysterious and ambiguous energies simultaneously in man and in nature. No modern dramatist, for example, can recapture the pagan awe with which the *Agamemnon* regards the life-force itself and the force of violence ending it, as in Clytemnestra's speech where she refers to 'the sombre drizzle of bloody dew' from Agamemnon's body in which she 'rejoice[s] no less than in God's gift of rain'. Even less can he share Shakespeare's apparent sense of the natural order as ultimately embodying a moral and spiritual proportion with which human states can at moments be objectively identified and to which they may be metaphorically referred. In Shakespeare's language immoral acts are acts 'against nature'. The tempest in *King Lear*, for all its raging external force drowning Lear's own voice, is nevertheless bound up metaphorically with 'the tempest in [Lear's] mind' (III.iv.13); and 'Fair is foul and foul is fair' (*Macbeth*, I.i.10) is a state both of disturbed nature and of moral portent concerning Macbeth's overweening ambition in an already wartorn world. But the technological mastery of nature by man (or so it seemed) in the course of the eighteenth and particularly the nineteenth centuries and the erosion of religious and moral beliefs by the findings of science have left us with a more prosaic (that is, non-metaphoric) understanding of man and his world. Even Wordsworth, with all his feeling for 'the passions of men ...incorporated with the beautiful and permanent forms of nature' (Preface to the second edition of *Lyrical Ballads*), has the modern writer's more frequent recourse to simile in relating men to nature than to the compression and exhilaration of Shakespearean metaphor. It is not surprising, then, that in Chekhov's plays we find no Shakespearean robustness of natural metaphor, nor such density and profound inventiveness of poetic language. The 'poetic' life of his plays is made up of interconnecting patterns of imagery (supplied often through simile), of the lyrical cadences of some of the characters' speeches and of the delicately composed visual effects of the stage scenery, often associated with the changing atmospheres of the seasons. But of all the naturalists, Chekhov did the most, in his own way, to acknowledge the physical bases of existence as they manifest themselves through and around the comforts and refinements not merely of bourgeois life but also of the life of the upper class. In fact, it could be said that he exploited the very discrepancy between men and the world around them which made metaphoric language so difficult, in order to project his own distinctive sense of the indifference of nature towards human affairs and the isolation of human consciousness in an impersonal world. Whereas, for example, landscape in Ibsen is made to carry a great symbolic weight, even while his characters seem almost completely insulated from the forces of the physical world, Chekhov seems constantly to strive to make us feel both the objectivity and impersonality of natural phenomena and the subjective influence they may have, either in *seeming* to objectify a character's situation for him or else in themselves becoming partial components of his feelings. One thinks of Nadyezhda Fyodorovna in 'The Duel' yielding to the warm air of the southern summer and the soft lights on the water, or of Yulia in 'Three Years' feeling suddenly and desperately alone as she goes over and over Laptev's proposal in her mind while the storm roars outside. The characters respond to, and are subtly influenced by, states in nature; but nature itself, as Chekhov reveals it, is indifferent to them, neutral and existential. Some of the saddest and most profound moments in all Chekhov occur, therefore, when he represents his own characters as feeling the need to locate values objectively in the natural world, but as being inevitably met, and resisted by, the impermeable material facts of that world. When Chekhov's characters make an appeal for a better life or attempt to identify to someone else their own deepest feelings, they instinctively reach (as did the great dramatists) for natural illustrative imagery. Nikolay Stepanovitch of 'A Dreary Story' and Dr Astrov in *Uncle Vanya* both identify the dignity and uprightness of a moral way of life with the loftiness and linearity of tall forest trees. Irina feels 'as though [she] were sailing with the great blue sky above [her] and big white birds flying over it'; and Tusenbach, identifying with the dead tree still swaying in the wind, voices the impulse which so many of these characters implicitly share: 'What beautiful trees, and, really, how beautiful life ought to be under them!'[9] Yet at the very moment of their fullest appeals to nature, at the high point of their own creativity, these characters perceive the isolation of that impulse in themselves as they are met with silence or with misunderstanding. Nikolay Stepanovitch is troubled by the sense 'that these pines and fir trees, birds, and white clouds on the sky, will not notice my absence when in three or four months I am dead' (V.200–1). There is no change in the mild placidity of the sky, and not much reaction from other people, when Tusenbach dies. The act of creative identification which Shakespeare had made between men and the natural has been transferred, in this modern drama, from artist to protagonist: as we watch the characters make it, we share with their author a sense of *their* fineness, *their* creativity, and a common sense of deprivation since that impulse is not reciprocated by the natural world, as we may ideally wish it to be.

Chekhov, then, in placing his characters in the wider physical context of their world, creates a particular understanding of the kind of place it is and also of the kinds of sensibilities with which people meet it. Furthermore, he understands the ways in which the needs of those sensibilities vary with age. Chekhov almost invariably gives us the exact ages of his characters in both his stories and his plays, and his insistence to the company of the Moscow Art Theatre that they consider appropriate age as one of the first principles in casting suggests the emphasis he put on this. For it was part of his realism and his profound understanding of human nature to recognize that neither temperament nor sensibility is an entirely stable thing. Anya believes in Trofimov because she is young: she may easily change. Tusenbach believes in personal happiness to a greater extent than Vershinin because he too is young, is in love, and has no experience of the domesticity of marriage. Even five years' difference in age between characters can mean crucial differences in understanding, and five years added to the same character's life can make him almost another man. In fact, this is one of the primary centres of Chekhov's interest, and, as I suggested earlier, one of the reasons why he was so much better served by the longer span of the four-act play.

Unlike Ibsen, whose dramas derive much of their power from their unity of place and the concentration of the action into two or three consecutive days, Chekhov, in both the stories and plays, set out to capture the less dramatic but subtler and ultimately perhaps more decisive changes which time effects in people's lives. So, unlike Ibsen's characters, who are introspective only in moral terms, the people in Chekhov's stories and plays are intensely aware of their biological beings: they recognize not only the material and moral conditions of their lives but the changes – biological, emotional and psychological – which take place naturally through time. The two outstanding examples from the stories are, of course, Olga Mihalovna of 'The Party' and Nikolay Stepanovitch of 'A Dreary Story'. Both of these characters are undergoing a crisis in their biological lives – crises which inevitably have their emotional and psychological concomitants; and, in capturing the combined physical and emotional aspects of such experiences, both stories are short masterpieces. But even outside times of overt crisis, we find Chekhov's characters – especially in the plays – talking about their bodies, their failing memories, their headaches and fatigue. They even register the changes taking place in themselves and others from day to day:

OLGA. You are radiant to-day and looking lovelier than usual. And Masha is lovely too. Andrey would be nice-looking, but he has grown too fat and that does not suit him. And I have grown older and ever so much thinner. I suppose it's because I get so cross with the girls at school. Today now I am free, I am at home, and my head doesn't ache, and I feel younger than yesterday.[10]

This is what makes Chekhov's people seem like real people: not because he captures 'what people actually say' – for few people actually speak of themselves and others as explicitly as this – but because they emerge very strongly as people subject to time and thus to the ageing process. They have not, nor has the world around them, a constant current of energy. It is spring at the opening of *The Cherry Orchard*, but there are still three degrees of morning frost. Olga in *Three Sisters* may at one moment be able to cope with the demands of her life, but the next moment she is liable to collapse. This instability of natural and human energy, together with the emphasis the characters themselves put on the passing of time, is a distinctive element of Chekhov's realism. But it is more than just realism, for (as *Uncle Vanya* shows) the wastage of people's energies, affections and talents through the course of time touched Chekhov deeply. In *Uncle Vanya* not only Vanya but all the characters in the play experience this wastage – wastage of talent through lack of opportunity, wastage through mis-direction of energy, wastage through personal inhibition and wastage by time. Vanya complains, 'I have no past, it has been stupidly wasted on trifles, and the present is awful in its senselessness.'[11] Astrov confesses that he gets drunk once a month because 'I don't think of myself as a crank at such times.'[12] Even Serebryakov feels like an exile – 'Every moment to be grieving for the past, watching the successes of others, dreading death.'[13] Moreover, through the turn of the season from the late summer afternoon of Act I to the autumn twilight of Act IV and through the series of echoing farewells which end the play, Chekhov makes us feel time passing as a narrowing down and closing off of even such limited possibilities as were open to the characters when the play began. But his real achievement is to have also made us feel the way in which people of different ages and temperaments experience such a situation differently and at different levels of intensity. Yelena and Serebryakov are the sort of shallow people who must physically escape any situation which requires that they acknowledge the deeper facts about their lives. Astrov, a younger man than Vanya and a more intellectual, less emotional one, is protected to a large extent by his more abstract justifications of his life and by the fact that, with time, he is actually becoming coarser and blunter in his feelings. Only Vanya and Sonya have those vulnerable, emotional natures which feel situations intensely and thus are prone to despair, and even Sonya has at least the compensation of her youth. It is not that there are any more opportunities open to Sonya than to Vanya himself, but since she is twenty-six where Vanya is forty-seven their perceptions of their situation simply cannot be quite the same. For all the piety and sentimentality of her final speech, Sonya manages a genuine stoicism; Vanya's last words, which may be too easily forgotten amid the formal rounding-out of Sonya's speech, are simply 'Oh, if only you knew how my heart aches!'[14]

Time itself, then, might be said to be one of the protagonists of Chekhov's drama and fiction. It exists in his work not as a force bearing upon people's lives, as in Ibsen, but as the active medium in which those lives occur and as a dramatized presence. In the very early stories, the passing of time tends to be conveyed visually, as in 'Misery' with its falling snow and the accumulating weight of snow on the mare's back and the old man's shoulders. In the later novella-length works, especially 'The Duel' and 'Three Years', time itself becomes the agent which accomplishes changes in people's lives which they never expected and for which they had perhaps never hoped. In those works Chekhov seems to take a somewhat harsh, impersonal comfort in the active autonomy of time, in the resiliency and unexpectedness of life, since the very fact of time ensures that there are potentialities – positive as well as negative – in people's lives which are not entirely predictable on the basis of the present. Unlike the traditional realist, he is not interested in pursuing the consequences of particular choices through a passive span of time, but tries instead to give a sense of 'what time itself may do, taking those actions and choices as a starting-point. By doing so, he develops in his narratives new shapes and structures which derive from a deep conviction about the fundamental unpredictablity of human events: it is no accident that his longest mature narrative is called simply 'Three Years'. But it is in the plays that time is most felt as a pressure and a weight upon the characters' lives, perhaps because the characters there carry in their speech and gesture so much of the aristocratic past. Their geographical displacement – as people from a highly urbanized culture who are disablingly at leisure in the countryside – intensifies our sense of the ways in which they are also displaced in time, for theirs are, essentially, aristocratic natures living in a bourgeois age. Their awareness of time as an element in their personal lives is continuous with their sense of a wider historical past, as when Lopahin's mind reaches back to his childhood memory of Lyubov as the young lady of the estate or when Firs recalls his own reaction to the Emancipation of the serfs and the rejoicing there was then. And the world of their past seems still so real to them, in all its apparent stability, that they never properly objectify their situations in the present: whatever they see or feel of the present is determined in the comparing context of their memories. In fact, it is one of Chekhov's distinctive achievements to have given such an introspective dimension to realist drama, since realist drama cannot afford the artifice of soliloquy. When Olga delivers her first long speech about her father's funeral, comparing it with Irina's Saint's Day exactly one year later, or when Lopahin recalls what Lyubov Andreyevna was like before her departure from the estate to which she is about to return, the effect is similar to that of soliloquy in both imparting information and opening up the speaker's state of mind and the very rhythms in which he feels and thinks. But the fact that there are other people present to whom the remarks are in part addressed, together with the atmosphere of reverie so finely evoked by the subdued lighting and the sense of people waiting, gives a naturalness and acceptability to such speeches: there is even a suggestion that they are partly elicited, in such length, by the distinctive conditions in which they are uttered. Thus, without loss to the basic realism of the drama – though there is a slight effect of stylization, of course – Chekhov extends our sense of the characters back into their senses of themselves as conditioned by their personal and social pasts (a true internalization of the drama which Ibsen, for example, almost never achieves) and immediately immerses his characters in the flux of time. The major characters are created as people whose own imaginations constantly refer the present to the past (the more so, since most of them are living reduced lives in the present), while the audience is invited to witness the continuing changes in their lives which take place as time passes within the drama itself. This immediate sense of time passing is unusually strong in Chekhov's plays since, by extending his basic realism into the area of stage sound-effects – as in Act IV of *Uncle Vanya*, when the characters on the stage sit silent, listening to the fading sound of harness bells as Astrov drives away, or when the recurrent striking of the axe against the cherry-tree is heard in *The Cherry Orchard* – he was able to create a sense of dramatic and psychological time actually elapsing before us on the stage.

In all these things Chekhov was a modern writer in the best sense. But he is not to be lost among other modern authors who superficially share his concerns. There is a classical stringency about Chekhov's works, something (as is often said) 'impeccable', which distinguishes them entirely from those of the modern absurdists and surrealists. Yet with their awareness of the world's essential impersonality, their deeply sceptical intelligence and unorthodox humour – his works do belong to a perceptibly more modern world than that of Tolstoy, Dostoevsky or George Eliot. They also reveal a breadth of humanity which (again with the notable exception of *Ulysses*) literature in our century has generally lacked. Concerned as he was with people, Chekhov consistently refused to allow his concerns to narrow or to become abstract. In his life as both an imaginative writer and a practical doctor he was restless, hospitable and gay, but tactful, reticent and always somewhat withdrawn: the greatness and versatility of his art derive from the integrity with which his works reflect his distinctiveness as a man.

NOTES

Introduction

1. 'Chekhov and the English', in Donald Davie (ed.), *Russian Literature and Modern English Fiction* (Chicago, 1965), pp. 203–4.

2. Ronald Hingley, *Chekhov* (London, 1966); Maurice Valency, *The Breaking String* (Oxford, 1966); Logan Speirs, *Tolstoy and Chekhov* (Cambridge, 1971).

3. See particularly Nina Andronikova Toumanova, *Anton Chekhov: The Voice of Twilight Russia* (New York, 1937).

4. There are, I think, good psychological reasons why the novella is often the mode in which disputatious stances are openly adopted or in which literary or quasi-theological arguments with other writers tend to be taken up. The short story by nature has not sufficient space in which to accumulate the extreme moral or argumentative pressure which the sheer weight of detail in the novella can build up; while the novel, on the other hand, has so much space that it implicitly demands a more comprehensive inclusion of imaginative fact, which in all probability would dissipate the powerful consistency of a polemical approach.

5. See Irving Howe, 'Dostoevsky: The Politics of Salvation', in *Politics and the Novel* (New York, 1957). Howe argues persuasively that the almost prophetically intense seriousness of the Russian novel (particularly in Dostoevsky and Tolstoy), its 'mania for totality', derived from the particular position of the intelligentsia in Czarist Russia. Given, he says, 'an intelligentsia of a kind found only in "backward" countries: ablaze with activity yet brutally confined in its power to communicate, brimming with the boldest ideas yet without a tradition of freedom, aspiring to independence yet reduced to an appendage of the city poor', the Russian novel was uniquely energized by ideas from other fields – politics, religion and philosophy – to which the Czarist censorship likewise denied a proper outlet.

   The same can presumably be argued about the rise of the novella in Russia, with its still greater concentration of purpose and the powerful self-containment (in moral terms) of its represented world. Contributing to this intensity and seriousness about ideas – and, in the case of late Tolstoy, to what is virtually a messianic sense of purpose – was a critical climate itself morally serious and intense. Its most prominent figure, the influential Russian critic Belinsky, seems indeed to have made demands on art of a kind which we would now recognize as purposefully, but simply and limitingly, didactic.

6. Raymond Williams, 'Anton Chekhov', in *Drama from Ibsen to Eliot* (Harmondsworth, 1964).

7. *Three Sisters and Other Plays* (Garnett), p. 40.

Chapter 1. *The Cherry Orchard*

1. Quoted in Ernest Simmons, *Chekhov: A Biography* (London, 1963), p. 608.
2. Letter to V. I. Nemirovich-Danchenko (Yalta, 2 September 1903), in Louis S. Friedland (ed.), *Letters on the Short Story, the Drama, and Other Literary Topics by Anton Chekhov* (New York, 1966), p. 158.
3. Letter to Madame Stanislavsky (Yalta, 15 September 1903), ibid. p. 159.
4. Quoted in Simmons, *Chekhov*, p. 606.
5. See letter to Olga Knipper, 23 November 1903: 'Stanislavsky wants to have a train going past in the second act. He has to be stopped. He also wants to have frogs and landrails.' (Quoted in David Magarshack, *The Real Chekhov* (London, 1972), p. 192.)
6. See letter to Olga Knipper, 29 March 1904: 'Stanislavsky is acting abominably in the fourth act by dragging it out so terribly. This is dreadful! An act which should last at most twelve minutes lasts forty minutes. One thing I can say: Stanislavsky has ruined my play. Oh well, I don't suppose anything can be done about it.' (Ibid. p. 192.)
7. Quoted in Simmons, *Chekhov*, p. 617.
8. Magarshack, *Chekhov the Dramatist* (London, 1952), p. 286.
9. Valency, *The Breaking String*, p. 280.
10. Speirs, *Tolstoy and Chekhov*, p. 213.
11. J. L. Styan, *Chekhov in Performance* (Cambridge, 1971); Harvey Pitcher, *The Chekhov Play* (London, 1973).
12. *The Cherry Orchard and Other Plays* (Garnett), pp. 25–6.
13. Ibid. pp. 15–16.
14. Ibid. pp. 36–7.
15. Ibid. pp. 40–1.
16. Ibid. p. 43.
17. Ibid. p. 67.
18. Ibid. p. 5.
19. Ibid. p. 31.
20. Ibid. p. 16.
21. The subtly stylized elements of Chekhov's play would, after all, be foreign to the spirit of Stanislavsky's naturalistic practices, and the robust stage comedies of the Russian tradition provided little precedent for the variations of texture we find in Chekhov's work. In his early account of the play, Magarshack (in *Chekhov the Dramatist*) adheres stubbornly and literally to a gusty notion of comedy, accepting Chekhov at what he takes to be Chekhov's word, and finding situations and even characters throughout the play 'ludicrous'. His account thus has the air of being somewhat willed out of respect for Chekhov's stated 'intentions' (as Magarshack understands them, interpreting 'comedy' as something closely akin to farce), rather than proceeding from a direct response to the art as actually achieved.
22. *The Cherry Orchard and Other Plays* (Garnett), p. 3.
23. Ibid. p. 3.
24. Ibid. pp. 3–4.
25. Ibid. p. 20.
26. Ibid. pp. 53–4.

27. See *The Chekhov Play*, pp. 193–8.
28. *The Cherry Orchard and Other Plays* (Garnett), p. 28.
29. Letter to Nemirovich-Danchenko (Yalta, 22 August 1903), in Friedland (ed.), *Letters by Anton Chekhov*, p. 158.
30. *The Cherry Orchard and Other Plays* (Garnett), pp. 28–9.
31. Though many of Trofimov's speeches are in a more florid style than Chekhov would have permitted himself and are therefore intended to reflect upon the rhetorical and unrealistic nature of Trofimov's hopes, nevertheless his social conscience about the serfdom of the past, distrust of the intelligentsia and belief in a work ethic as the means to a better future find many echoes in Chekhov's own letters. In some cases, though certainly not in all, Trofimov's speeches and the passages from the letters are even tonally and syntactically similar, as in this instance of Trofimov's condemnation of the intelligentsia and Chekhov's letter to I. I. Orlov, (Yalta, 22 February 1899): 'I have no faith in our intelligentsia, hypocritical, false, hysterical, ill-bred, lazy. . .' (Friedland (ed.), *Letters by Anton Chekhov*, pp. 286–7.)
32. *The Cherry Orchard and Other Plays* (Garnett), p. 39.
33. Ibid. pp. 39–40.
34. Magarshack, *The Real Chekhov*, p. 217.
35. *The Cherry Orchard and Other Plays* (Garnett), p. 48.
36. Ibid. p. 46.
37. Ibid. p. 47.
38. Ibid. pp. 48–9.
39. Ibid. p. 64.
40. Ibid. pp. 67–8.
41. Ibid. p. 77.
42. Ibid. p. 78.
43. *Chekhov in Performance*, p. 335.

Chapter 2. Beginnings

1. It is difficult to define this class exactly. Lyubov and Gaev do not belong to the Russian aristocracy, since they do not possess a title; but, as Ronald Hingley points out in *Russian Writers and Society* (pp. 132–4), the titled aristocracy in nineteenth-century Russia formed only a small section of the gentry as a whole. For a fuller account of the composition of this class of gentry, see Hingley, Chapter 10.
2. 'Dostoevsky: The Politics of Salvation'. (I am referring here to the reprinted article in René Wellek (ed.), *Dostoevsky: A Collection of Critical Essays*, Twentieth Century Views series (Englewood Cliffs, N. J., 1962), p. 54.)
3. Simmons, *Chekhov*, pp. 64–5.
4. Ronald Hingley, *Chekhov: A Biographical and Critical Study* (London, 1966), p. 40.
5. See p. 52, where Grigorovich's letter and its decisive influence on Chekhov's development are discussed.
6. Letter to N. A. Leikin (Moscow, 24 December 1886), in Friedland (ed.), *Letters by Anton Chekhov*, p. 108.
7. Hingley, *Chekhov*, p. 45.

8. Stories marked with an asterisk are not included in the Garnett selection. 'Sergeant Prishibeyev' is translated by Avrahm Yarmolinsky in *The Portable Chekhov* (New York, 1965).
9. Letter to A. S. Souvorin (Moscow, 7 January 1889), in Friedland (ed.), *Letters by Anton Chekhov*, pp. 100–1.
10. *Anton Chekhov: Selected Stories*, translated by Ann Dunnigan (New York, 1960).
11. *The Note-Books of Anton Tchekhov Together with Reminiscences of Tchekhov by Maxim Gorky*, translated by S. S. Koteliansky and Leonard Woolf (London, 1967), p. 4.
12. See W. H. Bruford, *Chekhov and His Russia: A Sociological Study* (London, 1948).

Chapter 3. The short story – I

1. D. V. Grigorovich, at this time aged sixty-five, was an eminent figure in Russian literary circles. He was one of the influential figures in the rise of the Russian realist novel in the late 1840s, having written two minor classics, *The Village* and *Anton Goremyka*. Chekhov later dedicated his third book of selected stories, *In the Twilight*, to him; and Grigorovich, in his turn, was a member of the Division of Russian Language and Letters of the Academy of Sciences which in 1888 unanimously voted to award the Pushkin Prize to that same book of stories. While always grateful for the part Grigorovich played in promoting his career, Chekhov seems in later life to have become somewhat estranged from him, suspecting him of originating some of the rumours against his friend Souvorin.
2. The two letters are quoted in Simmons, *Chekhov*, pp. 95–9.
3. Ivan Turgenev, 'The Tryst', in *The Hunting Sketches*, translated by Bernard Guilbert Guerney (New York: New American Library, 1962), pp. 278–9.
4. Letter to Mariya Kiseleva (14 January 1887), quoted in Simmons, *Chekhov*, p. 131.
5. Letter to Mitrofan Chekhov (18 January 1887), ibid., p. 132.
6. Lev Shestov, 'Anton Tchekhov (Creation from the Void)', in *Chekhov and Other Essays* (Ann Arbor, Mich., 1966), pp. 4–5.

Chapter 4. The short story – II

1. See letter to A. S. Souvorin (Moscow, 27 October 1888), in Friedland (ed.), *Letters by Anton Chekhov*, pp. 59–60: 'You are right in demanding that an artist should take an intelligent attitude to his work, but you confuse two things: *solving a problem* and *stating a problem correctly*. It is only the second that is obligatory for the artist.'

Chapter 5. The steppe stories

1. Letter to A. S. Souvorin (10 February 1887), quoted in Simmons, *Chekhov*, p. 118.
2. Letter to A. S. Souvorin (Sumi, 30 May 1888), in Friedland (ed.), *Letters by Anton Chekhov*, p. 58.

3. Letter to A. P. Chekhov (Babkin, 10 May 1886), ibid., pp. 70–1.
4. Gogol, 'Taras Bulba', in *The Diary of a Madman and Other Stories*, translated by Andrew R. MacAndrew (New York: New American Library, 1960), pp. 114–15.
5. Letter to Y. P. Polonsky (Moscow, 18 January 1888), in Friedland (ed.), *Letters by Anton Chekhov*, p. 3.
6. There seem to me to be sufficient echoes of this passage in Pasternak's description of the clods falling on the coffin lid ('drumm[ing] on the lid like rain') at Yura's mother's funeral, and of Yura's fear that night that 'the snow would drift over the field in which his mother, powerless to resist it, would sink deeper and further away from him into the ground', to suggest that Chekhov was at least one quite important influence on *Doctor Zhivago*. Later, too, when Anna, fearful of death, asks Yura for reassurance – 'You're clever, talented... That makes you different... Say something to me... Set my mind at rest' – the influence is, fairly obviously, Katya's plea to Nikolay Stepanovitch in Chekhov's 'A Dreary Story' (see *Doctor Zhivago*, translated by Max Hayward and Manya Harari (London: Collins Fontana, 1969), pp. 11–13, 80).
7. Simmons, *Chekhov*, p. 133.

Chapter 6. 'Lights'

1. Tolstoy, *War and Peace*, translated by Rosemary Edmonds (Harmondsworth: Penguin, 1957), vol. 1, pp. 494–5.
2. Lawrence, *Sons and Lovers* (London: Penguin, 1966 (originally published 1913)), pp. 34–5.
3. See the previous chapter for a fuller discussion of the significance of these remarks, made in a letter to A. S. Souvorin (Sumi, 30 May 1888), in Friedland (ed.), *Letters by Anton Chekhov*, p. 58.

Chapter 7. Chekhov and Tolstoy

1. Letter to A. S. Souvorin (Moscow, 11 December 1891), in Friedland (ed.), *Letters by Anton Chekhov*, p. 208.
2. Letter to A. N. Pleshcheyev (Moscow, 15 February 1890), ibid., p. 205.
3. Letter to A. S. Souvorin (Moscow, 1 April 1890), ibid., p. 64.
4. This story was more fully discussed in chapter 2.
5. There is no certain evidence that Chekhov wrote 'A Dreary Story' directly in reaction to 'The Death of Ivan Ilych', but some internal characteristics of the writing, plus Chekhov's developing interest in Tolstoy and Tolstoyanism (evident in his letters at this time), make it seem very probable. Certainly it is standard practice to compare the two; and Logan Speirs's recent formal study, *Tolstoy and Chekhov*, does compare them, though in terms somewhat different from the ones I shall subsequently pursue.
6. Tolstoy, 'The Death of Ivan Ilych', translated by Aylmer Maude (New York: New American Library, 1964), p. 117.
7. Ibid., pp. 146–7.
8. John Bayley, *Tolstoy and the Novel* (London, 1966), p. 85.
9. Letter to A. S. Souvorin (Moscow, 8 September 1891), in Friedland (ed.), *Letters by Anton Chekhov*, p. 207.

10. I have used the phrase 'redemption of his past', since 'salvation' or simply 'redemption' may imply a Christian after-life. It is, of course, widely known that one of Tolstoy's heresies concerned that after-life, whose existence he denied in any orthodox Christian terms. As I go on to argue at a later point in this chapter, he seems to have put an absolute value on each person's moral recognition of himself: by that means one 'redeems' one's life in a personal sense, which is what is signalled by Ivan Ilych's sense of psychological release and the appearance of the light. One notices what an odd ambiguity this gives to the appearance of the light at the end of the story. Tolstoy's position also differs from that of orthodox Christianity in that, in his work, the fact of repentance seems to be the only condition of salvation; whereas to find salvation in more orthodox Christian terms further requires God's act of grace.

11. Despite my likening of some of the prose habits of 'Enemies' to those of George Eliot, Chekhov is like the middle-period Tolstoy in being probably most authoritative in the area of psychological generalization. Neither writer (if we think of Tolstoy at that stage of his career) typically feels situations in predominantly moral terms, as the major English novelists tend to do. As Logan Speirs has said, both Tolstoy and Chekhov see the purpose of their art in terms of its accuracy: 'Beauty for them is the reward of clear vision' (*Tolstoy and Chekhov*, p. 3). Of course, their art inevitably involves them in adopting certain moral positions, but each is a realist rather than a moralist in the English sense.

12. Lev Shestov, *Potestas Clavium* (Athens, Ohio: Ohio University Press, 1968), p. 64.

13. Letter to A. S. Souvorin (Yalta, 27 March 1894), in Friedland (ed.), *Letters by Anton Chekhov*, p. 208.

14. Letter to A. S. Souvorin (Yalta, 27 March 1894), in *Letters of Anton Chekhov*, translated by Michael Henry Heim and Simon Karlinsky (London, 1973), pp. 261–2.

15. Letter to M. O. Menshikov (Yalta, 28 January 1900), in Friedland (ed.), *Letters by Anton Chekhov*, p. 212.

Chapter 8. 'A Dreary Story'

1. See particularly Lionel Trilling in his 'Commentary' on 'The Death of Ivan Ilych', in *The Experience of Literature: Fiction* (New York: Holt, Rinehart and Winston, 1967), p. 103; but it is a commonplace elsewhere.

2. Speirs, *Tolstoy and Chekhov*, p. 149.

3. Letter to A. N. Pleshcheyev (Moscow, 30 September 1889), in Friedland (ed.), *Letters by Anton Chekhov*, pp. 16–17.

4. I am, however, inclined to agree with John Bayley's implicit criticism of this as a probable distortion of Ivan Ilych's predicament (*Tolstoy and the Novel*, p. 88). Much of the power of the scene comes from the suggestion that Ivan Ilych is both unconscious and yet somehow conscious of the sensation of unconsciousness – a form of literary double-vision made possible by the third-person narrative, but one which (at least in that particularly stark form) is unlikely to answer to the facts.

5. Tolstoy, 'The Death of Ivan Ilych', p. 154.
6. *Tolstoy and Chekhov*, p. 151.

Chapter 9. 'The Duel' and note on 'Three Years'

1. Letter to A. N. Pleshcheyev (Moscow, 15 February 1890), in Friedland (ed.), *Letters by Anton Chekhov*, p. 205.
2. *Tolstoy and Chekhov*, pp. 169–82.
3. Ibid., pp. 170–1.

Chapter 10. Chekhov's women

1. Letter to Alexander Chekhov (Moscow, April 1883), in Friedland (ed.), *Letters by Anton Chekhov*, p. 297.
2. Lawrence, *The Rainbow*, chapter 6 (Harmondsworth: Penguin, 1965), p. 169.
3. Nearly thirty years separate the two passages, the Chekhov being published in 1886.
4. *Anton Chekhov and the Lady with the Dog* (Oxford, 1973). This book appeared, in fact, after I had written this chapter, and I therefore cannot engage in detailed argument with it. But there seems to me something self-defeating about a procedure which establishes such categories as 'heroine' and 'anti-heroine' (each of which is specified as severely limited in conception) and then subdues some of Chekhov's best women characters to these terms while yet conceding them success (as, for example, in the argument that both Masha and Irina of *Three Sisters* are 'successful' romantic heroines). Furthermore, some distortions have, in my view, been introduced into the argument by Dr Llewellyn Smith's almost exclusive concentration on women (except in the chapter 'The Cynical Hero'), which leads her to assume – without sufficiently questioning Chekhov's general attitudes to people and the world – that there is some anti-feminine prejudice involved in the fact that many of Chekhov's women are portrayed as frivolous, or that the outcome of sexual love is rarely happy in Chekhov's stories. I think a much more comprehensive and careful study is needed before such arguments are accepted as conclusive.
5. Lawrence, *The Rainbow*, chapter 15, p. 458.
6. From 'Readings for Every Day in the Year', 'Tolstoy's Criticism on "The Darling"'.
7. Ibid.

Chapter 11. 'The Party'

1. Letter to A. S. Souvorin (Moscow, 15 November 1888), in Friedland (ed.), *Letters by Anton Chekhov*, p. 10.
2. Virginia Llewellyn Smith, *Anton Chekhov and the Lady with the Dog*, pp. 189–90.

Chapter 12. 'The Lady with the Dog'

1. A comparison of *Anna Karenina* with even such acknowledged masterpieces as *Le Rouge et le noir*, with its ironic composure about the subject, or *Madame Bovary* and its rather cynical satire should, I think, make this clear.

Chapter 13. 'A Woman's Kingdom'

1. 'Introduction: A Note on Tchehov's Art', in *The Darling and Other Stories* (Garnett Vol. I), p. v:
    'Tchehov's range of subject, scene, and situation is so varied that it will be convenient here to classify his Tales as follows:
    '(*a*) The short humorous sketches, of which the author wrote many hundreds, chiefly in early life.
    '(*b*) Stories of the life of the town "Intelligentsia"; family and domestic pieces, of which "The Duel" and "Three Years" – a study of Moscow atmosphere and environment – are the longest.
    '(*c*) Stories of provincial life, in which a great variety of types – landowners, officials, doctors, clergy, school-teachers, merchants, inn-keepers, etc. – appear.
    '(*d*) Stories of peasant life – settled types.
    '(*e*) Stories of unconventional and lawless types – roving characters.
    '(*f*) Psychological studies, such as "The Black Monk", "Ward No. 6".
    'One must recall here, also, Tchehov's plays, his short farces, and his descriptive account of Sahalin life.'
2. Letter to A. S. Souvorin (Moscow, 1 April 1890), in Friedland (ed.), *Letters by Anton Chekhov*, p. 64.
3. 'Daughters of the Vicar', in *The Tales of D. H. Lawrence* (London: Martin Secker, 1934), p. 79.
4. *Three Sisters and Other Plays* (Garnett), p. 93.
5. See his well-known letter to Souvorin (Yalta, 27 March 1894): 'Prudence and justice tell me there is more love for mankind in electricity and steam than in chastity and absention from meat etc.' (Heim and Karlinsky (translators), *Letters of Anton Chekhov*, p. 261). These remarks are made in the context of Chekhov's critique of Tolstoyanism, which I have discussed elsewhere (see especially chapter 7, 'Chekhov and Tolstoy').

Chapter 14. *Three Sisters*

1. 'Chekhov and the English', in Davie (ed.), *Russian Literature*, p. 206.
2. *Three Sisters and Other Plays* (Garnett), p. 27.
3. Ibid. p. 40.
4. Ibid. p. 25.
5. *Chekhov and His Russia: A Sociological Study* (London, 1948), p. 36.
6. *Three Sisters and Other Plays* (Garnett), p. 26.
7. Ibid. p. 5. The tense-structure of the original is actually ambiguous: it might be translated in the present, as here, or cast more strongly in the past.
8. Ibid. p. 65.
9. Ibid. p. 79.
10. Ibid. p. 24.
11. Ibid. p. 80.
12. Ibid. pp. 18–19.
13. Ibid. p. 28.
14. Ibid. p. 95.
15. Ibid. p. 64.

16. Ibid. p. 8.
17 Ibid. p. 33.
18 Ibid. p. 4.
19. Unpublished lectures on Chekhov, delivered at the University of Melbourne, 1970.
20. *Three Sisters and Other Plays* (Garnett), p. 3. I have inserted the word 'outside' into the Garnett translation of the stage directions here, as this detail seems to me important for a proper understanding of the scene and is clearly indicated in the original text (*на дворе* солнечно, весело.). Incidentally, the Fen translation of this particular work does seem to me on the whole rather more careful and exact than the Garnett; but I have kept to the Garnett for this quotation, for the sake of consistency.
21. Ibid. p. 35.
22. Ibid. p. 55.
23. Ibid. p. 58.
24. Ibid. pp. 85–6.
25. Ibid. p. 7.
26. Ibid. pp. 94–5.

Chapter 15. Chekhov's modernity

1. Chapter 10, 'Chekhov the Humanist', pp. 125–34.
2. See Letter to A. N. Pleshcheyev (Moscow, October 1889), in Friedland (ed.), *Letters by Anton Chekhov*, p. 63.
3. Gifford, *The Novel in Russia*, p. 129.
4. Letter to V. V. Bilibin (February 1886), quoted in Simmons, *Chekhov*, p. 81.
5. *Tolstoy and Chekhov*, p. 190.
6. This is the title most frequently given to a long play which Chekhov wrote during his second year at university and subsequently destroyed. A rough-draft version of it emerged after his death and appears among his collected works.
7. *Three Sisters and Other Plays* (Garnett), pp. 9–10.
8. See Ronald Gaskell, *Drama and Reality: The European Theatre since Ibsen* (London, 1972).
9. *Three Sisters and Other Plays* (Garnett), p. 85.
10. Ibid. p. 5.
11. *The Cherry Orchard and Other Plays* (Garnett), p. 103.
12. Ibid. p. 106.
13. Ibid. p. 99.
14. Ibid. p. 148.

CHRONOLOGICAL TABLE

Year	Works	Life
1860		Anton Pavlovich Chekhov born at Taganrog on the Black Sea, third son of the merchant Pavel Yegorovich Chekhov and Evgenia Yakovlevna Chekhova (née Morozova).
1868		Attends Taganrog School for Boys after unsuccessful beginning at Greek Parish School.
1873	Devises comic sketches for performance at home.	Shows early interest in theatre. Sees local productions of *Hamlet, The Inspector-General* and Griboedov's *Woe from Wit*.
1875	Begins his own humorous magazine (*Stammerer*) for circulation in the family. Comic sketches of Taganrog life.	
1876		Father declared bankrupt. Family escapes, in hardship, to Moscow; Chekhov left alone in Taganrog to complete schooling. Reads Russian fiction and literary criticism: Buckle, Schopenhauer and Humboldt. Also reads humorous magazines *Alarm Clock* and *Dragonfly*. Fleeting visits to the steppe region.
1877	Produces 'little trifles' like those in humorous magazines. Two submitted to *Alarm Clock* (it is not known whether they were published).	First visit to Moscow: family in hardship, but the city itself a revelation to Chekhov.
1878	*Without Fathers* (full-length drama); *Diamond Cut Diamond* (comedy); *Why the Hen Clucks* (vaudeville): all unpublished.	

Year	Works	Life
1879	Begins more regular submission of short items to *Alarm Clock* and *Dragonfly*.	Goes to live in Moscow and becomes virtual head of his family. Begins studies at School of Medicine, Moscow University, August.
1880	First sketch published in *Dragonfly* (9 March), 'A Letter from the Don Landowner Stepan Vladimirovitch N., to His Learned Neighbour Dr Frederick'. Nine more stories in *Dragonfly* in this year, under various pseudonyms (especially 'Antosha Chekhonte'). Also writes the long 'Play without a Title' (*Platonov*), rejected by Maly Theatre; attempts to destroy the MS. in disgust.	Introduced by brother Nikolai to Russian landscape painter Levitan: beginning of important friendship between the two.
1881	Eight short pieces published in humorous magazines. With brother Nikolai, associated with new comic journal *Spectator*.	Visit of Sarah Bernhardt to Moscow: Chekhov calls her acting 'artificial'.
1882	*The Unnecessary Victory* (short novel) appears serially in *Alarm Clock*. Thirty-two stories published by this time, including the first in *Fragments*.	Now writing, along with medical studies, in order to support family. Meets Leikin, editor of *Fragments*, a Petersburg weekly.
1883	A further 90 short tales, published largely in *Fragments*. Regular column (in *Fragments*), 'Fragments of Moscow Life'.	Gains practical experience in medicine at rural hospital, Chikino. Interest in Saltykov-Shchedrin, Turgenev, Nekrasov. Introduced by Leikin to Leskov.
1884	Total of stories published in humorous magazines almost 300 by end of this year. Publication of first book of selected stories, *Tales of Melpomene*. Another short novel, *Drama at a Hunting Party*, serialized in *Daily News*.	Completes medical degree, 25 June. Associated with Chikino Hospital as practising physician. In December displays first symptoms of tuberculosis.
1885–86	More than 100 new short stories, including the first in *St Petersburg Gazette* (for which he wrote regularly until end of 1888). First story published under his own name, and first in *New*	Has Moscow medical practice. Intermittent illness and constant financial worries. First visit to St Petersburg, December 1885. Meets Souvorin (editor of *New Times*) and the writers Grigorovich and

Year	Works	Life
	Times (largest-circulation daily newspaper in Russia), February 1886. Influential letter from Grigorovich. Second volume of selected tales, *Motley Tales*, mid-1886.	V. P. Burenin. Special interest in Darwin at this period, and developing interest in music.
1887	Fewer contributions to humorous magazines. Third book of selected stories, *In the Twilight* (dedicated to Grigorovich). Fourth book, *Innocent Speeches*, hurriedly produced in response to financial need. First published vaudeville, *Swansong*. Initial version of *Ivanov* written at request of proprietor of Korsch Theatre, Moscow. *Ivanov* first performed there, 19 November: causes uproar.	Elected member of Literary Fund. Leaves in April for tour of the Don Steppe. Later visits Petersburg again; meets I. E. Repin, Leontiev-Shcheglov and A. N. Pleshcheyev.
1888	Completes 'The Steppe' and 'Lights' for serious journal *Northern Herald*. Also works, without final success, on novel tentatively entitled *Tales from the Life of My Friends*. *Swansong* staged for the first time, Korsch Theatre, 19 February; The Bear, written in February, staged October. New collection of stories, *Tales*, appears in June. Writes 'The Party'. Begins work on *The Wood Demon* (later, in drastically revised form, to become *Uncle Vanya*: see 1897). Writes one-act farce *The Proposal*. Revises *Ivanov* for first Petersburg performance (revision completed December: radical changes in Acts II and IV, clarification of character of Ivanov).	Pushkin Prize, 'for the best literary production distinguished by high artistic worth', awarded to *In the Twilight* by Division of Russian Language and Letters of the Academy of Sciences. First meets Stanislavsky at meeting of Society of Arts and Literature, November. Attends many performances at Maly and Korsch Theatres, becoming widely acquainted with actors and with the stage. First meets Tchaikovsky, December.
1889	Favourable reception of Petersburg première of revised *Ivanov*, Alexandrinsky Theatre, 31 January. Publishes collection of stories, *Children*. Working on *Tales from the Life of My Friends*. Writes and	Meets Lidiya Avilova, whose memoirs (*A. P. Chekhov in My Life*, 1947) claim that she and Chekhov shared a secret love. Tolstoy begins to read Chekhov. Chekhov elected to

Year	Works	Life
	publishes 'The Princess' (short story), 'A Dreary Story' (novella); *The Wedding* and *A Tragedian in Spite of Himself* (one-act plays). Work on *The Wood Demon*: first draft rejected by the Alexandrinsky Theatre; revised version performed by Moscow Abramov Theatre, November, and unanimously condemned. (Chekhov never permitted publication of this original form of *The Wood Demon* in his lifetime.)	Society of Lovers of Russian Literature; becomes member of Society of Russian Dramatic Writers and Opera Composers. Nurses his brother Nikolai, dying of tuberculosis.
1890	New selection of tales, *Gloomy People*, March (dedicated to Tchaikovsky). 'Gusev' the only story published this year.	Feels need of change after Nikolai's death and failure of *The Wood Demon*: 'There is a sort of stagnation in my soul.' Undertakes extraordinary journey across Siberia by horse-drawn vehicle and river-boat, to investigate conditions on penal island of Sakhalin: departs 21 April, returns to Moscow 8 December.
1891	Work on *The Island of Sakhalin* (non-fictional study) and on 'The Duel'. 'The Duel' published serially in *New Times*, October–November. 'Peasant Wives' published in *New Times*. Writes 'The Grasshopper'; completes *The Jubilee* in December.	Six-week tour of western Europe with Souvorin. More intense, though always wary, relationship with Lika Mizinova ('lovely Lika'). Late in 1891, attempts to give practical relief to famine victims in central and south-east Russia.
1892–93	Stories begin to be translated into other languages. Twenty-one stories over these two years, including 'Ward No. 6' (1892) and 'Tale of an Unknown Man' (1893): these stories published in serious monthly *Russian Thought*. Works on 'The Black Monk'. Publishes 'A Woman's Kingdom'. *The Island of Sakhalin* completed; appears serially in *Russian Thought*, late 1893 and early 1894 ('I am glad that this rough convict's garment hangs in my literary wardrobe. Let it hang there!').	Buys small estate, Melikhovo, near Moscow: family moves there 5 March 1892. Performs medical services for local peasants along with his writing. Begins to keep notebooks. Re-reading Turgenev at this stage; but regards him as clearly inferior to Tolstoy and is critical of Turgenev's heroines.

Year	Works	Life
1894	Publishes 'The Student', 'The Teacher of Literature' and 'At a Country House'. Another volume of selected stories, *Stories and Tales*. Working on 'Three Years'.	Further excursion to western Europe, September.
1895	'Three Years' published in *Russian Thought*. *The Island of Sakhalin* appears in book form. Writes 'Ariadne', 'The Help-mate', 'The Murder', 'Anna on the Neck'. First draft of *The Seagull*, October–November.	Spends two days at Yasnaya Polyana, August. First meets Tolstoy, Ivan Bunin.
1896	'My Life' in monthly literary supplements of *Niva*. Early part of year spent revising *The Seagull* for première, Alexandrinsky Theatre, Petersburg, 17 October. Hostile first reaction (but audience untypical); published in *Russian Thought*, December, after more favourable reaction to later performances.	Personal agitation for, and contribution to, projects in rural education, transport etc., including building of village school at Talezh. Collects books to supplement library in Taganrog.
1897	Writes 'Peasants' (published in *Russian Thought*, April). Three short tales in *Russian News*: 'The Pecheneg', 'At Home' and 'In the Cart'. Publishes *Uncle Vanya* (revised version of *The Wood Demon*: see 1888–9) but refuses to allow performance until 1899.	Undertakes work for national census, builds second rural school. Crisis in health, March: committed to Moscow clinic, haemorrhage of the lungs. Visits Europe in August, during convalescence. Stays at Nice, reads French authors and periodicals.
1898	Four short stories published, July–August: 'Ionych', 'The Man in a Shell', 'About Love' and 'Gooseberries'. 'A Doctor's Visit' published in *Russian Thought*, December. First performance of *The Seagull* by Moscow Art Theatre (M.A.T.), 17 December. Enormous success; establishes Chekhov as a playwright and	Indignant over Dreyfus affair and trial of Zola; conflict with Souvorin over this. Returns to Russia, 2 May. Nemirovich–Danchenko requests permission for new People's Art Theatre (later Moscow Art Theatre) to perform *The Seagull*. Chekhov refuses but relents under pressure. Attends Moscow Art Theatre rehearsals of *The Seagull*, September. Attracted to the actress Olga Knipper; but leaves almost immediately for the Crimea.

Year	Works	Life
	saves the newly formed M.A.T. from financial ruin. Intimate relationship thereafter between Chekhov and M.A.T.	Meets Rachmaninov. Begins first correspondence with Gorky. After father's death and own illness, buys land near Yalta and engages architect to build a house.
1899	'The Darling' published in *Family*, January. Two short sketches, 'The New Country House' (*Russian News*) and 'On Official Duty' (*Books of the Week*). Signs contract with publisher A. F. Marx for Complete Edition of works, 26 January. Begins work at once on compiling first two volumes (most of early part of the year spent on this). Private performance of *The Seagull* by M.A.T., in effort to persuade Chekhov to give them *Uncle Vanya* (see 1897). First performance of *Uncle Vanya* at M.A.T., 26 October; moderate success. 'The Lady with the Dog' published in *Russian Thought*, December. Plans 'The Bishop'; completes 'In the Ravine'. First thoughts on *Three Sisters*.	Breaks with Souvorin over question of student riots. Olga Knipper visits Melikhovo. Sells Melikhovo in June and moves, with mother and sister, to Yalta. First meeting with Gorky. Awarded Order of St Stanislav for work in the cause of national education, December; elected (with Tolstoy and Korolenko) to newly formed Pushkin Section of Belles Lettres of Academy of Sciences.
1900	First two volumes of Marx Edition appear. Begins serious work on *Three Sisters*, August; completed in October. Reads first draft to M.A.T. in November. In December goes to Nice to revise last two acts while the first two are in rehearsal: makes a number of changes, especially in Act IV.	Settled in the Yalta house. M.A.T. visits Sevastopol and Yalta at Chekhov's request, April. He sees *Uncle Vanya* performed for the first time, and M.A.T. for the first time before the public. Admires Hauptmann but decides that 'Ibsen is really not a dramatist'. Becomes intimate with Olga Knipper.
1901	Première of *Three Sisters*, M.A.T., 21 January. Olga Knipper as Masha. Moderate success. Published in *Russian Thought*, February. Ten of the 11 volumes of	Turbulent year in Russian politics: riots, universities closed, attempt to assassinate Pobedonostsev (Procurator of Holy Synod), Tolstoy excommunicated.

Chronological table

Year	Works	Life
	Marx edition published by the end of 1901. Work on 'The Bishop'.	Chekhov marries Olga Leonardovna Knipper, 25 May.
1902	Completes 'The Bishop'; begins 'The Betrothed'. Begins work on *The Cherry Orchard*. Revises 'On the Harmfulness of Tobacco' (1886) for Marx Edition.	Receives Griboedov Prize from Society of Dramatic Writers and Opera Composers for *Three Sisters*. Resigns from Academy of Sciences (along with Korolenko) in protest at action of Nicholas II to exclude Gorky from membership.
1903	Completes 'The Betrothed'; works on final volume of Marx Edition. Accepts editorship of literary section of *Russian Thought*. Finishes first draft of *The Cherry Orchard*, 26 September, but undertakes second and third drafts; not completed until 12 October.	Elected provisional president of Society of Lovers of Russian Literature. Arrives Moscow, 4 December, for M.A.T. rehearsals of *The Cherry Orchard*. Disagreements with Stanislavsky over interpretation of the play.
1904	Première of *The Cherry Orchard*, M.A.T., 17 January. Published in *Znanie Annual* (owned by Gorky), Petersburg.	Chekhov dies of tuberculosis at Badenweiler in the Black Forest, 1 July.

BIBLIOGRAPHY

Texts of works by Chekhov

The Tales of Tchehov, translated by Constance Garnett, 13 vols. London: Chatto & Windus, 1916–23. (See the Note on Translations, p. x above.)

The Plays of Tchehov, translated by Constance Garnett, 2 vols. London: Chatto & Windus, 1922–3 (reprinted 1965–70). (See the Note on Translations, p. x above.)

Selected Stories, translated by Ann Dunnigan. New York: New American Library, 1960.

Ward No. 6 and Other Stories, translated by Ann Dunnigan. New York: New American Library, 1965.

Chekhov Plays, translated by Elisaveta Fen. Harmondsworth: Penguin, 1951.

Stories 1889–1891, translated by Ronald Hingley ('The Oxford Chekhov', vol. V). London: Oxford University Press, 1970.

Stories 1895–1897, translated by Ronald Hingley ('The Oxford Chekhov', vol. VIII). London: Oxford University Press, 1965.

Tchekov's Plays and Stories, translated by S. S. Koteliansky. London: Everyman, 1937.

Lady with Lapdog and Other Stories, translated by David Magarshack. Harmondsworth: Penguin, 1964.

The Portable Chekhov, translated by Avrahm Yarmolinsky. New York: Viking, 1965.

Source material

Friedland, Louis S. (ed.), *Letters on the Short Story, the Drama and Other Literary Topics by Anton Chekhov*. New York: Dover, 1966 (first published London: Geoffrey Bles, 1924).

Heim, Michael Henry, and Simon Karlinsky (translators), *Letters of Anton Chekhov*. London: Bodley Head, 1973.

Koteliansky, S. S. (ed.), *Anton Tchekhov: Literary and Theatrical Reminiscences*. New York: Benjamin Blom, 1965.

Koteliansky, S. S., and Leonard Woolf (translators), *The Note-Books of Anton Tchekov, Together with Reminiscences of Tchekhov by Maxim Gorky*. London: Hogarth Press, 1967.

Biographies

Hingley, Ronald, *Chekhov: A Biographical and Critical Study*. London: George Allen & Unwin, 1966.

Simmons, Ernest J., *Chekhov: A Biography. London: Jonathan Cape, 1963.*

Critical books

Bruford, W. H., *Anton Chekhov*. London: Bowes & Bowes, 1957.
Davie, Donald (ed.), *Russian Literature and Modern English Fiction*. University of Chicago Press, 1965.
Hingley, Ronald, *Chekhov: A Biographical and Critical Study*. London: George Allen & Unwin, 1966.
Jackson, Robert Louis (ed.), *Chekhov: A Collection of Critical Essays* (Twentieth Century Views series). Englewood Cliffs, N.J.: Prentice–Hall, 1967.
Llewellyn Smith, Virginia, *Anton Chekhov and the Lady with the Dog*. London: Oxford University Press, 1973.
Magarshack, David, *Chekhov the Dramatist*. London: John Lehmann, 1952.
– *The Real Chekhov*. London: George Allen & Unwin. 1972.
Pitcher, Harvey, *The Chekhov Play*. London: Chatto & Windus, 1973.
Speirs, Logan, *Tolstoy and Chekhov*. Cambridge University Press, 1971.
Styan, J. L., *Chekhov in Performance*. Cambridge University Press, 1971.
Toumanova, Nina Andronikova, *Anton Chekhov: The Voice of Twilight Russia*. New York: Columbia University Press, 1937.
Valency, Maurice, *The Breaking String*. New York: Oxford University Press, 1966.

Critical essays

Bentley, Eric, 'Chekhov as Playwright', *Kenyon Review* 11 (1949), pp. 226–50.
Curtis, Penelope, 'Chekhov', *Quadrant*, June 1972, pp. 13–45.
Davies, Ruth, 'Chekhov: The Axe to the Tree', in *The Great Books of Russia*. Norman: University of Oklahoma Press, 1968, pp. 309–45.
Gifford, Henry, 'Chekhov the Humanist', in *The Novel in Russia*. London: Hutchinson University Library, 1964, pp. 125–34.
Jarrell, Randall, 'Six Russian Short Novels', in *Third Book of Criticism*, New York: Farrer, Straus & Giroux, 1965, pp. 235–78.
Mirsky, D. S. 'Chekhov and the English' (1927), in Donald Davie (ed.), *Russian Literature and Modern English Fiction*. University of Chicago Press, 1965, pp. 203–13.
Poggioli, Renato, 'Storytelling in a Double Key' (Part 2), in *The Phoenix and the Spider*. Cambridge, Mass.: Harvard University Press, 1957, pp. 122–30.
Shestov, Lev, 'Anton Tchekhov (Creation from the Void)' (1916), in *Chekhov and Other Essays*. Ann Arbor: University of Michigan Press, 1966, pp. 3–60.

Other secondary material

Bayley, John, *Tolstoy and the Novel*. London: Chatto & Windus, 1966.
Bruford, W. H. *Chekhov and His Russia: A Sociological Study*. London: Kegan Paul, Trench, Truebner & Co., 1948.
Gaskell, Ronald, *Drama and Reality: The European Theatre since Ibsen*. London: Routledge & Kegan Paul, 1972.

Hingley, Ronald, *Russian Writers and Society 1825–1904* (World University Library). London: Weidenfeld & Nicolson, 1967.

Howe, Irving, 'Dostoievsky: The Politics of Salvation', in *Politics and the Novel.* New York: Horizon Press, 1957. (Reprinted in René Wellek (ed.), *Dostoevsky: A Collection of Critical Essays*, Twentieth Century Views series. Englewood Cliffs, N.J.: Prentice-Hall, 1962.)

Williams, Raymond, 'Anton Chekhov', in *Drama from Ibsen to Eliot.* Harmondsworth: Peregrine, 1964.

INDEX

Chekhov's works are indexed by title; others are indexed under their authors.